65-00

65-00

ETHICS, LAW AND SOCIETY

Ethics, Law and Society
Volume II

JENNIFER GUNNING AND SØREN HOLM
Cardiff Law School, Cardiff University, UK

ASHGATE

Published by
Ashgate Publishing Limited
Gower House
Croft Road
Aldershot
Hampshire GU11 3HR
England

Ashgate Publishing Company
Suite 420
101 Cherry Street
Burlington, VT 05401-4405
USA

Ashgate website: http://www.ashgate.com

British Library Cataloguing in Publication Data
Ethics, law and society
  Vol. 2
  1.Professional ethics 2.Law and ethics 3.Bioethics 4.Social
  ethics 5.Human rights
  I.Gunning, Jennifer II.Holm, Søren
  174

Library of Congress Control Number:
Ethics, law and society / edited by Jennifer Gunning and Søren Holm.
    p. cm.
  Includes bibliographical references and index.
  ISBN 0-7546-4881-8
    1. Applied ethics. 2. Law. 3. Civilization. I. Gunning, Jennifer. II. Holm,
  Søren.

  BJ1581.2.E85 2005
  170--dc22

2005007351

ISBN-10: 0 7546 4881 8
ISBN-13: 978-0-7546-4881-9

Printed and bound in Great Britain by Antony Rowe Ltd, Chippenham, Wiltshire.

Contents

List of Figures and Tables

Figures

Tables

List of Contributors

David Archard is Professor of Philosophy and Public Policy at Lancaster University. He previously taught at the Universities of Ulster and St Andrews. He has written extensively in moral, political, social and legal philosophy, including *Children, Rights and Childhood* 2nd edition 2004; *Children, Family and the State* 2003, and *Sexual Consent* 1998. He is currently a member of the Nuffield Council on Bioethics Working Party on the ethics of prolonging life in fetuses and the newborn, and is Honorary Treasurer of the Society for Applied Philosophy.

Karen Birmingham has a background in general and psychiatric nursing with a particular interest in psychosocial nursing and therapeutic communities. Karen began working at the University of Bristol, Institute of Child Health, in 1988 and was involved in piloting and setting up the Avon Longitudinal Study of Parents and Children (ALSPAC). Responsible for abstraction of data from medical records for this study. Secretary of the ALSPAC Law & Ethics Committee since 1999.

Cathy Cobley, LLB, LLM is a lecturer in Law at Cardiff Law School where she teaches on the undergraduate degree schemes in Criminal Law and Evidence and also contributes to teaching on the postgraduate degree in Legal Aspects of Medical Practice. She has written widely on the topics of child abuse and sex offenders and, together with colleagues from Cardiff Family Studies Research Centre, she has recently completed a two year retrospective research project, funded by the Nuffield Foundation, on the legal and social consequences when children sustain a subdural haemorrhage.

Gillian Douglas, LLB (Manchester), LLM (London), is Professor of Law and Head of the Cardiff Law School. She writes and researches extensively in the field of family law and is the co-author of *Bromley's Family Law* and the author of *An Introduction to Family Law*. She is also co-editor of the *Child and Family Law Quarterly* and co-editor of 'Case Reports' in the journal, *Family Law*. She is a former member of the Judicial Studies Board Family Committee, and has just completed five years as Secretary General of the International Society of Family Law. She is currently engaged in research (with Professor Mervyn Murch) for the Department of Constitutional Affairs into the separate representation of children in private family law proceedings.

Elizabeth Dowler is reader in food and social policy at the Department of Sociology of the University of Warwick. Elizabeth's research and professional experience is in the social and policy aspects of nutrition and food. Current work is on food and nutrition in mediating inequalities in health and exclusion; evaluation of policy intervention in food at local and national level; consumers' identities and perceptions of 'risk' and 'trust' in relation to food and new technologies, and implications of negotiated new relationships with producers and the food system. Elizabeth is a member of the Food Ethics Council UK, the Council of the Nutrition Society, and the UK National Heart Forum

Yulia Egorova is a Research Fellow at the School of Religious and Theological Studies working on a project on 'The meanings of Genetics' with Prof Pattison and Dr Edgar. She received her PhD from the School of Oriental and African Studies, London University, where she also worked on a project on 'The Impact of genetic research on the religious identity of the Lemba Judaising movement of Southern Africa'.

Philip Fennell B.A. (Hons) Law (Kent), M.Phil. (Law) (Kent), PhD (Law) (University of Wales, Cardiff) is Professor of Medical Law and Human Rights at Cardiff Law School, University of Wales, College of Cardiff, where he teaches Medical Law and European Community Law. He is a member of the Law Society's Mental Health and Disability Committee and was a member of the Mental Health Act Commission from 1983-1989. He has published many articles on law and psychiatry. He is honorary legal advisor to Wales MIND, the National Association for Mental Health, and works extensively with Hafal (which means equal in Welsh, and which is the new name for the National Schizophrenia Fellowship). He also writes the Annual Review of Medical Law cases for the *All England Law Reports* (Butterworths). He is co-author of Gostin and Fennell, *Mental Health: Tribunal Procedure* (Longman) 1992 and his book entitled *Treatment Without Consent: Law, Psychiatry and the Treatment of Mental Disorder since 1845*, was published by Routledge in 1996. He has lectured on the Human Rights Act 1998 to the judiciary on behalf of the Judicial Studies Board, and is involved in training of mental health review tribunal members and advocates.

Michael Furmston studied law at Oxford and taught at Birmingham, Belfast and Oxford before going to Bristol in 1978 to be Professor of Law. He retired in 1998 and is now an Emeritus Professor and Senior Research Fellow. He was called to the Bar at Gray's Inn in 1960 and has been a Bencher of Gray's Inn since 1989. He is a member of the UNIDROIT working group which has produced a set of General Principles for International Commercial Contracts. He is the Editor of the Construction Law Reports.

Jennifer Gunning originally trained as a scientist but, over the years, has become an expert on the regulatory and legislative aspects of assisted reproduction, following her term as secretary to the Voluntary Licensing Authority for Human in vitro

Fertilisation and Embryology, which regulated human embryo research and IVF before statutory regulation was introduced. She has provided advice both to the European Commission and the British government. She is now a Senior Research Fellow in bioethics and law at Cardiff Law School, where she co-ordinates the Cardiff Centre for Ethics, Law & Society, and works as an independent consultant in bioethics and science affairs.

Andreas Hasman is a Research Associate at Picker Institute Europe, an independent health care survey and research organisation in Oxford. He obtained his doctorate from the University of Oxford.

Clem Henricson is a social policy analyst who has specialised in investigating the relationship between the state and the family. She has a particular interest in human rights and has assessed the government's family policy from a social rights perspective in *Government and Parenting*, 2000, and the interaction between child and family policy in *The Child and Family Policy Divide*, 2004. She is the secretary of the *Commission into Families and the Well -Being of Children*, and wrote its report *Families and the State: Two-way support and responsibilities* (2005). As Director of Research and Policy at the National Family and Parenting Institute, Clem Henricson edits the Institute's research and policy publications and directs a multidisciplinary academic team of developmental and social psychologists, and comparative cultural and social policy analysts. She serves on government and academic advisory committees concerned with family policy.

Stephen Hogan is a principal lecturer and teaches marketing, international marketing and ethics. His industry background is in international sales and marketing where he worked for a number of world-leading multi-nationals. In addition to his course leader duties, he has been heavily involved in the marketing of the School and the recruitment/admissions of students. He is a former chair of the University's Admissions Forum. Steve is currently studying for a PhD in the area of ethics and marketing to children.

Søren Holm is Professorial Fellow in Bioethics and Director of the Cardiff Centre for Ethics, Law and Society at the University of Cardiff, UK, as well as Professor of Medical Ethics at the Centre for Medical Ethics at the University of Oslo, Norway. He holds degrees in medicine, philosophy, and health care ethics, and two doctoral degrees in medical ethics. He has written extensively on reproductive ethics, cloning, genetics and research ethics.

Matthias Kaiser (Dr. phil. University of Frankfurt) is Director of the National Committee for Research Ethics in Science and Technology (NENT), a position including 50 per cent of work time for own research, with acknowledged competence as full professor in philosophy of science since 1996. He is also adjunct professor for philosophy of science in the doctoral education program at the College of Architecture

(AHO) in Oslo. His main work and areas of expertise are in the fields of philosophy of science, ethics of science, and technology assessment. His areas of competence include social studies of science and technology, history of science, ethics, logic, and history of philosophy. Due to his position at the National Committees for Research Ethics he is familiar with, and directly involved in matters of science and technology policy. Through detailed case studies he has furthermore considerable insights in diverse fields of science, such as the history of plate tectonics, aquaculture, and biotechnology. Another topic of detailed study is the Precautionary Principle, particularly in environmental science. His leading role in the conduct of three Norwegian consensus conferences has led to a special interest in participatory policy tools and their use in ethical debate. He has published two books, co-published two further books, written several committee studies and edited three thematic issues of scientific journals. In addition he has published approximately 50 articles in various journals and anthologies. Most publications are in English or in Norwegian, some in German, and some are translated into Russian, Chinese, and Serbo-Croatian.

Kelechi A. Kalu is Professor of Political Science at The University of Northern Colorado, Greeley, CO 80639. He was a Mellon Research Fellow in Government at Connecticut College, New London in 1994/95 academic year. He is a past President of the Southwestern International Studies Association. Professor Kalu is the author of *Economic Development and Nigerian Foreign Policy* (New York: The Edwin Mellen Press, 2000). His publications include articles in the *International Journal of Politics, Culture and Society, Africa Today*, *Journal of Nigerian Affairs*, *Journal of Asian and African Studies*, *Journal of Third World Studies* and several book chapters on African and Third World issues. His is editor of *Agenda Setting and Public Policy in Africa* (Aldershot, UK and Burlington, VT. US 2004). Dr. Kalu is currently working on a manuscript on constitutionalism and political restructuring in post-conflict states in Africa.

Julian Kinderlerer is the Assistant Director of the Sheffield Institute of Biotechnological Law and Ethics (SIBLE) based in the University of Sheffield. He is a biochemist who has moved from research interests in theoretical aspects of enzymology and enzyme kinetics to looking at law, ethics, risk assessment and risk analysis in biotechnology. He is now in the Faculty of Law at the University of Sheffield.

Geoffrey Klempner worked briefly as an assistant to an advertising photographer in the early 70s. After discovering an interest in Philosophy, he gained a 1st class BA degree at Birkbeck College London, followed by a B.Phil and D.Phil at University College Oxford. His book *Naive Metaphysics: a theory of subjective and objective worlds* was published by Avebury in 1994. In 1995 he started the Pathways to Philosophy Distance Learning Program, an independent correspondence school for academic philosophy which today has students in over 40 countries. In 2002, he founded the International Society for Philosophers in order to 'bring together students and teachers of philosophy, and amateur philosophers from all over the world'. In 2003 he launched the *Philosophy for Business* electronic newsletter, aimed at a broad readership of philosophers and business people. He is married, with three children.

Nicola Langlands – transplant patient.

Christian Lopez-Silva is a full-time PhD student at the Sheffield Law Department since 2003. His research interests are primarily in the legal implications of green biotechnology, i.e. agricultural applications. This includes Access to Genetic Resources and Benefit Sharing as well as Biosafety and Trade matters. He is examining the implications of the recent EU-US trade dispute on biotech products and its impact for developing countries. This is framed in the wider interaction of trade and environment international regulation of Genetically Modified Organisms. He has worked in the environmental sector as legal advisor for the Mexican government in the regulation of biotechnology. Christian holds a LLB (Hons) from the Technological Autonomous Institute of Mexico and a Master in Biotechnological Law and Ethics (MABLE) from the University of Sheffield.

Tom MacMillan is Executive Director of the Food Ethics Council (www. foodethicscouncil.org), a research and advocacy network that aims to make the food system fairer and healthier. He was previously an ESRC postdoctoral fellow at the University of Manchester, where his research focused on the politics of science in food regulation. He is an Honorary Fellow of the School of Geography at Manchester University.

Deirdre Madden is a lecturer in the Faculty of Law, University College Cork, Ireland. Her research interests and publications are primarily in the area of Medical Law, in particular assisted reproduction and genetics. She was appointed by the Minister for Health and Children to the Commission on Assisted Human Reproduction in 2000. She is also a member of the Research Ethics Committee of the Irish College of General Practitioners, and has recently been appointed to the Irish Medical Council. She is the author of *Medicine, Ethics and the Law*, (Butterworths, Dublin, 2002).

Donato Masciandaro is Full Professor of Monetary Economics at Paolo Baffi Centre, Bocconi University, Milan, and Department of Economics, Mathematics and Statistics, University of Lecce. He is Associated Fellow of the Institute for International Political Studies (ISPI), Milan. He has been Consultant to the World Bank since 2002 and, prior to that, the Inter-American Development Bank (1999-2001) and the United Nations (1998-99).

Máire Messenger Davies is Professor of Media Studies and Director of the Centre for Media Research, in the School of Media and Performing Arts at the University of Ulster, Coleraine. A former journalist, with a BA in English from Trinity College

Dublin and a PhD in Psychology from the University of East London, she has taught in universities on both sides of the Atlantic. Her research interests focus particularly on audience reception of both storytelling and of news/ factual material, and the ways in which these audience studies intersect with public policy issues in media and in education. She is particularly interested in child audiences and has written widely on this issue, producing both policy documents such as her report (2004) *Review of BBC Digital Services: Cbeebies and CBBC*, for the Department of Culture, Media and Sport (http://www.culture.gov.uk/global/publications/archive_2004/review_ bbc_digital_tv_services+.htm) and books such as '*Dear BBC': Children, television-storytelling and the public sphere,* (2001) Cambridge: Cambridge University Press.

Richard Moorhead's main interests are legal aid, the legal profession, regulation of professions and legal systems and socio-legal research methods. He is a member of the Legal Services Consultative Panel (formerly ACLEC) which advises the Lord Chancellor on issues of professional ethics and conduct, a board member of the Journal of Law and Society and an editorial advisory board member of The International Journal of the Legal Profession. He is currently a specialist advisor to the Consitutional Affairs Select Committee. Richard is currently Deputy Head of Cardiff Law School, Cardiff University.

Tony Newman is Principal Research Officer with Barnardo's, one of the UK's oldest child care charities, which was established in 1866 and now provides around 360 services to children and families in England, Scotland, Wales and Northern Ireland. Tony has worked as a social worker in the USA and UK, and as a manager of community-based learning disability services in South Wales. Since becoming a researcher and academic, he has written a number of books, most recently *Evidence-Based Social Work: a guide for the perplexed* (Russell House, 2005); *What Works in Building Resilience?* (Barnardo's, 2004); *What Works for Parents with Learning Disabilities?* (Barnardo's, 2004); *Children of Disabled Parents* (Russell House, 2003) and *What Works for Children?: effective services for children and families* (Open University Press, 2002), as well as many papers and articles. Tony's main research interests are the impact of parental disability on children, the promotion of resilience and the implementation of evidence-based practice. He is currently writing a book about child migration from the UK to Canada between 1919 and 1939. Tony grew up in South Wales but has recently moved to Totnes, in Devon. On secondment from Barnardo's, he spent the first half of 2005 developing a new research utilisation organisation for adult social care services at the Dartington Hall Trust. He is married and has three adult daughters.

Jirí Pribán graduated from Charles University in Prague in 1989 and joined Cardiff University as a full-time member of staff in 2001. Jirí received his LLD in 2002 and was appointed visiting professor of legal philosophy and sociology at Charles University by President of the Czech Republic Václav Havel in November 2001. He was also visiting professor or scholar at European University Institute in Florence, New York University (Prague Office), University of

California in Berkeley, University of San Francisco, and University of Pretoria. Jirí Pribán has published extensively in the areas of sociology of law, legal philosophy, constitutional and European comparative law, and theory of human rights. He is an editor of the Journal of Law and Society and a regular contributor to the BBC World Service, the Czech TV, newspapers and other periodicals.

Sarah-Jane Richards is a qualified psychologist, neuro-anatomist and lawyer specialising in pharmaceutical product liability. She was awarded a senior fellowship at King's College Cambridge in 1989 while simultaneously establishing a research team within the Department of Medicine, at Addenbrooke's Hospital, Cambridge investigating cellular and molecular replacement for the treatment of neurodegenerative disease. In 1998, in response to the Medical Research Council's 40 year age limitation for funding senior fellows, she re-trained as a lawyer in the Claimant Division of Hugh James solicitors, Cardiff. She is a professional musician and holds a private pilot's licence.

Henriette d.c. Roscam Abbing is professor of health law at the University of Utrecht and legal counsellor on health law at the Ministry of Health, Welfare and Sport. Before that she worked at the Council of Europe (Strasbourg), Health Division, the Dutch Sick Fund Council, and the University of Maastricht. She is co-editor of the *Dutch Journal on Health Law*, one of the chief editors of the *European Journal of Health Law* and a member of the Dutch Health Council. She is representative of the Minister of Health at the Steering Committee on health and the Steering Committee on Bioethics of the Council of Europe. Her scientific activities and publications cover the whole range of health law. At present she specifically focuses upon new biotechnological developments and their impact on rights of the patient, from a national international and European Union perspective.

Tom Sanders, BA, MSc, PhD is a Post-doc Research training Fellow in Health Services Research at the Department of Applied Social Science, University of Manchester. Before taking up his current post, he worked with the Cardiff Family Studies Research Centre, conducting the research on subdural haemorrhages in children with Cathy Cobley. He is currently working on a Department of Health study to investigate the communication process between health care professionals and patients diagnsoed with heart failure.

Shaila Seshia works as a consultant to the Food Ethics Council on its project Agri-Food Research: An Ethical Audit. She previously worked at the Institute of Development Studies, University of Sussex where her work focused on governance, sustainable livelihoods, and agricultural development. Shaila began a PhD in Anthropology at Yale University in autumn 2004.

Gerry Simpson is Reader in Public International Law at the London School of Economics and Political Science. He is the author of *Great Powers and Outlaw*

States (Cambridge, 2004) (awarded the American Society of International Law's annual prize for Pre-eminent Contribution to Creative Legal Scholarship) and is co-editor (with Tim McCormack) of *The Law of War Crimes: National and International Approaches*. His most recent books were *War Crimes Law Volumes I and II* (Ashgate, 2005) and he is currently completing two books: *Law, War and Crime*, (Polity, 2006) and *Iraq and Just War* (ed. Ashgate, 2006).

Jason Söderblom is a Director of the World-ICE Group – Legal and Security Advisors – and is an Analyst with Clive Williams' Terrorism Intelligence Centre (TIC) in Canberra, Australia. He holds a double degree in Bachelor of Laws with Honours and a Bachelor of Arts from the Australian National University (ANU). His recent publications include *Opening the Intelligence Window: Realist Logic and the Invasion of Iraq, Combating Al-Qaeda: The Clever Hand of Anti-Terrorism, and Risk Analysis in Suicide Bioterrorism*. He has written on the trial of Saddam Hussein for the *American Foreign Service Journal* and *Lawyers' Weekly* (Australia). The views expressed in this article are not necessarily those of the TIC.

Philip A. Thomas was educated at the universities of Cardiff, Aberystwyth and Michigan. He has held academic positions at the universities of Yale, Dar es Salaam, and Lusaka. In addition, he has been a visiting professor in a number of law schools including, Oslo, Utrecht, Prague, Kuala Lumpur, Hong Kong and Macquarie. He currently teaches a course on 'Civil Liberties'. His research is focused in the area of socio legal studies and he is a founding member, and former executive committee member of the Socio Legal Studies Association. In addition, he is the founding and current editor of the *Journal of Law and Society* which is a leading international socio legal journal.

David Watkinson graduated in Archaeological Conservation from University College London Institute of Archaeology in 1975 and later gained a research based MSc at Cardiff University. His thesis assessed selected conservation methods for archaeological iron. After a brief period working in museums and on excavation material he entered teaching and research at Cardiff University, where he is currently Senior Lecturer responsible for BSc and MSc artifact conservation courses. Research interests and publications lie mostly in the areas of archaeological iron, glass, practical conservation and conservation training design and implementation. Professionally he is a fellow if the International Institute for Conservation and an Accredited Member of United Kingdom Institute for Conservation. He has been Chair of the Archaeology Section of the United Kingdom Institute for Conservation and a committee member of that body. He is also a past editor of *Conservation News*.

Elspeth Webb grew up on a farm in North Wales, trained in St. George's Hospital, London, and subsequently worked in a variety of settings across the UK – of which the most memorable was in General Practice in the Isle of Skye – and also in Africa.

She has two children, and has worked for the last 14 years as a part-time senior lecturer in the Department of Child Health in the College of Medicine, Cardiff University, Wales, UK. Like all medical academics she spends half her working week as a clinician. Her clinical work includes autism, child protection, and improving service access for marginalised communities. She has a longstanding commitment to the promotion of children's rights and to combating discrimination, particularly against children who are socially marginalised. These interests are reflected in her clinical commitments, teaching, research, and publication record. When not at work she enjoys reading, art galleries, walks that take in a medieval castle or other suitable ruin, and singing in any choir that will have her.

Peter Wells, after a varied background in Geography and then Urban Planning during which he gained his BA, MSc and PhD, joined Cardiff Business School and became a founder member of the Centre for Automotive Industry Research in 1990. He then became a founder member of the ESRC-funded BRASS research centre, also at Cardiff University. He has been a contract researcher for almost twenty years, preferring the excitement, interest and variety of this life to the discipline that mainstream lecturing brings. Dr Wells has published widely on the automotive industry, particularly environmental matters and is currently exploring the scope of industrial ecology to inform a redesign of the industry.

Joy Wingfield, LLM, MPhil, BPharm, FRPharmS, Dip Ag Vet Pharm, FCPP is Boots Special Professor of Pharmacy Law and Ethics at the University of Nottingham and a pharmacy practice consultant for Boots The Chemists Ltd. She qualified as a pharmacist in 1971 and then worked for five years in community pharmacy. She joined the staff of the Pharmaceutical Society in 1976 as an inspector under the Pharmacy Acts, covering almost a thousand community pharmacies and registered agricultural outlets as well as many other retailers of medicines. From 1986 to 1991 she joined the headquarters staff at the Society in the law department, first as senior administrator and later Head of the Ethics division dealing with aspects of registration, disciplinary and professional matters. During this period she obtained postgraduate qualifications in European law and later in law and medical practice. This was followed by nine years as the assistant pharmacy superintendent for Boots, being responsible for risk management across the company's 1000 plus UK pharmacies. In 2000 she was appointed to a chair as Boots special professor of pharmacy law and ethics at Nottingham University, a post which includes teaching, development and research. Since taking this post, she has secured government funding for a three-year project to advance the teaching of pharmacy law and ethics. Her publications include joint authorship of the standard textbook, *Dale and Appelbe's Pharmacy Law and Ethics* and a companion volume, *Practical Exercises in Pharmacy Law and Ethics*. She is a regular journal contributor and speaks widely on pharmacy law and ethics. She is founder and chairman of the Pharmacy Law and Ethics Association and a Governor and examiner for the College of Pharmacy Practice.

Acknowledgement

We would like to thank Kate Reeves, Matthew Davies and Sarah Kennedy for their help in gathering material and putting this book together.

Jennifer Gunning
Søren Holm

List of Abbreviations

ADHD	Attention deficit hyperactivity disorder
ADISCO	Associazione Donatrici Italiani Sangue di Cordone Ombelicale
ADR	Adverse drug reactions
AHR	Assisted human reproduction
ALSPAC	Avon Longitudinal Study of Parents and Children
BBSRC	Biotechnology and Biological Sciences Research Council
BEM	Black or ethnic minority
BTHA	British Toy and Hobby Association
CAFCASS	Children and Family Court Advisory and Support Services
CAMHS	Child and Adolescent Mental Health Services
CAMS	Court of Appeal Mediation Scheme
CBU	Cord blood unit
CFA	Conditional fee agreement
CPA	Coalition Provisional Authority
CRC	Childrens' Rights Commissioner
CSM	Committee for the Safety of Medicines (UK)
CST	House of Lords Select Committee on Science and Technology
DCA	Department for Constitutional Affairs (UK)
DEFRA	Department for the Environment, Food and Rural Affairs (UK)
DfES	Department for Education and Skills (UK)
DNA	Deoxyribonucleic acid
DTI	Department of Trade and Industry (UK)
ECHR	European Convention on Human Rights
EHRR	European Human Rights Reports
EPEG	Ethical Protection in Epidemiological Genetics
ESRC	Economic and Social Research Council
EU	European Union
EWHC	England and Wales High Court
FACT	Foundation for the Accreditation of Cellular Therapy
FAO	Food and Agriculture Organization of the United Nations
FATF	Financial Action Task Force
FDA	Food and Drugs Administration (US)
FGM	Female genital mutilation
FSA	Food Standards Agency (UK)
GAfREC	Governance Arrangements for NHS Research Ethics Committees
GATT	General Agreement on Tariffs and Trade

GM	Genetically modified
GMC	General Medical Council
GMP	Good manufacturing practice
GP	General practitioner
GPE	Growth, poverty and environment
GSK	GlaxoSmithKline
GSL	General Sale List
GVHD	Graft versus host disease
HFEA	Human Fertilisation and Embryology Authority (UK)
HIV	Human immunodeficiency virus
HLA	Human leukocyte antigen
HRA	UK Human Rights Act
HSC	Haematopoietic stem cell
ICCPR	International Covenant on Civil and Political Rights
ICTI	International Congress of Toy Industries
ICTR	International Criminal Tribunal for Rwanda
ICTY	International Criminal Tribunal for Yugoslavia
IFI	International financial institution
IHCC	Iraqi Higher Criminal Court
IMF	International Monetary Fund
IOSCO	International Organization of Securities Commissions
IP	Intellectual property
IST	Iraqi special tribunal
ITC	Independent Television Commission (UK)
IVF	In vitro fertilization
JOMEC	Cardiff University School of Journalism and Media Studies
LAFQAS	Legal Aid Franchise Quality Standard
LDC	Less developed country
LREC	Local research ethics committee
MCA	Medicines Control Agency (UK)
MHRA	Medicines and Healthcare products Regulatory Agency (UK)
MHT	Mental Health Tribunal
MIND	The National Association for Mental Health (UK)
MNC	Multinational Corporation
NAMA	Non-agricultural market access
NAO	National Audit Office (UK)
NCCT	Non-cooperative Countries and Territories
NCDS	UK National Child Development Study
NERC	Natural Environment Research Council
NGO	Non-governmental organization
NHS	National Health Service (UK)
NIH	National Institutes of Health (US)
NOD/SCID	Non-obese diabetic/severe combined immunodeficiency mutation
NSPCC	National Society for Prevention of Cruelty to Children

OECD	Organisation for Economic Co-operation and Development
OFC	Offshore financial centre
Ofcom	Office of Communications (UK)
OFT	Office of Fair Trading
OSCE	Organization for Security and Co-operation in Europe
OTC	Over the counter
POST	Parliamentary Office of Science and Technology
RCT	Rhondda Cynon Taff
RELU	Rural Economy and Land Use programme
RPM	Retail Price Maintenance
SAP	Structural Adjustment Policies
SCSL	Special Criminal Court for Sierra Leone
SNP	Single nucleotide polymorphism
SPUC	Society for the Protection of the Unborn Child
SSA	Sub-Saharan Africa
SSRI	Selective serotonin reuptake inhibitor
UN	United Nations
UNCRC	United Nations Convention on the Rights of the Child
UNDP	United Nations Development Programme
UNICEF	United Nations Children's Fund
USSC	Unrestricted somatic stem cells
WAG	Welsh Assembly Government
WHO	World Health Organization
WTO	World Trade Organization

INTRODUCTION

Chapter 1

Introduction

Jennifer Gunning
Søren Holm

When people get to know that you are working in ethics two quite opposite questions are often raised. The first of these is 'But haven't you solved most problems already?. I am a doctor and everyone now gets informed consent from patients and has been taught ethics in medical school'. The second is 'That is interesting, there are all these new technologies being developed and they all seem to create huge ethical problems'. The papers in this book show that both these responses are misguided. There are many of the traditional areas of ethical concern that are still not resolved and therefore still require analysis, and there are many newly discovered areas of ethical interest that have nothing to do with new technologies. The papers also show that the interface between law and applied ethics opens up possibilities for very creative scholarship. The book has a highly multi-disciplinary team of contributors and as editors we have tried to get the individual authors to think outside their own disciplinary box, so that the book will be of value to a multi-disciplinary readership.

The papers in the first part of the book are all concerned with bioethics (or biolaw), one of the traditional core areas of applied ethics and one of the topics that is discussed in many of them is the issue of consent to interventions, treatment and research. The issue of consent has been discussed since the birth of modern medical ethics in the late 1960s and even if there are large areas of consensus concerning what constitutes valid consent and why, the papers in this section clearly illustrate that the analysis of consent is far from being exhausted, and that it is not only trivial and unimportant issues that still need further analysis.

The papers in the second part of the book 'Ethics and society' covers a wider range of current issues, but many of them deal specifically with the way societies handle disputes and conflicts concerning its most vulnerable members, including children. From the papers it becomes clear that well-meaning regulation can have very problematic side-effects and even more strongly that our societies have not yet reached a stable conceptualisation of childhood and children. The perceived vulnerability of children is in conflict with an increased realisation that children can in many circumstances be competent decision makers even in stressful situations.

The third part of the book analyses current issues in business and professional ethics, some of these are traditional issues in business ethics, but others are quite new, not because they are not important or not worth analysing, but simply because they have been overlooked. Although we have had a toy industry for many years, the number of papers giving an in-depth analysis of the ethics (or lack of ethics) of the toy industry is very small. But anyone reading Stephen Hogan's paper on this issue must quickly realise that an ethical analysis of the activities of the toy industry is neither trivial nor simple, and that it is strange that there is not a thriving academic 'industry' in toy ethics.

The fourth part of the book illustrates the power of ethical and legal analysis to illuminate current societal developments ranging from the Orange revolution in Ukraine to the rebuilding of Iraq. In a media culture characterised by the sound-bite and the short life of most news stories, there is a growing need for insightful analysis of the bigger or deeper picture. The short commentaries in part four seek to fill some of that need.

Although each of the papers in the book focuses on a particular topic and is therefore of value primarily to readers interested in that topic, the book as a whole should be of interest to anyone interested in the broader area of ethics, law and society; both as a compendium of current thinking across a range of issues, but also, and perhaps more importantly as a source of inspiration for further work.

PART I
BIOETHICS

Chapter 2

Human Tissue Research, Individual Rights and Bio-banks

Henriette d.c. Roscam Abbing

'The interests and welfare of the human being prevail over the sole interest of science and society' (Article 2 of the Convention on human rights and biomedicine)[1]

Introduction

Medical progress is based on research. The human body is an indispensable resource for progress in medicine. Human related medical scientific research includes research involving direct interventions on research subjects and research with personal information and/or human biological material (human tissue). Important breakthroughs in knowledge of the human genome and of the influence that genes (may) have on individuals' health, as well as advances in computer technology, account for the increased use of human tissue in human health related research. Thanks to the advances in science and technology, the medical (genetic) information contained in human tissue may be uncovered and placed in its genetic context. Human tissue thus has become a valuable resource of health related information.

As such, the use of human tissue in research is not a new phenomenon. But scientific and technological developments have drastically changed the nature and design of research. The focus of new research possibilities involving human tissue is upon genetic characteristics. The research is carried out on a large scale, involving huge quantities of human tissue in combination with personal information, and may extend over a life span and over generations. The objective of such large scale tissue research is to find genetic variations among individuals and among groups of the population, including the interaction of genes with environment and lifestyle. The research findings may allow for personalised medicine.

This area of research is continuously moving. As a consequence of the developments in human tissue research, the status of the human tissue has changed from a res derelicta into a substance which has personal (informational) value; because of the commercial prospects the research offers, human tissue has also become a commodity.

These developments have implications for the implementation of the individual right to private life (article 8 of the Council of Europe Convention on human rights and fundamental freedoms). In October 2005, a first international legal instrument on research on human biological materials that addresses the human rights aspects was drawn up by the Council of Europe Committee on bioethics.[2] The purpose of the recommendation is to set out and safeguard rights of individuals whose biological materials are used in biomedical research, while recognizing the importance of freedom of research. Because this is a quickly developing area of research, the provisions of the recommendation are mostly of a general nature; they have to be complemented by practice guidelines that will give substance to the general principles. This allows for flexible application of the norms in a variety of situations and for adaptation of the practice guidelines in the light of changing circumstances. The recommendation includes provisions on managing tissue collections (e.g. transparency and accountability), documentation of human biological samples, quality and safety requirements, conditions for access to the biological materials for research uses, supervision of collections. A distinct chapter is devoted to population bio-banks.

The main guiding principle of the recommendation is the professional obligation to provide information to and ask consent from patients and research subjects when biological materials are stored and used for research purposes. Protection of the individual's private sphere when utilising human biological material and personal data in research is another important element of the recommendation.

There is discussion on how best to implement these individual rights in research practice.[3] This paper analyses the conditions necessary to safeguard the right to private life of individuals whose personal informational sources are used in the research. It focuses primarily on information and consent and on protection of privacy (with particular emphasis on bio-banks). Issues of an organisational and procedural nature are less controversial.[4]

The Picture

Research with a combination of large scale (population) collections of (DNA) tissue samples, medical data, family history genealogical information and environmental factors holds many prospects for improvements in health.

To find the key to individual differences and among groups of the population for predominantly genetically determined diseases means finding the key for making effective medicaments. Explanation of the reason why individuals show varieties in responses to medicaments will allow for prediction of whether and if so in how far someone may positively respond to medicaments. It is assumed also that eventually the research will allow for establishing environmental and lifestyle links to the risk of developing a specific disease. This will allow for timely preventive measures. Huge collections of human tissue and associated personal information must be available for such research activities, now and in the future.

For the purpose of human tissue research, use can be made of tissue which is left over after a medical (research) intervention and subsequently stored for future uses. These tissue collections are assembled for the medical interest of the patient from whom the tissue is taken, and/or for their use in other patients' care, and/or for research activities. Health care and related research account for the existence of a great number of collections of human tissue. Some of those collections are disease specific, others unspecified. With information and communication technology, existing collections can be mutually linked and combined with personal information, thus creating a virtual data base as a source for human tissue research.

A relatively new method to collect tissue is to ask individuals to donate bodily tissue for research purposes. These tissue samples are stored after a physical intervention for (future) use in a variety of research activities, often in combination with personal data.

In principle every human tissue collection constitutes a 'bio-bank', in case the tissue contains nucleated cells, also referred to as a 'genetic database'. However, these terms are mostly reserved for structured collections of large quantities of (DNA) tissue samples, mostly donated, allowing for research activities that link the genetic information contained in the tissue sample with personal information collected over time and over generations. Bio-banks contain 'dynamic' collections. With the contribution of 'depositors' of tissue, a bio-bank creates resources for present and future research activities, including for purposes other than those specified at the time of the collection and storage of the tissue.

Bio-banks are set up in the public sphere and on a commercial basis. If created in the public sector, access to the material is in principle open to a great number of researchers for a variety of research activities. Research activities may involve a considerable cross border flow of data and tissue.

Changes in Research Focus – Changes in Normative Concerns

The changes in the focus of human tissue research give rise to a number of concerns in relation to the rights of those whose tissue and personal information are involved.

Tissue research has many parallels with medical research on individual research participants and with research using personal (coded) medical data, but there are also differences. The parallels are that in research use is made of personal human resources, which are altruistically made available and may involve a physical intervention; that the research is not primarily undertaken for the benefit of the individual, that the research involves third party interests and that the research may have implications for those whose tissue and personal information are involved. Under these circumstances, the rights of those whose tissue is involved in the research deserve similar protection as in the case of biomedical research on research subjects and with personal medical data. This includes the independent examination of the scientific merit and legal and ethical acceptability of the research activity.

However, unlike the case of research on individual research participants, physical integrity is not per se at stake in tissue research. This is the case when use is made of left over tissue. In that situation, the focus of the protection is on the control the source has over his biological material. Another difference is that the prevalent standards address living persons only, whilst the new tissue research activities may also involve tissue from the deceased. This aspect however can be addressed by soliciting people to express their wishes during life (e.g. as terms of the will).

Because of the informational value of human tissue in research, the standards on the protection of individuals with regard to the processing of personal data apply[5] in the various stages of the research process, from the moment the data are solicited for the purpose of a research project, data handling during the research, as well as when the research is finished (the research results).

The requirements pertain to quality of data, data security and safeguards for the data subject.

As in the case of data research, whenever feasible, non-identifiable biological materials should be used in a research activity. Non-identifiable materials are materials that (alone or in combination with associated data) do not allow with reasonable efforts the identification of the person concerned. These materials are often referred to as unlinked anonymized materials. If the research does not allow for the use of unlinked anonymized materials, they should be anonymized as far as appropriate for the research activity and they should remain identifiable only as long as necessary for the purpose of the research activity. Depending on the nature of the research the materials (alone or in combination with associated data) may allow the identification of the person directly, or through the use of a code to which the research user has direct access (coded materials) or does not have access (linked anonymized materials). The latter is the case when the code is under the control of a third party. The burden of proof of the necessity of using the one or the other form of identifiable material lies with the researcher (principles of necessity and subsidiarity).

When the samples are stored in a bio-bank, the individual is traceable by the person(s) who are responsible for the collection, but not necessarily by the researcher. Anonymous storage in a bio-bank by removal of the identifiable characteristics after a certain period of storage, so that tissue and data can no longer be linked to identifiable individuals, may substantially diminish the value and functions of bio-banks. But anonymized research use is not always necessary. However, even if human tissue and associated data are rendered unlinked anonymous prior to their handing over to the research user, they may become identifiable during the process. The application of bio-informatic technologies in pharmacogenetic studies for instance increases the chance that individuals whose data are kept in a biobank may be identified through their single-nucleotide polymorphism (SNPs) data.[6]

Where research involves genetic information, the concerns extend beyond the individual who has provided the tissue, as the information contained in the tissue also pertains to the person's blood relatives and future offspring. The combination of tissue and data in this area of research can yield new information in itself, so that it is possible to build up a rather comprehensive picture of an individual's health (present and future). Because the research may reveal genetic information which can be of importance for the health of the individuals concerned, the right to know and the right not to know are important.

Private Life Within the Family: A Case

The family interest in protection of privacy was recently recognised in an Icelandic Supreme Court decision.[7] The Icelandic Health Sector Data Base Act of 1998, set up for the purpose of genetically related human tissue research, provides for the right of patients to refuse permission for information concerning them to be entered into the Health Database. In this case, the court recognised the interest a daughter may have, on the basis of the right to protection of privacy in the Icelandic Constitution, in preventing the transfer of health information in medical records pertaining to her deceased father into the database. Icelandic medical records contain extensive information on medical treatment, life style and social conditions, employment and family circumstances together with detailed information of the person that the information concerns. Information could be inferred from data relating to the hereditary characteristics of the daughter's father which might also apply to her. The Act provides for a one way encryption prior to the transfer of the information to the database, making it virtually impossible to read the encrypted data. But it does not specify to what information of medical records such encryption applies. The court concluded that various forms of monitoring of the creation and operation of the database are no substitute in the light of the obligations under the Constitution without foundation in definite statutory norms.

The court also concluded that though the Act stipulates that health information in the Health Sector Data base should be non-personally identifiable, it is far from adequately ensured under statutory law that this stated objective will be achieved.

Information and Consent: General Requirements

Because of the personal informational value human tissue represents, it is generally acknowledged nowadays that the sample 'source' should have explicit control over it.[8] As in other human related medical research, respect for autonomy (private life) implies that everyone has a right to accept or to refuse to have his human tissue (and associated data) used in research activities. Consent should be voluntary, should be based on information that allows for a meaningful decision and should be obtained before any research activity is undertaken. This notion is reflected in the Council of Europe Convention on human rights and biomedicine (in particular article 22), in the additional protocol concerning biomedical research and in the recommendation on research on humans biological materials.

The right to have control over one's bodily tissue samples implies that everybody has the right to be informed whether, if so and for what research purposes human tissue is or will be stored and used. This right is a fundamental premise irrespective of the manner in which the consent for research use is modelled (express consent or opting out). The provision of information is an active, dynamic process that starts the moment human tissue (left over or donated) will be stored and used in research. The quality of the information is determinant for the validity of the consent to the use of human tissue in research. The informed consent delineates the scope of legitimate research.

The information to be provided from the onset should include the rights of the source of the human tissue to withhold consent to (some of the envisaged) research uses, to be re-contacted when a new research activity is envisaged, to withdraw or change the scope of the consent, to have the material and data destroyed or rendered absolute anonymous and/or removed from the collection, during life or after death.

In conformity with the principles of data protection, the information on the research objectives should be as specified as possible at the time of collection and storage of the tissue. For instance, storage of left over tissue from a breast cancer related intervention for research in that specific disease area would be a sufficiently clear determination for obtaining valid consent for future research uses in that area; 'storage for cancer research' would be an insufficiently defined purpose.

If the research is genetically related, the possible implications of a new research activity for the source of the material and his relatives will make a new explicit informed consent necessary.

Likely risks and consequences of the specific research uses should in any case be part of the information. Furthermore, general (written) information should be provided on the (content of the) independent overview of the research activities, on privacy protective measures and other safeguards, such as the anonymization techniques to be used, on measures to prevent unauthorised access to the tissue collection, on the management of the collection and on control measures. The principles governing access to and use of the samples should be communicated, including the contractual obligations of researchers. It should be made known to the source of the material that such obligations always reflect his wishes in relation to the research uses. Policies regarding transborder transfer of material and data should also be communicated.

The nature, content and context of the informational aspects of a specific research are important factors for the content of the information to be given for acquiring valid consent. In case of genetically related research the risks of intrusion into the private sphere of the source and his relatives are more serious as with not genetically related research. Therefore, when the envisaged research use is genetically related, the information should be more specific regarding the content of the information the research activity will generate, the kind of other information it may bring about, the need for feedback of health related information becoming available during the research, whether relatives have to be involved in the research, or may have interest in new information.

Information and Consent: Bio-banks

As with other collections, research with biological materials and associated personal information contained in a bio-bank likewise is legitimate only in as far as it is in the scope of the consent, based on information that is sufficiently specific to make the consent valid.

In as far as the research implies further processing of resources of the bio-bank for purposes which were not conceived at the time of their collection and storage, or that fall outside the originally specified research purposes, the source of the material and data should be re-contacted. This re-contacting is sometimes perceived as problematic in research terms. Re-contacting would be unfeasible (in particular if the source of the tissue has died without leaving any instructions); it would be impracticable to re-contact large groups of the population, especially in longitudinal studies; re-contacting has a risk of insufficient positive response, which will undermine the value of the research. To overcome these (perceived) hindrances, simplification of the consent procedures is sometimes suggested as an alternative. The simplification of the consent requirements then is sought in asking for a broad and general consent, in dispensing with the offer of options in the information and consent process for the use of left over tissue obtained during medical care. Moreover, a waiver of consent is considered justified if the researcher has no access to the code. In such an approach, withdrawal of the research uses will be respected, unless anonymization takes place.

General consent so as to avoid re-contacting the source, and waiver of consent in case of 'pseudo-anonymized' (coded) material and data, are not compatible with the right to private life. In the medical research context that right implies the obligation to provide sufficient information to allow the source of the biological material to make a well-founded decision. Moreover, other than the 'general consent' approach seems to imply, information is not a one time event, namely at the moment of seeking consent. The right to withdrawal for instance cannot be knowingly exercised without knowledge of the developments with the research.

In the alternative approach to the information and consent requirements, the direct guarantees for the right of the source to hold control over his biological material are shifted towards procedural protection, namely the review of a research project by an independent research ethics committee and the oversight by a data protection officer, unless the data and samples are anonymous or anonymized.[9] When looked upon from the right to informational privacy the latter exception is not unproblematic. Failing an objective control, there are no guarantees that anonymity and anonymization are indeed properly performed.

The informed consent may be considered impractical and a hindrance from the perspective of the research users, but the arguments do not as such justify that research in essence departs from the rights of individual whose personal informational resources are involved. Protective organisational and procedural measures are indispensable, but they cannot come in the place of the rights of the individual.

The suggested simplification of consent procedures implies an erosion of the informed consent requirement that is neither necessary, nor proportional, and therefore not legally justified.

In the particular context of bio-bank research, departure from the scope of the (original) explicit consent by assuming that people consent unless they indicate otherwise (opting out) can be justified under the conditions which are generally accepted in personal medical data research. They are that the research has an important potential significance for public health that cannot be reasonably achieved in another way, that active re-contacting is not possible or reasonably cannot be required, and provided all necessary safeguards for the protection of the personal sphere are in place. The burden of proof lies with the researcher.

Re-contacting the source of human tissue might prove less unfeasible than it is perceived. Re-contacting is nowadays much facilitated by information and communication technology, and because virtually everybody can be traced through a personal identification number. There are also other possibilities such as re-contacting the depositors as a matter of routine, at regular intervals, to reassess their specific wishes. If no instructions on future re-use are left by a deceased in the case of genetic oriented research, a next of kin should be contacted.

The modelling of consent as an opting out may be justified by the circumstances, in particular with high quality anonymization in place, but the obligation to provide appropriate and sufficient information remains. These requirements are determinant factors for the validity of any kind of consent procedure. As was indicated before, the provision of information is an active, ongoing, dynamic process. With the application of information and communication technology depositors of tissue in a bio-bank can be actively and adequately informed and communicated with. The website of the biobank should be used to provide regular update information on ongoing research projects, on the progress made and on future research activities. The functioning of a bio-bank ought to be an open process so that consent procedures are embedded in a human rights enabling environment. This will also contribute to public trust and to the continued participation in the functioning of the bio-bank.

Freedom of Medical Research: Freedom Within Restraints

Modern medical research activities increasingly give rise to claims for (more) freedom of medical research.[10] Often heard arguments are, time, effort and money involved with obtaining informed consent from persons to use their medical records or data entered in other registries and to use their biological material, that informed consent would result in insufficient participation in the research to be able to draw valid conclusions from it and that thereby the public interest in the discovery and findings of research might be harmed. For making progress in medicine, freedom of medical research is of paramount importance.

But medical research is not a free play area. Human rights, human dignity and ethical and moral values set limits.

Freedom of medical scientific research is a privilege that depends on the readiness of people to freely participate. With changing research practices come changing rules, but the basic human rights standards remain unchanged.

The interest society has in medical research as the essential precursor for new knowledge and experience to improve the individual health and the health of the population, goes hand in hand with the interest society has in respect for human rights, social and moral values.

Notes

[1] Council of Europe, Oviedo, 4 April 1997.
[2] The recommendation is submitted to the Committee of Ministers for approval. <www.coe.int/bioethics>
[3] Melissa A. Austin e.e., Genebanks: A comparison of eight proposed international genetic databases, Community genetics, 2003, 6: 37–45. T. Caulfield, tissue banking, patient rights and confidentiality: lessons in law and policy, Medicine and law, 2004, 23: 39–49. Jane Kaye e.a. Population genetic databases: a comparative analysis of the law in Iceland, Sweden, Estonia and the UK, TRAMES 2004, 1/2: 15–33.
[4] The World Health Organisation partnership on patients' rights and citizens' empowerment network has issued the document 'Genetic Databases, assessing the benefits and the impact on human and patient rights' which was produced by Graeme T. Laurie as the principal author. The key recommendations of the document are published in the *European Journal of Health Law*, 2004, 11: 87–92.
[5] Data Protection Working Party, set up under article 29 of Directive 95/46/EC. Working document on genetic data, 17 March 2004, 12178/03/EN – WP91.
[6] Data privacy may not be 'technically' feasible for pharmacogenetics studies. See newsletter Public Health Genetics Unit, 2-7 September 2004. <http://www.phu.org.uk/newsletter/index.shtm#fletcher>
[7] Icelandic supreme court, no. 151/2003.
[8] The specific position of persons not able to consent is not discussed.
[9] Nationaler Ethikrat, Biobanks for research, Opinion, the German National Ethics council, Berlin 2004 www.ethikrat.org and a commentary by Bartha Knoppers, Biobanks: symplifying consent, Nature reviews/genetics, Research Highlights: ethics watch, July 2004, p. 485.
[10] See for instance George J. Annas, Medical privacy and medical research, judging the new federal regulations, *New England Journal of Medicine*, 2002, pp. 216–p219. David Price, The human tissue saga continues, *Medical Law Review*, 2003, p. 1–66. Cancer registries: should informed consent be required? *Journal of the National Cancer Institute*, 2002, p. 1269.

Chapter 3

Umbilical Cord Cell Banking: A Surprisingly Controversial Issue

Jennifer Gunning

Introduction

Stem cells from umbilical cord blood probably now form one of the most commonly banked types of human tissue. Originally stored for the treatment of haematological disorders these stem cells have now been found to be more versatile, even pluripotent, with potential for use in the treatment of a broader range of disorders and diseases and may be particularly valuable in cell therapy and regenerative medicine.

The storage of umbilical cord cells has not been without controversy and there is a rapidly growing private sector involvement. A number of ethical issues continue to be debated involving questions of regulation and quality assurance, ownership and commercialisation and patenting. This paper aims to investigate some of these issues.

Background

Historically bone marrow transplantation has been used in the treatment of patients with blood and immune disorders requiring a source of haematopoietic stem cells (HSC). Until recently, the blood remaining in the placenta and umbilical cord following the birth of a baby was discarded as a waste product. But in 1988 the first successful cord cell transplant to a sibling with Fanconi's anaemia took place[1] and this proven utility of cord blood led to the establishment of cord blood banks.

It has been determined that umbilical cord blood is some ten times richer than bone marrow in its proportion of progenitors of haematopoietic stem cells.[2] Moreover, lymphocytes in cord blood appear to be less immunologically active than those found in bone marrow[3] and the incidence of graft versus host disease (GVHD) lower. These factors make cord blood an attractive alternative to bone marrow for a number of conditions and, following the report of the 1988 case, cord blood banks were established first in the USA and Europe and now there are over 100 such banks worldwide both in the public and private sectors. Early transplants were to siblings but with the establishment of public cord blood banks unrelated cord cell transplants were enabled first in children and then to a lesser extent, in adults.

The use of cord blood cells has a number of advantages over the use of bone marrow, particularly in the paediatric context. Cord blood units (CBU) are more rapidly available than bone marrow. Bone marrow is obtained from volunteer donors who are recruited by blood and transplantation services and other organisations. Donor details, including ethnicity, human leukocyte antigen (HLA) and blood type, are held in registers. If a transplant is needed by a patient, their clinician will search the bone marrow registries for a match. The volunteer will then be approached for a bone marrow donation and tests for disease and other exclusion criteria will be carried out. This process is time consuming and it may take many weeks before a suitable donation becomes available, if at all, for the critically ill patient. There is always a risk that the volunteer will change their mind about donating. Cord blood units are stored frozen after thorough testing for contamination and specified diseases, such as Hepatitis B and C and HIV, and there is no risk of last minute consent refusal.

Cord blood is less risky to collect. The collection of cord blood following delivery is a harmless process that should not affect the mother or her newborn. Cord blood can, therefore, be collected with little or no risk to the donor and stored, frozen, until needed. The harvesting of bone marrow is an invasive process that can cause some risk and discomfort to the donor. Bone marrow is therefore not collected until it is needed.

The number of potential donors is high. Recruitment of cord blood donors from antenatal clinics is relatively easy and only a very small number of women, from amongst those who might be willing to donate, is ever approached. Potential bone marrow donors are not so readily identifiable although many will be blood donors.

There is a decreased risk of GVHD. The cells in cord blood appear to be more 'naive' than their counterparts in bone marrow because of the immune immaturity of the newborn. It has also been shown that the low number or absence of $CD8^+$ natural killer (NK) T cells in cord blood may also be a relevant factor.[4] Cord blood units do not have to be a perfect HLA match because of the reduced incidence of GVHD. This means that it is possible to use unrelated and mismatched donors.[5,6] While sibling donors were used in early cord blood transplants, the establishment of cord blood banks means that it has been possible increasingly to use unrelated donors.

The risk of transmission of infectious disease is diminished for cord blood because all CBU are screened for disease and any infected or contaminated units discarded.

Cord cells would, therefore, seem to be the perfect alternative to bone marrow but there are some important disadvantages. The time to platelet engraftment is prolonged in the transplantation of cord blood in comparison to bone marrow[7] – this study also showed that engraftment time was strongly related to cell dose – and the cell dose of CBU is generally insufficient for adults. Although cord blood is enriched in HSC its volume is less than is collected from bone marrow. This makes CBU more suited to paediatric use. Clinical experience has shown that to successfully treat an adult the nucleated cell dose in the CBU must be at least $1.5–2.01 \times 10^7$ per kilogram body weight[8,9] and it has been shown that a cord blood nucleated cell dose of 0.37×10^8 per kilo increased the speed and probability of engraftment (E Gluckman personal communication). The Düsseldorf NetCord bank has had a policy of collecting only units larger than 80ml since 1997. In these units the median number of nucleated cells was $10 \pm 5 \times 10^8$ per unit yet only 25 per cent of the units contained enough cells to engraft patients of 50–70 kilograms. To overcome this problem multiple units of cord blood have been transplanted but usually only one CBU engrafts. There is also a risk that hereditary disorders, undiagnosed in the donor at birth, may be transmitted to the recipient.

The problem of cell dose is being addressed. Cord blood has a higher potential for in vitro proliferation than adult bone marrow[10] and, currently, a considerable body of research is being undertaken into cell expansion to overcome the cell dose problem. Most of this research is being validated in mouse models[11, 12] but some expanded units have already been used in the human clinical context as part of a trial.[13,14] Eurocord III, funded by the EU under the Cell Factory area of Framework 5, will also carry out an evaluation of umbilical cord blood transplant engraftment using ex vivo haematopoietic stem expansion.

Cord blood units may be stored in for-profit private banks where parents pay for the storage of their child's cord blood or in non-profit public banks where parents donate their child's cord blood for unrelated use. There is a tension between private cord blood banks, which store blood for autologous or family use, and public banks, which store blood for unrelated use. There is an inference that private banks are taking out of circulation cord blood units which might otherwise be used for unrelated recipients. It is not clear that this is the case since public banks restrict their collection to a local network of hospitals and it is difficult for women outside their target population to donate. Private banks have no such restrictions. But a recent study found that women in antenatal clinics had very little knowledge about cord blood banking although 86 per cent of those questioned would have been willing to donate altruistically; 14 per cent would have elected to bank privately.[15]

Private banks recruit clients from obstetric clinics, via the internet and through other promotional material. Some provide inducements, such as, one American company which offers incentives to recruiters with commission on every 'sale' and to parents in the form of club membership for the child which gives entry to a sweepstake providing access to four $10,000 college scholarships per year.

Cord blood collected for private banks may come from obstetric clinics which are far from their processing and storage facilities. Cord blood units are therefore shipped by courier/delivery service. Although some private banks do provide training materials for obstetric staff undertaking collection, they have no control over collection standards and the obstetricians or midwives collecting CBU for private banking may have little or no experience. Often the collection kits are provided directly to the parents requesting the service and they give them to their obstetrician. The risk of contamination must be higher where those responsible for the collection of cord blood do not carry out the procedure regularly and have little formal training.

Private cord blood banks currently offer contracts for 18–20 years' storage. Recent research indicates that this may be reasonable as CBU stored for 15 years have been thawed successfully and been able to undergo cell expansion. Engraftment into NOD/SCID (Non-obese diabetic/sever combined immunodeficiency mutation) mice was comparable to fresh cord blood.[16] People using private storage are usually required to pay a non-refundable enrolment fee of about $150 (€175), which includes the cost of the collection kit, there will then be the costs of processing and storing the cord blood unit, following a successful collection, which may bring the cost up to nearly $1,000 (€855). Private banks usually offer prepaid storage deals. In Europe this can range from €1,185 to €1,800 for 20 years' storage.

Non-profit, or public banks predominate in Europe. They too recruit from obstetric clinics but usually within a local or regional network. They will generally have a policy of collecting CBU from as wide a diversity of ethnic groups as possible and patients wishing to donate cord blood may find difficulty in doing so if they do not come from within the catchment area of a public bank. Collection methods for the CBU are effectively the same as within the private sector and will differ principally as to whether blood collection is undertaken by trained blood services or obstetric staff.

The funding of the non-profit banks comes from a number of sources and in some cases is precarious. Sources of funding in the USA are US Federal Government support through National Institutes of Health (NIH) grants, contributions from charitable foundations, support from American Red Cross Biomedical Services or from running parallel private banking services. Red Cross funding also supports public banks elsewhere in the world. The only Canadian public cord cell bank has no secure long-term funding arrangements although it has received Canadian and Provincial government funding in the past and it is now actively soliciting funds from the private sector. In Europe the José Carreras Foundation is an important source of charitable funds and other charitable foundations, such as l'Associazione Donatrici Italiane Sangue di Cordone Ombelicale (ADISCO) in Italy, also contribute. The cord cell bank in Milan also receives regional government funding. State funding is also provided to banks in Australia, Japan, Poland and Spain. In Australia all the public banks have been funded by Commonwealth, States and Territories governments since 2001. Previously, the banks in Queensland and New South Wales were dependent on research, charitable and community funds and grants. Public banks also receive income from charging the users of CBU and these can be substantial (in Italy sample charges are €17,000 (Bologna) and €17,675 (Milan)). But use is low with only 1-3 per cent of units stored being used in any one year while the setting up and maintenance costs are high. Moreover, public banks which supply data to international registries have to undertake sophisticated tissue typing and DNA tests which private banks storing for autologous use do not. Both types of bank would be expected to carry out contamination and communicable disease tests. Private banks pass these processing costs on to their customers. However, tissue typing costs are high and these tests would not routinely be offered by private banks in their storage contracts.

Recently it has been discovered that cord blood also contains pluripotent stem cells which have the capacity to develop into neuronal, muscle and bone forming cells[17] and into endothelial cells.[18,19] McGuckin et al[20] also reported a population of adherent CD34 negative cells which differentiated into neural progenitor cells in vitro. More recently McGuckin has reported the world's first reproducible production of cord blood cells expressing embryonic stem cell markers, – cord-blood-derived embryonic-like stem cells (CBEs).[21] The CBEs grew as tight adherent clusters forming embryoid like bodies and showed exponential expansion in liquid culture. The CBE colonies expressed specific stage embryonic antigens (SSEA) 3 and 4 and a number of other embryonic stem cell markers. It is suggested that CBEs represent a primitive cell group with an embryonic stem cell phenotype. The authors were also able to differentiate CBEs into potential hepatic precursor cells. Given that it has been reported that autologous bone marrow cell transplantation has been used successfully in the treatment of patients with severe heart failure[22] it is likely that cord blood cells would have similar properties and, in the longer-term future, it would seem that stem cells from umbilical cord blood might have a significant role to play in cell therapy and regenerative medicine.

Regulation and Quality Assurance

Until recently there has been virtually no regulation of cord cell banks. In March 2004 the European Directive (2004/23/EC) on setting standards for quality and safety for the donation, procurement, testing, processing, preservation, storage and distribution of human tissues and cells came into force. This tissue banking directive will apply to all biobanks, including cord cell banks (though not banks storing blood or blood products), in the public sector. In the UK the Human Tissue Act 2004, which meets the Directive requirements, came into force on 1 April 2006. Other countries, notably Australia, Germany and France, already impose good manufacturing practice (GMP) standards. Elsewhere, standards apply which have been developed by bone marrow transplant organisations or blood services such as the Foundation for the Accreditation of Cellular Therapy (FACT) and the American Association of Blood Banks.[23] There have probably been over a dozen organisations around the world setting quality standards for cord blood banking, all varying slightly, and accreditation has been voluntary. This means that, even in the public sector some CBU released for transplant have been sub-standard. Increasing acceptance of FACT accreditation as the gold standard should lead to improvements in this sector. But accreditation in the private sector, outside those countries that require GMP standards, remains voluntary. Standards for registries holding details of haematopoietic stem cell donors are set by the World Marrow Donor Association. In the USA the FDA is in the process of drawing up tissue banking regulations and it has been agreed that the Health Resources and Services Administration will put $10,000,000 into funding a National Cord Blood Stem Cell Bank Program but this expenditure will await a report on the issue from the Institute of Medicine. In the meantime there is disagreement between cord blood banks and registries as to how the program should work.[24] Up to the present the use of cord blood cells has been facilitated through registries established by blood and bone marrow transplant organisations: the continued appropriateness of this is now being questioned by some cord cell banks in the US.

In Europe the current mood is principally against private cord cell banking. A recent opinion on the ethical aspects of umbilical cord blood banking[25] states that the likelihood of an individual to need an autologous graft of HSC was, at the present time, non-existent and that, so far, there is no proven utility of other stem cells from cord blood. These would have to meet stringent criteria before they could be used clinically and there was no evidence, if they did, that the subject's own bone marrow or a well-matched donation from an allogeneic donor would not suffice. The opinion mentions the draft recommendation of the European Health Committee of the Council of Europe which states, 'the promotion of donation for autologous use should not be supported by member States or their health services.' In February 2002 the French National Consultative Ethics Committee, in its Opinion No. 74, warns of private banks that '... setting up such banks is likely to contradict the principle of solidarity, without which no society can survive' and that 'such banks raise hopes of utopia and disguise a mercantile project using assistance to children as a screen'. Private cord blood banking is prohibited by law in Italy[26] and forbidden by the Ministry of Health in China. In the US, on the other hand, private cord blood banks have had relatively free rein. However, they are now coming under attack from within the mercantile system itself.

Ownership

Biologically cord blood belongs to the newborn child but a newborn child is unable to exert its property rights or give consent to its use. It is the mother's consent that is required if the blood is to be stored for the child's own future use or donated to another. Annas[27] makes an analogy with consent to the use of fetal tissue. Once it is given away to a third party, cord blood ceases to be the property of the child. If the mother decides to store the cord blood in a private cord blood bank it remains the property of the child who can, when he or she is of age, decide whether or not to continue storage. One might also wonder if a child would have a right to sue its parents for failing to store its cord blood for future use. Some banks notably offer 18-year storage, presumably to coincide with the child's majority. Problems can arise if the parents fail to continue storage payments. Some private banks have policies that, if storage fees are not paid, the CBU becomes the property of the company[28], others will destroy the CBU.

Recently the issue of saviour siblings has been the subject of debate in the UK following decisions by the Human Fertilisation and Embryology Authority[29] to permit the selection of tissue matched IVF siblings for families where an older child has suffered from a disorder which was amenable to treatment using a cord cell transplant. Again, the mother is making the altruistic decision to donate cord blood cells on behalf of her newborn.

Commercialisation and Patenting

The discovery that cord blood is a source of pluripotent stem cells opens their utility to a new range of medical applications in cellular therapy and regenerative medicine and makes them a less ethically contentious alternative to embryonic stem cells. It is, therefore, not surprising to find biotech companies being established alongside cord blood banking facilities. In this way, these companies have access to CBU which are insufficient for transplantation purposes. In Europe, Kourion Therapeutics AG was established alongside the non-profit Düsseldorf Cord Blood Bank with the Director of the Cord Blood Bank as a Scientific Advisor and on the Board of Directors of the company. The company, which estimates that the total cell therapy market will amount to more than $30 billion by the end of the decade, is developing cell therapies for the treatment of bone defects and for myocardial regeneration using a proprietary lineage of Unrestricted Somatic Stem Cells (USSC) isolated from umbilical cord blood. Kourion Therapeutics has recently been taken over by the American company Viacell, the parent company of the Viacord private cord blood bank. Also in the for-profit cord blood banking sector, Cryo-Cell Europe has recently acquired MainGen GmbH, a company located in Frankfurt that specialises in the processing, preparation and expansion of stem cells from cord blood and bone marrow with interests in cell and gene therapy.

In 1987 the American biotechnology company Biocyte Corporation filed for a US patent on 'the isolation and preservation of fetal and neonatal hematopoietic stem and progenitor cells of the blood'. This was granted as US Patent No. 5,004,681 on 2 April 1991. A continuation application was filed in 1988 and US Patent No. 5,192,553 was granted on 9 March 1993. In 1996 Biocyte was granted a further patent in Europe under reference EP O 343 217. In effect, these patents gave Biocyte patent monopoly rights over all stored cord blood cells and their therapeutic use and cord blood banks would be forced to operate under licence. In Europe, the cord blood banking and transplantation community began to lobby for the revocation of the patent both on legal and ethical grounds. The patent was contrary to the resolution of the International Society of Transplantation that no part of the human body should be commercialised and that the donation of all organs or cells should be free and anonymous. Subsequently Biocyte was acquired by PharmaStem Therapeutics who had the patents assigned to them. After four years' legal battle, the European Patent Office revoked PharmaStem's European patent on 7 April 2003. European cord blood banks can therefore continue to operate without threat of legal action.

In the US the legal battle continues. In February 2002 PharmaStem filed a lawsuit for patent infringement against eight American cord blood banking companies; ViaCell Inc., Cryo-Cell International Inc., CorCell Inc., StemCyte Inc., Nu Stem Technologies Inc., Cord Blood Registry Inc., Bio-Cell Inc. and Birthcells Technology Inc. In November 2002 PharmaStem was awarded a third US Patent No. 6,462,645. In November 2003 PharmaStem achieved success in the courts, being awarded $7.1 million in damages against four of the defendant companies (ViaCell, CorCell, Cord Blood Registry and Cryo-Cell). The remainder either settled or went out of business.

This judgment is has now been successfully challenged.[30] In addition, NetCord and the cryostorage manufacturer Thermogenesis Corp made submissions to the US Patent Office (USPTO) for the re-examination of PharmaStem's US patents. As a result The USPTO has thrown out patents '553 and '681, which were the basis of the 2002 lawsuit against private cord blood banks. PharmaStem is now pursuing the private banks on the basis of another patent.[31]

Conclusion

Umbilical cord cell transplantation has moved over the last 15 years from being an experimental procedure to an accepted treatment for a number of haematological diseases and genetic disorders. As it has done so the banking of this human tissue has increased exponentially around the world. The proliferation of private cord cell banks has been particularly strong in the US and Asia while, in Europe, where there are one or two old established private banks, the emphasis has been on public cord cell banking. But, whether in the private or public cord cell banking sector, there remains a heterogeneity of quality assurance standards that needs addressing. This will become particularly important if cord blood stem cells are to play an important part in the cellular therapies of the future. As the utility of these cells increases countries may have to consider whether cord blood should be collected from all newborn but this will be a costly process and maybe the promotion of cord blood donation but with the acknowledgement of the right to private storage may prove a pragmatic way forward. It is also clear, within this dynamic field, that new ethical questions will continue to arise.

Notes

[1]   Gluckman E., Broxmeyer H.E., Auerbach A.D. et al. (1989), *N Eng J Med,* vol. 321, pp.1174–78.
[2]   Broxmeyer H.E., G.W. Douglas H.E., Hangoe G. et al. (1989), *Proc Natl Acad Sci USA,* vol. 86, pp. 3828–32.
[3]   Cohen S.B.A., Madrigal J.A. (1998), *Bone Marrow Transplant,* vol. 21 (suppl 3), S9-S12.
[4]   Kim Y.J., Broxmeyer H.E. (1996), *Blood ,* (suppl 1, pt 1), 240a abstract 1031.
[5]   Wagner J.E., Rosenthal J., Sweetman R. et al. (1996) *Blood.* Vol. 88, pp.795–802.
[6]   Gluckman E., Rocha V., Bayer-Chammard A. et al. (1997), *N Engl J Med.,* vol. 337, pp. 373–78.
[7]   Rubinstein P., Carrier C., Scaradovou A. et al. (1998), *N Engl J Med.,* vol. 22, pp.1565–1577.
[8]   Ballen K., Broxmeyer H.E., McCullough J. et al. (2001), *Biology of Blood and Marrow Transplantation.,* vol. 7, pp. 635–645.
[9]   Gluckman E., Rocha V., Chastang C. on behalf of Eurocord-Cord Blood Transplant Group, 'Cord blood hematopoietic stem cells: biology and transplantation' in: *Haematology* (American Society of Hematology, Washington DC, 1998) pp. 1–14.

[10] Piacibello W., Sanavio F., Garetto L. et al. (1997), *Blood.* vol. 89, pp. 2644–2653.

[11] Ohishi K., Varnum-Finney B., Bernstein I.D. (2002), *J Clin Invest.* Vol. 110(8), pp. 1165–74.

[12] Encabo A., Mateu E., Carbonell-Uberos F., Minana M.D. (2003) *Transfusion.* Vol. 43(3), pp. 383–89.

[13] Jaroscak J., Martin P.L., Waters-Pick B. et al. (1998), *Blood.* Vol. 92, 646a (suppl 1, part 1).

[14] Stiff P., Pecora A., Parthasarathy M. et al. (1998), *Blood.* Vol. 92, 646a (suppl 1, part 1).

[15] Fernandez C.V., Gordon K., Van den Hof et al. (2003), *CMAJ.* vol.168(6), pp. 695–98.

[16] Broxmeyer H.E., Srour E.F., Hangoc G. et al. (2003), *Proc Natl Acad Sci USA.* vol. 100(2), pp. 645–650.

[17] Kögler G. et al, (2004), 'A New Human Somatic Stem Cell from Placental Cord Blood with Intrinsic Pluripotent Differentiation Potential', *Journal of Experimental Medicine*, vol 200(2), pp.123–135.

[18] Bompais H., Chagraoui J. et al. (2003), *Blood*, Nov 20.

[19] Le Ricousse-Roussane A., Barateau V., Contreres J.O. et al. (2004), *Cardiovasc. Res.* vol.62(1), pp. 176–84.

[20] McGuckin, C.P., Forraz, N., Allouard, Q., Pettengell, R.(2004) 'Umbilical cord blood stem cells can expand hematopoietic and neuroglial progenitors in vitro.' *Exp Cell Res.* vol. 295, (2), pp. 350–59.

[21] McGuckin, C.P., Forraz, N., Baradez, M-O, (2005) 'Production of stem cells with embryonic characteristics from human umbilical cord blood. *Cell Prolif* vol. 38, pp. 245–255.

[22] Perin H.F., Dohmann E.C, Borohevic R. et al., epub circulated ahead of print April 2003.

[23] Gunning J., 'A worldwide study of umbilical cord cell banking.' European Commission (EGE and DG Research), Brussels, March 2004.

[24] Reed A., 'Blood Treatment's Promise Mired in Bureaucracy', *New York Times*, May 29, 2004.

[25] European Group on Ethics in Science and New Technologies to the European Commission, Opinion No. 19, Brussels, 16 March 2004.

[26] Gazetta Ufficiale n. 31 January 2002.

[27] Annas, G.J. (1999), 'Waste and Longing – The Legal Status of Placental Blood Banking.' *NEJM*, vol. 340,(19), pp.1521–24.

[28] Ibid.

[29] Human Fertilisation and Embryology Authority, Press Release, 21 July 2004. <http://www.hfea.gov.uk/PressOffice/Archive/1090427358>

[30] <http://www.viacord.com/documents/sleete.pdf>

[31] <http://lists.essential.org/pipermail/ip-health/2005-March/007548.html>

Chapter 4

Assisted Reproduction in the Republic of Ireland – A Legal Quagmire

Deirdre Madden

Introduction

In vitro fertilisation (IVF) has been practised in the Republic of Ireland since 1987 and there are at present nine units in Ireland carrying out assisted reproduction treatment services. Donor insemination is available, though only through importation of the sperm from the UK and elsewhere. Egg donation has recently become available in one clinic, and, to date, there have been no reports of embryo donation or surrogate motherhood carried out in the jurisdiction.

Assisted human reproduction (AHR) services are carried out in Ireland in the absence of any legislative provisions, and with only very general guidance from the Irish Medical Council. The Minister for Health set up the Commission on Assisted Human Reproduction (CAHR) in 2000, and its report was published in May 2005. (available at <http://www.dohc.ie/publications/cahr.html>)

Despite the Commission's strong recommendation in favour of legislation in the area, the possibilities of legislating for AHR in Ireland are complicated, not least by the ethically controversial nature of the treatments themselves, but by the potential impact of the provisions of the Irish Constitution, *Bunreacht na hÉireann*, 1937. This paper describes the current position in relation to the provision of AHR services in the Republic of Ireland, and outlines some of the difficulties that may face legislators in this jurisdiction in attempting to regulate the area. It also sets out some of the main recommendations of the Commission on Assisted Human Reproduction.

Existing Provisions

The Medical Council of Ireland is the statutory body empowered to regulate the medical profession in the Republic of Ireland (<http://www.medicalcouncil.ie>). Its functions include giving guidance to the medical profession on matters relating to ethical conduct and behaviour. To that effect it issues a Guide to Ethical Conduct and Behaviour every five years, the most recent edition (6th) was published in March 2004. In relation to AHR, the Guide (section F) provides for sperm/ova freezing for use by those from whom the gametes were taken, and advises doctors who consider donor programmes for their patients to be cautious in relation to the source of the material and the advice given to patients regarding the consequences of the donation.

In relation to IVF the Guide stipulates that 'any fertilised ovum must be used for normal implantation and must not be deliberately destroyed'. The Guide does not expressly stipulate when implantation must take place and therefore embryo freezing, followed at a later stage by embryo transfer, is presumed to be within the terms of the Guide. Destruction of the embryos, with or without the consent of the gamete providers, is not permissible under the terms of the Guide. The only change made to the paragraph dealing with IVF in the most recent guide states that 'if couples have validly decided they do not wish to make use of their own fertilised ova, the potential for voluntary donation to other recipients may be considered'. The Council might have seen this as a pragmatic way of dealing with surplus embryos without transgressing the prohibition on embryo destruction, and its members were no doubt also mindful of the provisions of the Irish Constitution, which oblige the state to respect the right to life of the unborn. This is discussed further below.

Although the Guide is described by the Council itself as 'an articulation of general principles of ethical conduct' rather than a binding legal code, nonetheless it is clear that medical practitioners in Ireland do adhere to the Guide in practice. One of the difficulties in the AHR area is that not all of those involved in the provision of AHR treatments would in fact be registered medical practitioners, and would therefore fall outside of the remit of the Medical Council. However, it would be seen as the responsibility of the clinic's medical director to ensure that the clinic's practices do not contravene the Medical Council's Guide, or risk an application being made to the Fitness to Practise Committee of the Medical Council in order to have his/her name erased from the medical register.

There is no central licensing body in Ireland with responsibility for collecting details from clinics in respect of treatments carried out, or children born as a result of treatment services.

The Commission recommends the establishment of a regulatory body whose functions would include the compilation of national statistics on AHR and the long-term monitoring of health and safety issues for all participants.

Irish Constitutional Provisions

There are a number of Constitutional provisions that potentially affect the provision of AHR services in Ireland. These include Constitutional rights to privacy and bodily integrity, custody of a child, equality before the law, and other personal and family rights. However, probably the most important provision in the Constitution in this context is Article 40.3.3, which states as follows:

'The State acknowledges the right to life of the unborn and, with due regard to the equal right to life of the mother, guarantees in its laws to respect, and, as far as practicable, by its laws to defend and vindicate that right.'

This provision has been the subject of much controversy in Ireland, predominantly in the area of abortion, since its incorporation into the Constitution in 1983. However, the article also may have an impact on IVF, and is a factor that the Irish government will have to grapple with in any attempt to legislate for the provision of AHR services in Ireland for the future.

It is often presumed, without much analysis, that the Irish Constitution prohibits embryo research and destruction, but such an interpretation may not be strictly accurate. The most significant word in the article for IVF purposes is 'unborn'. If this word is interpreted by the Irish Supreme Court to mean the fertilised ovum/ embryo, then the rights ascribed to the unborn in the Constitution, specifically the right to life, come into play. Thus, the state would be obliged to respect and, as far as practicable, vindicate those rights. This would cause difficulties in relation to the storage of embryos, and most certainly, in relation to embryo/stem cell research, as by facilitating storage and research the state could be seen as failing in its obligation to vindicate the right to life of the unborn.

On the other hand, if the word 'unborn' were interpreted as extending only to the embryo *after* implantation in the uterus, then it would seem that embryo freezing and research would not violate the Constitutional provisions. There is little guidance from the limited Constitutional jurisprudence in existence in relation to this article. In *Attorney General (SPUC) v Open Door Counselling Ltd.*[1] Hamilton J. held that the Offences Against the Person Act 1861 protects the foetus in the womb, and that 'protection dates from conception'. It is not, however, clear from the context whether conception means fertilisation or implantation, a crucial distinction in relation to IVF.

In *Attorney General v X*[2] in 1992, the Supreme Court considered the article in the context of a young girl who had become pregnant as a result of rape, and who was considered to be at risk of suicide as a result of the pregnancy. The Court interpreted the Constitutional provision to mean that the termination of pregnancy was permissible only when it was established as a matter of probability that there was a real and substantial risk to the life of the mother if such termination were not effected.

In relation to the question of when Constitutional protection begins, and therefore whether the pre-implantation embryo falls within the scope of the article, there is little to be gained from a reading of the judgments in the case. Given that the facts of the case pertained to an established pregnancy, the court did not have to consider the question as to whether or not the provision applied to the embryo prior to implantation. The language of the court relates to the 'life of the infant in the womb', and Hederman J. (dissenting) states that 'one cannot make distinctions between individual phases of unborn life before birth, or between unborn and born life.' Unfortunately it is far from clear from this case, or any other, to what extent, if any, the Court would apply the protection of Article 40.3.3. to the embryo outside the womb.

Academic commentators can only conclude that 'it cannot be said with certainty whether the protection afforded by Article 40.3.3 to the "unborn" applies from the moment of fertilisation, the moment of implantation, or from some later date'.[3] The Constitution Review Group[4] agree that definition is needed as to when the 'unborn' acquires the protection of the law. Their report states that the word 'unborn' seems to imply 'on the way to being born' or 'capable of being born', but whether the Court would accept either of those definitions is as yet a moot point.

Sherlock[5] argues that it is likely that the courts would hold the *in vitro* embryo to come within the protection of the Constitution and, if this were the case, it would rule out embryo research and embryo destruction. 'It would also have implications for infertility treatments involving in vitro fertilisation (IVF) as it would undoubtedly require that all embryos produced would have to be placed in the woman's uterus.' However, Madden argues that 'if the "unborn" means "not yet born" or "with the potential to be born" then, in the light of the biological development of the early embryo and the absence of potential in the pre-implantation embryo, it is likely that the embryo in the laboratory does not qualify for this Constitutional protection.'[6]

Ultimately, as acknowledged by the Commission's report, the meaning of the word will fall to be interpreted by the Irish Supreme Court or by constitutional referendum of the people. However, the Commission (with one member dissenting) recommended that the embryo created by IVF should not attract legal protection until placed in the human body, at which stage it should attract the same level of protection as the embryo formed in vivo.

Gamete Donation

As has been stated above, there is an implicit permission given to medical practitioners to provide gamete donation services to patients under the provisions of the Medical Council's guide. However, the legal consequences of such donations, for example in relation to parental responsibilities, or the rights of those conceived by this method, have not been dealt with by any legislation. Apart from the inherent difficulties that arise in ascribing parental rights in this context, the issue of donor anonymity is also problematic. At the present time no sperm bank exists in Ireland to provide donor sperm for insemination services here and therefore the sperm used in such procedures is imported, mostly from the UK. Presuming that the sperm is imported from licensed clinics in the UK, such clinics would be obliged to comply with the provisions of the Human Fertilisation and Embryology Act 1990, and the Code of Practice issued by the licensing authority, the HFEA. Thus, whatever provisions exist in relation to the provision of information to children under the UK Act, will also apply to the sperm currently imported into Ireland.

The Commission recommends that donation of sperm, ova, and embryos, should be permitted subject to regulation. It also recommends that donors should only receive reasonable expenses and that children born through donation should, on maturity, be entitled to access to the identity of their genetic parents.

Access to Treatment Services

Another controversial issue that arises in relation to AHR is that of access to services. The Irish Constitution provides recognition for the family as 'the natural and fundamental unit group of society', and further, pledges to guard with special care the institution of marriage on which the family is founded, and protect it against attack (Article 41.3.1). A question arises as to whether, if AHR treatment services were provided to single persons or same-sex couples, such a policy would be in keeping with this constitutional provision. A seemingly straightforward solution might be to restrict access to services to married couples, but this is not in line with current practices of treating unmarried couples, the Medical Council guide (which no longer provides such a restriction), or equality law in Ireland.

A further complication is the Equal Status Act 2000, which prohibits discrimination in the provision of services, on the basis of, *inter alia,* marital status, race, gender, disability and sexual orientation. There is no derogation given in the Act for AHR clinics and therefore it must be assumed that the Act currently applies to the provision of AHR treatment services. This means that clinics may not refuse to treat on the basis of, for example, marital status or sexual orientation, though discrimination will not be considered unlawful if made on clinical grounds, such as, for example, age or health of the mother. However, discrimination on grounds of disability may not be unlawful if the treatment of that person less favourably to other persons is deemed necessary to prevent harm to that person or others. It remains to be seen whether complaints will be made against clinics under the provisions of this Act, and if so, what attitude the courts will take to the potential conflict with the Constitutional protection of the marital family.

The Commission recommended that AHR treatments should be made available without discrimination on grounds of gender, marital status or sexual orientation subject to consideration of the best interests of any child who may be born as a result of the treatment. Where there is objective evidence of a serious risk of harm to any child that may be conceived through AHR, there should be a presumption against treatment.

Surrogate Motherhood

Irish clinics have not provided surrogacy treatment services to date. However, Irish couples have travelled to the UK and the US in furtherance of surrogacy arrangements made in those jurisdictions. As the law currently stands, the children born through such arrangements are in a legal limbo due to the absence of legislative means by which their status might be regularised. The Commission recommends that surrogacy be permitted subject to regulation.

Adoption legislation in Ireland provides that the payment or receipt of money in connection with an adoption is a criminal offence (Adoption Act 1952, s. 42(1)). However, it is not entirely clear whether adoption law would come into operation in a surrogacy case due to the lack of definition as to who the legal mother of the child is. If the legal mother of the child were the commissioning mother (who may also of course be the genetic mother), then the question of adoption would not arise. She and her husband would be registered on the birth certificate of the child, and would have custody. However, if the birth mother of the child were regarded as the legal mother, then in order for the commissioning couple to establish a legal relationship with the child, she would have to relinquish her constitutional rights to custody, and give the child up for adoption.

In order for this to comply with adoption law, such an arrangement could not be done privately, but only through a recognised adoption agency. The Adoption Acts provide that it is not lawful for any person to give a child to any other person for the purpose of having that child adopted unless the person who intends to adopt the child is a relative, or the spouse of a relative of the child (Adoption Act 1952, s.34, as amended). Therefore, it may be possible to arrange an adoption directly with the Adoption Board where the commissioning couple are genetically related to the child. However, the question of payment might arise in this context and raise the spectre of criminality for both the surrogate mother and the commissioning couple. The Commission recommends that surrogate mothers be entitled to reimbursement of expenses directly related to their participation.

In terms of the rights of the father in this situation, a man who is married to the legal mother of a child is presumed by law to be the child's father. Therefore, if the surrogate mother is the legal mother and she is married, her husband is presumed to be the father, though this is a rebuttable presumption. This raises other problems as the child is then a child of the marital family and cannot easily be given up for adoption. In exceptional cases, the High Court may make orders under section 3 of the Adoption Act, 1988, authorising the adoption of children whose parents have failed in their duty of care towards them. Children born within marriage may be adopted under this provision. A child born to a married woman but whose husband is not the father, is eligible for adoption provided the facts of the child's paternity can be proven to the satisfaction of the Adoption Board. The child must reside in the state, be at least six weeks old and under 18 years of age. The child need not have been born in this country.

If the surrogate mother is unmarried and the commissioning man is the genetic father, he may apply to court for guardianship rights in relation to the child, but this is not an automatic entitlement. The difficulty remains that even if he is appointed guardian of the child, his partner may not have any legal relationship with the child unless they jointly apply for an adoption order in respect of the child. This again raises the question as to whether the Adoption Board and the High Court would be likely to view any payment made to the surrogate mother as failing within the prohibitions in the Act, and therefore constituting a criminal offence.

The Commission, with one member dissenting, recommends that the child born through surrogacy should be presumed to be that of the commissioning couple, based on the intent of all parties to the arrangement.

Stem Cell Research

As in other European Member States, stem cell research is a controversial topic in Ireland, with the constitutional protection of the unborn being called in aid of the embryos from which the stem cells might be derived. In the recent attempt to establish guidelines for European Commission funding for embryonic stem cell research, politicians in Ireland were divided, as indeed was the population at large. The decision was ultimately made that, irrespective of whether such research might ever be carried out in this jurisdiction, Ireland should not stand in the way of such research being pursued elsewhere and should contribute to the formulation of strict guidelines to that effect. In the event, no consensus was reached across the Member States in relation to the issue of guidelines, but the stance adopted by the Irish government on the subject took many commentators by surprise. It was presumed that the traditional pro-life policies in Ireland would ensure a strong opposition to stem cell research, and the position adopted may indicate either a weakening of the position of the Catholic Church in Ireland, or a prioritisation of the economic interests of medical research over traditional ethical values.

The Commission recommends that embryo research, including embryonic stem cell research, be permitted under regulation and subject to stringent conditions, on embryos donated specifically for research.

Cloning

The Irish government has stated its opposition to cloning, both therapeutic and reproductive, on a number of occasions and therefore it is thought unlikely that the legal position on this issue will change in the near future. However, the Commission recommends that regenerative medicine or therapeutic cloning be allowed. Reproductive cloning should be prohibited.

Conclusion

The area of AHR is one that has proved controversial and divisive in every jurisdiction in which it has been debated. Irish social and political history, as well as the Irish Constitution and the small number of potentially relevant legislative provisions, will no doubt exacerbate the difficulties involved in any legislative attempt to regulate the provision of AHR services in this jurisdiction. The recommendations of the Commission on Assisted Human Reproduction will be the first attempt at debating the issues and arriving at some consensus in the area. Whether the Irish Government will take it upon themselves to act on the report remains to be seen.

References

[1]   Attorney General (SPUC) v Open Door Counselling Ltd. [1988] IR 593.
[2]   Attorney General v X [1992] 1 I.R. 1.
[3]   Kingston, Whelan and Bacik, *Abortion and the Law* Round Hall/Sweet & Maxwell, 1997.
[4]   Report of the Constitution Review Group, May 1996.
[5]   Sherlock "The right to life of the unborn and the Irish Constitution" (1989) XXIV Ir. Jur. (n.s.) 13.
[6]   Madden D., *Medicine, Ethics and the Law* Butterworths, 2002.

Chapter 5

Practical Ethics in Search of a Toolbox: Ethics of Science and Technology at the Crossroads

Matthias Kaiser

Say you have a moral dilemma and are sincerely uncertain what to do. One of the things you might do is to ask a good friend for ethical advice. How do you know the advice you get is a good advice? Well, you might ask yourself a number of questions along the lines of: How well does this friend know me? How well does this friend understand the problem I face? How experienced is she in addressing moral dilemmas? How much do I trust her judgement? Can this friend provide reasons for the advice that seem convincing to me? In the end it is your personal choice and sole moral responsibility what you do, but if your friend takes the question put to her seriously she might admit some moral co-responsibility in helping you to find the morally best response. Advising on ethical issues is in itself a moral action.

What happens if we change the perspective from the individual to a public body or a governmental institution? Obviously, moral dilemmas and ethical uncertainty may arise as well. Examples of this ethical uncertainty by public decision makers can be found e.g. in the debate about biotechnology and GM food. The problem is that ethical advice is not that easy to come by, not because of a lack of people willing to provide it, but because the standards for what constitutes a good advice for public decision making are in themselves problematic. In the public arena there simply is no equivalent to the good friend and trusted and skilled morally competent person. A public body or governmental institution may carry moral responsibility for its decisions, but in modern democracies it is by its mandate and institutional basis accountable to the public at large. Advice on ethical issues for public bodies needs a quality assurance that anchors the advice firmly both within the values of pluralist societies and within a high level of argumentative backing. In other words, ethical advice to public bodies appeals not only to the moral integrity and co-responsibility of the advisor, but also to the set of standards whereby the advice is generated and eventually evaluated.

In this brief and summary paper I make the claim that the important turn to ethics that one has experienced in the realm of science and technology during the 1990s (and partially earlier) now brings about a need to develop a toolbox for practical ethics that makes ethical advice amenable to quality assurance and democratic transparency. I believe many ethicists have as yet only partially recognised the need to put their own activity on much firmer grounds that answer the needs of a modern and deliberative democracy. Much needs to be done to develop such a toolbox if ethics of science and technology is not to come out of the debate as a mere smokescreen or a passing fashion of terms.

Let us briefly examine the possibilities that the advisor will want to consider. First, the advisor may take recourse to existing ethical theories and academic traditions of discourse. Obviously, a variety of choices offers itself. There are those that adhere to the utilitarian traditions of various kinds, but there are also others who adhere to more deontological traditions (e.g. of a Kantian kind) or others who defend some sort of contractarianism or versions of virtue ethics. Whatever one chooses, the definite advantage of such an approach is that it will – if followed competently – provide a thorough and coherent level of argumentation. Spelling out reasons for the advice and embedding in it a larger ethical framework or theory opens the advice for rational critique. Those that disagree may criticize it by showing which of the presuppositions they deem as problematic and contested. In other words, ethical advice based on academic ethical theories answers to ideals of modern society and modern social institutions (as e.g. expressed by Max Weber). But in the end there are serious problems that face any such approach, whatever the theoretical foundation may be. For instance, all these theories are in some sense controversial, and it does not seem a good starting point to use controversial theories to solve controversial societal problems. Each theory will have areas where the implications of the theory seem to contradict the moral intuitions of a great number of people. Another difficulty is that these theories do not in any straightforward sense of the term have direct applications in those areas that are debated. In ethics, there is no 'applied ethics' in the same sense as, say, in applied mechanics. In order for these theories to be useful in practice one has to spell out particular interpretative contexts and specifications that do not have the same appeal to generality as the more fundamental principles. Providing these contexts has the ring of being ad hoc, at least to those who are sceptical to the theoretical starting point. Also the context will typically leave out many considerations that others deem ethically relevant. In sum, I think the thrust of the objections to this approach is that it does not live up to the recognition of value diversity and essential pluralism in modern democracies. In the background lurks the objection of implicit paternalism, or the suspicion that ethics is used as a smokescreen to hide underlying powerful sector interests.

Second the advisor may try to live up to the ideals of modern deliberative democracies by turning the above approach on its head and resting the advice on a truly bottom-up and participatory approach. The art of the advice then consists in bracketing the advisors' own ethical standpoint and organizing a process that reveals values and moral judgements of the people, i.e. those that are not deemed experts in ethics but hold values and convictions of importance to the societal decision in question. Obviously, there is again a variety of approaches that one may choose from. Prima facie, the most democratic one seems a survey method that charts existing values and attitudes. Apart from the impracticality of conducting large surveys on each and every issue on which one wants ethical advice, there is also the problem that a survey cannot reveal what ethicists call 'considered judgements', i.e. judgements that are informed by all relevant facts and considerations. Most people will not be in a position, nor have the interest, to evaluate and weigh all ethically relevant factors of an issue. Other approaches rectify this shortcoming to some extent. Public hearings with stakeholders or other participatory approaches like critical system heuristics aim at revealing different value judgements of stakeholders. Stakeholders can by definition be assumed to have an interest in the issue at stake and thus to bring at least some kind of relevant knowledge and information to the fore. But again, in democratic societies stakeholders with some kind of direct interest may not be the only legitimate source of information on relevant moral considerations. Civic society as such may have an overriding interest because of how the issue relates to the general welfare and fundamental principles of society. Thus, one has developed approaches that capture not so much the moral judgements of stakeholders, but rather the value-based judgements of a selection of the general public. The consensus conferences developed first in Denmark are a typical example of such an approach. One of the advantages of this approach is that those issuing the recommendation are first offered the best information available on the issue, and their final statement is based on argumentative consensus within the panel. All of these approaches are oriented towards the recognition of pluralism in modern societies and seek to base their advice on how the plurality of ethical viewpoints relates to the issue at hand. All of them are also bottom-up in methodological outlook. Yet, they also face some more fundamental objections. One such objection is that recommendations based on participatory approaches are easily targeted as incoherent in the long run and lacking reference to more principal considerations, like e.g. universalism, i.e. treating ethically similar cases alike. They are vulnerable to who is consulted when, and the framing of the issue is often decisive for the outcome. From an ethical point of view, one may criticize that participatory approaches of this kind are short on rational ethical argument, short on coherence over time, but long on admissions to ethical subjectivism or relativism.

If we turn back to our initial formulation of the problem, i.e. issuing advice to a public body on ethical issues in policy formation, we may thus conclude that there is a dilemma. It appears to be one of choosing between the Scylla of relying on expert culture in ethics (thus risking to sacrifice important aspects of modern deliberative democracies) and the Charybdis of relying on the voice of the people (thus risking to sacrifice coherent rational argument to some extent). Obviously, the public body that seeks advice wants both considerations to be taken into account.

My claim is that in spite of many years with practical ethics, and in spite of some years with debates about the ethics of science and technology in particular, we have not yet managed to answer this challenge satisfactorily. Let us consider two related developments in particular.

The typical response to re-occurring ethical issues related to the policy work of a public body or governmental institution is to appoint an ethics committee of some sort. This is the institutionalisation of ethics. In the context of issues relating to developments in science and technology, the European countries have indeed witnessed a significant increase in the number of regional, national or trans-national ethics committees during the last 10-15 years. Some of them are specific to certain fields, like the bioethics committees in the life-sciences, while others are more generic dealing with the sciences in general and turning their attention to a variety of issues. Their composition often reflects some of the same considerations that we described above. In some countries these committees are restricted to scientific experts, in others they also include ethicists and other specialists that professionally deal with the range of issues that the committee has to confront. In some countries, like e.g. the Scandinavian countries, these experts are typically supplemented by members of the general public. Whatever their composition, they face the fundamental problem of democratic legitimacy and rationality. Normally one expects a certain degree of independence and transparency of such a committee. This, in combination with the fact that they are appointed to provide ethical advice, provides at least some justification for the recommendations they issue. Yet this is merely restricted to the formal level of their operations. This still leaves the more substantial level of how they reach their outcome basically untouched. Accordingly one finds great differences between countries how these committees work. Some of them can perhaps be described as striving to reach some ideal of discourse ethics (in the Habermasian sense) based on the deliberations in the committee. Some seek explicitly expert advice from ethicists that provides a coherent string of arguments. Others again seek to initiate public discourse by means of some of the participatory measures described above. And perhaps the majority of them do not have a clear philosophy that provides guidelines for their operations, or even a clear conception of what an ethical issue or a moral judgement is and what it demands. In this sense, from the perspective of the advice seeking public body, the resulting recommendation may seem to come out of a black box. Quality assurance of the advice seems thus to be limited and to be mainly restricted to the assumed trust that the committee operates according to its task. Typically, even if the public body may trust the committee to operate professionally, the public may not share this view. They may simply open the issue again, and not be impressed by the fact that a committee has come to a conclusion on the matter. The underlying problem is really that there exists no consensus on what a competent dealing with an ethical issue by an ethics committee demands in terms of method.

There is another area where we have some experience with practical ethics. This field is medical research ethics. Arguably within medicine and medical research important ethical problems are now by and large handled rather competently. This is due to a combination of factors. First ethics committees are established on several levels and integrated into the workings of medical research. Second, guidelines such as the Helsinki Declaration, provide a checklist of issues that are to be dealt with by those that issue ethical advice. These guidelines are also supported by a majority of actors. Third, practical approaches are spelled out that essentially side-step the controversies of ethical theory and provide for a variety of broad considerations to be taken into consideration that together seem to cover major ethical intuitions. This is basically the principlism that was first propagated by Beauchamp and Childress.

These factors together seem to work rather well for ethical issues that involve medical research vis à vis patient considerations. For more complex issues however, like e.g. xenotransplantation where also overarching societal issues like risks of infections matter, this framework seems to meet some limitations.

My conclusion from this brief summary of the state of the art in practical ethics is that we need to develop a toolbox for practical ethics that works for addressing ethical issues related to science and technology in general. The major function of such a toolbox would be to make possible some kind of quality assurance of the ethical advice and to make ethical advice amenable to democratic transparency and ideals of deliberative democracy.

I want to make it clear that I do not nourish any hopes of developing a kind of decision algorithm that would solve any practical problems in ethics. To my mind, ethics will always rest on some process of judgement and weighing that cannot be delegated to impersonal procedures or strict logic. But this is not what the term 'tool' implies. A tool in general is always a means to an end, but typically we may apply different tools to the same ends or the same tools to different ends. Tools become useful only in the hands of the skilful and experienced user. The effectiveness of any tool is always dependent on the skills and judgement of the practitioner. Thus tools become an integral part of human practice, forming assets for skilful practice and quality work. A well-equipped toolbox and skilful, well-trained personnel are hallmarks of professional services. Quality assurance of a practice typically implies assessment of the tools brought to the task and the skills of the personnel performing it. Good tool design always depends on good theoretical understanding of structural features of the issues and tasks to which they may be applied.

Ethical tools would structure the basic considerations that need to be taken into consideration and they would relate these considerations to the specific facts and the social context that pertain in regard to the issue. This would be done in methodical and transparent fashion so that criticism may be directed to each step in the method (e.g. for not being sophisticated enough). Yet, an ethical tool will not relieve us of having to make a final judgement. Once our judgement is preceded by the application of an ethical tool, however, others will have the possibility to check whether disagreement is based on a criticism of our incompetent use of the tool or merely restricted to disagreement with our judgement.

There are already some tools discussed in the literature on practical ethics. One prominent tool is e.g. the ethical matrix first developed by Ben Mepham and inspired by the principlist approach in medical research ethics. This tool has been modified by others, among others by our group at NENT in Oslo, and has been suggested in various contexts. Recently it has entered the joint recommendations of an expert consultation on GM animals organized by the WHO and the FAO (see the chapter on ethics in: <http://www.who.int/foodsafety/biotech/meetings/en/gmanimal_reportnov03_en.pdf>)

Here is briefly – by way of example – how an ethical matrix works. Assume you want to assess the ethical issues of a certain genetic modification of a fish species for food production in aquaculture. The first important step is to identify all the relevant stakeholders. This is not necessarily an easy or uncontroversial part of the job. Some people may insist that e.g. the fish that is modified does not deserve to be ranked as a stakeholder along the lines of consumers and producers. They ascribe only instrumental value to the animal. However, others feel strongly that even animals or the environment (biota) should be treated with moral respect akin to ascribing some degree of inherent value to animals. Instead of deciding who is right on the issue, the ethical matrix approach implies to include as stakeholders all those with sufficiently homogenous interests and of whom many people believe they enjoy some moral standing. It is one matter to be generous in the inclusion of stakeholder and another to assign sufficient weight to their being affected by the technology.

The next step is then to establish a set of ethical principles. Ideally, the combination of the selected principles reflects the variety in ethical theory that is known from the literature. Being too restrictive in the choice of principles may be punished by incompleteness of the ethical analysis, while a generosity at worst may complicate the picture and lead to non-obvious considerations. Personally I suggest that the combination of: welfare as elimination of negative utilities, welfare as promotion of positive utilities, dignity/autonomy, and justice as fairness works well in most settings. The reason for differentiating between negative and positive utilities – instead of only considering their aggregated net result – is purely pragmatic, not theoretically founded. Many decision makers need to see separately what the problems are to which a technology is supposed to be the remedy, and to see what the good-making qualities are that we strive for. Furthermore, if our only stakeholders were human beings, the principle of autonomy would be sufficient, but since we want to include animals and nature among stakeholders it seems more adequate to describe the general moral principle in terms of respecting dignity.

Having set up the frame of the ethical matrix, one needs now to specify what each principle means more specifically when seen from each stakeholder's own point of view. Respect for consumer autonomy means mainly to respect the consumer's right to choose between alternative and clearly labelled products. One ends with a first matrix in which all principles are specified in individual cells.

The next step is then to investigate in what way the suggested technology, e.g. the GM-fish, will affect each and every cell that is specified in the first matrix. In other words, one starts to construct a consequence matrix. For instance, having genetically modified fish in fish farms may provide adequate and stable income for small producers, may increase their dependence on large corporations, may be neutral with respect to nutritional quality, and may threaten biodiversity or secure biodiversity (always depending on the technology, e.g. whether or not one uses sterile fish).

The final step consists then in the considered judgement of what is ethically acceptable, taking all these different implications into account. Typically, the situation may be a little more complex. One may e.g. want to ascribe different weight to different cells, thus expressing the view that some harms or some benefits are more important in principle than others. One may also want to differentiate between effects that are certain and others that are merely possible. However one does this, the important point is to make sure that the ethical matrix captures precisely those considerations that people consider morally relevant to an issue.

In principle the ethical matrix approach can be an exercise that a scholar pursues in isolation from actual stakeholders. In this case, the matrix merely serves the purpose of clarifying the scholar's mind on an issue and providing a checklist whether all relevant considerations have been considered. But the matrix may also be used as an instrument in a participatory stakeholder process, where stakeholders themselves agree on what the ethically relevant features of an issue are. In this case, it typically helps (some) stakeholders to recognize that their perspective on an issue is not the only relevant consideration. They may recognize more easily when a controversial issue may have to be solved by finding a compromise that satisfies several important interest, and when the issue is based on a fundamental conflict of different interest constellations. Advice that comes out of an ethical matrix approach, in particular when generated by a participatory approach, will be amenable to demands of transparency, democratic pluralism, and some argumentative backing (given that the principles are well chosen from a variety of ethical theories). Here is how a simplified ethical matrix may look like for this case:

Table 5.1 Ethical matrix for GM fish

	Welfare as eliminating negative utilities	Welfare as promoting positive utilities	Dignity/ autonomy	Justice as fairness
Small producers	Dependence on nature and corporations	Adequate income and work security	Freedom to adopt or not adopt	Fair treatment in trade
Consumers	Safe food	Nutritional quality	Respect for consumer choice (labelling)	General affordability of product
Treated fish	Proper animal welfare	Improved disease resistance	Behavioural freedom	Respect for natural capacities (telos)
Biota	Pollution and strain on natural resources	Increasing sustainability	Maintenance of biodiversity	No additional strain on regional natural resources

My point here is not to propagate the ethical matrix as a wonder-tool in practical ethics. This it is not. There are problems and difficulties connected to this method. However, my point is rather to make plausible the claim that tools of practical ethics can be worked out. I try to show this by pointing out that the ethical matrix is one such tool.

Other tools are suggested in the literature, but in general there is little discussion and even less empirical testing about them in the literature. In the meantime, some projects have started to pay attention to the need to developing ethical tools, e.g. the 'Ethical BioTA Tools'-project funded by the EC (see: <http://www.lei-meta.nl/ethicalbiotatools/>). I hope that ethicists and other scholars will pay more attention to the need to develop ethical tools and that this will contribute to put ethical advice on a more firm and democratic basis.

Some Suggested Further Reading:

On the general background on ethics and new technology:

Bauer, M., Gaskell, G. (eds.) 2002, *Biotechnology: The making of a global controversy* Cambridge, Cambridge University Press.

Beck, Ulrich 1992, *Risk Society*, London, Sage.

Clarke, S.G. and Simpson, E. (eds.) 1989: *Anti-Theory in Ethics and Moral Conservatism*, State University of New York Press, Albany.

Fischer, Frank 2000, *Citizens, Experts, and the Environment*, Duke University Press, Durham and London.

Gaskell, G. et al. 1997, 'Europe ambivalent on biotechnology.' *Nature* vol. 387, 26. June.

Habermas, J. 1991, *Erläuterungen zur Diskursethik*. Suhrkamp, Frankfurt/Main.

Kettner, M. 1993, ,Scientific knowledge, discourse ethics, and consensus formation in the public domain', in: Winkler, E.R. and Coombs J.R. (eds.) *Applied Ethics: A Reader*. Blackwell.

Schomberg, R. von (ed.) 1995, 'Contested Technology: Ethics, Risk and Public Debate', *International centre for Human and Public Affairs, series B: Social Studies of Science and Technology*, Tilburg, Buenos Aires.

Webler, T., Renn, O. and Wiedemann, P. (eds.) 1995, 'Fairness and Competence in Citizen Participation: Evaluating Models for Environmental Discourse.' *Technology, Risk, and Society* vol. 10, Kluwer Academic Publishers, Dordrecht.

On some aspects of practical ethics:

Arras, J.D. (1991), 'Getting Down to Cases: The Revival of Casuistry in Bioethics.' *Journal of Medicine and Philosophy* vol. 16, pp. 29–51.

Beauchamp, T and Childress, J. (1979, 1983, 1989, 1994, 2001) *Principles of Biomedical Ethics*. Oxford University Press, Oxford.

Beauchamp, Tom. (1995), 'Principlism and its alleged competitors.' *Kennedy Institute of Ethics Journal* vol. 5, pp. 181–198.

Carr, S. & Levidow, L. (2000), 'Exploring the links between science, risk, uncertainty, and ethics in regulatory controversies about genetically modified crops.' *Journal of Agricultural and Environmental Ethics* vol. 12, pp. 29–39.

Checkland, P.B. (1981), *Systems Thinking, Systems Practice*. John Wiley & Sons, Chichester.

Danner Clouser, K. and Gert, B. (1990), 'A Critique of Principlism.' *The Journal of Medicine and Philosophy* vol. 15, pp. 219–236.

Jonsen, A.R. and Toulmin, S. (1988), *The Abuse of Casuistry: A History of Moral Reasoning*. University of California Press Berkeley.

Jonsen, A.R. (1991), 'Casuistry as Methodology in Clinical Ethics'. *Theoretical Medicine* vol. 12, pp. 295–307.

Kaiser, M. and Forsberg, E.M. (2000), 'Assessing fisheries – Using an ethical matrix in a participatory process.' *Journal of Agricultural and Environmental Ethics* vol.14, pp. 91–200

Keenan, J.F. and Shannon, T. (1995); *The Context of Casuistry*. Georgetown University Press, Washington DC.

Mayer, S. and Stirling, A. (2002), 'Finding a precautionary approach to technological developments - lessons for the evaluation of GM crops' *Journal of Environmental and Agricultural Ethics*. vol 15, pp. 57–71.

Mepham T.B. (1996), 'Ethical analysis of food biotechnologies: an evaluative framework.' in *Food Ethics*, T.B. Mepham (ed.), Routledge, London, pp. 101–119.

Mepham, T B (1996), 'Ethical impacts of biotechnology in dairying', in *Progress in Dairy Science*. Phillips C.J. (ed.), CAB International, Wallingford.

Mepham T.B., Moore C.J. and Crilly R.E. (1996), 'An ethical analysis of the use of xenografts in human transplant surgery'. *Bulletin of Medical Ethics* vol. 116, pp.13–18.

Mepham T.B. (2000), *Farming animals for food: towards a moral menu*. Food Ethics Council, Southwell.

Mepham T.B. (2000), 'A framework for the ethical analysis of novel foods: the ethical matrix.' *Journal of Agricultural and Environmental Ethics* vol. 12, pp. 165–176.

Mepham T.B. (2000), 'The role of food ethics in food policy.' *Proceedings of the Nutrition Society* vol. 59, pp. 609-18.

Mepham T.B. (2001), 'Novel foods.' in *The Encyclopedia of Ethics of New Technologies* ed. R. F. Chadwick (ed.), Academic Press, San Diego. pp. 299–313.

Midgley, G. (2000), *Systemic Intervention: Philosophy, Methodology, and Practice*, Kluwer/Plenum, New York.

Romm, N. (1994), *Continuing tensions between soft systems methodology and critical systems heuristics*. Centre for Systems Studies, University of Hull, UK, Working paper no. 5.

Ruyter, K. (1995), 'Kasuistikk som saksbasert problemløsning i medisinsk etikk. Om medisinsk assistert befruktning.' Doktorgradsavhandling Det teologiske fakultet, Universitetet i Oslo.

Schroeder D. and Palmer C. (2003), 'Technology assessment and the ethical matrix' *Poiesis and Praxis* vol.1, pp. 295–307.

Stirling, A. (2000), 'Rethinking risk: application of a novel technique to GM crops.' *Technology, Innovation & Society* vol.18, pp. 21–23.

Stirling, A. and Mayer, S. (2002), 'Confronting Risk and Precaution: a Multi-Criteria Mapping of a GM Crop.' in Michael Gletzner (ed.) *Developing Alternatives for Valuing Nature*. Edward Elgar.

Stirling, A. and Mayer, S. (2001), 'A novel approach to the appraisal of technological risk: a multi-criteria mapping pilot study of a genetically modified crop in the UK.' *Environment and Planning C Government and Policy* vol.19, pp. 529–555.

Stirling, A. and Mayer, S. (2000), 'Precautionary approaches to the appraisal of risk: a case study of a GM crop.' *International Journal of Occupational and Environmental Health* vol. 6, pp. 342–357.

Stirling, A. and Mayer, S. (2000), 'A precautionary approach to technology appraisal?: a multi-criteria mapping of genetic modification in UK agriculture' *TA-Datenbank-Nachrichten* vol. 3, pp. 39–50.

Stirling, A. and Mayer, S. (1999), 'Rethinking Risk.' *A Pilot Multi-Criteria Mapping of a Genetically Modified Crop in Agriculture in the UK*. SPRU, University of Sussex, Brighton

Ulrich, W. 1983, *Critical Heuristics of Social Planning: A New Approach to Practical Philosophy*. Haupt: Berne.

Chapter 6

'Up in the Sky': Human and Social Sciences' Responses to Genetics

Yulia Egorova

James Watson, one of the discoverers of the DNA structure, has observed in one of his characteristically eloquent speeches that the objective of genetics is to respond to human needs, and 'to try and give it more meaning than it deserves in some quasi-mystical way is for Steven Spielberg or somebody like that. It's just plain aura, up in the sky'.[1]

The development of genetic research has intensified both public engagement with the subject and academic responses outside of the domain of natural sciences. There is a considerable body of literature belonging mainly to the fields of Sociology, Anthropology and Bioethics examining such topics as the impact of genetic research on particular communities and social groups, their attitude towards various types of genetic screening, ethical implications of genetic research and its possible positive and negative outcomes. What about the more general impact of genetics on our self-perception? Has it changed basic understandings of what it means to be human and the relationship between nature and culture? In this paper I would like to outline how this potential impact has been perceived and assayed by contemporary 'non-scientific' academic community, i.e. by humanities scholars, sociologists and cultural anthropologists.

Meaning, Ethics and Post-humanism

The issue of genetics has been discussed quite at length by contemporary philosophers and social theorists who have engaged with the subject of post-humanism and the future of human nature. To highlight this trend we would like to use the work by Habermas, Fukuyama, Baudrillard and Derrida.

Jurgen Habermas in his recent publication 'Debate on the Ethical Self-Understanding of the Species' discussed the impact that biotechnology and specifically genetics may have on the humanity's self-perception. Habermas states that he is 'not taking the attitude of a cultural critic opposed to welcome advances of scientific knowledge' but is rather asking 'whether, and if so how, the implementation of these achievements affects our self-understanding as responsible agents.'[2] The author is apprehensive of the possibility of the future genetic engineering when parents could get an opportunity to intervene with the genome of their child. He argues that once the latter realizes that he had been programmed before his birth he will be affected on an existential level: his being a body will be subordinated to his having a body.[3] Habermas adds that he does not wish to undermine the importance of 'non-genetic' parental guidance and influence on the child, but maintains that the latter impact may be resolved through psycho-therapy, while a genetic intervention would be 'a mute and ... unanswerable act.'[4]

He argues that this position should not be taken for genetic determinism. For him it does not even matter how deeply genetic interventions can alter a child's physicality or determine his behaviour. Even if it is negligible the '*post factum* knowledge of this circumstance may intervene in the self-relation of the person.'[5] I suggest that this thesis may be easily construed as an example of genetic determinism because in Habermas's critique of genetics, environmental influences appear to be easy to 'undo' while genetic impact, however small, is forever. What Habermas does not seem to consider here is what is going to determine this *post factum* knowledge and why it needs to be so crucial for the self-relation of the person. What could be explored in this respect is whether for this *post factum* knowledge to affect one's self-relation on an existential level it does not need to be based on a very deterministic image of the gene to begin with. Would not this relationship between genetics and identity be secondary to the humanity's perception of genetics? Would it be really genetics that will influence identity and not the image of the gene? Elsewhere Habermas observes that genetic involvement will change 'the initial conditions for the identity formation of another person' who as a result 'may suffer from the consciousness of sharing the authorship of her own life and her own destiny with somebody else.'[6] It may be suggested that the author links genetics to identity and ascribes to genetics a very particular type of importance putting it at a higher premium than, for instance, parental guidance, which, in the popular perception and the mass media representations, has a significant determinative power as well.[7]

Another recently published book almost totally devoted to the question of the impact of biotechnology on human life is Francis Fukuyama's *Our Posthuman Future*. Fukuyama advocates the idea of the common human essence and the restoration of a universal concept of human rights. He argues that the possibility of 'buying' genes for one's children, which he reckons will become one of the inevitable consequences of the 'genetic revolution', will have a disastrous social effect on humanity: society will be divided into 'GenRich', well-off strata who can afford buying 'good' genes for their offspring and 'GenPoor', short of wealth and short of advantageous genetic make-up.[8]

Fukuyama quite clearly opposes social constructivist ideas about human nature and promotes the idea of the biological 'essence of life'. The essence, as it follows from his analysis of biotechnology, is in the genes. Like Habermas, Fukuyama assigns the genes this very special meaning, but he does not even try to engage with the question of their actual deterministic power.

An interesting perspective on the meanings of contemporary genetics in the history of humanity is provided by Jean Baudrillard in the context of his discussion of cloning. He construes scientific attempts at cloning and particularly at human cloning as a technique which will make humans immortal. According to Baudrillard, this is involution, a return into the state of continuity and immortality that the first creations of nature, e.g. bacteria, lived in: 'We are in the process of reactivating this pathological immortality, the immortality of the cancer cell, both at the individual level and at the level of the species as a whole. This is the revenge taken on mortal and sexed beings by immortal and undifferentiated life forms.'[9] This will lead to the destruction of the humans, the first species who will disappear due to an unnatural cause. He doubts that it will be possible to call the species that will succeed in reaching immortality human beings and it is only 'whatever survives', i.e. fails to get cloned or programmed could be called human: 'some inalienable and indestructible human quality could finally be identified.'[10]

The whole struggle for immortality is described as a purely Western condition, as, according to Baudrillard, it is Westerners that invented the very distinction between the 'human' and the 'inhuman' and are now trying to eliminate it not by reconciling the two but by technological intervention. However, by arguing that we are experiencing involution, as opposed to evolution, he situates biotechnology and its implications within the history of the development of organic/non-organic, human/inhuman dichotomy, which he himself views as a Western construction.

The question of the status of the gene is addressed also by Jacques Derrida in his essay 'The Aforementioned So-called Human Genome'. Derrida has two sets of feelings about genetic advances. On the one hand he is concerned about the possibility of them resulting in eugenic practices, with identification of the super-human and the sub-human, but on the other hand, he gets a 'relativizing' and 'demystifying' feeling based on the assumption that to map the genome is not yet the ability to manipulate it.

Describing his first, rather negative feeling about genetic advances, Derrida argues that genetics has led us to this 'unique moment in the history of humanity where the question, *What is man?* could no longer wait as it seems to have done formerly, considering the time and patience of theological or metaphysical speculations'. Today it is 'taking on, here, now, a terribly concrete and urgent form at an infinitely accelerated rate in the very place where decision about the processing of the aforementioned so-called *human genome* could no longer wait.'[11] Derrida engages with the idea of the essence of human life and maintains that we are now running 'the risk of new crimes being committed against humanity and not only … against millions of human beings as was the case, but a crime such that a sorcerer's apprentice who was very cunning, the author of potential genetic manipulations, might in the future commit or supply the means for committing – in the name of science, of techno-science – against man, against the very humanity of man.'[12]. It may be suggested that this discussion implies that genome is an important component of what it is to be human if intervening in it will threaten 'the essence-itself of humanity'. A similar representation of the genome appears in Derrida's discussion of its patentability. He expresses his deep concern about the possibility of patenting the genome on the grounds that it will be appropriated by the more powerful nation-states. Derrida appears to construct genome as the essence of life thus giving it an exclusive ontological significance.

Genetics, Meaning and Society

A more detailed analysis of the impact of genetics on the reconceptualisation of the notion of life has been offered in the work by cultural anthropologists and historians who have looked at the way genetics has affected various social practices, such as, for instance, health care and jurisprudence.

Paul Rabinow has suggested that 'the new genetics will prove to be an infinitely greater force for reshaping society and life than was the revolution in physics, because it will be embedded throughout the social fabric at the microlevel by medical practices and a variety of other discourses.'[13] Writing at the dawn of the Human Genome Project he argues that '[i]n the future, the new genetics will cease to be a biological metaphor for modern society and will become instead a circulation network of identity terms and restriction loci, around which and through which a truly new type of autoproduction will emerge'. This type of autoproduction Rabinow calls biosociality, where 'nature will be modeled on culture understood as practice.'[14] In his view, nature will be changed through culture and thus will become artificial, which would bridge the gap between nature and culture. Rabinow suggests that new identities will emerge on the basis of biotechnological screening with new social groups forming around specific diseases, who would lobby their interests and educate their children.[15] This positive vision of the future development of genetics highlights the possible beneficial outcomes of genetic technology, such as more opportunities and better psychological and social climate for the disabled. At the same time, Rabinow does not deny that genetics may be used to reinforce older cultural constructions of biological identities, such as race and gender identities and that 'post-social-biological classifications will only gradually colonize older cultural grids.'[16]

A similar engagement with the changing patterns in the relationship between nature and culture caused by genetics appears in the work by the historian of science Hans-Jorg Rheinberger. He stresses that new genetic technology for the first time in history allowed us to alter the natural world, which also changed the meaning of biology. The task of this discipline has always been 'understanding life' with biologists trying to recreate in a test-tube the processes occurring in real-life organisms. With the new genetics, biologists, on the contrary, are trying to implant into living organisms new structures that they have developed in the lab, which means that the result of their work is 'no longer the extracellular representation of intracellular processes... but rather the intracellular representation of an extracellular project, i.e. the deliberate "re-writing" of life'.[17]

Quite apart from that, Rheinberger suggests that contemporary genetic technology opens a new page not only in the history of biology but also in the history of the human ability to write, instruct and legislate, which has shaped the entire social and political system of the Western world. Now we have got access to the system of legislation that only nature has so far been able to construct, i.e. to the instruction of the organic existence.[18] On this backdrop, the author comes to the conclusion that the traditional nature/nurture, biology/culture dichotomies are about to collapse:

> We come to realize that the *natural* condition of our genetic makeup might turn into a social construct... We could say as well that the future *social* conditions of man will become based on natural constructs. The "natural" and the "social" can no longer be seen as ontologically different.[19] *

A different view of the impact of genetics on the nature/culture dichotomy is expressed by the anthropologist Sarah Franklin, who has put the achievements of the new genetics into the context of the anthropology of kinship and gender studies. Franklin has assayed Rabinow and Rheinberger's critique of the natural facts/cultural facts dichotomy as very fruitful but has suggested that it obscures the fact that this dichotomy has not become obsolete yet.[20] Thus she has argued that on the one hand genetics may be viewed as dissolving and re-genealogising gender. In this respect she has coined the term *autopaternity*, a condition resulting from 'a decoupling of paternity from heterosexuality', when 'the gene, as "author" of the message, becomes the agent of its own instrumentality' and does not need 'matrix' at all. In Franklin's view, contemporary genetics reinvents the notion of maternity along similar lines, as in those cases of surrogacy, where both partners provide their sex-cells to the surrogate mother.[21]

However, she has also demonstrated that though contemporary genetics-related technology appears to have given a new meaning to parenthood and reproduction (reproduction became divorced from heterosexuality), it has been employed in society to reinforce 'the old heterosexual essentialism' with mainly heterosexual couples gaining permission to IVF and the donors of sperm and eggs recognized as the 'real' parents of the child in cases of surrogate motherhood.[22]

Geneticization and 'Gene talk'

A generally (but not completely) more skeptical assessment of the actual or possible impact of genetics on 'life itself' and the nature/culture dichotomy is offered by a number of scholars belonging to the fields of cultural and critical theory who have explored the representations and rhetoric of genetics. Their studies more often than not focus on the effect of the 'scientific propaganda' on the public perceptions of genetics and argue that the claims of geneticists are exaggerated.

This analysis has led many to criticizing a set of phenomena, which has been defined as geneticization or genetic essentialism. The former term was coined by Abby Lippman and means 'the ongoing process by which priority is given to differences

---

* For an excellent analysis of the effect of genetics on the reconceptualization of 'life' in biology see Keller 1992: 96–7.

between individuals based on their DNA codes, with most disorders, behaviors and physiological variations … structured as, at least in part, hereditary'.[23]

The expression 'genetic essentialism' first appears in the work by Sarah Franklin, who defined it as 'scientific discourse… with the potential to establish social categories based on an essential truth about the body'.[24] The idea was developed by a number of scholars including Nelkin and Lindee. Their study *DNA Mystique* considers the way various genetic practices and achievements are portrayed in the North American mass media and some semi-academic and popular accounts of genetics. It is argued that the symbolic meaning of the gene is already quite independent of its 'scientific' meaning. The authors have demonstrated that often the myth about genes being 'the essence of life' originates in the accounts of geneticists themselves.

The explanation that the authors give to this phenomenon is that these days when many social boundaries are getting blurred genetics provides one with a solid structure that helps to mark these boundaries. It is also argued that quite often genetics is used to reinforce traditional stereotypes, e.g., the idea that families should be based on real, i.e. 'blood' ties, that races may be essentialised or that some social problems (like alcoholism) have biological roots. Hence, their conclusion is that at least in public debates genetics has turned into a rhetorical device which can be used to support all kinds of agendas.[25]

A similar critique is offered by Elaine Graham, who opposes the idea of the relationship between the genome and the meaning of being human and argues that there are a lot of culturally constructed notions surrounding contemporary genetics which are promoted as objective and real blueprint for human nature. In Graham's view this is likely to reduce diversity in favour of standardisation.[26]

Donna Haraway, a cultural theorist and a feminist scholar, also draws on the notions of genetic essentialism and genetic fetishism. Having been trained as a biologist and as a historian of science, Haraway is very well situated to engage both with the mass media representations of genetics and with the discourse of the geneticists themselves. She has highlighted the constructivist nature of the term 'gene' and the way it is mediated by the wider cultural discourses of the Western society. Thus she has argued that 'the discourses of genetics and information are replete with instances of barely secularized Christian realism at work'.[27]

Another important work coming from the field of cultural studies is José Van Dijck's *Imagenation*[28] where the author examines the popular representations of the gene since the 1950s. Like Nelkin and Lindee, Van Dijck suggests that both academic and popular literature tends to construe DNA as the 'essence of life' and 'on a more philosophical level, DNA-manipulation and genome research stir up profound agitation over the integrity of the human body and the corrosion of human identity'.[29] Like some of the previous authors Van Dijck suggests that the development of new biotechnologies paradoxically has been accompanied by the reinforcement of the older ideologies of hereditary determinism. Contributing to the critique by Franklin and Nelkin and Lindee, the author insists that 'while the new genetics, and especially genomics, is motivating an implosion of categories at various levels, the ontological categories that distinguish the technical from the organic, the natural, and the textual are vigorously reinstated'.[30] This, according to Van Dijck, is generally symptomatic of post-modern culture, which shares the nature/culture, science/society, fact/image oppositions of modernity. Thus, in postmodern theory genetics would become a linguistic practice, which in itself constructs a contradistinction between the material and the textual world. Van Dijck neither endorses this view, nor does she argue that genetics is totally separate from its representation. For her genetics neither equals its image, nor is it separable from it. What the author has attempted to demonstrate is rather that 'there has never been a distinct separation between science and its images'.[31]

In this discussion Van Dijck uses the concept of geneticization too. She argues that '[t]he premise of the "geneticization" of society does not necessarily mean that genetics has become more "popular", but that its axioms and principles have spread out through an ever-growing number of discourses'.[32] The role of language in scientific discourse itself has been discussed by Evelyn Fox Keller, a scientist, philosopher and a feminist scholar, who uses the expression 'gene talk' to describe the wide usage of the term gene in scientific, academic, mass media and public discourses. The words 'genes' and 'genetic', according to Keller, carry too much of 'historical baggage' of hopes for a simple and clear explanatory framework that nowadays, even though biologists face increasing difficulties in defining the gene, they cannot stop using this word. Hence, to stop talking about genes would take the development of a whole new vocabulary rather than just a new word.[33]

Conclusion

It appears that human and social sciences have indeed been eager to engage with genetics, which is demonstrated by the growing literature addressing the cultural implications of this field including the reconceptualization of ourselves in the light of the new genetic research.

The assessed response proved to be theoretically and methodologically varied but I would suggest that there are a number of points that unite it. First, most of our authors have considered the emergence of the new genetic knowledge as a contribution to the long-standing debate about the relationship between nature and nurture in human nature and about the nature/culture dichotomy. There is no unanimity among humanities scholars when it comes to the actual determinative power of the gene. Writers like Habermas and Fukuyama take it for granted that genes (whatever the term itself means) have a profound determinative power on humans and are going to affect the relationship between the made and the given in human nature. Some authors construe the impact of genetics on human life as the largest that science has ever had on us. The Copernican or the Darwinian revolutions, for instance, against which genetics is often measured, introduced some radically new knowledge, however, they did not provide humanity with any tools for changing life itself on such a qualitatively different level. Genetics is described as a breakthrough which gives us hope/threatens us to be able one day to change human nature on the level of instruction.

Others argue that the power of the genes is exaggerated by geneticists (Nelkin and Lindee, Van Dijck) and that genetics is sometimes used as an empty term to prove whatever is on the agenda of the speaker (Franklin, Van Dijck, Nelkin). However, they also agree that genetics does offer us a lot on the level of the imaginary, and appears to have a lot of potential to have a huge impact upon human life.

Secondly, what most (though not all) of these studies have in common is that they discuss mainly biotechnology stemming from genetics research, rather than the 'pure science' or the theory and method of genetics. Those who produced what could be defined as normative rather than descriptive research about genetics often refer to the future potential of biotechnology, e.g. the horror of cloning. Needless to say, there is an extensive scholarship in the fields of the history and philosophy of science which engages with the development of the concepts of the science of genetics. However, those scholars who address the question of its ontological meanings prefer to deal with genetics translated into concrete social practices. It is noteworthy that practically all the studies described above are published after 1992, i.e. after the beginning of the Human Genome Project. In other words, the interest in the cultural implications of genetics was prompted by its technological advances, rather than by the new developments in its theory.

Finally, it should be noted that practically all the studies described above rely on the evidence coming solely from the 'West' and mainly from English-speaking countries. There seems to be a need for research based on sources deriving from a wider range of cultural and linguistic settings. This research would indicate to what extent the demonstrated meanings of genetics are universal and to what extent they are culturally mediated. Do we all think about genetics in same metaphors? Needless to say, such research would require a number of studies.

References

[1]   Fukuyama, F. (2002), *Our Posthuman Future. Consequences of the Biotechnology Revolution.* Profile, London, p. 105.
[2]   Habermas, J. (2003), *The Future of Human Nature.* Polity, Oxford, p. 12.
[3]   Ibid., p. 54.
[4]   Ibid., p. 62.
[5]   Ibid., p. 53.
[6]   Ibid., p. 81.
[7]   Nelkin, D. and Lindee, S. (1995), *DNA Mystique. The Gene as a Cultural Icon.* Freedman, New York, p.14.
[8]   Fukuyama, F., *Our Posthuman Future. Consequences of the Biotechnology Revolution.* p. 154.
[9]   Baudrillard, J. (2000), *The Vital Illusion.* New York: Columbia University Press. p. 8
[10] Ibid., pp.15–16.
[11] Derrida, J. (2002), 'The Aforementioned So-called Human Genome.' in E. Rottenberg (ed.), *Negotiations*, Stanford University Press, Stanford, p. 209.

[12] Ibid, p. 208.
[13] Rabinow, P. (1992), 'Artificiality and Enlightenment: From Sociobiology to Biosocialty' in J.C. Winter (ed.), *Incorporations.* New York, Zone, p. 241.
[14] Ibid.
[15] Ibid., p. 244.
[16] Ibid., p. 245.
[17] Rheinberger, H.-J. (2000), 'Beyond Nature and Culture: Modes of Reasoning in the Age of Molecular Biology and Medicine'. in M. Lock, A. Young and A. Cambrosio (eds.), *Living and Working with the New Medical Technologies: Intersection of Enquiry.* C.U.P. Cambridge, p. 25.
[18] Ibid., p. 28.
[19] Ibid., pp. 28–29, emphasis original.
[20] Franklin, S. (2003), 'Re-thinking Nature-Culture. Anthropology and the New Genetics.' *Anthropological Theory*, vol. 3,(1), pp. 65–85.
[21] Franklin, S. (1995), 'Romancing the Helix: Nature and Scientific Discovery.' in L. Pearce and J. Stacey (eds.), *Romance Revisited* Lawrence & Wishart, London, p. 70.
[22] Franklin, S. (1993), 'Essentialism, Which Essentialism? Some Implications of Reproductive and Genetic Technoscience.' in J. Dececco (ed.), *Issues in Biological Essentialism versus Social Constructionism in Gay and Lesbian Identities* Harrington Park Press, London.
[23] Lippman, A. (1993), Prenatal Genetic Testing and Geneticization: Mother Matters for All. *Fetal Diagn Ther*, vol. 8, pp. 175–188.
[24] Franklin, Essentialism, Which Essentialism? Some Implications of Reproductive and Genetic Technoscience, p. 34.
[25] Nelkin, D. and Lindee, DNA Mystique. The Gene as a Cultural Icon, p. 124.
[26] Graham, E. (2002), 'Representations of the Post/human. Monsters, Aliens and Others' in *Popular Culture*. Manchester University Press, p. 122.
[27] Haraway, D. (1997), *Modest_Witness@Second_Millennium FemaleMan_Meets_ Oncomouse. Feminism and Technoscience.* Routledge, New York, p. 10.
[28] Dijck, José, van. (1998, *Imagenation. Popular Images of Genetics.* Macmillan, London.
[29] Ibid., p. 7.
[30] Ibid., p. 194.
[31] Ibid., p. 196.
[32] Ibid., p. 28.
[33] Keller, E. Fox. (2000), *The Century of the Gene.* Harvard University Press, Cambridge (MA), pp.136–37.

Chapter 7

Family Decision Making – A Victim to the Hegemony of Autonomy?

Søren Holm

'**Family** Basic social unit of Islamic society. In Arabic, *ahl* or *aila* is a comprehensive term that may include grandparents, uncles, aunts, and cousins on both sides of the family. The *Quran* enjoins mutual respect and responsibility between spouses and among family members. Spouses and children have duties and rights protected by law. Men and women remain members of their natal families even after marriage. In modern times, the family has been subjected to economic and social pressures that have disrupted the traditional extended family patterns, including changing responsibilities for women. Nevertheless, it remains a flexible unit of social organization in Muslim societies.'[1]

Introduction

For many people the fact that they are members of a family or some other closely knit group of people is extremely important, and even in Western societies where the stable nuclear family may no longer be the norm,[2] people tend to live in a succession of family like arrangements. The importance of the family to people shows itself in many ways from an interest in genealogy,[3] to a willingness to help family members to a greater extent than other people.

Family decision making, i.e. decision making where the views of family members are heard and a common, consensual (or at least agreed) decision is reached is also very commonly practised (concerning where to go on holiday, which car to buy, whether to have another child etc. etc.). In many instances of family decision making some, or all family members will agree to a decision they would not have made if they were the sole (dictatorial) decision maker.

However, in modern bioethics the family is not mentioned that often and when it is mentioned it is almost invariably as a problem. In the bioethical literature families create conflicts (see for instance the extensive commentary on the recent Terry Schiavo case) or they prevent family members from pursuing their legitimate and autonomous choices.

The only two places in the bioethics literature where family is taken seriously are in discussions about proxy decision making for children and in genetics,[4] but even in that literature there is a tendency to see joint, family decision making as an exception and individual decision-making as the norm. The extensive literature on proxy decision making for children does, for instance, often proceed as if there was only one parent to take account of.

This is a strange state of affairs, not only because families are important to many people and because family decision making is so common, but also because many health care decisions people make impact directly on the members of their family. A prime example is the lifestyle advice often given to patients with ischaemic heart disease. They are told to alter their diet and take up exercise, but altering your diet when you are living in a family will almost inevitably impact other family members, and suddenly spending more time exercising may also lead to changes in the family dynamic. Family involvement in care of the elderly or persons with disability is also still expected, even in societies where many elderly people are not cared for in the family but in nursing homes. Research, for instance, shows that when people are in nursing homes family involvement in their care is expected, even when staff won't let the family take part in decisions about the care.[5]

In this paper I want to try to advance our understanding of why the family is seen as problematic in bioethics and to suggest ways in which bioethics could engage more constructively with the reality of family decision making. The focus will be on family decision making involving the competent, adult person since family involvement in that context is viewed much more negatively in bioethics than family involvement in decisions concerning incompetent children or adults. If convincing arguments can be found for the involvement of family in some health care decisions involving competent adults much will have been achieved.

Autonomy Rules

Like genetics, biomedical ethics may be said to have a central dogma. In the case of biomedical ethics the central dogma is that Mill's liberal analysis holds true for all health care decisions involving competent patients.

> '…that the sole end for which mankind are warranted, individually or collectively, in interfering with the liberty of action of any of their number, is self-protection. That the only purpose for which power can be rightly exercised over any member of a civilised community, against his will, is to prevent harm to others.'[6]

The acceptance of Mill's dictum leads to a situation where an adult, competent patient can make any health care decision he or she wants, as long as this decision does not harm other people directly. Such a patient can refuse life saving treatment, and can, if he can find a doctor willing to help him have any 'treatment' he desires as long as he pays for it himself. No competent patient can be forced to have treatment for the benefits of others, except in rare circumstances involving communicable diseases. Even if he could save someone's life by giving one unit of blood, he cannot be forced to donate his blood.

This liberty focused, individualist approach to health care decision making also underlies the recent appropriation of human rights language into medical ethics, and the attempts to turn bioethics into a branch of human rights discourse.

This liberal reasoning leading to an almost exclusive emphasis on individual, autonomy based decision making, does not deny that it may be morally good to help other people, or to take the interests of other people into account when a person decides what to do, but it does deny that the moral goodness of a specific choice can ever be a reason to enforce it on anyone.

If scepticism is expressed concerning the force or scope of the liberal principle two further considerations are brought into play. One is a principle claiming a strong right to bodily integrity, and the other is the libertarian argument that since we are 'moral strangers', i.e. we hold different moral values and cannot know which values other people hold unless they directly express them, there will be many situations in which we cannot say whether a choice is morally good or not from a third person perspective, because we cannot know whether it is good seen from the value system of the agent him- or herself. Both of these additional considerations are based on sound ethical considerations, but their weight may be questioned (see below).

The Groups We Live In

As noted above many people do live in families and this raises the question of to what degree family life, or life in some other close knit group is compatible with full individual autonomy.

Families come in many shapes and sizes, but here I will focus on those groups of people that comprise a number of people (>1), live together for an extended period of time and self-identify as a family. Given this focus it follows that no one who sincerely claims not to be part of a given family can be taken to be a part of that family. Family membership is thus optional in the sense that it is always possible to secede unilaterally.[7]

Living in a family of this kind has many consequences. It will mean that there is a group of people who know much more about you than anyone else. It will mean that there is a group of people who will in many cases be more directly and more significantly affected by your actions and the consequences of your actions than most other people will. It will mean that there are people you know a lot about and whose actions affect you very directly. And it will mean that you will often be involved in some kind of shared decision making with these people. This will be the case whether your family is held together by (romantic) love, cultural tradition, religious obligation, legal necessity or economic forces or some combination of these.

Decision making in families may take many forms, and many of these are ethically extremely problematic since they entail the subjugation of the liberty and interests of some family members. This is, for instance, the case where only one family member takes decisions for the whole family, where only family members of one gender are allowed to be involved in decision making[8] or where only certain generations are involved in the process.

There are, however also ethically non-problematic types of family decision making. Decisions about common activities will often have a form so that the first preference of all family members cannot be satisfied. This incompatibility of first preferences has to be resolved in some way, and if it is resolved through open negotiation, voting, or some form of consensus building process the decision will be ethically unproblematic and legitimate, even if some or all family members end up not getting what they most wanted.[9] Sometimes getting the second best option is all each of us can hope for when we interact with other people, as exemplified by many game theoretic problems.

The Alleged Clash Between Family and Individual Reconsidered

If we go back to Mill and the putative central dogma of biomedical ethics we see that the fact that many people live in families must have implications for our understanding of under what circumstances interference is warranted in the actions of an individual actor. First we should again note that the family is often the circle in which 'harm to others' will occur in the health care context, and second that the family (other family members) are often those best placed to judge whether such harm will occur and what its magnitude will be. This is the case not only when the family is put at risk of contracting a communicable disease, but also when the decision imposes a burden of care on the family, emotional stress or large economic costs.

This entails that one of the standard liberal arguments against enforcing morals does not work in the family context. It is often claimed that even if a certain action is potentially harmful (e.g. allowing the open sale of pornographic material) no specific person can be shown to be harmed, and diffuse harm does not count enough to curtail liberties. But in the family situation the harm is often not diffuse, but rather precisely situated.

Furthermore, if, outside of the family context, a person made a decision that imposed large economic costs on somebody else there would at least be a *prima facie* case that the person on whom this burden had been imposed had been harmed, and that imposing such a harm has to be justified by something stronger than a right to self-determination.

This seems to indicate that the family might be justified in interfering with the liberty of one of its members in a case where an outsider would not be justified in interfering because the family is in a privileged epistemic position to assess likelihood and magnitude of harm, and using the self-determination argument so beloved by modern bioethics, in a privileged position to say whether it (as individuals) is willing to accept the imposition of this harm.

The Family Re-introduced

How can bioethics take account of the legitimate role of family members in decision making without condoning rampant paternalism or maternalism?

Let me suggest four different avenues that need to be explored. All of them focus on the relationships that constitute family ties but they do so in slightly different ways:

1. an extension of the harm based analysis;
2. common values;
3. the family as a deliberative community;
4. a contractarian or promise-based approach

First we could pursue the harm based analysis outlined above in greater depth in order to get a more precise delineation of the obligations I have toward my family, and the circumstances in which my family is justified in influencing me to discharge my obligations.

The harm argument indicates that I sometimes have moral obligations towards family members that I do not have towards other people. Not because my family is more important, but because it is more affected by my actions. These include positive obligations to offer them assistance, but also negative obligations to allow them to perform actions that I do not need to allow other people to perform. An obvious example is that I may in many circumstances have an obligation to inform other family members about my health state, and to allow them to try to influence my health care decision making, for instance through persuasion, moral pressure or even in some cases threats of non-health related consequences. Whereas it would be wrong for my dentist to nag me to come for a check up if I have stated clearly that I do not want to, or to threaten me with cold dinners until I see sense, it is not always wrong for my partner to do so if she can see that I badly need the attention of a dentist, and that it will affect our future life if I don't get my teeth sorted.

As noted above it is sometimes claimed that one of the reasons not to infringe on autonomous decisions is that we are 'moral strangers' to each other. We hold (potentially radically) different moral values, and only the agent is in a position to say whether an action is in accord with his values. Enforcing the morally right choice is, on this line of argument, simply moral imperialism at the personal level. But this argument is, again, much less convincing in the family context. Many families are formed, and sustained because their members have value systems that have significant overlaps. In long lasting families the members also mutually influence the value systems of each other. And even in cases where these two considerations are not true, i.e. where the family members have radically different value systems and where there is no mutual influence, family members are in a much better epistemic position to know the value systems of other family members than the average third person. It is thus much less likely that family members are really 'moral strangers'. This means that family members can be in a position to use legitimate moral persuasion, i.e. to point out that something is the morally right thing to do, that the person in question should do it for that very reason, and that they might think less of him or her if he does not act as he should. Holding a family member to those values he or she has professed is not moral imperialism.

As we have noted above families come in all shapes and sizes, and some are characterised by the fact that their inner decision-making processes are discursive and reason based. Such families may have internal moral or religious tensions, but these are not resolved by force but by continued discussion and reason giving. Their decision-making processes share many characteristics with the accounts of legitimate decision processes in morally pluralistic societies developed in the literature on deliberative democracy in political philosophy.[10] And just like political decision-making legitimacy can flow from proper deliberative political processes, familial decision-making legitimacy can flow from proper deliberative processes within the family.

What exactly are the requirements for participants in the public debate in a deliberative democracy, the features that should also distinguish legitimate family decision making?

The main requirement is a requirement for reciprocity in family discourse. Reciprocity has two components, it entails that the principles and standards that are proposed have to be principles and standards that are viewed as reasonable for everyone to accept as fair terms of cooperation, and that there is a willingness to discuss the fair terms that others propose. As Guttmann and Thompson point out true reciprocity can only occur if there is mutual respect, and if the participants in the debate evince two particular civic virtues: the virtue of integrity and the virtue of magnanimity. Integrity in this context requires consistency of speech in different situations, performative consistency, and the willingness to recognise all the broader implications of the position one puts forward. Magnanimity requires the recognition of the sincerity of the opposing position, openness to the possibility that I might come to change my own position, and a commitment to 'search for significant points of convergence between our own understandings and those of citizens whose positions, taken in their more comprehensive form, we must reject'.[11]

When we enter the realm of family discourse we have minimally to accept that there are other reasonable views than those we hold, and that the purpose of the discourse is not to 'win', but to reach a solution that is mutually acceptable and respectful.

A final avenue for exploring the role of the family would pursue a contractarian line of argument. Although families are not always formed based on an explicit contract or original founding promise – but some are – many families do have a semi-contractual nature. Promises are made between family members during the life of the family, and like all promises these promises constrain the future possible actions of the promise giver.[12] The promises may be substantial (e.g. promises to do certain specific things), or they may be procedural (e.g. promises to engage in certain kinds of decision-making processes before making certain kinds of decisions), and they may be explicit or implicit.[13] Members of many families have given each other explicit procedural promises, for instance regarding the purchase of major items for the household, in effect giving other family members a legitimate say or maybe even a veto in future decisions concerning the area in question. One of the common implicit, but never the less clearly discernable procedural promise existing in many families is a promise to involve other family members in decisions that significantly affect the future of the family or its individual members.[14] Many health care decisions belong to this genus and other family members may therefore have a legitimate interest in my health care decisions, because I have committed myself to giving them a say.

How do these lines of possible argument relate to children? For children who are incompetent to make a certain decision for reasons of immaturity the main reason for allowing family decision making is probably not along these lines. We should instead look at exploring the wide range of contexts where we can argue 1) that the family is the best judge of the best interests of its incompetent child members, partly because of its epistemic position, partly because of its continuing caring role, or 2) that the child's best interest cannot be determined in isolation without consideration of what kind of family it lives in, including what values that family holds.

With regard to children who are old enough to make their own decisions, but not old enough to lead independent lives the issue is more complicated. Remember that one premise for the whole paper is that the kind of family we are talking about is a family you can leave (although not necessarily without substantial cost). This means that if the decisions made are so inconsistent with a family member's conception of his or her interests or value system that they are intolerable, that family member can dissociate themselves from the family and from the decision. A child (or for that matter any other family member) who cannot lead an independent life does not have this escape, or it is at least a much more costly option. This brings into question the relevance of those justifications for family decision making that does not allow this special situation to be taken into account for such persons. The justification which seems most secure is the third based on legitimate decision-making procedures, since such procedures would be able to take account of the special burden imposed by the impossibility to exit the family.

All of these ways of exploring the legitimate role of the family in health care decision making leaves the standard bioethics analysis of the role of the doctor mainly intact. The doctor stands outside of the family relation and cannot avail himself of any of the family based justification to justify **medical** paternalism. He is not specifically likely to be harmed by decisions of the patient, he is not in a privileged epistemic position concerning the patient's values and he is not part of the patient's circle of commitment. The doctor therefore has to accept the patient's decisions, whether or not he agrees with them. The only difference in the doctor–patient relationship would be to change the current default assumption concerning information giving to family members, in those cases where the patient is part of a family. Instead of assuming that information can only be shared if the patient gives explicit consent, the assumption must be that the family has a *prima facie* right to be informed, unless the patient objects on the basis of good, moral reasons.

Conclusion

In this paper I have argued for the following conclusions:

1. Any serious bioethics need to engage with the fact that many people do not live their lives alone, but in different kinds of families.
2. A default presumption of individual decision making is problematic in health care (and also in many other areas).

I have also made some tentative suggestions concerning how the family can be re-introduced in bioethics thinking. Bioethics needs to take note of the facts that:

1. Family members are in an epistemically privileged position to judge the likelihood and magnitude of certain kinds of harms to persons.
2. Family decision making is a perfectly legitimate sub-type of collective decision making.[15]
3. Families are one of the ways in which we legitimately bind our future selves and re-orientate our future options for action.

Notes

[1] *Oxford Dictionary of Islam*. John L. Esposito, ed. Oxford University Press Inc. (2003), *Oxford Reference Online*. Oxford University Press.

[2] It is questionable whether the stable nuclear family has ever been the statistical norm in Western societies, but it has definitely been the type of family held up as the ideal.

[3] An age old preoccupation of human beings already pursued in great detail in the Hebrew Bible.

[4] Hallowell N., Ardern-Jones A., Eeles R., Foster C., Lucassen A., Moynihan C., Watson M. (2005), 'Men's decision-making about predictive BRCA1/2 testing: the role of family'. *Journal of Genetic Counselling* vol. 14, pp. 207–217.

[5] Ryan, A.A. & Scullion H.F. (2000), 'Family and staff perceptions of the role of families in nursing homes'. *Journal of Advanced Nursing* vol. 32, pp. 626–634.

[6] Mill, J.S. (1987), *Utilitarianism, On Liberty, and Considerations on Representative Government*. Dent, London, p. 78.

[7] This does not entail the claim that deciding to leave a family is easy or without significant costs.

[8] The latter is most commonly a problem in strongly patriarchal societies, but is also a problem in the few strongly matriarchal societies, as well as in more egalitarian societies.

[9] The fact that my family does not spend all its holidays in Hay on Wye (the antiquarian bookshop capital of the UK) does not in itself show that my autonomy has been infringed.

[10] For a range of different approaches to deliberative democracy, including applications to health care see the following. Daniels, N., and Sabin, J. (2002), *Setting Limits Fairly: Can We Learn to Share Medical Resources?* Oxford University Press, Oxford.

Guttman, A. (1993), 'Democracy', in R.E. Goodin, and P. Pettit (eds.). *A Companion to Contemporary Political Philosophy.* Blackwell, Oxford, pp. 411–21.

Guttman, A., Thompson, D. (1990), 'Moral Conflict and Political Consensus'. *Ethics,* 101(1): 64–88.

Habermas, J. (1992), *Faktizität und Geltung.* Frankfurt am Main: Suhrkamp.

Holm, S. (Forthcoming). 'Policy making in pluralistic societies'. in: B. Steinbock (ed.). *Oxford Handbook of Bioethics.* Oxford University Press, Oxford.

Rawls, J. (1996), *Political Liberalism (With a New Introduction and the "Reply to Habermas").* Columbia University Press, New York.

11   Guttman & Thompson, 'Moral Conflict and Political Consensus', p. 82.

12   I here assume without argument that promises have *prima facie* moral force. If I voluntarily promise to do something, or not to do something I need overriding justification for not keeping the promise. Just saying that 'I have changed my mind' is in most cases not a sufficient reason to break a promise.

13   For those who do not believe that there is such a thing as an implicit promise, precisely the same argument can be made in terms of commitment.

14   A common implicit substantial promise is the promise not to harm other family members.

15   Only hard core libertarians believe that collective decision making is in itself problematic.

Chapter 8

Avon Longitudinal Study of Parents And Children (ALSPAC): Ethical Process

Karen Birmingham and Michael Furmston

Introduction

The Avon Longitudinal Study of Parents and Children (ALSPAC)[1] also known as 'Children of the 90s' is a longitudinal study aimed at identifying ways in which to optimise the health and development of children. Over 14,000 pregnant mothers were enrolled with expected dates of delivery between April 1991 and December 1992. This cohort, with their partners and children continue to give vast amounts of data: physical, psychological, social, educational, environmental, biological and genetic. ALSPAC's main goal, in collaboration with local, national and international scientists, is to understand the ways in which the physical and social environment interact, over time, with genetic inheritance to affect a child's health, behaviour and development. From the outset of the study it became clear that sound legal and ethical advice would be necessary in order to guarantee appropriate protection for the study participants including those yet to be born.

The ALSPAC Law & Ethics Committee was set up in 1989, in order to advise on all legal and ethical aspects of the study. The early work of the committee has been well described and put into the context of the legal and ethical milieu of that time by a founding member and the first secretary of the committee, Elizabeth Mumford.[2,3]

Further ethical review for most aspects of the study was, and continues to be, obtained from the Local Research Ethics Committees (LRECs). These committees are required by the Department of Health to advise NHS bodies on the ethical acceptability of research proposals involving human participants. At the beginning of the study it was necessary to seek approval from the three LRECs in the area as: i) ALSPAC enrolled the majority of its mothers with substantial cooperation from local midwives and other NHS staff; ii) ALSPAC staff used NHS premises to approach mothers and display posters; iii) ALSPAC collected initial bio-samples on NHS premises, again with the cooperation of NHS staff. The LRECs also provided essential authoritative independent ethical review, which the new ALSPAC Law & Ethics Committee did not claim to provide at the time.

Much has changed in the last sixteen years in relation to the laws, ethics and governance of medical research. The ethical complexities involved with running a study such as ALSPAC multiply relentlessly as does the bureaucracy, risking the ethical protection of the study participants. This article describes how ALSPAC has maintained the process of ethical review without compromising any of the many people involved whilst trying to minimise duplication of the considerable workload.

ALSPAC Law & Ethics Committee: Membership and Remit

Membership

The governance of ALSPAC has changed over time both within the University of Bristol and because of changes introduced when substantial funding was provided by the Medical Research Council and the Wellcome Trust. This later development led to the setting up of a Steering Committee including external members and an external Chair. The Chairman of the ALSPAC Law & Ethics committee has for the last several years been a member of the ALSPAC Steering Committee. The ALSPAC Scientific Director and Executive Director attend the ALSPAC Law & Ethics Committee in order to provide information and to listen to the committee's deliberations and advice. If the committee were ever to conduct their business by voting, they would be non-voting members. Some other members of the committee have associations with ALSPAC; there are always two members on the committee who are enrolled study mothers. Local professionals, with enough interest in the ethics of longitudinal birth cohorts to be willing to give up considerable unpaid time every month, are sometimes in some way associated with the study, for example as past, present or potential scientific collaborators. The committee is chaired by a lawyer and has broad membership, each member representing a certain 'constituency': medical ethicist, legal medical expert, philosopher, paediatrician, general practitioner, child psychiatrist, teacher, school nurse and the aforementioned study mothers and ALSPAC personnel. It is likely that the committee will appoint an adult psychiatrist, and at least one social scientist in the future as the breadth of ALSPAC's research requires such experts on the committee if it is to adequately meet its remit.

The committee has discussed on several occasions whether teenage members of the cohort should contribute to the committee's decisions. There are already quarterly focus groups of cohort teenagers, providing invaluable information to the ALSPAC family liaison, publicity and clinic teams about the preferences and interests of this age group but ethical issues are not specifically on the agenda. The committee have discussed having one or two teenage study participants as full committee members or as members who attend regular but extraordinary meetings dealing with particular issues. Another possibility is to have an ethics subcommittee of teenage cohort members.

The committee's interest in the study of children's understanding of ALSPAC and their role in it, led to a three-year qualitative study which took place when the children were still in primary school: Ethical Protection in Epidemiological Genetics; Participants' Perspectives (EPEG).[4,5,6,7,8,9] Focus groups and in-depth interviews with ALSPAC study children, ALSPAC parents and non-ALSPAC parents, took place in order to investigate amongst other questions what 'genetics research' means to participants, and whether this category is perceived as ethically different to other categories of research. Interestingly the EPEG team 'found that genetic research as such did not pose special ethical problems for parents or children – but that commercialisation of research, confidentiality between parents, children and researchers, and the use of schools as a research site did'.[10]

Remit

The devil in the detail

The committee's prime concern is for the ethical protection of the study participants. They believe 'the devil is in the detail' and insist on reviewing the detail of each set of new questions to be sent to the study mothers, partners and children. They also review the protocols and other documents associated with all hands-on measurements, observations and biological samples. They try to avoid scientific review as there are other, frequently better qualified, committees within ALSPAC to do this. Also, most funding bodies pay rigorous attention to the quality of the science before agreeing to fund any study. The committee pays particular attention to the concerns raised by such an extensively studied cohort and frequently asks why it is necessary to conduct certain sub-studies on the ALSPAC cohort. The cohort could be inappropriately used for many research projects, such as some cross-sectional studies, as ALSPAC has the infrastructure which allows for relatively easy contact and subsequent collection and processing of data in many formats (paper, computer files, video, biological samples, etc). Constructive linkage to and analyses of other time specific ALSPAC data sets are usually necessary for approval.

Confidentiality and anonymity

The committee continually reviews issues of confidentiality and anonymity. With approval by the committee, ALSPAC maintains a strict ethical 'divide' between those staff who have access to names, addresses or other identifying data and those who are able to link and analyse the many different data sets. This is at times cumbersome but has been essential for the trust, now well established, that the cohort has for the researchers, and allows exceptionally sensitive information to be collected and used. This 'divide' has to be explained simply, clearly and frequently in communications to the cohort, particularly to the children as their capacity to understand ethical issues has developed. It also has to be explained to the many collaborators as it impacts on specialised data collectors, for example psychologists conducting qualitative research who are unable themselves to link and analyse these data.

Data access

Related to confidentiality and anonymity is data protection and who may have access to ALSPAC data. The committee feel that even if data are kept strictly anonymous, as they are, they may be misused if analysed and published irresponsibly. It is the committee's duty to try to prevent this especially as there is increasing pressure by funding and government bodies to allow greater access to large data sets. At the same time it is important that responsible collaborators are encouraged to access the data and allowed to do so with the minimum of difficulties; obstructing bona fide research would itself be unethical. Under the close supervision of the committee, ALSPAC is currently in discussion with the UK Data Archive (funded by the Economic & Social Research Council and the Joint Information Systems Committee), which provides access for secondary analysis of large data sets to researchers and other academics mostly in the fields of economics and other social sciences.

Consent

Consent, assent, proxy consent, retrospective consent or withdrawal of consent are issues grappled with by the committee on a regular basis as not only do concerns change as the cohort grows up but legal and ethical matters change over time too. The children's cooperation or assent has always been paramount but the committee decided that from the age of 12, signed consent for biological samples and certain other measurements was necessary. This was regarded as important as it would provide a formal opportunity for the children to address their concerns to the researchers. More recently the committee has explored at what time consent from parents will no longer be necessary, as increasingly the young study participants arrive at the annual research clinics on their own. The common law governing consent for research is not wholly clear. The leading discussion came in the Gillick case in which the House of Lords considered whether Mrs Gillick had rights in relation to the possible offering of advice to daughters under the age of 16. The House of Lords decided that she did not have such rights but only by 3 to 2 and the judgments making up the majority do not say exactly the same thing. Perhaps the best test is that propounded by Lord Scarman who said that a young person who showed a good understanding of the nature of the procedure, the broader context in which it arose and any potential risk would probably be entitled to give consent. The committee is currently considering whether to seek formal advice on this question.

Feedback: Prospective Decisions

When the study mothers enrolled and regularly since then, they and their families have been told that there is very little benefit for them in participating in the study, apart from the satisfaction of knowing that they are helping future generations. Individual feedback is exceptional and only given with the approval of the Law & Ethics committee. ALSPAC is a research organisation, not a clinical one. In general therefore, it has been thought right to take the position that those attending tests should not be advised on the results. Nevertheless it would be going too far to treat this as a rigid rule. Every measure is assessed prospectively and the committee decides if is ethically necessary to inform the participant of the results of a particular measure. Such measures are few but include deficient hearing, deficient eyesight, anaemia and perhaps controversially high blood pressure. It is not yet known what cut-off point should be regarded as high blood pressure among children. ALSPAC is in the process of defining such baselines. More importantly, the implications that high blood pressure in children might have in later life are yet to be established fully; again ALSPAC is in a prime position to answer this question eventually. Nevertheless the committee felt that parents should be informed if the systolic reading was over 140 mmHg and given a letter to take to their GP if they so wished.

Feedback: Retrospective decisions

Often professionals or study participants themselves, ask the Director of ALSPAC for individual data, for example: a clinical psychologist asked for a child's I.Q. results; and a study mother concerned about her child's development asked for her baby's APGAR scores (evaluation of a newborn's physical condition). The decision to release such data is made by the committee and as yet they have never agreed to do so as it goes against all ALSPAC protocols for keeping data anonymous. They endeavour to be helpful and in the case of the request for APGAR scores explained to the mother their reasons for seeming obstructive and suggested she contacted the hospital consultant (address supplied) who would not only have the APGAR scores but possibly other useful information about her child at birth.

Another case the committee reviewed involved the rare death of a study child from a relatively common disease. A post-mortem had taken place and it was considered that linking the results with other tests that had been conducted at the Focus Clinics could be medically valuable. If something important came from such linking and the results of such an investigation published, it would be extremely difficult to keep the child's identity anonymous as such deaths are so rare. Informed consent would be needed from the family but even so, to be linking an individual's results in this way was not the usual ALSPAC policy when asked by parents or clinicians. The committee thought the chance of discovering a vital 'key' was minimal and that the linking should not take place. It was suggested that a study looking at the factors associated with this type of death could be carried out. If all children with this particular condition needing either intensive care admission or frequent admissions were selected the deceased child's identity could be concealed. The committee decided not to recommend data linkage in this case although, if necessary, the case could be reviewed again in the future.

The committee believes that the review of such requests is an important part of their remit and, in life or death circumstances, they may have to decide to release certain data or identify participants. They therefore insist that all requests are referred to the committee.

Child and staff protection

The committee has established protocols for staff, should they have concerns about a study child, for example if they suspect abuse, neglect or self-harm. The protocol is reviewed annually, as is the protocol for the protection of staff, who are increasingly vulnerable to certain types of accusations if interviewing children by themselves. To date we have operated the policy that children are only alone with a member of staff in interview sessions and that the rooms are so organised that there is no possibility of physical contact between member of staff and child. There is always a window in the door of the interviewing rooms through which both can be seen clearly. In other sessions if there is not a parent or carer available, a second member of staff attends the session as well as the tester. This situation arises occasionally, for example when twins come with a single carer. Increasingly the young study participants are beginning to come to the 'clinics' alone. Staff are never alone with the children in 'measuring' sessions which requires some clothing to be removed and some physical contact to take place. However, the situation is less clear in 'activity' or 'hearing' sessions where some physical contact may be needed, to adjust a heart monitor or use an otoscope for example. It is not possible to employ sufficient staff to be able to act as chaperones for all sessions. The committee recently updated the policy: a chaperone is always present in the measuring sessions; a chaperone is not offered to a young person in other sessions, including blood taking, but one will be provided if they seem uneasy or request one; there are windows in doors to all rooms where a young person may be alone with a tester; staff endeavour to avoid physical contact with the young person; a record is kept of all incidents where the tester has felt uncomfortable because of inappropriate speech or behaviour; any tester who feels uncomfortable should end the session as soon as possible and failing that should open the door.

Laws

As illustrated previously in relation to consent, knowledge of the laws which impact on decisions concerning this sort of research is essential. The committee relies on advice from the two lawyers on the committee but on occasions has to seek further advice. There are several pieces of legislation that the committee pays particular attention to in order to ensure that ALSPAC complies with the law: the Data Protection Act 1998 and research exemptions; the Health & Social Care Act 2001, Section 60 and access to NHS data; the Human Tissue Act 2004 in relation to stored and newly acquired samples; the Freedom of Information Act 2000 in regard to both research data and decision making within ALSPAC.

Sub-studies

The committee reviews all sub-studies that require extra data collections. The committee does not, unless under exceptional circumstances such as biosamples being sent abroad for analysis, review studies that only involve secondary analysis of ALSPAC data. Frequently the sub-studies have undergone ethical review by committees attached to the collaborators' institutions, for example, faculty committees in other universities. The ALSPAC committee is aware of the previous reviews and takes into account the evaluations made by the other committees. They are eager not to duplicate the work involved in ethical reviews, usually involving reading extensive documentation, but also recognise that they have a particular role, as they have a broader understanding of the cohort and the other studies or interventions that have taken place.

Institutional review board

American collaborators sometimes have to have their studies reviewed by their own Institutional Review Boards (IRBs), the equivalent of a faculty committee or perhaps LREC, but as the ALSPAC Law & Ethics Committee is recognised as an IRB,[11] the ALSPAC committee's approval is, on occasions, all that is necessary. Interestingly, the United States Department of Health and Human Services recognises the ALSPAC committee as independent enough to provide conscientious ethical review, with assurance from the University of Bristol Ethics of Research committee[11], but independent status has not been established locally. This recognition as an IRB has led to the referral of a non-ALSPAC study to the committee for review and approval. The study was to be carried out in an East European country and had already had ethical review by an IRB in the United States as the main part of the study was to be carried out from the US. Further local review was necessary for the investigators based in Avon. The ALSPAC Law and Ethics Committee were unsure if their review was valid as there was no forum for discussion between the ethical panel and frontline researchers. The committee decided they would tell the Avon investigators the advice that they would give if it was an ALSPAC study. The committee, already committed to a substantial workload, is not prepared to jeopardise the conscientious review of ALSPAC studies in favour of others, and is currently considering the implications of this extension to its work.

Local research ethics committees

ALSPAC has always, and continues to seek, approval from these NHS committees. The Governance Arrangements for NHS Research Ethics Committees (GAfREC)[12] published by the Department of Health states under 'The Remit of an NHS REC':

> Ethical advice from the appropriate NHS REC is required for any research proposal involving:
>
> • patients and users of the NHS. This includes all potential research participants recruited by virtue of the patient or user's past or present treatment by, or use of, the NHS. It includes NHS patients treated under contracts with private sector institutions;

- individuals identified as potential research participants because of their status as relatives or carers of patients and users of the NHS, as defined above;
- access to data, organs or other bodily material of past and present NHS patients;
- fetal material and IVF involving NHS patients;
- the recently dead in NHS premises;
- the use of, or potential access to, NHS premises or facilities;
- NHS staff – recruited as research participants by virtue of their professional role.

There is no question that the LREC's approval at the beginning of the study was mandatory but by now continuing approval for all the research carried out by ALSPAC is less clear. Many but not all of the study mothers were recruited through the NHS, the cohort children were recruited in utero and partners of the study mothers are usually relatives by marriage but not always so. Some of the other points could be addressed too, but to no purpose. ALSPAC employ all their own staff and rarely use any NHS facilities. It is clear that LREC approval is a necessity for those few sub-studies involving the use of NHS facilities and staff but for many other studies it seems an unnecessary load to impose on the LREC.

The LREC usually meets 10 times per year in order to review research projects (monthly, with a break in the summer and at Christmas). It obviously mostly reviews non-ALSPAC projects. In 2004 the ALSPAC Law & Ethics committee met 11 times and in 2005 they were due to meet 13 times. It is quite obvious that the ALSPAC committee is spending significantly more time on individual items than could possibly be spent by the LREC. The ALSPAC committee also falls within the supervisory remit of the University of Bristol Ethics of Research Committee.

It is surprising, considering the work involved in reviewing ALSPAC research, that the LREC have not asked ALSPAC to find another independent ethics committee to review most of the research. The work involved, for the committee members, the Trust Research and Development department, the Trust Paediatric R&D Peer Support Group (compulsory in the local Trust), and administrators has proved to be overwhelming. Not only have their own deadlines been exceeded by months, but contradictory approvals have been given to identical paperwork submitted to the same committee meeting and the expertise required for reviewing psychological, social, educational, environmental and even genetic studies is in question. This has had serious consequences for ALSPAC. Over 1,500 parents who attended the 'clinic' willing and expecting to give samples for DNA extraction or transformation to cell lines could not, due to the LREC missing their deadline. We currently have over 20,000 DNA samples being used or available for genotyping but another rapidly increasing subset of identical type samples are in storage but unavailable for any 'further research' without going back for full approval from the LREC and possible re-consent from the participants.

Some researchers of ALSPAC sub-studies are also in a curious position as regards ethical approval. As they are recruiting through ALSPAC not the NHS and do not conform to any other of the above GAfREC stipulations, is it necessary to seek LREC approval? Others, for example psychologists, have sought ethical approval from their own institutions and rightly query the necessity to seek approval from another less qualified committee. Yet other social scientists believed that there was no formal requirement to obtain ethical approval for a social research project.[13]

Conclusion

Unlike UKBiobank,[14] ALSPAC was not able to spend many years planning an ethical framework. The ALSPAC Law & Ethics Committee and LRECs have since 1989 ensured that all ALSPAC research has been comprehensively reviewed and that the study participants have been well protected. The ALSPAC committee has provided an integrated legal and ethical perspective and thorough scrutiny of detail not possible by the LRECs. The LRECs have provided a necessary independent perspective. Many other groups and committees have contributed in part to the ethical review. Sixteen years on, the system is not entirely satisfactory or efficient and puts at risk the responsible use of data that the participants expect and the researchers are obliged to carry out. The process of ethical review must adapt and change with the ethical and legal constraints of the times whilst ALSPAC must continue to provide the study participants with the protection to which they have a right.

References

1   <http://www.alspac.bris.ac.uk/welcome/index.shtml>
2   Mumford, S.E. (1999), 'Children of the 90s: ethical guidance for a longitudinal study.' *Arch Dis Child Fetal Neonatal Ed*, vol. 81(2), F146–51.
3   Mumford, S.E. (1999), 'Children of the 90s II: challenges for the ethics and law committee.' *Arch Dis Child Fetal Neonatal Ed.* vol. 81(3):F228–31.
4   Goodenough, T., Williamson, E., Kent, J., and Ashcroft, R.E., (2003), 'What did you think about that? Researching children's perceptions of participation in a longitudinal genetic epidemiological study.' *Children and Society* vol. 17, pp 113–125.
5   Ashcroft, R.E., Goodenough, T., Williamson, E., Kent, J. (2003), 'Children's consent to research participation: social context and personal experience invalidate fixed cut-off rules.' *American Journal of Bioethics* vol. 3, iss. 4, pp. 16–18.
6   Williamson, E., Goodenough, T., Kent, J., Ashcroft, R.E. (2004), 'Children's participation in genetic epidemiology: consent and control' in Tutton R., Corrigan O.(eds.) *Genetic Databases: Socio-ethical issues in the collection and use of DNA* Routledge, London, pp. 139–160.
7   Goodenough, T. Williamson, E., Kent, J., and Ashcroft, R. (2004),'Ethical Protection: Participants' Views. Including Children in the Debate', in Smyth, M. & Williamson, E. (eds) *Researchers and their 'Subjects': Ethics, Power, Knowledge and Consent in Research*, Policy Press, pp 55–72.
8   Goodenough, Trudy (2004), 'Children's Focus Groups: Location, Location, Location' in Hallowell, N., Lawton, J., Gregory, S. (eds.) *Reflections on Research: The realities of doing research in the social sciences*, O.U.P.

[9]   Williamson Emma, Goodenough Trudy, Kent Julie, Ashcroft Richard (Accepted) Conducting Research with Children: The limits of confidentiality and child protection.

[10] Ethical Protection in Epidemiological Genetic Research: Participants Perspectives (EPEG): End of study report to the Wellcome Trust.

[11] <http://ohrp.cit.nih.gov/search/iasurdtl.asp?asuid=FWA00004516&asutyp=X> (IRB00003312 & FWA00004516)

[12] <http://dh.gov.uk/assetRoot/04/05/86/09/04058609.pdf>

[13] Kent, J., Williamson, E., Goodenough, T., Ashcroft, R.E. (2002), 'Social Science Gets the Ethics Treatment: Research Governance and Ethical Review.' *Sociological Research Online* vol 7, no 4, para 2.1. <http://www.socresonline.org.uk/7/4/williamson.html>

[14] +<http://www.ukbiobank.ac.uk/ethics/ethicsgov.php>

PART II
ETHICS AND SOCIETY

Chapter 9

Restrictive or Engaging:
Redefining Public Health Promotion

Andreas Hasman

Public health seems to have become a timely issue which takes up a still more prominent position in public and political debate. Very publicised public health issues relating to for example smoking, drinking, diet, exercise and sexually transmitted disease may be the cause of this renewed interest. This paper is not an attempt to debate what constitutes good public health or what should be the objective of efforts to promote it. Most people would agree that good or perhaps better health for the population is what we are aiming for, although there is of course considerable disagreement on how to measure and assess improvements in the health of the public. In the paper I will instead try to discuss what means of health promotion should be applied in order to achieve that goal most effectively and appropriately.

Focusing on a draft strategy for public health in the European Union I argue that *patient engagement* is the most appropriate and efficient means to promote health. Engaging patients in their own care through self-care, and self-management of chronic conditions not only empowers individual patients and members of the public to make the choices that are right for them, it also leads to more effective utilisation of services and improved public health outcomes.

A New Focus in Public Health Promotion

On 15th July 2004 David Byrne, European Commissioner for Health and Consumer Protection, launched a reflection process on the EU's health policy strategy. This process was intended to help shape the future of EU health strategy and stakeholders and interested organisations and individuals were encouraged to contribute. To kick off the reflection process a supporting paper, *Enabling Good Health for All*, set out the priorities of the European Commission's DG Sanco (Department for Health and Consumer Protection) in relation to the development of EU health policy over the coming years.[1]

The fundamental argument put forward in the paper is that the perspective in public health must necessarily change:

> Europe should take positive action to avoid ill health in the first place. Pro-active, forward looking, long-term measures to promote good health are needed. The time has come for

a change of emphasis from treating ill health to promoting good health (…) The EU must empower citizens to make healthy choices and involve them in policy-making from the start.

Commissioner Byrne's reflection process and proposed new strategy for the European Union was the latest initiative in what has now turned out to be a much wider attempt to redefine public health.[2,3,4]

New and exacerbated public health problems have led policy makers to contest a traditional perception of health care as primarily catering for the sick and the injured; instead they have suggested and defined the role of health systems which involves emphasis on combating determinants of disease and improvements in public health. This new approach re-emphasises classic public health objectives of promoting health by targeting the causes and determinants of ill health, such as unhealthy lifestyle choices and social inequities, but where public health efforts in the past involved giving information as their principal intervention, the new approach proposes more radical action.

A helpful way of understanding public health policy is to categorise initiatives as either encouraging, in which case they serve to inform or advise people about health; enabling, which are policies that aim to create favourable social, economic conditions that promote health; or restrictive. Restrictive policies are legal or fiscal measures that actively prevent the individual from acting in ways that put others' health at risk, or increase his or her own risk of getting sick or disabled.[5] As health policy makers have grown increasingly discontented with the impact of non-restrictive means they are now, arguably, more inclined to accept that forcing choices on people, either through selective bans or fiscal measures, is necessary if those at risk do not (or will not) listen to repeated health warnings. That restrictive health promotion is gaining momentum is illustrated by newly implemented bans on smoking in Ireland and New York and by plans in the UK for a 'children's watershed' for food advertising to restrict TV ads of foods high in fat, sugar and salt during children's viewing times.[4]

Commissioner Byrne finds that the challenges currently facing health care planners, such as for example an ageing population, and growing problems of obesity, tobacco consumption and sexually transmitted disease, are best (or most efficiently) tackled through a coordinated approach to public health planning, which involves legislation as a prominent component. Effective health promotion is, he argues, a prerequisite for long-term prosperity in the European Union and the legislator should play the key role in this – involving the public only at policy level. What is also at the heart of *Enabling Good Health for All*, and indeed the wider current developments in policy, is a belief that unhealthy individual lifestyle choices and social inequalities in health status are the principal *preventable* causes of ill health and that these choices should be the focus of attention for public health planners. Byrnes writes:

Europe increasingly suffers from lifestyle related diseases triggered by an unbalanced diet, physical inactivity, smoking or alcohol abuse. This means that citizens' health is, to a great extent, determined by individual choices on what people eat, smoke, drink and do.

And later on in the paper:

> By increasingly putting EU policies at the service of good health, we bring Europe closer
> to its citizens and help them enjoy longer, happier, more productive lives (...) Enabling
> citizens to make the right choices is indispensable.

These policies can take different forms, but the Commissioner points explicitly to legislation on mandatory food labelling and other initiatives procuring high quality consumer information, legislation on quality and safety standards for medical products and devices, and a ban on tobacco smoking in public places, as examples of health policies which have the potential to facilitate people making those right choices. It is also suggested that public health planning authorities should seek to improve the knowledge base on determinants of ill health through research and disseminate experiences and best practice among those responsible for public health.

These arguments clearly lend themselves to the assumption that there indeed is an *objectively right choice* as far as individual decision making on lifestyle and health is concerned. The underlying idea seems to be that if only sufficient information can be made available, people at large will necessarily choose good health over poor health and therefore healthier lifestyles over unhealthy lifestyles. Consequently, if sufficient information *is* available, and a minority of people still fail to make the decisions which will lead to better public health, then it is only rational and fully legitimate for legislators to force these choices on them.

There is evidence from the UK to show that the general public supports the renewed focus on prevention and health improvement and for public health planners to have access to more restrictive means. A recent investigation, carried out by Opinion Leader Research for the King's Fund and the Department of Health[5] showed that a majority is in favour of giving government agencies more power to directly intervene in individual lifestyle choices, provided this can improve health and reduce public spending on health care. This finding was to some extent reproduced in the reflection process. Most of the hundreds of national and regional authorities, non-governmental organisations (NGOs), universities, individual citizens and companies who made contributions to Byrne's reflection process, also agreed that provision of consumer information and protection from harm and 'wrong choices' is imperative; and that health policies and objectives can legitimately be enforced through legislation if information and support are no longer effective and sufficient. A number of contributors even found that the suggested strategy did not go far enough in suggesting means of outlawing unhealthy behaviour, particularly as this relates to tobacco and alcohol consumption.[6]

The question which remains, however, is whether restrictive policies are actually the best way to persuade the public to make healthier lifestyle choices. We have ample evidence from everyday life that people at large do not agree on what constitutes a 'right choice' of lifestyle, even when they know that that choice has ramifications for future health. For decades we have known that smoking causes disease but still some people choose to smoke, even when there are no apparent determinants in their social background or environment, which cause them to do so. Tobacco smoking has both positive and negative consequences for social life and health and most people are, provided of course they have access to sufficient information to make an informed choice, fully able to assess and balance advantages and disadvantages.[7] Banning smoking or levying heavy taxes on tobacco may be right for other purposes, but it does nothing to involve, or indeed empower, individual patients and members of the public who smoke or may want to start smoking.[8] The same could be said about patients who are obese – banning certain kinds of processed foods may promote health in a restrictive and authoritarian sense, but will not empower those who consume those products to make informed, autonomous choices for themselves. Quite a separate issue relates to whether restrictive public health policies are justified or legitimate in the first place. I will not go into details on that here, although I feel very strongly that at least some restrictive policies are clearly not legitimate. I will instead focus on whether there are not other ways of promoting health which will more appropriately empower the individual citizen and patient.

Patient Engagement and Health Promotion

In his review of future funding needs for the British National Health Service, Derek Wanless established that health care provision is currently not sufficiently centred on the needs and preferences of patients, and suggested ways in which demand for services can be modified by investment in effective health promotion and disease management with the aim of actively involving individual patients and local communities.[3] Social research evidence had shown that patients in the UK generally felt insufficiently involved in decisions relating to their care; that tests and treatments were in most cases not properly explained to them; that information was often insufficient and inappropriate; and that there was rarely anyone for patients to talk to about their anxieties and concerns. The review concluded that radical changes would be needed to rectify these shortfalls.[9] The Wanless team modelled three economic scenarios (the *solid process*, the *slow uptake* and the *fully engaged* scenario) which varied in the extent to which patients and members of the general public were engaged in health service provision. Although the *fully engaged scenario*, which entailed a radical change in professional and public roles, was the most ambitious of the three alternatives, it was also proven to offer the best and most cost effective, long-term, means of matching demand to supply of health care. The scenario forecasted (1) more *healthy behaviour*, resulting in, for example, reduced smoking rates, increased exercise, and more balanced diets; (2) more *health seeking behaviour*, for example more frequent visits to GPs and increased use of prophylactic medicines; (3) more *self-care*, for example when patients are capable of self-diagnosing and self-treating minor ailments and injuries, are more directly involved in treatment decisions, and supported in active self-management of chronic conditions; and (4) faster uptake of new *medical technology*. Wanless singled out increased access to health information, and increased *health literacy* within the population as the main driving force behind greater patient engagement, which would again result in healthier lifestyles, increased life expectancy, reduced long-term and acute ill health among the elderly, as well as increased productivity. The degree of engagement would therefore impact on the future resources required for the health service by moderating overall demand for health services, and by reducing the cost and configuration of the supply of care. This strategy is now, to an extent at least, enshrined in official policy for the NHS in England.[10,11]

Research shows that engagement of patients in managing their own health care can not only improve their experience, but that it often also results in more effective utilisation of health services and better public health outcomes. Yet health care systems have been slow to develop explicit training tools which enable doctors to partner with patients, to support them in self-care and self-management of chronic conditions, and to share decisions with them. The key to greater patient engagement lies in building health literacy and ensuring that doctors help patients to help themselves in managing their own health. Health care systems have different options available to promote this development.[11] It is clear, however, that regardless of how it is achieved, ensuring full patient engagement in health is far from a quick fix. It is nothing short of a long-term reorientation of the health sector which requires not only careful strategic planning and reform of the health service infrastructure but also, more importantly perhaps, fundamental changes in public and professional roles and attitudes. There are, as I see it, two essential components to this: first, health planners need to provide the tools which patients and members of the public require in order to get engaged in health and health care; second, there is a need to prepare providers of care, i.e. the health professionals, through education and training so that they are able to help and facilitate the patient's and public's engagement.[12]

There is a clear need for finding ways to broaden public and patient access to high quality information on health and health care issues which they can use to make decisions relating to their choice of life style and treatment. The proposed European strategy for public health goes some way to address the first of these issues. Commissioner Byrne suggests the implementation of an effective health impact assessment system and the creation of a new European equivalent to the National Institutes of Health in the United States with the purpose of conducting research on determinants of health and assembling and sharing best practice expertise among policy makers. These suggestions signal a strong commitment to ensuring that health policies and legislation are well informed by quality research, but do less to empower patients with sufficient information to make informed autonomous choices for themselves. Consequently, the European strategy for public health seems clearly biased in favour of an approach involving informed policy and legislation rather then encouragement and enabling through patient information. Although the document briefly refers to a need for helping citizens make informed choices, and mentions the development of supporting networking of patients' organisations and internet based information gateways for patients as examples of how this might be done in practice, it never seems to take this need explicitly into account. A bureaucratic emphasis on policy making and legislation fails, I argue, in the quest to empower patients and members of the general public. In order to do that successfully, public health systems will need to give highest priority to the development of information sources which suit the requirement of patients – not legislators and other policy makers.

The second important component of a drive towards increased patient and public engagement in health, and hence improved public health outcomes, has to do with the way in which doctors and other health care professionals are educated and trained. Medical education plays an essential role both in developing and sustaining good medical practice and in shaping the health care professionals of the future. Education should facilitate doctors' awareness and responsiveness to patients' evolving needs, and help them adjust their attitudes and practices to meet changing requirements and expectations. They have to form partnerships with patients, and other members of the public who come to them for help and advice, where each party respects the importance of the other party's knowledge and contributions. The health care professional will of course bring technical knowledge and clinical experience to this partnership, but if they are ignorant of patients' values and preferences, they may provide treatment and care which is inappropriate to patients' needs. It is therefore crucial that patients' contributions are part of decision making. Only patients have knowledge of their own personal circumstances and preferences; they should be encouraged to express their views and these should be accepted as instrumental to clinical decisions. Education and training should help to facilitate the creation of this partnership. It should create, in effect, doctors with mindsets appropriate to modern day requirements.[12]

Conclusion

A new breed of policy strategies for public health gives too much emphasis to restrictive means of health promotion through legislation. Drawing on a draft strategy for the European Union I have tried to illustrate some of the shortfalls of this approach. More attention should be paid to finding ways of engaging patients directly in their own care through self-care, and self-management of chronic conditions. Although legislators may have some role to play in this, real change must happen from the bottom up. Public health planners must ensure that high quality information is available, but it is even more crucial that this information is of a kind which will enable patients and members of the public to make decisions that are right for them. Developing the way in which health care professionals are educated and trained, to fully prepare them to form partnerships with patients and to ensure their responsiveness to patients' evolving needs, may well be another key component of a move towards greater patient and public engagement – and hence towards better public health. Changes along these lines to the way health care is delivered will not only have the potential to improve public health, they will be genuinely empowering for patients and members of the public.

Notes

[1] David Byrne, *Enabling Good Health for all. A reflection process for a new EU Health Strategy*, DG SANCO 2004. <http://europa.eu.int/comm/health/ph_overview/Documents/byrne_reflection_en.pdf> (accessed July 2004)

[2] WHO The Fifth Global Conference on Health Promotion: Bridging the Equity Gap, Conference report, World Health Organisation 2000, <http://www.who.int/hpr/NPH/docs/mxconf_report_en.pdf> (accessed November 2004)

[3] Wanless, D. (2002), *Securing our future health: taking a long-term view (final report)*. London, HM Treasury.

[4] Public Health Whitepaper: *Choosing Health – Making healthy choices easier*, London, Department of Health 2004.

[5] King's Fund, Public Attitudes to Public Health Policy, London: King's Fund Publications, <http://www.kingsfund.org.uk/pdf/publicattitudesreport.pdf> (accessed August 2004).

[6] Enabling good health for all: Report on responses received, DG SANCO 2004.

[7] Hasman, A., Holm, S., (2004), 'Nicotine conjugate vaccine: is there a right to a smoking future?', *Journal of Medical Ethics* vol. 30, pp. 344–45.

[8] I make the argument although, with regards to smoking at least, the issues involved may be more complex, since some bans may empower non-smokers to avoid passive smoking. A ban on smoking in public places may, for example, give non-smokers more choice as to where to go out and where to work. Such a ban would, nevertheless, still not empower those who choose to smoke – quite the opposite in fact.

[9] Wanless, D. (2001), *Securing our Future Health: Taking a Long-Term View* (Interim Report), HM Treasury, London.

[10] Secretary of State for Health. *Building on the best: choice, responsiveness and equity in the NHS*. Cm 6079. London, Department of Health, 2003.

[11] Coulter, A., Rozansky, D. (2004), 'Full engagement in health', *British Medical Journal* vol. 329, pp. 1197–98. <http://bmj.bmjjournals.com/cgi/content/full/329/7476/1197 > (accessed November 2004).

[12] Picker Institute Europe, *Principles of Good Medical Education and Training: Response to the GMC's Consultation,* Picker Institute Europe, Oxford. <http://www.pickereurope.org>

Chapter 10

Enemies of Mankind

Gerry Simpson

The Certainties of Empire

Three months after the invasion of Iraq by US–UK-led forces in March 2003, Iraqis and allied troops began to uncover mass graves; sites of atrocities committed by the Iraqi regime. The relatives of victims called for some form of punishment of those responsible. One relative spoke bluntly: 'Either the people who did this must be brought to court or we should ask for the authority to kill them'.[1] To some extent, this mirrored the views of many within the Bush Administration and Blair Cabinet about the decision to go to war in the first place. While the neo-conservatives within the Bush Administration were willing (reluctantly) to tolerate Security Council debate and involvement in the decision-making process (they were happy for Iraq to be 'brought to court' as it were), they also were very prepared to take political action to eliminate the regime outside the parameters of strict legality. As Jack Straw put it prior to the intervention:

> We are completely committed to the United Nations route, if that is successful. If, for example, we end up being vetoed…then of course we are in a different situation.[2]

The movement between law and politics in the field of war and crime is also, then, a movement between the use of judicial processes to punish enemies on one hand, and resort to non-judicial methods to remove these enemies from the political scene on the other. But the relationship between law and politics in this regard is not straightforward. In a forthcoming book I argue that war crimes trials are political trials (in a very particular sense). Equally, though, political action directed at defeated enemies turns out to be, very often, grounded in legal forms (Simpson, 2006). In 1943, as the Allies began to contemplate war crimes trials, there was inevitably resistance among those of a more punitive inclination. Anthony Eden took the position, shared by Churchill, that Nazi guilt fell outside the framework of law (Overy, 7). He was in favour of summary execution or political action arguing that there was simply no international law capable of confronting the sort of evil seen in the 1930s and 40s. But, of course, this was not quite political action. Summary execution, after all, required some legal authority. The Lord Chancellor, Lord Simon, suggested that Nazi fugitives be treated like the outlaws of mediaeval Britain. This pseudo-legal procedure permitted any citizen to kill an outlaw declared such by the

Grand Jury: '...the Sheriff did not try the outlaw or bring him before any court for trial; he merely hanged him' (Overy at 4).

This idea of outlawry was taking hold, too, among prominent academics. Georg Schwarzenberger shared the Eden view that the Nazis fell outside the ambit of decent international law. In his book, *Totalitarian Lawlessness and International Law*, he called for the Nazi Regime to be designated an outlaw regime or pirate state, one that could no longer avail itself of the protections of international law, and one in relation to whom the term neutrality could have no meaning (Schwarzenberger, 1941). Henry Morgenthau, Roosevelt's Treasury Secretary, meanwhile, was busy working on a plan that would combine the two ideas of state piracy and individual outlawry in one overarching scheme for an emasculated post-war Germany (Bass, 166).

In contemporary international society, too, the idea of piracy has enjoyed a renaissance on a number of fronts. The pirate state, for example, is a readily identifiable figure in the practices of the international community and in the rhetoric of the Great Powers (Simpson, *Great Powers,* passim). In addition, terrorism often is regarded as the new 'piracy'. Arguments are being increasingly made for placing terrorists in a parallel legal regime subject to universal jurisdiction or relatively unfettered enforcement action (Halberstam, 1996). Recalling Anthony Eden's language, President Bush has called the Guantanamo Bay detainees, the 'evil of the evil'. And, of course, there is the revival of old-fashioned free-market piracy itself in the South-east Asian shipping lanes and enclaves, and elsewhere.[3]

But how ought we to understand the identity of our enemies? Now, and in history? Take the use of the term 'criminal' to describe the state of Afghanistan or the Taliban or Osama Bin Laden. To describe an adversary as 'criminal' might be a useful rhetorical ploy: creating the impression of an enemy to be destroyed and without mercy. I think this is what the Bush administration was getting at when it used this term. Indeed, President Bush's deployment of the mythic imagery of the Wild West plays well in this regard. The chief characteristic of the Wild West was that it was wild and lawless; criminals got smoked out dead or alive. So, the use of this language seemed to me to be a way of positing retribution as an alternative to trial.

But in liberal legal traditions criminals get tried and convicted not killed or liquidated by Special Forces. Inevitably, then in characterising Bin Laden as 'criminal', U.S. officials were signalling or bringing into play two contradictory images: the image of lawlessness and vigilantism on one hand and the image of trial and conviction on the other. The President might think that calling Bin Laden a criminal means that he must be killed more ruthlessly than if he were just an enemy (after all we accord honour and respect to our enemies, criminals should be denied that respect), amongst international lawyers (and not just international lawyers), though, it means that we should set up a court and try Bin Laden offering him the privileges and immunities of criminal suspects (after all, he is no longer an enemy to be killed but a criminal to be defended in court).

But what we are really conjuring into existence is a figure, or identity, who sits outside these two categories: not quite an enemy (entitled, after all, to certain protections under the Geneva Conventions and Protocols) nor quite criminal (entitled to due process and civil rights) (nor of course friend). The illegal combatant, the terrorist and the Islamic 'fanatic' all seem to fall between these stools. What are they? If a criminal is at war with a particular society, and an enemy is at war with a particular state, then we might suggest that this new (or revivified) character is at war with everyone or international society or the international community. This, in turn, invokes 'the enemy of mankind' but in invoking this term, we inevitably call up another figure, that of the pirate.

This then, we might say, is the age of outlawry with the pirate as our defining motif. Pirates were, of course, international law's original enemies of humankind. Indeed, piracy is a founding metaphor for a whole sub-discipline of public international law: international criminal law or the law of war crimes. Piracy is international law's foundational *bête noire*. The international legal order's own imperial ambitions rest on the presence of outsiders like pirates. But piracy also seems to belong to law's past or international society's past. The category has the ring of obsolescence about it. The modernisation of the international legal order surely rendered piracy an old-fashioned category and pirates no longer a threat to the state system?

Bert Roling, the Dutch judge at the Tokyo War Crimes Trials, in his famous interview with Nino Cassese, worried that the piracy metaphor could not extend to war crimes or terrorism precisely because of the lack of solidarity in the international system, because the 'international community' did not exist (Roling at 97). But Roling came at this the wrong way surely. The pirate category is precisely how international community is made. The presence of mere 'enemies', in the old Geneva Convention sense of the word (enemy personnel entitled to certain protections under the laws of war), is evidence of a lack of community, and the continued presence of legitimate ideological or political disputation and conflict, or pluralism. In order to *construct* international community, adversaries must be transmuted into pirates. Enemies become outlaws, criminals become pirates. *Our* enemies become enemies of humankind. Pirates are enemies of particular political projects that happen to have been universalised: Empire, globalisation, Christianity, America. We could go further and suggest that Empire needs pirates: this contains a literal truth about empire: pirates (transformed into privateers) are agents of imperial ambition and regulation and, at the same time, subject to it. Osama Bin Laden, after all, was once 'licensed' as one of our privateers or terrorists just as the High Court of Admiralty issued licenses to pirates to become privateers. But at a deeper level, enemies of humankind are one way of ensuring the continued purchase of 'humankind' as a category capable of waging perpetual war. So, when the particular is universalised, particular enemies must become enemies of humankind. In this sense, piracy might also be characterised as international law's future. The concept of piracy, applied widely enough, anticipates a future deepening or homogenisation (forced or otherwise) of international society.

All of this recalls Carl Schmitt's distinction between foes and enemies (Schmitt, 2004). The revival of piracy (initially, the pirate state at the end of the Great War) signals, for him, the beginning of a post-duellist international order marked by police action rather than war. In this international order, the international community fights humanitarian wars against outlaws and pirates. Old wars, between equal sovereigns, are abolished. The pirate, then, represents the passing of a tradition in warfare between equal combat to police actions. The transformation of the Iraqi resistance from legitimate military adversaries to terrorist brigands is a perfect example of this. Almost at every instance where the US army met serious resistance this opposition was instantly converted into piracy or terror. This is the second story of new wars, alongside the idea of them as predominantly internal and chaotic affairs (Kaldor, 1999). When the US and its allies fight wars, these wars will always be elevated with the dignity of wars but the war will be the war against pirates or terror never the old-style war between two states with conflicting political projects or territorial ambitions. Pirate states will be subject to territorial intrusion as part of an enforcement action on the part of the legally-empowered Great Powers acting in a policing capacity; not the 'war between' but the 'war against'. These will not be wars between sovereigns but enforcement actions against some transcendent evil, represented by a particular sovereign. Imperial projections are publicised as wars *against* say terror but at the same time not wars *with* (this is not a war with Iraq or with the Iraqi people but a war against the regime or the pirates using the state's territory as a base). In the occupation phase, a similar process occurs. The police action, very temporarily an invasion in the case of Iraq, is converted back to counter-piracy policing or vigilantism within days of occupation. There can be no legitimate resistance (implying the possibility of politics and disagreement) only the pathology of counter-imperialist piracy.

This points to a paradox in the construction of new international law. If the problem of international law is a problem of social solidarity then piracy will have its uses. The completion of international law, for some, would be marked by the final consummation of the 'international community', marking a movement from the pluralistic, competitive society international law that has sought to ameliorate the effects of war or to the idea of international law as a sort of moral community defined in part by the presence of outsiders. But these outsiders are configured as *beyond* international law, too. These are not enemies of society whose prosecution, conviction and incarceration confirms the majesty of law but rather radically estranged outlaws whose lack of law is also a lack for international law.

The ongoing attempts at the international level to define enemies of humankind whether they be terrorists or aggressors has met with failure precisely because these always have the potential to become self-definitions. We, too, are pirates and aggressors. This ambiguity is not simply an accident of contemporary politics or late-modern indeterminacy, but is found in the very origins of the original enemy.

The Ambiguities of Piracy

It is important here to do more than simply make an argument about the return of the pirate or, indeed, produce a Schmittian volley in the direction of Empire. What I want to suggest is that the pirate is a deeply ambiguous figure, and therefore entirely appropriate as a motif for the age. This ambiguity emerges precisely because of efforts to inject clear moral distinctions into our dealings with enemies and at the same time erase some of international law's most enduring distinctions.

One feature of the modernisation of international law has been the effort to distinguish between different categories of identity e.g. neutrals–non-neutrals, combatants–non-combatants, war–peace, pirates–enemies and so on (it is also a feature of this process that the identity of sovereignty itself is fixed as neither good not bad but simply sovereign). Now, a counter-trend appears to have emerged in which more and more actors are assimilated to piracy and in which these various distinctions are being eroded, and in which sovereigns are unequal (Simpson, 2004). We need think only of 'infinite justice' or the assault on neutrality or the shift in risk from combatants to non-combatants during humanitarian wars or, as I have already noted, the way in which members of the Iraqi resistance were repositioned as 'terrorists' even as the initial stage of the war was being fought or of the rise of the pirate state to be contrasted with the decent (Rawls, 1999) sovereign.[4]

Yet this counter-trend perhaps returns us to our foundations in the regulation of piracy. If the pirate is our foundational figure here – the original enemy of humankind to whom all others are to be assimilated – then it is little wonder that categories are blurring as we recover this figure. Because the return of the pirate is a return to ambiguity.

What are (or were) pirates? Piracy was defined by King James as 'depredations committed on the seas by certain lewd and ill-disposed persons'. In the English common law, for example, piracy has been characterised as, '...acts of robbery on the high seas' (Russell on Crimes). But these are over-inclusive definitions and most international law definitions focus on the presence of a private motive or purpose. The UN Law of the Sea Convention defines piracy as an illegal act of '...violence or detention, or any act of depredation committed for private ends by the crew or the passengers of a private ship...'.[5]

States and state actors cannot, on the conventional definition, commit acts of piracy (except when they mutiny and cease to be publicly authorised) but nor, seemingly, can private actors acting for public or political ends (e.g. insurgents or belligerents) commit acts of piracy.

What, then, are private ends? In another set of definitions, the emphasis is on the absence of authorisation rather than the presence of pecuniary motives on the part of the individuals involved (Brierly, *Law of Nations* 154 1928; Oppenheim, *International Law* 8th ed. 608). So that while in the earlier cases, private acts are assimilated to selfish motives or an intent to plunder, the later definitions begin to emphasise the absence of a official mandate. In this way, the sailor is reduced to the status of pirate in the act of mutiny. The pirate, then, is not marked by his or her plundering psychology but rather by the absence of public authority. It is very much who they are as well as what they do.

Elsewhere, in case law and literature on piracy, there are further complications. In one case, failure to act within the laws of warfare or beyond the law on the use of force becomes a defining feature of piracy (In *Re Piracy Jure Gentium*, 1934 App.

Cas. 586, 598). In an early US case, piracy is defined as an absence of public authority including a 'lawless appetite for mischief' or 'plunder' or 'not commissioned and engaged in lawful warfare'. Pirates, then, are not those acting from selfish motives (or not just that) but also those who engage in illegal warfare. They are, perhaps, illegal combatants.

This distinction between private and public was explored in greater detail in a case called In The Republic of Bolivia v Indemnity Mutual Marine Assurance. Here, an English Court was obliged to determine the status of a group of rebels operating on the Bolivian-Brazilian border. The case required consideration of some exclusions in an insurance policy in the aftermath of losses incurred after an attack on the insured shipping by Bolivian rebels representing the 'Free Republic of Acre'. Acts of piracy were indemnified but not acts of rebellion. The key definition in the insurance schedule referred to piracy as 'plunder for private gain...not for a public, political end'. Despite the presence of some private motives these motives were not enough to deprive the Bolivian insurgents of the privilege of public action. The activities of the Acre 'Privateers' were essentially political. The Acre Rebels were dedicated to the overthrow of a particular state authority in a particular place. Theirs was not plunder for personal greed and gain but for political change.

It is clear, then, from Republic of Bolivia, and much of the writing around piracy, that private greed is not the controlling feature of what it means to be a pirate. It is a lack of politics that is the distinguishing mark. Pirates are not our enemies, with that term's implication of political contestation, but rather the enemies of all. The El Acre rebels were enemies of one particular state not of all states. So, though the activities of the El Acre insurgents may have been, in form, almost exactly that of pirates, their plunder had a public purpose. It was lawless but only in relation to the laws and sovereign authority of Bolivia. Theirs was behaviour lacking the '...spirit and intention of universal hostility' (In *Re Piracy Jure Gentium*). But this raises a question about groups who are neither insurgents nor plunderers. Is the political actor whose actions are indiscriminate, a pirate? Can we assimilate the idea of universal hostility to the concept of piracy? Are terrorists enemies of humankind? Are there different sorts of terrorists?

There is a problem with the attempt to analogise terrorists to pirates. Despite the inevitable parallels between some terrorists and the conventional imagery associated with piracy, terrorists, most often, *are* acting for political ends. Yet there has been an effort among some international lawyers to see Al Qaeda, or the PLO around the time of the Achille Lauro Affair, as fundamentally pirates.

These international lawyers have argued that Al Qaeda, say, are not acting in a private capacity for private gain but nor were they, so the characterisation goes, acting against one state. Doing the latter would constitute a political project along the same lines as the insurgents in *Republic of Bolivia* or the rebels in the *Santa Clara* incident (where naval officers took over a Portuguese vessel in act of rebellion in 1960 against the Salazar regime). Instead, they are configured, like pirates, as outside politics, acting in the name of inhumanity. The political project is *disallowed*, converted into an act of private madness directed at international society generally. Thus is probably what a League of Nations committee was suggesting in 1926 when it concluded that for the purposes of piracy, 'private ends' could encompass 'anarchistic vengeful motivations'. The contrast, then, is between international terrorism and activities of the El Acre rebels who were as the court put it: 'Not only not the enemy of the human race but he is the enemy of a particular state' (at 4) and therefore not pirates.

So, one might say a pirate is either acting in a private capacity or is acting publicly against the whole world. Pirates are either individuals acting for private ends or political actors acting indiscriminately. The lack of discrimination in definitions of piracy goes the absence of a particular enemy, a sovereign one wants to displace or overthrow.

Here it is not the quality of the act that is decisive but rather the personality of the actor. Is this terrorist, an enemy of humankind, all states or simply an enemy of one state? Michael Reisman, has pursued this line in distinguishing previous 'crimes' of terrorism (by, for example, the IRA or Basque separatists) from the attack on the Twin Towers. The activities of the IRA were directed at particular political ends whereas, according to Reisman, the terrorist attack on the United States was an 'aggression' against the 'values of the system of world public order.' As a result of the attack, 'all peoples who value freedom and human rights' have been forced into a war of self-defence (Reisman, 2001). Thus the attack on the United States was not simply an hideous breach of international law and an attack on a particular set of values (say, capitalism or US foreign policy in the Middle-East) but an assault on international society by those outside this society aimed at the destruction of that society. The key attribute of piracy was an animus against the whole world.

So, the conflation of certain forms of terrorism with the idea of piracy results in a combination of universal jurisdiction over pirate-terrorists (anyone can try them) with their increasing vulnerability to unilateral, discretionary political action (pirates could be simply executed without trial in the 17th Century). In the words of Judge Moore, in the *Lotus Case*, the pirate is to be treated as: 'outlaw, as the enemy of mankind...whom any nation may in the interest of all capture and punish'.

This return to piracy comes with some baggage, though. There is a rigid demarcation between good and evil and, paradoxically at the same time, a blurring of categories. There seems to be a search for the clarity of categories: If they are pirates, they must be bad. If they are assimilable to pirates, they must be enemies of mankind. But at the same time, there is a lack of (jurisprudential) certainty about the nature and identity of pirates themselves. Maybe this failure to achieve the requisite level of certainty can be traced back to piracy's origins. Indeed, were pirates, enemies of (hu)mankind? Were they, historically, acting in their private capacity or with an animus against the world? Were they the evil of the evil?

There are passages in *The History of the Peloponnesian Wars* in which Thucididyes describes a transition from a pirate class to a more static, civilised life usually adopted by the most successful pirates or by those colonisers who had expelled the pirates. The pirates, then, begin as romantic heroes, a respectable job for a young Hellene.[6] At some point, these pirates must have ceased to be respectable. This occurs at the very point when their power becomes a threat to the state (or the state system). But this is the point at which pirates are on the cusp of becoming respectable citizens of international society. So, we have the spectre of pirates becoming states or the state system finding its violent foundations in the successes of piracy. And of course there are states that become pirate states. Again the history of piracy is dotted with examples of states that simply pursue their economic and political interests through piracy. These pirate states may be forerunners to the contemporary outlaw states: partially demonised, partially tolerated. Illyria, for example, was regarded as a 'predatory state' by the Romans (Ormerod, 19). Indeed, the whole distinction between pirates and a multiplicity of other agents was often very obscure. This is reflected best in the transformation of the Barbary pirates, through association with the Great Powers, from pirate to privateer, and the pirate becomes a confident, land-based actor capable of generating acts of recognition on the parts of others. The Barbary states in Tunis and Algiers, for example, acquired such recognition after years of piracy, and the US began paying tribute to the Barbary pirates at the turn of the 18th century. So here, we see a transformation from private greed to public respectability (all the while engaging in the *actus* of piracy). But as one of the textbooks on piracy puts it: 'At different stages of their history, most of the maritime peoples have belonged to first one class, then another' (Ormerod at 13).[7]

Indeed, it is not always clear that piracy was even criminal at all times. Piracy was a mode of production supported by the Great Powers and Empires (akin to today's narco-terrorism, perhaps) and there is great uncertainty surrounding the legitimacy of piracy in, say, the ancient Mediterranean where it was, at various times, regarded as a form of production, a cheap way of getting slaves to market and a method of harassing competitors. At other times, pirates were the enemies of civilisation. Sometimes they were both at the same time.

The pirate, rather like the 'contemporary enemy of humankind', was simply the enemy of particular political projects. It is clear that in the ancient Mediterranean, for example, pirates are enemies of humankind subject to policing action only where there is Empire. At other times they find themselves in a melting pot of rebellions, wars and revolutions.

So, the counter-trend towards moralising clarities in the international system (good and evil) perhaps returns us to our foundations in the regulation of piracy. If the pirate is our foundational figure here, the original enemy of humankind to whom all others are to be assimilated, then it is little wonder that categories are blurring as we recover this figure. This is because the return of the pirate is a return to ambivalence and because the identity and identification of pirates has always raised difficult questions about war and peace, about sovereigns and non-sovereigns, and about policing and warfare. Pirates turn out to be not enemies of humankind but humankind in its plural guises.

References

Athens Maritime Enterprises Corp. v. Hellenic Mutual War Risks Assn. Ltd., (1983) QB 647.

Gary Bass, *Stay the Hand of Vengeance*, (Princeton, 2000).

James Brierly, *The Law of Nations*, (Oxford, 1928).

Cameron v. H.M Advocate, (1971) SC 50.*Oppenheim's International law* (9th ed. 1992) 746.

Green, L.C., 'The Santa Maria: Rebels or Pirates', 37 *British Yearbook of International Law* 496 (1961).

Halberstam, 'Terrorism on the High Seas: The Achille Lauro, Piracy and the IMO Convention on Maritime Safety', 82 *AJIL* 269 (1988).

IMO Convention on the Suppression of Unlawful Acts Against the Safety of Maritime Navigation, 27 ILM 668 (1988). <http://untreaty.un.org/English/Terrorism/ Conv8.pdf>.

Mary Kaldor, *New and Old Wars*, (Polity, 1999).

H. Ormerod, *Piracy in the Ancient World*, (Liverpool University Press, 1924).

Richard Overy, *Interrogations*, (Penguin , 2001).

John Rawls, *The Law of Peoples* 1999.

Re Piracy Jure Gentium, (1934) AC 586.

Republic of Bolivia v. Indemnity Mutual Marine Assurance Co., (1909) 1 KB 785.

M. Reisman, 'In Defence of Public Order' 95(4) *American Journal of International Law*, (2001) at 833.

B. Roling, *The Tokyo Trial and Beyond*, Polity (1991).

C. Schmitt, *The Concept of the Political* (Chicago, 2004).

Georg Schwarzenberger, *International Law and Totalitarian Lawlessness* (Cape, 1943).

Gerry Simpson, *Rebellious Subjects: War, Law and Crime* (forthcoming Polity, 2006).

Gerry Simpson, *Great Powers and Outlaw States: Unequal Sovereigns in the International Legal Order*, (Cambridge, 2004).

United Nations Convention on the Law of the Sea, 1982, Articles 100–107, 21 *ILM* 1261.

Notes

[1] Rory McCarthy, *The Guardian*, June, 20, 2003 at 1.

[2] Julian Borger, 'Straw threat to bypass UN over attack on Iraq', *The Guardian*, 19 October 2002 at 1.

[3] E.g. J. Clayton, 'Warlords take piracy to new extremes', *The Times*, 14 October 2005; International Maritime Organisation, *Reports of Piracy and Armed Robbery against Ships*, MSC.4/Circ.75, (2005).

[4] "In dealing with states that are outright criminal, the United States may, at times, need to take unilateral action to protect its citizens, its interests, its integrity' John Kerry, *The New*

War: The Web of Crime that Threatens America's Security, New York, 1997 at 182 (in Cockburn, 'Surrendering Quietly', *NLR* 29 at 17).

5 Article 101, United Nations Convention on the Law of the Sea (1982); Article 15, Convention on the High Seas (1958).

6 'How strange it is to choose as our foundational baddie, a figure with so many romantic associations. Thucydides, again, talks about a period when piracy was a respectable source of livelihood for young Greeks: Old poets ask – "Are they pirates?" as if those who are asked the question would have no idea of disclaiming the imputation' (1.5, *Landmark Thucididyes*).

7 Individuals, too, underwent these transformations: Sextus Pompeius, a Roman legend, begins as a brigand in Spain, then is cast as a pirate before being appointed commander of the Roman naval forces, a position he uses to engage in more acts of plunder until the challenge from another Roman force obliges him to return again to piracy.

Chapter 11

Ethical Challenges in the Conservation of Cultural Material

David Watkinson

Preserving historical and cultural objects provides ethical challenges to conservators responsible for their continued existence. Decisions on preservation strategies involve the ethics of preservation techniques and materials; past and present cultural contexts of objects; financial and ownership considerations; as well as the needs of stakeholders. Conservation is a fusion of science, art, culture and logistics underpinned by situation ethics. This chapter explores factors influencing these ethics.

Introduction

All materials interact with their environment and decay. Conservation prevents or minimises change and is carried out by conservators. The preservation of favored or culturally significant objects is not a new concept. The Romans repaired Samian pottery with metal rivets and ancient mosaics were preserved by a state funded workshop in early 19th century France.[1] Today preserving cultural material is an integral feature of state and society in Western Europe.

> The fundamental role of the conservation professional is to preserve and restore, as appropriate, cultural property for present and future generations.[2]

Conservation involves the use of both science and art in the preservation of cultural material. Ethics in conservation range from discussions about whether an object should be conserved, through the choice of conservation materials, to the nature of the end goal. Besides their impact on objects, ethical decisions impinge on stakeholders ranging from owners and clients, through specialists, to groups with cultural investment or interest in an object. The differing ethical standpoints of stakeholders and the conservator's strong sense of unity with objects often make consensus agreement on ethical routes to conservation challenging.[3]

The conservator's role includes canvassing, co-coordinating and synthesizing the views of stakeholders and specialists into an integrated ethical framework, which is capable of underpinning the conservation procedure. A range of ethical and practical guidelines published by national conservation bodies exist to aid and guide them in this process.[4,5,6,7] These inform the conservator on matters such as standards, ownership, conservation materials, finance and history.

Conservation as a Profession

Professions produce codes of ethics and conduct to both regulate the actions of their members and to act as a platform for any disciplinary action.[8] As conservation is still an emerging profession in most countries, ethical frameworks also act to announce its arrival as a profession.[9] This progression is evident in the United Kingdom where several conservation bodies collaborated to introduce professional accreditation in 1998. Recently, the merger of several conservation bodies into The Institute of Conservation offered a move towards a central regulatory governing body for all conservation disciplines in the United Kingdom.

Similarity between ethical guidelines at an international level creates a degree of ethical uniformity within conservation, but not without subtle differences that reflect national characteristics. In contrast to other guidelines those produced by the American Institute for Conservation emphasize ethical procedures that guard against the more litigious environment that exists between the professional and client in the US.[10] Although national conservation bodies provide ethical guidelines, they do not either require or provide compulsory training in ethics. This is left to vocational conservation training courses in higher education.[11]

The Nature of Ethics in Conservation

Despite a high degree of uniformity between ethical codes within conservation, the extent to which they can dictate conservation processes is limited to core principles rather than detail. The diversity and complexity of cultural objects and their contexts requires a flexible use of ethics. While there is great similarity within material aspects of conservation, each cultural object, its context and stakeholder profile is unique. By necessity this places 'situation ethics' at the core of ethical decisions in conservation.[12]

Often several conservation options are feasible for any one object and each may broadly fit prevailing ethical codes. In contrast the nature of some objects dictates conservation options that only have a limited fit with standard conservation ethics. Survival of an object may mean that some basic conservation principles have to be compromised. In these instances adherence to an inflexible ethical approach would deny the object the treatment it requires to survive. Thus the importance of future reversibility of materials used to hold a fragile object together and the colour changes they produce may be downgraded as ethical imperatives when striving to save in-situ archaeological material, which is in an immediate state of collapse at some remote part of the globe. In this situation the materials available and the skill of the conservator will largely dictate ethical direction. All conservators must be prepared to use ethics flexibly within the complex equation involving material and cultural issues, which is used to design conservation practice. By entitling their paper, 'It was the least unethical thing we could do',[13] highlights the need for ethical compromises in conservation.

Physically intervening with objects in course of their preservation was a standard approach in conservation until the 1970s, which was when the concept of minimum intervention evolved. Early interventive conservation was often geared towards the aesthetics of the end result using either flawed ethics or lack of rigorous ethical justification. Routine use of intervention is now recognized as being unacceptable without first '...assessing and establishing the necessity and suitability for such intervention.'[14] This development of conservation practice and its ethical framework can be linked to a range of factors. These include the growth of a more ordered and professional conservation structure, increased science within conservation practice, greater understanding of material/environment interactions, empirical historical progression and, to some extent, fashion.

Situation ethics allow the adoption of pragmatic approaches to the conservation of objects within their various contexts. A central feature of conservation ethics must be inclusion and the conservator should take into account not only the needs of the object, but the views of stakeholders, whose agenda for an object may be quite different to that of the conservator. Integrating these with the context of an object leads to the design of conservation options, which are then ranked according to their effectiveness and broader ethical validity. While it is ethically important to canvass the views of the public and other associated parties, it is essential to recognize the degree to which these views are informed and weight them accordingly within the equation used to formulate conservation options. When conserving a mosaic pavement in-situ Nardi[15] used the views of the visiting public to his advantage, by making them a tool in support of the conservation programme that he proposed to his funding body.

By definition, if an object requires conservation it must be altered from its original form. Decay may have transformed its composition and appearance to make it dirty, weak and fragmentary. Additionally it may either have been deliberately modified during its lifetime or bear evidence of its working life. These factors constitute object history and to change them requires ethical justification. While it seems obvious that decay should be arrested and physical integrity restored, it is less clear whether either purpose made alterations or natural wear should be retained. Broader issues can enter the equation, as even arresting decay may be unethical in relation to the beliefs of some of those with a vested interest in the object.

Justifying Conservation

Reference has been made to revealing and preserving the 'true nature' of an object a conservation goal.[16] This terminology has now disappeared from current United Kingdom Institute for Conservation (2004) guidelines, as it is recognized that it is often unclear what constitutes the true nature of an object. Before implementing conservation it is necessary to decide first whether, and then why, an object is of sufficient cultural significance to merit preservation.

'Among all known cultures…individuals consider some object or artifact as being valuable.'[17] What makes a particular object more valuable to one society than another? In the case of a culturally significant, aesthetically pleasing and valuable object like an old master painting, whose imagery excites and extends the mind, ethical justification for its conservation is easily rationalized. In contrast justifying conservation of a badly damaged pen that belonged to a famous author cannot rely upon ethics related to aesthetic appearance. However, '… external objects can be a repository of feelings, beliefs and imaginings that stem from Western religious tradition and from its combination with the generic and personal inheritance explored by Freud and Klein.'[18] The concept of sentimental attachment creating emotive feelings can impart importance on the most mundane objects and, in some instances impart great financial value upon them. So a Fender Stratocaster guitar formerly belonging to Jimi Hendrix was sold in 1993 for $1,300,000. Does this alter the ethics of conserving such an item?

Prevailing views within society can justify the retention of everyday items to document and record obsolete industries, via the tools and buildings they involved. All these items were originally intended to have a finite life followed by recycling or destruction. It may be argued that the educational ethic attached to such collections far exceeds that of a pen belonging to a famous individual and therefore outstrips it in importance. Dealing with a mixture of tangible records and intangible emotive connections makes the ethical argument for prioritizing conservation resources a challenge. In cultural terms conservation encompasses the preservation of everything from fine art to ordinary utilitarian objects, but resources to facilitate conservation are finite. Where ownership and market forces are involved, ethical justification alone will rarely be found to be sufficient reason to attract funding to preserve an object.

Too Many Cultural Objects For Too Few Resources?

Is it rational and ethical to argue that purposely reducing the number of objects collected and retained is beneficial? Such action will reduce the strain on the resources allocated for their preservation and allow for better care of the objects retained. Many museums used to collect indiscriminately and are full of accessioned objects that are now in poor condition. Ethical arguments abound concerning de-accessioning objects to lower the storage and conservation burdens. What criteria would be required to de-accession material?

In view of the scarcity of resources is de-accessioning a simple case of financial logistics? Thomson[19] argues for more clearly defining what material is worth collecting and preserving, as well as a reduction in the current number of museums and collections.[20]

Discarding material after first recording it is an option adopted for some classes of material in archaeological conservation. The cost of treating waterlogged archaeological wood is prohibitively expensive, except for the most prestigious objects, yet cheap successful long-term storage for untreated material is difficult to achieve.[21] Limited availability of conservation resources means that most wet wood is recorded then discarded. It is accepted as a normal procedure and is seen as ethical in the prevailing circumstances. In contrast hundreds of thousands of archaeological iron nails are stored in museums in the United Kingdom where most corrode away due to poor storage environments. It must be asked whether they are retained because they are small and easily packed, thereby avoiding difficult ethical decisions on disposal, rather than because they are deemed to be more important than archaeological wood. The dilemma of what and how to collect is currently under review and options such as temporary collection, followed by de-accessioning after reassessment of cultural value, may be one of many options available to define and control collecting.[22]

The Influence of Ownership and 'Cultural' Ownership on Conservation

Different stakeholders in an object may have diverging views as to what its conservation should involve or, even, whether the object should be conserved at all. Should a particular range of religious or cultural beliefs, coupled to object ownership, override the preservation of that object as a piece of art or history? The cultural requirements of individuals and groups associated with the original context of an object are often taken into consideration as part of conservation planning. This is especially true where objects are of religious or ancestral significance. The influence of these views is often more marked where there is a clash of cultures, especially where this is linked to long-term cultural repression.

An awareness of object context is generally reflected in current publication. It would now be poor ethical practice to publish an article on the conservation of a Papuan shrunken head,[23] without a discussion about whether the conservation methods used breached its original cultural context. It is also possible that particular materials used in a conservation process are not acceptable to the beliefs of cultural stakeholders, which may compromise the preservation process.

Beliefs can make conservation ethics more complex. It is considered inappropriate that Jewish Sefer Torah scrolls are repaired by gentiles, even when there are no trained Jewish restorers.[24] The problem is made more complex when a scroll is in the ownership of a museum and is considered unfit for use. In this instance according to Jewish law it should be buried. Should these laws be observed or is there a duty to society as a whole to preserve these objects? Ethical arguments to support both points of view abound, but in a material society such as the West pressure will be for preservation. This may be influenced by the level and nature of the publicity surrounding such a decision and may swing the 'ethical' pendulum in the opposite direction.

Scientists are often at odds with indigenous groups concerning investigation, conservation and repatriation of human remains, especially in North America and the Pacific.[25] Repatriation of some sacred objects and biological materials from human burial contexts is allowed for in legislation for Native American Indians in the US.[26] Aboriginal objects on loan from Britain to Australia have recently been impounded, creating problems for possible future loans.[27]

This range of clash points highlights how cultural groups may define conservation in a completely different way to museum curators. The way forward is by communication between interested groups and exploration of their various ethical standpoints. Due to their close contact with objects, conservators are ideally placed to actively develop links between such groups.

What of owner responsibility? Unlike listed buildings, there is no legislation to stop an owner doing what they want to a cultural object. Although many owners are sympathetic to the needs of an object and seek conservation advice from professionals, should they be subject to the same ethical codes that guide conservators? Already conservation ethics bind conservators not to carry out inappropriate actions requested by owners.[28] A conservator should not in-fill areas of loss in ceramic vessels as being undetectable at the request of the owner, as this offers opportunity for deceit and possible fraud.[29] This type of action involves conservators with broader ethical issues within society.

The Role of Science in Conservation Ethics

Science has an important role in all aspects of conservation ethics. It is used to elucidate information about an object, which will contribute to investigative, historical and preservation debates. In many instances science can offer the evidence to support a particular course of action with an object. The International Council of Museums recognizes science as an integral part of ethical conservation. They cite that '…all interventions must be preceded by a methodical and scientific examination aimed at understanding the object in all its aspects, and the consequences of each manipulation…' and later, '…this approach enhances our ability to decipher the object's scientific message and thereby contribute knowledge…'.[30]

Science is used to investigate the performance of materials used to adhere, consolidate and coat objects during conservation. Understanding the properties and performance of materials now and in the future is an essential part of conservation ethics, since future reversibility of materials applied to objects is a central conservation ethic.[31,32,33] Yet science often falls short of absolute answers. Testing the lifespan of polymers to be used in conservation by accelerated ageing can provide misleading results.[34] Even a real-time 10-year test programme may only provide partially useful results and at a very high financial cost.[35] Further, even when highly reversible polymeric materials are identified, their future removal from an object may be impossible due to the damage this would inflict on the object.[36]

It is tempting to think that by using proven scientific methods conservators avoid subjective judgements but '...the science of restoration is neither immutable nor infallible. Techniques become discredited and human beings are incapable of acting with absolute objectivity...'.[37] Scientific investigation is not able to provide an indisputable ethical framework for conservation practice. Possibly one of the most high profile examples of this is the conservation of the ceiling of the Sistine chapel. Although the painted ceiling was subjected to extensive scientific research before conservation, including cross sectioning thousands of paint samples to determine the juxtaposition of the paint layers and varnishes, disputes continue as to whether the conservation restored the painting to a former glory or damaged its appearance, history and integrity. These arguments utilize historical record, conservation techniques, analysis and contemporary comment to press their point.

Art-History enters conservation ethics, often alongside science. In relation to the Sistine Chapel ceiling, Daly[38] cites descriptions of Michelangelo's work and his character recorded by one of his contemporaries, as well as the loss of added detail and shadow from the paintings, as reasons to doubt the result of the cleaning process. In contrast Kirkby-Tally Jr[39] cites contemporary and historical records to support the conservation techniques carried out and considers that cleaning rediscovered Michelangelo as a colourist. He also cites the removal of extensive poor quality repairs and additions, as well as a flaking glue coating as good reasons for the conservation action. Interestingly, debate involving subjective comment on appearance in relation about what to remove from objects is not new. Similar disagreements about the ethical validity were recorded in 19th century Holland for the *Wedding of Pelus and Thetis* painted in 1593.[40]

The Ethics of Minimum Intervention

In recent years conservation science has concentrated on discovering more about the properties, ageing and decay of materials forming cultural objects. Focus on understanding interaction with the environment allows for its control to minimize object decay, which leads to the concept of minimum intervention. This is defined as, 'all actions taken to retard deterioration of, or to prevent damage to, cultural property through the provision of optimum conditions of storage, exhibition, use, handling and transport.'[41] This preventive conservation has found strong ethical acceptance within conservation. Intervention is normally a slow expensive procedure carried out on a single object, but preventive conservation offers cost-effective opportunities for the long-term preservation of many objects. Naturally, such a cost-effective and statistic-friendly methodology is seen as ethical in political terms.

Archaeological Conservation – A Special Case for Ethics?

Archaeological conservation illustrates the malleability of conservation ethics. Its goal is to reveal evidence about technology and life history, hidden either in decay and corrosion or within the object material itself (United Kingdom Institute for Conservation Archaeology Section 2001). Although non-destructive approaches such as x-radiography are employed wherever possible, revealing evidence normally involves irretrievably removing existing information in order to expose new. This is ethically acceptable under the Code of Ethics statement that '…each member must strive to preserve cultural property for the benefit of future generations but he/she must make every effort to maintain a balance between preservation of cultural property and the need to appreciate it and understand it.'[42] Interventions of an aesthetic nature, which do not reveal further information, are ethically unacceptable, as in the case of reshaping a prehistoric gold object for cosmetic effect.[43]

Restoration

Although there have always been voices raised against restoration[44], at one time repair and restoration of objects to mimic their original state was common within conservation. The term restorer has only slowly been supplanted by that of conservator to describe those involved with the preservation of cultural material. Today the circumstances in which restoration could be considered an option are carefully documented and linked to the concept of 'aesthetic reintegration'.[45] Restoration should '…reveal the aesthetic and historical value of a cultural property. Restoration is based on respect for the remaining original material and clear evidence of the earlier state…'.[46]

Ethical Dilemmas?

Restoration may be considered more ethically acceptable with certain classes of object, where new parts were routinely manufactured to replace originals worn out during a working lifetime. Whether previously working objects that are now of cultural significance should continue to work (and wear) is open to debate. Mann[47] considers that in technical museums, working exhibits are providing functional evidence as well as material evidence, but that this damages the material evidence and is … 'exploitation of the artifact for the public benefit'. As objects are for the benefit of society and thus the public, is this exploitation? Is it the artifact or the process that should be preserved? Is an object expendable, when it is subordinate to a process? Answers to these questions influence the construct of the ethical argument regarding how they are treated as museum objects.

The World War II 'Memphis Belle' B17 flying fortress survives today. What should the conservation approach be to an object like this? The 'Belle' flew 25 daylight bombing missions over Europe and had several sets of engines, new wings and virtually every other part replaced during its working life. If it is possible, should it be kept in flying condition? Should corroded parts be replaced with new? Should conservation identify how its construction materials are decaying and develop strategies for conserving them without replacement? Is the attraction of the plane its association with events, rather than as a piece of equipment? These questions reveal the complexities of the ethical debate. The 'Belle' is currently undergoing conservation with a clearly defined policy for each section of the aircraft, which involves retention of as much original material as possible, replacement of damaged parts with salvaged originals and correction or replacement of corroded areas.[48] A pragmatic approach has produced a blend of ethical solutions that have been formed into a policy that sees both cosmetic appearance and structural integrity as important parts of the conservation programme.

Ethical issues abound when considering the jacket Nelson was wearing when he was shot at Trafalgar in 1805, Jaeskche[49] asks where does the history of an object end? Without doubt the jacket is an important cultural object in terms of national psyche and emotional association. At some stage of its life it was 'improved' using red paint because the blood stain was fading. Is the paint now part of the history of the object? How far should the conservator strip back history, if at all, when preserving the jacket? Should Nelson's jacket be preserved exactly as it is, as the paint has now become part of its history? Alternatively is some restoration necessary?

Funding Conservation

While all conservation codes of ethics imply that money should not influence the conservation process, it would be naïve to think that the financial worth of an object has no influence on whether and how an object is conserved. Cultural objects as assets worth many millions of pounds are likely to receive priority conservation over those worth a few hundred pounds. Owners, whether private, public or corporate will demand this and the use of art as financial investment will promote it. Measuring the cultural worth of financially valuable cultural objects against that of worthless, but culturally significant collections will always challenge ethical principles. Is a painting produced by a prolific painter, which is worth millions of pounds, more deserving of conservation than an extensive and unique collection of obsolete tools that illustrate the technology of mining and reveal much about the lives and work of our ancestors? Such direct financial choices may occur in museums with mixed collections. Well funded conservation of a valuable item does not guarantee a better ethical outcome, as the owner may place more emphasis on the appearance of an object than its integrity.

Justifying cultural worth is increasingly an important part of grant applications for conservation programmes. Proving the international cultural significance of Brunel's steamship *ss Great Britain* and her dry dock, as well as their viability as a cultural attraction, was an essential part of a successful application for a Heritage Lottery Fund conservation grant.[50] Business and ethics often sit close together and finance may intervene, to the extent that what is ethically preferred is financially impossible. In these circumstances conservation has to offer alternative solutions that have ethical validity; as Barov and Faber[51] did when preserving an ancient tomb.

Ethics and the Law

As expected, if conservators have reason to believe they are working on stolen property or material that has been exported or imported illegally, they are required to report it to the appropriate authorities[52,53,54] This clear observance of law is more ethically challenging in circumstances where sales and auctions offer dubious provenance for antiquities. Greater ownership dilemmas occur when national, ethnographic and cultural arguments are cited. The longstanding dialogue about ownership of the Parthenon Marbles held in the British Museum illustrates this, but fortunately all parties recognize that the marbles should be cared for and conserved to the best possible standard wherever they are.

Ethics and Professional Exploitation

Responsibility for the survival of cultural objects enters conservation ethics. Some conservators believe that the commitment to preserve objects should be compared to the doctor-patient relationship, despite the difference between inanimate objects and sentient beings. While this belief may increase the conservator's degree of engagement with the object, it may also have more worldly undertones. If conservators feel they are the primary custodians of object welfare, it may open them to pressure to produce preservation outcomes for low financial return. The pretext for this being that without their input the object would disappear. The ethical commitment of conservators should not be used for manipulative exploitation. There is a broader context of responsibility to be considered. Many individuals have an interest in cultural objects, whether it is via ownership or as a member of the society that gains cultural benefit from the objects within its care. Each has an ethical responsibility to their culture and its survival; the conservator is merely the individual that interfaces with the object in course of its preservation.

Summary

Parts of this chapter offer more questions than answers about conservation ethics. There will continue to be differing ethical approaches within conservation and few conservators can state that their defined route is the only feasible option. As science, society and fashion change, so what was reasoned to be ethical yesterday may not be tomorrow. The growth of ethical codes within conservation will stimulate debate, but the diversity and uniqueness of cultural objects will always require the conservator to be flexible in thought and action. Professional conservation must guard against the development of ethical guidelines that are so detailed that they constrain freedom to develop ethical frameworks that meet the needs of the wide variety of cultural material facing conservators.

References

[1] Lavagne, H. (1977), 'The Conservation of Pavement mosaics before modern times: A selection from the mosaics of Gaul.' *Mosaics Number 1. Deterioration and Conservation* ICCROM Rome, pp. 15–19.

[2] Canadian Association for the Conservation of Cultural Property (2000), *Code of ethics and Guidance for Practice.* 3rd edition. <http://www.cac-accr.ca > (13th January 2006).

[3] Drysdale L., 1988, The eternal triangle: Relationships between conservators and their objects. *Conservation Today. UKIC Anniversary Conference.* V. Todd (ed). UKIC, pp. 19–20.

[4] United Kingdom Institute for Conservation (2004), *Code of Ethics and Rules of Practice.* <http://www.ukic.org.uk/ukic_ethics.doc> (11th January 2006).

[5] International Council of Museums Committee for Conservation. (1984), *The Conservator Restorer: A Definition of the Profession.* <http://icom-c.icom.museum/index.php?page_id=28>

[6] American Institute for Conservation of Historic and Artistic Works (1994) *Code of ethics and guidelines for practice.* <http://www.aic.stanford.edu/pubs/ethics.html> (13th January 2006).

[7] Canadian Association for the Conservation of Cultural Property, (2000), *Code of ethics and Guidance for Practice.*

[8] Pritchard, J. (1997), 'Codes of Ethics'. *Encyclopedia of Applied Ethics*, Academic Press, London, pp. 527–533.

[9] Ashley-Smith, J. (1982), 'The ethics of conservation.' *The Conservator*, vol.6, pp. 1–5.

[10] American Institute for Conservation of Historic and Artistic Works, *Code of ethics and guidelines for practice.*

[11] Pearson, C. and Ferguson, R. (1993), 'Code of Practice for Conservation Education and Training.' in J. Bridgland (ed.). *International Council of Museums Committee for Conservation 10th Triennial Washington.* James and James, pp. 731–37.

[12] Ashley-Smith, J., 'The ethics of conservation.'

[13] Nether, A. (1993), 'It was the least unethical thing we could do' V*ictoria and Albert Museum Conservation Journal* no. 7, April 1993, pp. 18–19.

[14] United Kingdom Institute for Conservation, *Code of Ethics and Rules of Practice.*

[15] Nardi, R. (1996), 'Zippori Israel: the conservation of the mosaics of the building of the Nile.' *Archaeological Conservation and its Consequences*, A. Roy and P. Smith (eds.) Preprints of the contributions to the Copenhagen Congress, 26–30 August 1996, IIC London, pp. 127–32.

[16] Child, R. (1988), 'Ethics in the conservation of social history objects'. *Conservation Today. UKIC Anniversary Conference.* V. Todd (ed.) UKIC, pp. 8–9.

[17] Daifuku, H. (1967), 'The significance of Cultural Property.' *The Conservation of Cultural Property.* UNESCO Switzerland, pp. 19–26.

[18] Drysdale L., 'The eternal triangle: Relationships between conservators and their objects.'

[19] Thomson, K. (2002), *Treasures on Earth*, Faber, London.

[20] Morison, J. (2002), 'Museums full of modern junk, says top curator'. *The Independent on Sunday* 16th January 2002.

[21] Fry, M. (1996), 'Buried but not forgotten: sensitivity in disposing of major archaeological timbers' in *Archaeological Conservation and its Consequences.* A. Roy and P. Smith (eds.) International Institute for Conservation, pp. 52–4.

22   Museums Association – Collections Inquiry 2004, Interim report of the group on collecting.
     <www.museumassociation.org.asset_arena/text/up/policy_collections_workgroup.doc>
23   Van-Dyke Lee D. (1974), 'The Conservation of a preserved human head.' *Studies in Conservation*, vol. 19, pp. 222–226.
24   Thomson, J. C. (1998), 'On Restoring Sacred Objects.' *Leather Conservation News* vol.14, no. 2.
25   Peers, L. (2004), 'Relative values.' *Museums Journal* September 2004, pp. 18–19.
26   Welsh, E. C. (1991), 'A new era in museum-Native American relations.' *Western Association for Art Conservation Newsletter* vol. 13, no. 1, p. 9.
27   Morris, J. (2004), 'The root of the problem.' *Museums Journal* September 2004, pp. 10–11.
28   American Institute for Conservation of Historic and Artistic Works, *Code of ethics and guidelines for practice.*
29   Hodges, H.W.M. (1975), 'Problems and ethics of the restoration of pottery.' *Conservation in Archaeology and the Applied Arts. IIC Stockholm Congress.* N. Bromelle and P. Smith (eds.) International Institute for Conservation, pp. 37–39.
30   International Council of Museums Committee for Conservation, The Conservator Restorer: A Definition of the Profession.
31   United Kingdom Institute for Conservation, *Code of Ethics and Rules of Practice.*
32   American Institute for Conservation of Historic and Artistic Works, *Code of ethics and guidelines for practice.*
33   Canadian Association for the Conservation of Cultural Property, *Code of ethics and Guidance for Practice.*
34   Down, J. (1984), 'Adhesive testing at the CCI, past and future' in *Adhesives and Consolidants* N. Bromelle, E. Pye, P. Smith and G. Thomson (eds.) International Institute for Conservation Paris Congress 2–8 September 1984. IIC, pp. 18–21.
35   Down, J. L., Macdonald, M. Tetreault, J. and Williams, S. (1996), 'Adhesive testing at the Canadian Conservation Institute – an evaluation of selected poly(vinyl acetate) and acrylic adhesives.' *Studies in Conservation* vol. 41, pp. 19–44.
36   Horie, C.V. (1983), 'Reversibility of Polymer Treatments' in *Proceedings of the conference on resins held in Edinburgh 21–22nd May 1982.* J. O. Tate, N. Tennent and J. Townsend (eds.), Scottish Society for Conservation and Restoration. Edinburgh, pp. 31–36.
37   Daly, M (1993), 'A restoration tragedy' *Times Higher Education Supplement.* June 4th 1993, p. 17.
38   Daly, M. (1990), 'Michelangelo: Lost or found?' *The Independent on Sunday* 25th March 1990, p. 8.
39   Kirkby-Tally Jr. M. (1987), 'Michelangelo rediscovered.' *Art News,* Summer 1987, pp. 159–170.
40   Levy-Van-Halm, K. and Hendriks, E. (1993), 'A case history of restoration, ideas and working methods in 19th century Holland' in *International Council of Museums Committee for Conservation 10th Triennial Washington.* J. Bridgland (ed.) James and James, pp. 377–80.
41   United Kingdom Institute for Conservation, *Code of Ethics and Rules of Practice.*
42   Ibid.
43   Corfield, M. 1988, The reshaping of archaeological metal objects: some ethical considerations. *Antiquity* vol. 62, pp. 261–65.
44   Corfield, M. 1988, Towards a conservation profession in *Conservation Today. UKIC Anniversary Conference.* V. Todd (ed.) UKIC, pp. 4–7.

[45] American Institute for Conservation of Historic and Artistic Works, *Code of ethics and guidelines for practice*.

[46] Canadian Association for the Conservation of Cultural Property, *Code of ethics and Guidance for Practice*.

[47] Mann, R. P. 1989, Working exhibits and the destruction of evidence in the Science Museum. *The International Journal of Museums Management and Curation* vol. 8, pp. 369–387.

[48] Loy J. (2004) Memphis Belle Restoration Plan. <http://www.memphisbelle.com/module.php?op=modload&name=news&file=index> (13th January 2006).

[49] Jaeschke, R. 1996, When does History end ? in *Archaeological Conservation and its Consequences.* A. Roy and P. Smith (eds.), International Institute for Conservation, pp. 86–88.

[50] Cox, J. and Tanner, M. 1999, *Conservation Plan for the Great Western Steamship Company Dockyard and the ss Great Britain.* ss Great Britain Trust internal report.

[51] Barov, Z. and Faber, C. 1996, Affordable versus optimal conservation: considerations in preserving an ancient tomb. in *Archaeological Conservation and its Consequences.* A. Roy and P. Smith (eds.) IIC, pp. 1–15.

[52] United Kingdom Institute for Conservation, *Code of Ethics and Rules of Practice*.

[53] American Institute for Conservation of Historic and Artistic Works, *Code of ethics and guidelines for practice*.

[54] Canadian Association for the Conservation of Cultural Property, *Code of ethics and Guidance for Practice*.

Chapter 12

Farming and Food Research: Participation and the Public Good

Tom MacMillan and Shaila Seshia

Each year, over £100 million of public money is spent on agricultural and food research in the UK. The British public have a double stake in this science, both financing it and feeling its consequences. Publicly sponsored research shapes the choices that are available to farmers, to food workers and to consumers, and the environments in which they live. Should citizens participate more directly in this research and, if so, how?

This article sketches some of the issues of principle and practice that policy makers face in answering this question.

Context

A little over a third of all research and development in the UK is state financed. The size of the public slice varies from sector to sector. Private research in food processing dwarfs publicly funded studies of nutrition, food safety and the sociology of food. By contrast, in agricultural research, the public sector has traditionally been a major player.

The government spends money on farming and food research in two main ways. On the one hand, government departments buy research to help them meet their policy objectives for food and agriculture. The big spenders are the Department for the Environment, Food and Rural Affairs (DEFRA), which procures about £40 million of farming and food research per year, the Food Standards Agency (FSA), which procures over £20 million, and the Department for International Development, which spends a further £40 million on rural livelihoods research.[1]

On the other hand, the government also funds research that is less immediately relevant to policy. The bulk of funding is granted to universities and to research institutes by the research councils, which fall under the Department of Trade and Industry's (DTI) Office of Science and Technology. The Biotechnology and Biological Sciences Research Council (BBSRC) spends over £40 million on farming and food research.[2] The Natural Environment Research Council (NERC) and the Economic and Social Research Council (ESRC) also fund research in this area. Jointly, the BBSRC, NERC and the ESRC are spending £20 million over three years on a new Rural Economy and Land Use (RELU) programme.[3]

In addition to financing research directly, the government influences privately funded science by shaping the market for research on food and agriculture. For example, health and environmental regulation can stimulate innovation, as well as restricting potentially harmful technologies. Government also creates incentives for research, both directly, through tax breaks and fast-track technology approval schemes, and indirectly, by enforcing property and reward systems relating to science, such as patenting.

In practice there is overlap between procurement, funding and other aspects of research governance. For instance, a department may procure science from a research council. The LINK programmes, which encourage industry and academic research collaboration, are jointly funded by the research councils and government departments; DEFRA spends 18 per cent of its farming and food research budget on LINK.[4] Patenting affects publicly funded research, as well as commercial science, and it can be a cost or a source of revenue for government departments.

Because of this complexity, terms that are often used to describe research, such as 'basic', 'enabling' 'strategic' and 'applied', do not always correlate with reality. In general, though, the government only sponsors research that is some way from commercialisation and that does not compete with industrial activity.

It goes without saying, of course, that publicly sponsored research is also meant to be in the public interest. However, definitions of 'the public interest' or 'the public good', and the scope that is seen for public participation in achieving them, vary considerably amongst the institutions responsible for farming and food research.

Participation in Science Policy

The past decade has witnessed a succession of science-related crises. Several of these, including BSE, Foot and Mouth Disease and the controversy over GM crops, have concerned food and agriculture. They have stimulated unprecedented levels of public concern and media coverage, with high political and economic stakes riding on their resolution.

Until the late 1990s, it was widely thought that scientific illiteracy was responsible for public mistrust. In March 2000, a report by the House of Lords Select Committee on Science and Technology (CST) found that the crisis of public confidence was not in science as such, but in the governance of science and technology.[5] The report argued that this crisis became manifest when there was conflicting scientific evidence and where debate was couched only in terms of risk, sidelining ethical, social and economic concerns. The crisis related to an erosion of public trust in the institutions handling science and technology, particularly when they downplayed public concerns as irrational or glossed over apparent uncertainties.

Since then, the government has trumpeted the demise of the old 'deficit model' of public mistrust, and placed increasing emphasis on transparency and public engagement in policies related to science. One of the most striking examples of this new approach is the 2003 *GM Nation?* debate, which centred on a programme of public events involving 36,000 people. The government has also sought to shore up the evidence base for policy, issuing new *Guidelines* on the use of science and a *Code of practice for scientific advisory committees*.

For the most part, however, public participation initiatives have focused on the use of science in policy and on technology assessment. Relatively few resources have been devoted to engaging the public in research and science policy *upstream*. Yet, at least in principle, the earlier that stakeholders and citizens become involved in science, the more likely it is that the outcomes will address their perceived needs and respect their values.

Making Participation Work

Certain areas of farming and food research, such as plant breeding, have established traditions of stakeholder engagement. Equally, in policy on food and farming, some stakeholder interests have long been well represented. The challenge for policy makers and scientists is thus not simply to increase participation, but to ensure that members of the public are involved more thoroughly and more even-handedly than in the past.

Formal processes of participation are designed to address this challenge. There are only a few examples of their use in UK farming and food research policy.[6] For instance, in 1994, the BBSRC convened a consensus conference on plant biotechnology. More recently, it has consulted stakeholders on priorities for crop science research.

In other areas of government, such processes have been used for over twenty years. There have also been a number of independent initiatives that have sought to engage citizens in policies about food and agriculture. These include the *Weekends away for a bigger voice* and the *GM Jury*.[7] From this wider experience, it is possible to identify at least six general conditions for effective participation.

Purpose	The purpose of involving members of the public should be clear to the organisers and to the participants.
Participation	The participants should be selected fairly and in a way that is appropriate to the purpose. They may be selected using statistical sampling techniques, but this is not always necessary. In some cases it will be suitable for people to take part as individual citizens and, in others, as stakeholder representatives.
Methods	An appropriate method of participation should be used. There is a wide range of methods for public policy participation, ranging from quantitative surveys to deliberative and inclusive processes such as citizens' juries. Sometimes more than one method may be appropriate.[8]
Resources	The organisers should have the money and skills that their chosen method demands. Depending on the method, costs may include

	travel and bursaries for participants. Under-resourcing can jeopardise success and alienate participants.
Outcomes	The intended outcomes should be clear to the participants and to observers. According to the government, public participation 'is waste of everyone's time unless the decision-maker is willing to listen to others' views and then do something which it would not have done otherwise'.[9]
Learning	The CST argues that there is a need to 'go beyond event-based initiatives like consensus conferences and citizens' juries' and calls for 'genuine changes in the cultures and constitutions of key decision-making institutions'.[10] Feedback processes to help institutions learn from their own and others' experiences are one means of encouraging this culture change.

Whilst processes that satisfy these conditions can boost the effectiveness and the legitimacy of policy, they are not sufficient to ensure that decisions are made accountably. Public participation can be used as 'deliberative fix' to avoid making decisions, suppress disagreement or displace responsibility.[11]

Andy Stirling argues that whether a process 'opens up' or 'closes down' policy matters more than whether it centres on the public or on experts.[12] Processes that open policy up produce 'plural and conditional' advice, raising neglected issues and including marginalised perspectives, whereas processes that close it down produce 'unitary and prescriptive' recommendations. Far from being radical or impractical, 'open' processes leave the responsibility for policy decisions clearly with traditional decision makers.

The Public Good

The different methods of public participation are all designed to steer policy towards 'the public interest' or 'the public good'. However, they rest on different notions of this objective. Some assume that the public good is 'out there', to be discovered, whereas others see it as a product of deliberation. Some treat is as the sum total of private interests, whereas others see it as a collective achievement. Some focus on building consensus, whereas others are designed to capture the heterogeneous priorities and values of multiple 'publics'.

Since public engagement processes are just one means of orientating farming and food research towards the public good, in practice an even greater range of assumptions about the public and the public interest come into play in research policy, in procurement, funding and technology regulation. Sometimes these complement approaches to public engagement and sometimes they compromise them.

When government departments procure research, they are supposed to meet the public interest as it is represented in their institutional policy objectives. For instance, DEFRA's six objectives include promoting 'a sustainable, competitive and safe food supply chain which meets consumers' requirements', and promoting 'sustainable, diverse, modern and adaptable farming through domestic and international actions'. In principle, democratically elected politicians are responsible for setting these objectives. Translating them into a research strategy is the responsibility of civil servants. In practice, however, the process of setting objectives and translating them into policy is rather more complex as institutions, and individuals within institutions, are subject to multiple pressures and face different opportunities and constraints that shape the decisions and actions they take.

The notions of the public interest underpinning government research funding are set out in strategy documents and in research council literature. A prominent theme is that research should boost the international economic competitiveness of UK Plc, thereby creating wealth and enhancing the nation's quality of life. For instance, the government's science strategy, *Investing in innovation*, claims that 'innovation is at the heart of productivity and social gain' and that science contributes 'the raw material for innovation'.[13] The DTI exhorts universities to 'embrace a new entrepreneurial role, bringing forward the businesses of the future'.[14]

Because companies only invest in technologies that appear to stand a good chance of gaining market approval, the regulatory assessment of new technologies, such as pesticides or veterinary drugs, also shapes farming and food research. The focus of regulatory assessment is on risk management, usually to the explicit exclusion of political, economic and social considerations. This rests on the view that, so long as a technology is harmless, market forces more or less service public needs. Regulators are advised by scientists on questions of risk, which are treated as separate from questions of value. The latter are often allocated to specialist 'ethics' committees, which can have the effect of shielding regulatory science from public involvement and scrutiny.[15]

How the public good is defined and assessed depends not only on the field of policy, but also on its scale. As a rule of thumb, the smaller the 'public', the simpler it would seem to determine the public interest. Yet there is also a case for up-scaling farming and food research, most notably through the EU, to encourage international collaboration and to make the best use of public funds. In practice, the institutional resources for representing the public interest are heavily concentrated in national government.

Public and private

Over the past several decades, private investment in agricultural research, in particular, has increased relative to public spending. It used to be that agricultural research was unattractive to commercial investors, because it was difficult to profit from new seeds or animal breeds that reproduced themselves, which farmers only needed to buy once.[16] The growth of patenting in agricultural research since the 1970s, which has gone hand-in-hand with the emergence of modern biotechnology, has helped to change that.

Patents are a form of 'intellectual property' (IP) protection, temporarily converting into private property knowledge that would, by default, be a free public good. The logic of granting this monopoly is that it should benefit the public by creating a profit incentive for innovation and by removing the motives for commercial secrecy. Patenting protects technical invention as opposed, say, to artistic creativity. Patents grant greater protection than other forms of IP relevant to agricultural research, such as plant breeders' rights.

The growth of patenting has not only contributed to a shift in the ratio of private to public agricultural research, but it has also changed the character of publicly funded research. Publicly sponsored scientists spend an increasing proportion of their budget on buying patented technology and protecting the products of their own research in order to keep them freely available. However, patenting can also be a source of revenue for the public sector, an 'IP management' strategy that DEFRA has been encouraged to pursue by the Public Accounts Committee in its 2003 report on *Reaping the rewards of agriculture.*[17]

Policy makers and scientists are amongst those who are worried that privatisation is diverting farming and research away from the public interest. There are four main areas of concern:

Cost	The growing number of patents on 'basic' research tools may gridlock innovation downstream.[18] Even if patents are made freely available, it is time-consuming for researchers to gain permission to use them. These costs can have the effect of stymieing innovation rather than promoting it. They can also cut into the resources available for public participation.
Distribution	The privatisation of agricultural research threatens to marginalise the needs of poor farmers and other stakeholders who cannot pay for technology. Patenting compromises the capacity of public sector researchers to address market failure by producing freely available 'public goods'. This concern is particularly acute in plant breeding and has prompted an upsurge in interest in the potential of public-private partnerships for pro-poor agricultural research.[19]
Value	Patents turn knowledge into a commodity with *market* value, and the broader *social* value of agricultural research recedes into the background.[20] Public participation in agricultural research, for instance in farmer field schools, can add social, cultural and economic value.
Power	Large companies have played a prominent part in shaping rules on IP, nationally and internationally. Many observers are concerned that both the principles of IP and their implementation reflect the interest of these powerful international actors, rather than the interests of the public at large.

With the growth of public-private partnerships nationally and internationally, and the spread of IP regimes that shape the environment in which research occurs, the boundaries between public and private are increasingly blurred. This trend presents new challenges for realising and protecting the public good in a research environment which is increasingly shaped and dominated by the private sector.

Conclusion

There is now widespread agreement that greater public engagement would be an asset to science. Yet, government pronouncements about the benefits of public engagement in science have focused mainly on technology assessment and risk. They have remained largely separate from economic policies on research and innovation, which have been oriented towards increasing the UK's international competitiveness. Until these two spheres of science policy are integrated, and a broader and more democratic notion of the public good comes to underpin decisions across the board, the public benefits afforded by citizen participation in farming and food research will be severely constrained.

This paper draws on the report of a workshop called 'Agri-food research: participation and the public good', funded by the Allen Lane Foundation.

Notes

1. These are approximate figures, based on DTI's 'Forward look' estimates for 2002/3 <www.ost.gov.uk/research/forwardlook03/>. They are not the most recent that are available, but they have been used for ease of comparison.
2. See note 1.
3. Details of RELU are available from www.esrc.ac.uk/relu/default.htm.
4. Murphy-Bokern, D. (2004), *Defra sustainable farming and food research*. Presentation delivered to FARM, FEC and others on 18th February 2004.
5. House of Lords Select Committee on Science and Technology 2000. *Science and society: third report of session 1999–2000*. TSO, London.
6. One example of a non-governmental initiative that aimed to increase public participation in farming and food policy is: London Centre for Governance Innovation and Science and the Genetics Forum. (1999*) Citizen foresight – a tool to enhance democratic policy-making: the future of food and agriculture*. Available online at www.peals.ncl.ac.uk. Members of the same team have also organised the *Weekends away for a bigger voice* and a citizen's jury on GM crops (<www.gmjury.org>).
7. Former participants of both of these processes took part in the workshop. See note 6.
8. Parliamentary Office of Science and Technology (2001), *Open channels: public dialogue in science and technology* (Report No. 153). POST, London, March.
9. Quoted in: Parliamentary Office of Science and Technology (2002) *Public dialogue on science and technology* (Postnote 189). POST, London, November: 2.
10. House of Lords Select Committee on Science and Technology 2000. *Science and society: third report of session 1999–2000*. TSO, London.

[11] Parliamentary Office of Science and Technology (2002), *Public dialogue on science and technology* (Postnote 189). POST, London, November.

[12] Stirling, A. (2004), 'Opening up or closing down? Analysis, participation and power in the social appraisal of technology' in: M .Leach, I. Scoones, and B. Wynne, (eds.), *Science, citizenship and globalisation*. Zed, London: forthcoming.

[13] Department of Trade and Industry, Department for Education and Skills and HM Treasury (2002), *Investing in innovation: a strategy for science, engineering and technology.* Department of Trade and Industry, Department for Education and Skills, HM Treasury, London, July: 3.

[14] Department of Trade and Industry (2001), *Excellence and opportunity: a science and innovation policy for the 21st century.* HMSO, London, p. 57.

[15] Wynne, B. (2001), 'Creating public alienation: expert cultures of risk and ethics on GMOs.' *Science as Culture* vol. 10, pp. 445–481.

[16] Kloppenburg, J. (1988), *First the seed: the political economy of plant biotechnology, 1492–2000.* Cambridge University Press, Cambridge.

[17] House of Commons Committee on Public Accounts (2003), *Reaping the rewards of agricultural research: Eighteenth report of session 2002–03.* TSO, London.

[18] Heller, M. A. and Eisenberg, R. S. (1998), 'Can patents deter innovation? The anticommons in biomedical research' *Science* vol. 280, pp. 698–701.

[19] Conway, G. and Toenniessen, G. (2003), 'Science for African food security'. *Science* vol. 299, pp. 1187–1188; Knight, J. (2003), 'A dying breed.' *Nature* vol. 421 pp. 568–70.

[20] Slaughter, S. and Leslie, L. L. (1997), *Academic capitalism: politics, policies, and the entrepreneurial university.* John Hopkins University Press, Baltimore.

Chapter 13

Do Mention the War:
Children and Media Coverage of
Traumatic Events

Máire Messenger Davies

When the attacks on the World Trade Centre took place on September 11th, 2001, a group of 11–12 year old primary school children in Glasgow wrote to Channel 4's news programme for Schools, *First Edition*, (now no longer broadcasting), expressing their shock, fear, concern and desire for explanation.

An 11-year-old girl wrote:

> I feel there is a need to write to you about my ideas and feelings. First of all, this letter has been written because of the bombing in America. Please will you feature something about it in the next programme? I feel very strongly about it and just looking at the pictures of the event makes you want to cry.

This essay discusses a research project on children and news conducted by myself, by Dr. Cynthia Carter and Dr. Karin Wahl-Jorgensen of the Cardiff School of Journalism, Media and Cultural Studies (JOMEC), and by Dr. Stuart Allan of the University of the West of England. The study originated directly from the way in which children's broadcasters dealt with the events of September 11th 2001, its aftermath, the war in Afghanistan, the subsequent war in Iraq, and the ways in which children responded to these events. When the programme ceased production, the producers of Channel 4's *First Edition* agreed to let us see the material they had collected, including regular weekly letters from children to the programme (with their identity protected, and with the children's and schools' permission). Our research is located within a contemporary debate about social constructions of childhood and children's agency.[1] As media scholars, we argue that media play a significant part in determining how we see children's social role; media representations of children as either potentially active citizens or as helpless victims of events (including violent media events) are particularly common, as are representations of the 'monster' child, the tearaway, the bully and – mercifully rarely – the child-murderer. Such children are not always represented as being at risk themselves (athough they clearly are), but are seen primarily as a risk to others. The construction of childhood as revealed in children's own responses to September 11th, casts some doubt on these simplistic versions of childhood.

The children's letters from which we drew data in studying children's responses to news events, were usually written to *First Edition* producers every week, after they had viewed and discussed the week's programme in their class. However, the attack on the World Trade Center occurred before the first programme of that season's series; the first batch of children's letters after the event responded to the events only as they were being presented in the *adult* news media and in discussions with peers, parents and teachers. The letters questioned why the planes crashed into the World Trade Center and the Pentagon; they expressed concern about those who died and their families; how the US should respond; and fear that it might lead to another world war. Said one young boy, 'If George W. Bush makes one wrong move, it could spark World War Three.' They clearly indicated, not only a sensitivity to the events themselves, but an awareness of their political implications – something that the producers were surprised by.

The following week's letters wrote about the preceding week's *First Edition* programme, so responded to the actual content of the story on the attacks and its presentation – responses which began to reveal the impact of the news coverage on children's perceptions on their own community. One Muslim girl reported:

> It is my point of view that it could be someone else who attacked America not Bin Laden. If they just start bombing Afghanistan and Iraq they are killing so many innocent Muslims. Even though they do catch him there are still so many people at there that might have done it. It could make World War Three and there's going to be a lot of chaos. I come to a school that is full of different religions and that is full of girls and boys. We all get on together very well.

On the internet, a group of school children from Ireland wrote short notes to the list with the subject line 'Our thoughts are with you' on September 14th. One child named Tom posted this notice expressing his sympathies with the children of New York:

> Hi. We have been hearing all about the terrorism in New York and Manhattan. It has been all over T.V.. I really hope that none of your friends or family have been hurt. It's really terrible. I hope nothing ever happens again like this. We all understand how scared you must feel. We also are scared. Good Luck (: From Tom (:

The work described in this essay is part of a number of research initiatives on children and news, arising from the *First Edition* material, which has been archived at JOMEC with funding from the British Academy <http://www.cardiff.ac.uk/jomec/en/research/28/71.html.> We were interested both in representational aspects of children in news media – the functions they serve in adult reporting particularly – and also in children's own responses.

Children's Functions in News

Children serve certain specific functions in news coverage of war and disaster – not all of these functions being in the child's broader interests, and often (because a child may be sick or unconscious) without the child's explicit consent. Part of our research looked at some of the ways in which representations of children were used in the coverage of the Iraqi war in March-April 2003, including news bulletins in the period during the lead up to war. Our research also included questionnaires and interviews with the children who wrote to *First Edition*, plus other younger children from the same school, and a comparable group of children from another school who did not write regularly to the programme. Children are often used in news coverage of war and disaster, not as active participants, but for signification purposes. In an earlier study, funded by the Broadcasting Standards Commission *Consenting Children?*[2] we did an analysis of a sample of broadcast output over two days in October 2000 and identified three main characteristics of the ways in which children were used in adult television programmes: (i) Passivity (Illustration); (ii) Entertainment; and (iii) Emotionalism.[3] In our sample of programming which featured children, by far the greatest number of child-related items were Advertisements (60 per cent) and the next most frequent category was News (20 per cent). Fifteen per cent of the sample was classified as Children's programmes, and 'General programming' (including family programmes, adult entertainment such as dramas, comedy shows, talk shows) comprised the rest of the sample.

Passivity and emotionalism were particular characteristics of the way in which children were portrayed in News.

We defined 'passivity' as a lack of participation of the child in the events; images of children were used to illustrate a subject, when children were the topic of debate, but the children had no intervention in it. They were not interviewed, and were not shown as central to any activity that was going on. In the 20 per cent of the programme sample which came into the News category, several items specifically referred to children: there were stories on the early release of the child murderers of the toddler James Bulger; on the BSE inquiry; on an appeal made by the Duke of York against child cruelty; on a toy fair; and on British schools failing black students. Most of the items concerned a subject related to children, but in none of them was the child an active participant. For example, in the first ITV news at 5.30 a.m. on 27 October 2000, the BSE inquiry was illustrated with images of 14-year-old Zoe Geoffrey infected with CJD, the BSE human variant, lying paralysed in bed, accompanied by two other young girls – an emotive scene. The children in this item did not speak, and obviously the sick girl could not have given her consent; their images were simply used as illustrative of a news item about the broader political and public health issue of BSE.

Children as 'Monsters'; Children as 'Innocents'

Our *Consenting Children?* analysis indicated a duality in the ways in which children are represented in the media: on the one hand, there was the innocent child who was allowed to play adult-like roles for the sake of entertainment or who was an innocent victim of disasters such as war, famine and disease; on the other hand, there was the controversial child, of interest to the audience because of his/her 'evil' nature, such as children who kill, as in the case of the Bulger killers. Both the 'innocent' and the 'evil' can be found in representations of children at war, often combined in the same children – as has happened with stories covering the child warriors of Liberia. Are they war criminals or victims? News reporters find it difficult to present stories about such children because of the duality of their roles. They are difficult to fit into the standard child-protagonist in media narratives – innocent victim or precociously evil 'monster'. They are clearly both. The children our research team interviewed in Glasgow, were sensitive to these polarised images of children. A 12-year-old boy pointed out: 'Children are only seen as hoolagins [*sic*] in adult news.' An 11 year old boy said, 'They're seen as crooks and vandalising.' On the other hand, references to victimhood – to 'murder', 'rape', 'kidnap' – were also very frequent in their responses. As an 11-year-old girl pointed out: 'Children are only seen in adult news when it's something serious.'

The Coverage of the War in Iraq

We were interested to see whether these impressions about the representation of children were supported by what had been shown in the media coverage of the Iraq war. We looked at a sample of 156 news items from BBC and ITN news, some – in December 2002 and February 2003 prior to the war – and some – (March 2003) – during it[4]. In this sample there were 47 (30 per cent) representations of children altogether: a 'representation' was any reference at all to a child or children, whether verbal or visual, and it included references to young people (teenagers). Of the 22 (30 per cent) out of 73 stories in the pre-war December bulletins which featured children, only two had any connection with the impending war. Both occurred in the BBC 10 pm bulletin on 25th February, 2003; one, from Egypt, showed a small boy on a man's shoulders yelling in protest, the other showed a close-up of a child accompanying her mother in a war protest in the UK (tight close-ups, an emotive technique, are a common feature of televisual representations of children). Other items included news about students demonstrating against university fees; Michael Jackson dangling his baby son over a balcony; children and their families fleeing fires in Australia; and a fatal accident on a school bus in South Wales, in which a 12-year-old boy was killed.

Although regular news items have a tendency to feature children in stories which are about accidents or disaster, in this sample most of these stories were directly about children themselves, whether as victims of accidents or of eccentric parenting or of callous governments. Only in one of these examples – the Australian fires story–were children used as incidental illustrations – i.e. 'passively' and 'emotionally' – in the shot of families sheltering in a community centre. In the other items, children/young people were actively featured speaking about their lost school friend (in the accident story) and about the difficulties of student debt (the fees story). In these cases, they appeared as agents.

In the analysis of war-time stories, children disappeared as active agents. Twenty-seven (33 per cent) of the 83 wartime stories featured children and 19 (over 70 per cent of the 27) were war-related. Among these 27 items, there was only one example of children/young people being active agents – the war protesters, mentioned above. Ironically, their way of protesting was to be passive: to lie down in the road and to pretend to be dead. All other examples of the use of children were passive. Children were shown as 'patients' both in the grammatical and medical sense; depicted as being on the receiving end of other people's actions, including being injured, and being medically treated. There was no footage of dead children, presumably arising from the news convention that to show footage of dead people is a mark of disrespect. While this may be the case, this convention certainly underestimates the true impact of war on children. The majority of visual representations in the war-story sample emphasised this overwhelming sense of passivity by showing children either lying down; being carried; or being held by the hand. No child spoke on camera. The repeated image of childhood here was one of persistent victimhood and lack of autonomy, with, in just one or two examples, an image of unruly, rebellious boyhood. Girls were not shown in even these limited active roles at all.

'Tory Tony WILL NOT CHANGE MY MIND.' Children as Active Agents

George Bush said: "This is a war against global terrorism".–This is a war against a dictator run and led by terrorists. Tony can't improve our transport, invest in our NHS or even give fire-fighters £30K a year each–but, ah, he can put aside a healthy £5.5 BILLION for a war. MADNESS as the Mirror said.11 year old boy, Glasgow, letter to *First Edition* (emphases in original)

From their representation in media coverage, it seems that children are not seen as having any active role to play in war news coverage. Their images serve the purpose of arousing horror (but not too much horror) and pity, but their voices are not heard.[5] This kind of coverage ignores the necessity of informed consent as identified in our BSC research on the use of children in factual programming. Furthermore, despite the government's emphasis on the Citizenship curriculum in UK schools, nowhere in all this is any evidence of 'citizens in the making'.

As the producers of *First Edition* reasoned in both showing and consulting children in their war coverage, wartime especially is an occasion for mobilising the political awareness and consciences of the young. Our research with primary school children suggests that they are not satisfied with a representation of themselves and their contemporaries in the media as innocent victims, grateful for adult intervention when they suffer horrific injuries, otherwise silently lying in the background while soldiers and embedded journalists do the real work of war and its reporting, and then dying off-camera later. Furthermore, the children we have interviewed have views on media coverage and news agendas which range more widely than the war itself; their responses indicate that many children are quite capable of making connections between the politics and economics of war, and other socio-political issues such as the fire-fighters' strike. The quote above gives a clear answer to the question: Should children accept a passive socio-political role at times of war? For the boy above, the answer (to use his favoured capitalisation) is NO.

Responding to *First Edition*: the Glasgow Children and News Survey

We carried out surveys and interviews with primary schoolchildren in Glasgow in both June 2002 and June 2003 (one of these schools included the children who had written regularly to *First Edition*). In 2002, the children's concerns focused on the war in Afghanistan. In 2003, concern had shifted to the Iraqi war, but there were many common concerns from one year to the next – and a sophisticated understanding of the political and ideological links between the two wars, some of which has to be attributed to the children's relationship with *First Edition* – their regular viewing of it, and their regular letters to it.

On both occasions, children answered a detailed questionnaire and took part in focus groups. For the purposes of this brief essay, I have looked at the answers to just one of the questions in the 2003 questionnaire: 'How are children shown in adult news? Can you give an example you've seen recently?' This question sought to establish what children thought about the ways in which their contemporaries were represented in the media and whether they, too, noticed elements of 'passivity', 'emotionalism' and general victimhood. The children's answers were listed and coded, and the largest proportion (20 per cent) were mentions of children being in danger in their own society: rape, murder, kidnap. This was also the case in 2002; it reinforced other findings in studies on children and violence which indicate that children are much more distressed by 'real' violence, in recognisable settings than they are with either remote violence (such as foreign war) or fantasy violence (see e.g. Buckingham, 1996).[6] Some specifically mentioned the Soham case, then already nearly a year old – one child gave a precise list: 'Jessica and Holly; Milly; Sara Pain' (sic). Nine children – just over 9 per cent – mentioned the Iraqi war specifically and a further six – just over 6 per cent – mentioned the other side of the coin of childhood innocence: 'hooligans'; 'vandals'; 'thugs'. Four mentioned children who were homeless or ill; three mentioned 'foreign children being ill' – one, optimistically, mentioned a positive view of 'foreign children', saying they were shown 'working and playing'. Altogether around 50 per cent of all responses talked about children being featured in a negative context, either as victims or as 'hooligans'. Leaving aside the 25 per cent who gave no response, only a quarter of the responses were positive – mentioning school stories, such as exam results; stories about Harry Potter and David Beckham and children making 'spectacular achievements'. Some were unspecific such as children being shown 'in pictures' or 'being interviewed.'

These answers relied on free recall – 'give an example you can remember'– and it is a feature of free recall that people will mention the most salient items in memory, with either very recent, or very strongly emotional or personally meaningful events being prioritised. The proportions in these answers do not necessarily reflect the actual distribution of these stories in the news (although my small content analysis does, in fact, reveal a preponderance of victim-based stories about children). The emphasis given in these answers to children like themselves being at risk, seems also a reflection of their anxieties about their own and their friends' safety. Such anxieties were also reflected in the focus group discussions – and are certainly there in the letters to *First Edition*.

We looked for evidence that children noticed and objected to the passivity and negativity with which the media represent other children. One boy aged 11 obviously did: 'It is usually sick children or children in poverty that are shown in children's news, like the two seriously injured Iraqi children that were saved in Kuwait.' Another boy pointed out that 'when they were hurt in the war was the last time I saw children in the adult news'. Some children took the opportunity to assert their 'citizenship' claims: 'Children play the same role as adults but aren't listened to as much. But children want their voices heard.' (Girl 11); 'Children don't make much of a difference and aren't shown as very important.' (Boy, 11); 'Children basically aren't seen in adult news–they don't care really. But I saw kids carried off in stretchers during the Iraqi war.' (Boy, 11); 'Children are shown as a responsibility in adult news … something which commits teenage crimes and eats unhealthily. THIS IS NOT RIGHT'. (Girl, 12). The following comment illustrates the paradox of using suffering children to emotionally heighten and soften media war coverage, when in fact such images may be perceived (by children at least) as condemnatory of the whole political and military enterprise:

> At the time of war in Iraq, children were shown in hospital near to death, which made us feel: why did we go to war if we are hurting innocent children? (Girl, 12)

Notes

[1] See e.g. James, A. & Prout, A. (1990), *Constructing and reconstructing childhood: Contemporary issues in the sociological study of childhood*, Falmer Press, London.

[2] Messenger Davies, M. and Mosdell, N. (2001), *Consenting Children? The Use of Children in Non-Fiction Television Programmes*. Broadcasting Standards Commission.

[3] Thanks are due to Ema Sofia Amarall Leitao, a PhD student in JOMEC, for her analysis of this material.

[4] BBC and ITN 6pm and 10 pm bulletins on 4 and 5 December 2002; 25 February 2003; and 28 March 2003. In the wartime bulletins (28 March) 61 (over 73 per cent) items out of 83, including local news, were war-related.

[5] There is a further article to be written about the role of schoolchildren in the UK and elsewhere in Europe, organising each other through mobile phone texting to leave school and join war protests in public places prior to the war in Iraq. Work is being done on this by one of my PhD students, Stephen Cushion – *'Well it beats doing your homework'* Re-representing protests against the war in Iraq: young people, politics and apathy.'

[6] David Buckingham, (1996) *Moving Images: Understanding Children's Emotional Responses to Television*. Manchester University Press, Manchester.

Chapter 14

Reducing Rights in the Name of Convention Compliance: Mental Health Law Reform and the New Human Rights Agenda

Philip Fennell

The Mental Health Bill was put out for consultation by the Department of Health in Summer 2002. The Bill was given a resounding thumbs down by what the government describes as the 'key stakeholders', known to the rest of us as patients/service users, carers, psychiatrists, psychologists, social workers, nurses and voluntary organisations. The essential features of the bill are that it broadens the statutory definitions of detainable mental disorder, it creates a single pathway to compulsory treatment for mental disorder, regardless of whether that treatment will take place under detention in hospital, and it is dominated by concerns of risk management. The predominant concerns are to seek to protect the public from possible assault by mentally disordered people.

These concerns are fuelled by the steady stream of inquiry reports into homicide and suicide by mentally disordered patients. There are two overarching policy goals. The first is to ensure that patients in the community are subject to an effective obligation to carry on with medication. Paul Boateng, then a minister at the Department of Health instructed the 'scoping committee' chaired by Professor Genevra Richardson[1] that their proposals should ensure that 'non-compliance with agreed treatment plans is not an option'. The second principal objective is to ensure that dangerous severely personality disordered patients who have committed no crime and cannot be imprisoned, can be subject to detention in the mental health system if they pose a risk to others.

The first point I want to make is that the Mental Health Bill is not simply a health measure, it is a constitutional reform. It is a reform of the relationship between not just individual psychiatric patients and the state, but also a reform of the relationship between the family and the state. As lawyers, we are very used to families not always being the people who act in the best interests of family members, and we are used to dealing with conflict about what is in the best interests of vulnerable family members. However, by and large we should recognise that in the case of people with mental illness, families do actually generally act in the best interests of their loved ones. They do try and care for them. They do try and protect their mentally ill family member, often provide home care for them, and will often want to object when the state wants to impose compulsory powers on them. These are not irrational impulses. Psychiatric hospitals, far from being asylums of tranquillity, are in the main overcrowded, underfunded places of dread, to which anyone would hesitate long before consigning any member of one's family. This is no reflection on the skills and dedication of mental health professionals. Under the Mental Health Act 1983 the patient's nearest relative has important rights to object to compulsory admission and to seek discharge, all of which will be lost if the Mental Health Bill in its present form becomes law.

Department of Health officials describe the Mental Health Bill as being 'Convention Compliant'. As I shall seek to demonstrate, achieving Convention compliance is not difficult. It requires the provision of only relatively basic safeguards for the individual rights of psychiatric patients. Department of Health officials talk of 'a new Human Rights agenda based on communitarian ideas', that is the community should have strong rights to protection against the depredations which might be visited upon them by mentally disordered people. In other words that the rights of the community should be weighed in the balance against those of individual psychiatric patients, and in certain cases should trump those individual rights. The new human rights agenda involves reading up the state's positive duty under Article 2 to uphold the public's right to life, the so-called Osman duty. In *Osman* v *United Kingdom* the European Court of Human Rights held that there was a breach of Article 2 if authorities knew or ought to have known at the time of the existence of a real and immediate risk to the life of identified individual or individuals from the criminal acts of a third party, and failed to take action within the scope of their powers which, judged reasonably, might have been expected to avoid that risk.[2] At the same time the new human rights agenda involves reading down the rights of psychiatric patients under Article 5 to protection against arbitrary detention and under Article 8 to protection or arbitrary use of compulsory treatment. What I am going to argue is that this self-proclaimed 'new human rights agenda' put forward by the government actually leads to a dumbing down of ethical debate because it is not hard to comply with the Convention when you are protecting the rights of persons of unsound mind.

The ethical issues are these. First, to what extent should the state have the power to overrule a family and take responsibility for the mental health care of a loved one? The second issue is under what circumstance should the State be able to treat compulsorily? The final issue which I wish to consider, and for carers and service users, the $64,000 dollar question, is how do we reduce the stigma and shame and fear and discrimination suffered by mentally disordered people and their families?

To What Extent should the State have the Power to Overrule a Family and Take Responsibility for the Mental Health Care of a Loved One?

Under the Mental Health Act 1983, if a person has a mental disorder which is of a nature or degree warranting detention they can be detained in the interests of their health *or* safety *or* for the protection of others. They do not have to be dangerous to be detained; we have a paternalist system of mental health law. But, as a counterweight to this strong paternalism, the 1983 Act gives substantive rights to the patient's nearest relative. Only the patient's nearest relative or an Approved Social Worker may apply for compulsory admission to hospital. Most applications are made by social workers as it is less destructive of family relations if the application to detain comes from someone independent of the family. Where an application for compulsory admission is being made by an Approved Social Worker, that social worker must, where practicable, consult the patient's nearest relative, as representative of the family.

If the patient is to be detained under s. 2 of the 1983 Act for assessment for up to 28 days (non-renewable), the nearest relative's objection may be overridden. However the nearest relative's objection to compulsory admission for treatment (s. 3) for up to six months may not be overridden, except through the county court procedure to displace a nearest relative whose objection to admission for treatment is unreasonable. The nearest relative may request the discharge of a detained patient and the authorities must discharge the patient unless the patient is likely to act in a manner dangerous to self or others.

So, the boundary between the power of the state and the rights of the family allows the state to detain on broad paternalist grounds. However, as a counterweight to these broad powers, if the family is willing, they can take responsibility for their family member's health needs, but not if that family member is dangerous to self or others. In cases of danger to self or to others, the state has the power to take over and provide care under detention, but the nearest relative retains rights to question the need for detention before the detaining authority and to seek discharge from the Mental Health Review Tribunal.

These important substantive rights will be taken away by the Bill. The nearest relative will be replaced by the patient's nominated person. The patient can nominate this person, who will not have any rights in the substantive sense. What they will have is the job of expressing the patient's wishes and feelings to the authorities. Nominated persons would have no rights to object to compulsory admission, no rights to seek discharge, in short no rights to act as a safeguard for the right to personal liberty of their family member. That family member's illness might prevent them from asserting their own rights. Hard edged rights for the nearest relative as the representative of the family are to be replaced with the right to express the patient's wishes and feelings, wishes and feelings which the mental health professionals are to take into account but not be bound by. The interesting thing about this is that rights are being stripped from families in the name of Convention compliance.

In *JT* v *United Kingdom*[3], the United Kingdom was held to be in breach of the right to respect for privacy under Article 8 of the European Convention On Human

Rights. Her complaint was that her nearest relative was her mother, who was living with a man who JT alleged had abused her in the past. Each time JT applied for discharge from detention to a Mental Health Review Tribunal, the tribunal rules required that her mother as nearest relative, be informed. JT objected to her mother being given information about her life. The Mental Health Act 1983 allows for the nearest relative to be displaced, but as noted there is currently no provision for the patient to nominate or replace his/her nearest relative. In *JT* v. *United Kingdom* the European Commission concluded that this deficiency contravened Article 8 of the European Convention on Human Rights. Article 8 of the Convention guarantees the right to respect for private and family life. The Commission stated that the absence of any possibility to apply to the County Court to change the applicant's nearest relative rendered the interference of her rights under Article 8(1) of the European Convention disproportionate to the aims pursued. The judgment of the European Court noted that a friendly settlement was reached between JT and the UK government, whereby the government undertook to introduce reform proposals to (1) enable a patient to make an application to the court to have his nearest relative replaced where the patient objected on reasonable grounds to a particular individual acting in that capacity, and (2) prevent certain persons from acting as the nearest relative of the patient.

It is now over three years since the European Court endorsed the friendly settlement. But the legislative changes anticipated by the friendly settlement have not taken place. This was openly acknowledged by the government in *R. (on the application of M)* v. *Secretary of State for Health*[4] and led Maurice Kay J. to declare that sections 26 and 29 of the Mental Health Act are incompatible with the ECHR.

The Draft Bill proposes to abolish the nearest relative in favour of a new 'nominated person' regime, but interestingly there is no provision to permit a patient to apply to the court for the replacement of the nominated person on reasonable grounds. Whilst clause 148 of the Draft Bill states that there would be a presumption in favour of the patient's choice, the clause goes on to provide that if the patient's nominee is 'unsuitable to perform the functions', or is 'of a description to be specified in ministerial regulations' he or she may be displaced. These conditions potentially allow for the patient's nominee to be displaced in a wide range of circumstances. The Parliamentary Joint Committee on Human Rights considered the Draft Bill and reported that patients with capacity to do so should have a fuller role in selecting their nominated persons, so as to ensure compatibility with the ECHR:

> ..the patient would have no power to revoke the appointment of a nominated person, or to insist on appointing someone of his or her choice. This would remain a potential interference with the patient's right to respect for private life under ECHR Article 8(1).[5]

Convention compliance requires that the patient be entitled to apply on reasonable grounds to the court to displace their nearest relative, and disqualifying those who have abused the patient in the past. The government's response in the draft Mental Health Bill was to remedy the breach by allowing the patient to nominate their representative, subject to broad exceptions, but at the same time to strip that representative of all legal powers, beyond the wishy-washy right to represent the wishes and feelings of the patient. This is insulting to the thousands of carers who take responsibility for providing community care of their loved ones but who are to be deprived of their rights to protect them against unnecessary deprivations of their liberty.

When Should the State be Able to Treat Compulsorily?

The key features of this Bill are that there is going to be a single pathway to compulsory treatment and that pathway will be via 28 days of assessment which can be authorised by mental health professionals. This will be followed, if necessary, by a care and treatment order which lasts for six months renewable, and which will have to be imposed by a Mental Health Tribunal (MHT). The MHT care and treatment order will provide either for treatment as a detained patient or compulsory treatment in the community. Compliance with it is mandatory. Clause 39 provides that the making of non-resident treatment order is sufficient authority for the clinical supervisor to require the patient to comply with the requirements specified in the order until the non-residency period ends. If the patient fails to comply with requirements or there is a material change in circumstances the clinical supervisor is to determine whether treatment should be provided as a resident.

The Bill provides clearly for the treatment order to be enforced in hospital settings. Resident detained patients may be required to accept medication using reasonable force. Non-resident patients may be required, again using reasonable force, to accept medication specified in an approved treatment plan if they have attended or been taken forcibly to a hospital. This reflects the concession made by Paul Boateng on behalf of the Government early on in the process that it was not intended to inject patients forcibly on their kitchen tables.

Clause 117 provides generally for compulsory medical treatment. Medical treatment means any treatment other than psychosurgery or Electro Convulsive Therapy.[6] It therefore includes medication. The clause further provides that both detained patients and patients subject to non-resident care and treatment orders may be treated without their consent. The consent of a patient who is liable to assessment and in respect of whom a care plan is in force shall not be required for any treatment which is specified in the care plan (cl 117(3)). The consent of a patient who is liable to a MHT care and treatment order shall not be required for any treatment which is specified in the care plan as approved or modified by the tribunal (cl 117(4),(5)). This means that reasonable force may be used to secure compliance. A detained patient who is in hospital may be required to accept treatment. So too may a non-resident patient who is subject to a requirement to attend a hospital, and who is at that hospital having attended voluntarily or having been taken and conveyed there compulsorily under cl 53. In the last resort, treatment will be enforced by taking recalcitrant patients to hospitals to enforce the medication requirement there.

Any care and treatment order made by the MHT may include requirements that the patient comply with a treatment plan, requirements that they reside at a specified place, and a new requirement (which is a criminal justice type of requirement) which is that the patient desist from any specified conduct. This is like an anti-social behaviour order for psychiatric patients. It is in this Bill because the Bill is what the government portrays as a shining example of 'joined up government'. The joining up is going on between the Department of Health and the Home Office who are jointly pushing forward a risk management agenda – how do we manage the risk posed by mentally disordered people in the community? How do we deal with mentally disordered persons who might commit serious sexual offences and how do we preventively detain them before they commit these offences? So we have got new criteria for compulsion under the legislation and there are different rules for what the government calls 'high-risk patients' and others. This is one of the most objectionable features of the Bill.

Here are the criteria for compulsion. First the person must be suffering from mental disorder. Under the Bill, 'mental disorder' will henceforth mean 'any disorder or disability in mind or brain which results in an impairment or disturbance of mental functioning'. It is a very broad definition. It replaces similarly broad definitions in the current legislation, but the government's aim in broadening this definition is so that people with personality disorders will clearly be included as people with mental disorder. The broad definition is Convention compliant because the Convention says you can detain people if they are of 'unsound mind', not the most stringent control on what the government can do.

The second criterion for compulsion is that 'the mental disorder must be of such a nature or degree as to warrant the provision of medical treatment to him'. Again, a very broad criterion. People have said that this could for example authorise the compulsory administration of Ritalin to teenage children because attention deficit hyperactivity disorder (ADHD) may be causing them to behave badly in school, and ADHD is a mental disorder. Convention compliance requires that if the patient is to be detained, Article 5 requires the unsoundness of mind to be of a kind or degree warranting compulsory confinement. If the patient is to be treated compulsorily in the community, there will be a breach of the right of privacy unless the treatment is justified and is a proportionate response for the protection of health or for the protection of the rights and freedoms of others. In respect of Article 8 there is a question mark whether in order to justify compulsory treatment the patient must lack capacity to make the treatment decision. Whether the condition warrants detention or compulsory treatment must be determined in relation to some adverse consequence which will probably happen if those interventions are not made. This is done in clause 6(4), which is one of the most objectionable parts of the Bill, as it fosters rather than combats stigma.

The third condition for compulsion depends on whether or not the patient is a 'high risk patient', reflecting the government's strange decision to issue two White Papers, one volume on reforming the Mental Health Act generally and the other on High Risk Patients.[7] Clause 6(4) (a) provides that 'In the case of a patient who is at substantial risk of causing serious harm to other persons' it must be 'necessary for the protection of those persons that medical treatment be provided to him'. Clause 6(4)(b) refers to the third condition which is to apply to 'any other case', that is patients who are not high risk. That condition is that it is necessary for the health or safety of the patient *or* for the protection of other persons that medical treatment be provided to him. This is very similar to the current position where a person can be detained if it is necessary for their health or safety or for the protection of other persons, and treatment cannot be provided unless the patient is detained (Mental Health Act 1983, s 3). Anyone who can be subject to a care and treatment order by virtue of 6(4)(a), would in any event be so subject by virtue of 6(4)(b). This prompts the question 'If this does not broaden the scope of powers to compel, what then is the point of 6(4)(a)?' The answer is that this division seeks to disapply the principle of proportionality to the high risk group. Proportionality is expressly applied to the any other case group by 6(4)(b)(ii) which requires that an order can only be made if the treatment needed cannot be provided to him unless he is subject to the provisions of this Act. Although expressly applied to the low risk group, proportionality is not applied to high risk patients (on the principle of *expressio unius exclusio alterius*). Clause 1(4) of the Bill allows for certain principles to be developed in the Code of Practice to be disapplied in respect of the high risk group. This is contrary to the principle established consistently by the court in Article 5 cases (see *Litwa* v *Poland)*[8] and in Article 8 cases (see *Pretty* v *United Kingdom)*[9] that proportionality applies to all deprivations of liberty and interventions with privacy. It is a pointless exercise to purport to disapply proportionality, because if a patient is high risk, detention will be a proportionate response. The only effect which this provision can have is to foster a connection in the public mind between behaviour which threatens others and mental disorder. What the government is doing is saying there are certain psychiatric patients that we do not like. And these are the high risk patients and we are going to remove fundamental human rights from those patients and we are applying very broad criteria. This sits very uneasily with Standard One of the National Service Framework for Adult Mental health Services which states that health and social services should: promote mental health for all, working with individuals and communities and combat discrimination against individuals and groups with mental health problems, and promote their social inclusion.[10]

The fourth criterion for compulsion is that appropriate medical treatment is available in the patient's case. This is the replacement of the treatability test in current legislation which is that medical treatment must be likely to alleviate or prevent deterioration in patient's condition. The 1983 Act focuses on the patient's condition, whilst appropriateness could focus on the rights of others to protection. Remember (3)(a) allows patients at substantial risk of causing serious harm to others to be subject to compulsory treatment if it is necessary for the protection of those persons that medical treatment be provided to him.

What the government is doing is saying there are certain psychiatric patients that we do not like. And these are the high risk patients and we are going to remove fundamental human rights from those patients and we are applying very broad criteria and furthermore we are going to require psychiatrists and others operating these compulsory procedures to give reasons why they do not use their compulsory powers. It is a fundamental principle of English medical law that a doctor cannot be ordered to do something which is against his or her clinical judgment [11] and the reasons for that you do not have to search far in your imagination or in history to see. The state should not be able to order doctors to do things which they consider against their clinical judgment, but what the State does do and what it is doing in this Mental Health Bill is require doctors and others to give reasons why they have not used their compulsory powers. If they have not used their compulsory powers and somebody is killed by that psychiatric patient or they commit suicide or harm themselves there will be an inquiry because there has to be a homicide inquiry.

If the new Mental Health Bill comes in there will be a paper trail back to the people who did not use their compulsory powers to protect the public. If there was an immediate risk to an identified individual or individuals (you remember the 'Osman formula' from *Osman–v– United Kingdom*), if such a risk exists from the criminal acts of a third party to an identified individual or individuals and that risk is immediate, the State has a duty to take action within the limits of its powers to protect against that risk. So if we have broad mental health legislation and if we have this group of people who suffer from an illness who have not necessarily committed a crime but who are seen as a risk group, you will have a great premium on risk management being placed on psychiatrists because they will be pushed into the direction of using these very broad compulsory powers. There will be no countervailing power in the family or in anybody else to resist what psychiatrists do.

I have cause to know from personal experience how important it is to be able to say to the psychiatric profession you can not admit this person because we are their nearest relative, they are not dangerous and if you try and detain this person we are going to take action against you. That substantive right will go away. We will not have that power any more under new legislation and indeed psychiatrists will be pushed in the direction of using compulsory powers and justifying themselves when they do not. I think for those reasons the relationship between the State, the family and the individual psychiatric patient are very severely threatened. We had a Royal Commission in 1957, the Percy Commission, which established the relationship between the family, the State and the patient enshrined in the Mental Health Act 1959 and in my opinion it is part of our constitution, our unwritten constitution, that that is the nature of our relationship. If we want to change it we should have a Royal Commission again and look at it properly and go through those processes. Instead what we have are devices like 'road testing' of various parts of the Bill before invited groups of key stakeholders, where selected groups are invited to the Department of Health to sit in rooms subject to Chatham House rules (I am probably breaking them by even saying that these things exist) and where everybody sits around road testing bits of a Bill which we have not seen yet in its entirety. There is going to be a new Bill because the last one was so comprehensively criticised by patients' groups, by carers, by psychiatrists, lawyers, nurses, social workers, (indeed anybody who knows anything about this).

What Can be Done to Reduce the Stigma Attached to Mental Disorder?

The answer to that is we must bring home to our legislators that they have a duty to introduce legislation which does not increase fear and stigma by drawing connections between mental ill health and risky behaviour, and which does not remove the rights of relatives to look after the liberty interest of their mentally disordered family member, and which does not ration mental health care by giving high priority to treating risky patients before others. Compliance with a Human Rights Convention which dates from 1950 is not an exacting ethical yardstick to apply, and is unlikely to yield the sort of enlightened mental health legislation appropriate to the 21st century. In terms of upholding the dignity and rights of mentally disordered people and their relatives, the new human rights agenda will be counterproductive. Convention compliance has become a device to reduce the rights of mentally disordered people and their carers.

Notes

[1] *Report of the Expert Committee Review of the Mental Health Act 1983* November 1999 DoH.
[2] [1998] 29 EHRR 245 at 305.
[3] [2000] 30 EHRR CD 77.
[4] [2003] EWHC. 1094.
[5] *Draft Menal Health Bill: Twenty Fifth Report of Session 2001–02*, HL Paper 181, HC 1294; London, HMSO, para. 84.
[6] And any kindred treatments to psychosurgery and ECT to be listed in regulations to be made under cl 112 or cl 118.
[7] *Reforming the Mental Health Act* Cm 5016-1; High Risk Patients Cm 5016-ll.
[8] *Witold Litwa Poland*, no. 26629/95 (Sect. 2), ECHR 2000-III.
[9] 66 BMLR 147.
[10] *A National Service Framework for Mental Health: Modern Standards & Service Models* Department of Health; September 1999, accessible at <www.doh.gov.uk/pub/docs/doh/mhmain.pdf>
[11] This has been reinforced by the recent House of Lords ruling in *R (on the application of IH)* v *Secretary of State for the Home Department* (2003) UKHL 59.

Chapter 15

The Impact of Leadership on Public Policy in Africa: Problems and Opportunities

Kelechi A. Kalu

Introduction

Many contemporary states in Africa are not economically viable and will remain mired in political crises because of the unsustainable and low levels of economic production and demand in the domestic markets. Affected nations include Equatorial Guinea, Rwanda, Burundi, Eritrea, Togo, Niger, and Chad. These and other African nations are currently unable to sustain viable export-oriented policies due to poor or non-existing comparative advantage in any product relevant to their natural and/or national resources. Existing institutional infrastructures – education, healthcare and information technology – remain inadequate or noncompetitive in the engineering of sustainable services industry in place of unlikely investments in manufacturing activities in these states. Also, as the imposed colonial state structures across Sub-Saharan Africa remain alien to most of the citizens, the character of the nations/ societies remain unintegrated into the structures and foundations of the state to generate nationalism, goodwill and the entrepreneurial spirit necessary for building strong viable modern states.

Further, as a result of colonialism, incorporation into the international political and economic systems by external western interests has exposed African states to a vulnerable level of external influence in both domestic and external management of their political and economic policies. And, some of the policy vulnerabilities – political conflicts, land tenure and debt managements – are largely sanctioned by the *extractive elites* based on policies aimed at continued domination and marginalization of African peoples. Subjectively, when political, economic, social and physical boundaries are externally imposed with the complicity of domestic leaders, those entrapped by such constraints often see the boundaries as artificial and alienating. However, and consistent with the game of international and domestic politics, most citizens are powerless to change the rules without deadly consequences as exemplified by Rwanda, Sudan, Nigeria and the Democratic Republic of the Congo. As a result, those with the resources to leave the continent often exercise that option, thereby exacerbating the absence of viable alternative ideas and policy frameworks.

Clarifying Indigenous and Extractive Elites

Unarguably, contemporary African states were established by Europeans during colonialism for purposes of expropriation, exploitation and imperial glory. The fragmentation of the continent is a direct result of colonial politics to which Africans were merely pawns in European colonial political chess games. Interestingly, political independence in Africa also came partly as a result of externally-induced European political games of domination and destruction ignited by Adolf Hitler's imperial design. However, Hitler's failed scheme had the unintended consequence of Africa's first liberation because most of the old colonialists lost the will and the capacity to hold on politically to their colonies. Perhaps, part of the unintended consequence of Africa's liberation is at the root of the long-term problem of the unwillingness and/or inability of most African states to institutionalize sustainable processes for solving national economic and political problems.

Some would argue that the problem with public policy in Africa remains external influences such as neocolonialism – where multinational corporations' emblems/logos have replaced former imperial flags; institutions such as the International Monetary Fund (IMF) and the World Bank's collective financial impact on African states through the draconian Structural Adjustment Policies (SAP); and, the irrelevance of African states in institutions such as the United Nations as demonstrated by that institution's lack of concern for the plight of Africans – exemplified by the seeming difficulty to resolve conflicts in Rwanda, Liberia, Sudan, Somalia, Democratic Republic of the Congo and elsewhere in the continent. However, others argue that the problem is internal to Africa. They cite corruption and poor management by the leaders; the apathy of the followers, ethnicity, religion and the lack of accountable government and institutions across much of the continent. While both of the above assessments of the problems of public policy in Africa are partially correct, they ignore a fundamental and perhaps dominant explanation with significant impact on public policy – the absence of an *indigenous elite*.

It is the lack of productive engagement in the public policy sector by indigenous elite with viable financial, intellectual and patriotic resources that remains an obstacle to the installation and maintenance of institutional structures that are consistent with modern statehood frameworks. While repugnant, what the colonialists did – first bringing the different nationalities together through an undemocratic process into one state for ease of exploitation and then exploiting their differences through autocratic strategies to keep them permanently divided – is not central to the problem of solving contemporary public economic problems today in much of Africa. The central problem in Africa has been the lack of a public leadership system that is nurtured by the core values of an *indigenous elite* across civil society and the national landscapes – family, politics, culture, religion, education and others. These problems remain irrespective of natural boundaries or near identical homogeneity in such states as Rwanda and Burundi where the boundary partitions in Berlin in 1884–85 did not affect these states.

The absence of a deep rooted, credible public leadership is directly related to the absence of national dialog and relevant action in many African states.[1] Especially since independence, there is no reliable vision and/or discussion on what the identity of each state and its citizens should be about and how the different nationalities that were brought together by colonialism should live and work together productively. In this respect, while European colonialists acted as *establishment and extractive elites*, post independence African leaders who also largely constituted themselves as *extractive elites* had no serious thought on the structural foundation and ideas that should under gird the post-colonial states they inherited at independence.

Indigenous elites build legacies using ideas and institutions. Significant to the roles and functions of indigenous elites is the fact that they also nurture dreams of current generations and, for the unborn, they leave their marks in sustainable and authentic educational institutions and structures, financial and judicial infrastructural legacies with enforceable norms and stable security across the country. Most importantly, indigenous elites produce a self-determined citizenry with the zeal to serve their country unselfishly. Extractive elites, on the other hand, leave legacies of dug up roads, wasted farmlands, uncompleted projects, corruption, malevolent leadership, false hopes, unfulfilled dreams, institutional decay represented by an externally weak state that is sustained internally by force of arms, while carting away the future of an already alienated, brutalized and emasculated citizenry as personal loots to foreign bank accounts. The Oscar Award (if there were one) in this regard goes to Nigerian leaders whose legacies are largely cash and carry mansions in the United Kingdom, United States and elsewhere, paid for with money stolen from the public treasury.

The above argument is not meant to suggest the absence of positive or negative external impact on public policy in Africa. Rather it points out that despite external constraints, resourceful and committed leadership (e.g. Nelson Mandela/Tom Mbeki administrations in South Africa) lays out a vision within a framework of ideas that galvanizes even the most stubborn citizens into working for the interest of the common good rather than forcing them to look for ways to thwart government efforts on the basis of their perceived irrelevance to the government. The extent to which the foregoing problems can be solved will largely be a function of how the relationship between the state and civil society can be enhanced and the extent both can mutually re-integrate public leadership with responsible citizenship in pursuit of the public good. In this respect, the colonially inherited culture of state violence and unresponsiveness to citizens must end to allow the state serve the larger interest of the whole within a framework of ideas that are internally generated in each state through citizens' commitment to building a society/state they would be proud to defend with the resources at their disposal. Unfortunately, over the years, the contested nature of state power by the various extractive elites has left most African states impoverished, economically underdeveloped by domestic elites in collaboration with multinational corporations (MNCs), irrelevant and without credibility relative to non-African states, and institutionally weak and undeveloped.

Institutionalism and Public Policy in Africa

For institutionalists, individuals and their preferences and the institutional contexts in which public policies are made are at the center of resolving public economic and political problems.[2] Understanding the differences in the economic and political contexts of public policy is important because the process in an economic context is mostly based on voluntary individual rational decision making in largely decentralized levels of interaction, with passive public purpose. In this sense, politics largely mediates the rules and governance structures that enable economic agents to more efficiently, optimally and securely interact to produce the desired effect of economic growth and development. The framework that guides economic decisions is different from the political context especially in a democratic decision-making structure because it is based on collectively made and binding decisions[3] that seek consensus, bargaining and at times acceptance of suboptimal outcomes in the interest of public interest. Critical to understanding the above is the idea that democracy intrinsically binds losers in the decision-making process to the will of the majority whose grievances (if any) are resolvable within the institutional structure of the state that mediates conflicts, apportions blames, awards compensations and/or sanctions in the name of the state.

However, making public policies within the context of transparent institutional structures presupposes that decision makers and the targets of such policies understand and accept the opportunities and constraints of such institutions. Consequently, while decision makers and recipients of such decisions often engage in strategic interactions that may produce a suboptimal outcome, it is the transparency of the decision-making process and the integrity of the institution that binds everyone to their relative positions on relevant issues and their impacts. In this sense then, 'rational individuals can take actions that lead to irrational social outcomes,'[4] but advance the interests of the common good. Neglecting this insight leads to consistent irrational choices and outcomes by leaders in most African states that advance the interests of the few that results in continuing institutional and infrastructural decay.[5] However, without institutional constraints, the head of state as the most powerful political and economic agent and his overzealous lieutenants and state agents resort to deliberate efforts that consistently undermine the public good using poor advice and/or outright looting of the public treasury. This situation mostly explains the persistent poverty, external debts, destroyed institutions and dysfunctional infrastructures in a socio-economic environment where the wealthiest individuals are government employees. By the same token, wealthy middlemen – past and present military officers and business persons – are mostly those whose access to government officials guarantees them contracts that are often the result of rent seeking rather than competence and entrepreneurial skills in the production of real economic goods. To avoid accountability, many successive African leaders have failed to enhance, install and/or renovate viable political institutions whose rule making and enforcement would mediate the suboptimal outcomes generated by inefficient policies, poor management and corruption. Consequently, the 'interests – the goals or policy objectives that the central actors in the political system and in the economy – individuals, firms, labor unions, other interest groups, and governments – [are supposed to deploy]'[6] for purposes of solving public economic problems lack a coherent framework because of deliberate ad hoc policy formulations and implementations by central administration. As such, political institutional structures like an independent judiciary and civil service that should transparently mediate between contested property rights and the enforcements of such policies, and therefore, invite the citizens and investors to risk their resources and energy to the benefit of the whole, remains either undeveloped or emasculated where they exist. To understand the economic preferences of most decision makers in Africa one only needs to examine where they prefer to bank their loots – in foreign banks; where they prefer to shop – in foreign markets; their preferred currencies – dollars, pounds and euros. The question becomes, in situations where the decision makers do not trust the institutions that they are responsible for maintaining, why should the IMF, the World Bank or the UN care. These crises, even if externally induced, dehumanize citizens who have no hope for recognizing and implementing a resolution because of the malevolence of their own leaders. Essentially, the ideas that frame public policies in most African states are either lacking in substance or poorly conceptualized because debates, alternative positions and policy preferences are often ad hoc and centrally controlled by the top echelon of government without regard or clue on the impact of such policies on ordinary citizens.

As I have argued elsewhere,[7] the most important task since political independence for African scholars and policy makers is how to achieve viable and sustainable economic growth and political stability. That task is at the core of public policy which the government or decision makers choose to do or not.[8] It involves the managing of political space to ensure that scarce economic resources are adequately utilized to achieve the most efficient government delivery of social and infrastructural services, which would enable individuals and/or groups to engage in entrepreneurial activities that add value to the economy, government's goals and implementation for the common good.

In this sense, change and transformation do not occur randomly or in a vacuum. The strategies and processes each state adopts in its approach to solving the puzzle of public problems affects the type of change that results from such a policy; and to the extent that the policy process is guided by clearly articulated ideas and implemented on the basis of promoting the general welfare, the resulting change is most likely to positively impact the lives of citizens in a transformative way. It is the nature of the political institution, its rules and mechanisms of enforcement of those rules, that empower change and transformative ideas/energies of the citizens across the board to move in a direction that changes the lives and social conditions of citizens in a given society. Thus, public officials have to be receptive to new ideas and willing to support a national framework for promoting new thinking. And, responsible private individuals, especially those in knowledge production institutions must be willing to think through and offer relevant ideas and insights that would creatively ensure improvement in the economic and political institutions and conditions of the people. Such conditions stabilize the general population and nurture people's sense of pride as citizens of a given nation.

As Thomas Dye cogently argues, public policy is an art as well as a craft. 'It is an art because it requires insight, creativity, and imagination in identifying societal problems and describing them, in devising public policies that might alleviate them, and then in finding out whether these policies end up making things better or worse.'[9] As a craft, public policy is the management of ideas, which are often embedded in the technical knowledge and ability of decision makers and their associates to translate the abstract ideas in governance, social structure and statistical data into practical and pragmatic policies for the society. Thus, for policies to be relevant to domestic realities, and for such technical knowledge to have the desired effect of changing the lives of people for the better, analysts and decision makers must be cognizant of the fact that changes are derived from preconceived ideas about how to correct perceived problems or enhance existing good in society.[10] Here, it is significant to say that, much of the ad hoc approach to public policy by many African leaders has been as a result of decision makers usually not wanting to adopt an incremental approach to policy issues because they are either uncertain about the likely impact of proposed new policies on policy elites and/or their associates.

In public policy, incrementalism – a strategy based on existing or previous policies or programs – is used by decision makers for modifying or framing new policies without radical changes to the status quo. A good example is increasing or decreasing budgets,[11] a characteristic of the various IMF-supported Structural Adjustment Programs in the continent. This approach results in transparently weak outcomes and is incapable of producing any real reform in any country. However, incrementalism is not only conservative, but complacent; and, as is true in the case of African states, this approach has not worked because rather than enhance existing policies and/or projects, most leaders engage in new ones, frequently for reasons that ensure maximization of their access to public funds for private gains. Also, incrementalism has not worked in enhancing public policy frameworks in Africa because both external and domestic elites have not been honest with the citizens in establishing the parameters of policy formulation that invites sacrifice and hard work; and, also because for much of Africa, especially South of the Sahara, there has not emerged an indigenous elite, except in South Africa with the necessary resources, commitment and patriotism to establish the parameters for institutionalizing a sustainable process of governance and stability that is empowering and supportive of collective decisions for the common good. This argument is powerfully illustrated through a close examination of how the coalitions at the international level remain consistent and resilient in protecting and advancing the interests of their citizens (including corporations) against the absence of serious coalitions and/or indigenous elites in Africa with the commitment to advance the interests of the citizens in various African states.

How Ideas and Politics Interact in Public Policy

The literature on democracy and war initiation – a law-like project of international politics scholars from the west that tends to ignore the conditions in much of African states – argues that, while democratic states are less likely to declare war against other democratic states, they are as war prone as non-democratic states in defense of their values, which includes economic, cultural, political and security issues. The effectiveness with which many advanced countries are able to formulate and implement public policies are largely influenced by the nature of domestic governance structure characterized by competition between special interests or elite groups for influence, which will tend to force advanced/democratic states to be weak in formulating domestic and foreign economic policies as institutional structures strategically move participants in the policy process toward accommodation and attention to alternative perspectives.[12] However, in interstate relations, what appears as democratic states' passive domestic position changes to a more assertive posture if the issue-area under discussion is relevant to national security, which is often redefined from military to economic security depending on the time frame. And, if the policy process involves a negotiation with dissimilar political structures and therefore values, the strategies are likewise changed consistent with the context in which the need arises for solving public problems.

The approaches are starkly different for many African states because of the weak institutions that resulted from the absence of indigenous elites willing and/ or able to establish relevant and sustainable institutional processes for formulating and implementing public policies. While a domestic coalition or interest group is important because it has access to decision makers and can influence public policy (the case of industrialized democratic states); in most Sub-Saharan African states, the groups that emerged after political independence simply transitioned themselves from nationalist agitators for political independence into *extractive elites* and proceeded to appropriate the state, using it as an instrument for advancing the interests of the particular group in power with little regard for the common good. That trend remains a critical part of the problem with making and implementing effective public policy in much of the region.

The problem here is that as the *extractive elites* proceeded to enhance their particular interests, they also succeeded in silencing both indigenous institutions and other formal civil society organizations that could have helped in advancing national goals and strengthening the new states. The extractive elites continue to preside over the weakening and decay of formal state institutions and the economies across the region. As a result educational institutions, road networks, electricity and healthcare facilities are in disrepair across Sub-Saharan Africa and economic structures, indigenous governance structures as well as local government institutions have been largely destroyed or weakened. Frequently, in addition to the unsustainable nature of much of the economies and state structures, rather than building on the existing strength of the states, which in most states was agricultural production, the extractive elites' poor policy visions and strategies resulted in the erasure of these strengths. Subsequently, this oversight turned agricultural producing countries like Nigeria, Ghana and Zimbabwe into food importing states. In the end, most of the states like Gabon, Chad, Niger, Gambia, Togo, Cape Verde, Rwanda and others are not only too small to sustain viable and consistent economic and political power without using force against the citizens, they are also too weak to consistently carry out the formal functions of government without external aid because of inadequate resources that constrain the projection of power beyond their territorial boundaries. Consequently, the leaders are largely unaccountable to anyone except to international financial institutions for purposes of continuous sourcing of military and economic aid that do not result in any of the donors' requests for reform.

Within the above context, the major external impact on public policies in contemporary African states comes from the fact that states in industrialized and democratic countries tend to be weak at the domestic level. This weakness allows such states to be effective in formulating and implementing their public policies that are strong at the international level where the major powers have economic and military advantages over African states whose domestic structures and external capabilities are characterized by the absence of indigenous elites presiding over weak states and with force that alienates most of the citizens from contributing to national development politically and economically.

For the advanced states, influential economic and political interest groups always compete with other coalitions to influence policy outcomes at the domestic level to strengthen the political and economic frameworks, but also, to strengthen the state's capacity to impact other states in the international system. Such influential coalitions have vested interest in the survival of the state as well as in the general welfare of the citizens who remain the most reliable consumer base for their products as well as a source of patriotic energies in defense of the state against external threat. Consequently, as a reliable base for nurturing and maintaining entrepreneurial spirit as well as for generating tax revenue at both the domestic and the international level, the state acts to protect the interest of the influential economic and political coalitions as well as the general interest of all its citizens.

For most Sub-Saharan African states, government officials constitute the only viable coalition and therefore the most important employer; this consequently leaves no room for serious economic production in the larger society. And, where government activities are characterized by 'contractocracy', rent seeking, the absence of a maintenance culture and the desire to accumulate without optimal productivity, the result is frequent awards of new giant project contracts that add nothing to either the aesthetic or material value to society. This crowding out of ideas for development and entrepreneurial spirit ultimately plays against viable solutions for public economic and political problems; causing ideas and other resources to flee the country to other regions of the world, which is best exemplified by the flight of medical practitioners and lecturers from across Sub-Saharan Africa to Europe and North America. With efficient institutional structures such as electricity, telephone lines, road networks, water supply and public safety and transparent judicial institutions, African states could take advantage of existing global infrastructures such as fiber-optic cables to establish service-based industries that will create private sector employment opportunities and generate incomes for the citizens and tax revenues for the government for further development.

And, because coalitions tend to form both at the domestic and across states – industrial democracies and the G-8 Summits – based on common economic interests, it is the absence of resourceful indigenous elites in many African states that have resulted in the unwillingness or inability of African states to strategically reposition public policies in ways that strengthen the various states. The absence of resourceful indigenous elites results in lack of/or poor vision for transcending the impact of the international system and exacerbates the effect of domestic economic and political weakness on public policy. Consequently, the tendency in most African states remains an 'anything but indigenous ideas' mentality especially in public policy regardless of their success or failure in advancing the common good.

Indeed, on issues involving economic development, where gains and losses have the potential to redistribute wealth, between the industrialized and African states, pure market mechanisms have to give way to politics with the tendency that the advanced states individually or in coalition with others will act to either minimize their losses or increase their gains. However, African leaders seem incapable of such simple insights that while the policy game table may remain the same, the issues, interests and rules determine the strategies by which participants play; and that effectiveness is fundamentally a function of existing domestic ideas and framework for advancing public policy. Indeed, on intellectual resources, most of the leaders through threats to freedom of action and/or co-optation actually 'encourage' the most educated Africans to migrate to Europe, North America and elsewhere without considering the implications of such policies to national development.

As Miles Kahler[13] has demonstrated, the liberal international political economy is characterized by states' intervention in both domestic and international economic policies; interventions that are either positive or negative to national development. Policy coordination among the G-7[plus 1] (the US, Japan, France, Germany, United Kingdom, Italy, Canada and Russia) in the international financial institutions (the IMF and the World Bank) ensures the dominance of the G-7[plus 1] through the rule of weighted voting and use of the intellectual power of their citizens who are directors and/or managers in these organizations. On issues such as monetary matters, 'special majorities voting requires more than a simple majority of votes'[14] in reaching a decision. This tends to encourage block voting between the US and the Europeans as a coalition against less developed states such as African states whose citizens were neither present at the decision-making tables, nor have any influence in changing the rules of the games. Kahler further argues that for most of the 1980s, the industrialized countries acted as a group to reduce the possibility that the less developed states such as those in Sub-Saharan Africa could have any serious gains in their negotiation with the IMF. In fact,

> The debt crisis, which began in late 1982, only heightened G-5 support of sharp adjustment in order to guarantee [LDCs] repayment to commercial creditors. These preferences in the design of IMF programs matched those of the bureaucratic actors who stood behind the Executive Board: usually the finance ministers and central banks of the industrialized countries.[15]

For Robert Putnam, domestic and international factors are essential in reaching an accord between the industrialized countries in their relationship with the less developed states. Thus, the role of resourceful indigenous elite in this regard is to first understand the nature of the rules and games that it is participating in. It has to understand the rules enough to know which can be changed, how and for what purpose and what resources can be used to play the game to its advantage. To the extent that indigenous elites in Africa use all their viable resources, especially its citizens' intellectual resources at the international level game to advance the common good for Africans, public policies will always be progressive in their effects on the citizens. But as Putnam insists, '[i]n the end, each leader believed that what he was doing was in his nation's interest — and probably in his own political interest too....'[16] The test for African leaders in this respect is whether or not such decisions advance or negate the interests of their respective states; and the jury is clearly in on this with regard to foreign economic issues such as external debts.

For example, the 'creditor coalition,' composed of the IMF, the World Bank, commercial banks and the industrialized countries, whose main interest is the maintenance of the global market economy, act as a block in their negotiation with debtor states. As a result, even though agreements with the international financial institutions (IFIs) do not enjoy the status of international treaties or law, and reneging on such agreements does not carry reputational consequences, the indebted states like those in Africa, by virtue of their weak economic and political positions relative to the industrialized countries in the international system, are constrained from exercising alternative choices like the formation of a debt cartel against their creditors because there is no emergent domestic coalition that thinks in terms of the national interest as evidenced by African states' recurring readjustment without progressive outcomes.[17] And, although some of the creditors are multinational corporations like Citibank, Chevron and Shell-BP without sovereign state standing, they are able to extract concessions from African states due largely to the political power of their home bases and the complementary interests of the *extractive elites* that rule many African states without efficient use of available resources to negotiate for the common good. As Putnam argues, agreements are possible in foreign economic policies if a powerful minority within each of the negotiating states favors the outcome of such an agreement.[18] In this case, Africa's *extractive elites* have effectively isolated competent and viable resources, thereby succeeding in collaborating with external entities in weakening state institutions, public policy frameworks and the standard of living of citizens in various states.

Although, there is no formal agreement for collaboration between the industrialized countries, the actions of the 'creditor coalition' which is based primarily on ideological acceptance of capitalism is consistent with the following assumptions of coalition politics:

- parties entering into a coalition must recognize their respective self-interests;
- each party must believe it will benefit from a cooperative relationship with the other or others;
- each party must have its own independent power base and also have control over its own decision making, and
- each party must recognize that the coalition is formed with specific and identifiable goals in mind.[19]

The industrialized countries generally work to ensure a capitalist international economic structure, theoretically free of governmental intervention by others, especially the less developed states, while ensuring that such government interventions remain consistent on the part of the industrialized states when it serves the interests of an influential economic coalition such as the interests of farmers and pharmaceutical companies. They work to ensure that established international institutions and regimes are sustained over time. To ensure the foregoing, such institutions as WTO, IMF and the World Bank are presented *as if* they are neutral economic agents without political support from the industrialized countries when in reality such institutions were created to advance the political and economic interests of the advanced states as evidenced by the persistent tendency of the United States and her allies to sidestep decisions that are inconsistent with its preferences. It is this posture that emergent resourceful indigenous elite in African states should work to overcome in order to ensure that public policies largely reflect the interests of the citizens that they serve rather than those of external entities. This needs to be done because for the 'creditor coalition,' the game of foreign economic policy, whether played at the domestic or international tables, is primarily based on the rules, regulations and sanctions established by the industrialized countries; and, a resourceful indigenous elite can strategically transcend such constraints in formulating and implementing relevant public policy frameworks in Africa.

But overcoming domestic political and economic weakness through the guided ideas of emergent resourceful indigenous elite also requires understanding that for the industrialized countries, whose policies impact African states' economic policies at home and abroad, foreign economic policies are played like a game on two tables.[20] At the international level, national governments seek to maximize their ability to satisfy domestic pressures, while minimizing the adverse consequences of foreign developments, especially in their relationships with important allies. Similarly, at the national level, domestic groups pursue their interests by pressuring the government to adopt favorable policies and politicians seek power by constructing coalitions among the various economic and political groups. As Putnam argues, 'neither of the two games can be ignored by central decision-makers, so long as their countries remain interdependent, yet sovereign'[21] and as long as the decision makers are guided by policies that aim to advance sustainable common interests of the states under their leadership.

Assuming a two-person game or coalition (for instance, an African state versus IMF on behalf of the 'creditor coalitions'), each negotiator or decision maker sits at both game boards. Across the international table sits his foreign counterpart, and across from the domestic table sit representatives of various domestic coalitions and advisors. Moves that are rational at the international game board (such as accepting IMF conditionalities that demand serious domestic reform, and thereby implementing SAP to please the IFIs) may be unwise for the same player at the domestic board where those who are likely to be negatively affected by such reforms will mobilize in opposition and potentially prevent effective implementation of the structural adjustment program. According to Putnam, 'there are powerful incentives for consistency, and ultimately differences in rhetoric between the two tables [which] may be tolerated.'[22] In the end the structural adjustment program is implemented as intended or it is poorly implemented, or it is not. However, the powerful incentive for consistency may not always be transformative or even progressive as evidenced by the consistency on the part of African decision makers with little overall progress in development or standard of living of the people. While there are political and economic costs which will affect the final decision; ultimately, the interests of the dominant economic and political coalitions will clearly control policy implementation. The question is: to whose benefit?

According to the IMF Managing Director, Michel Camdessus, if African countries are to be fully integrated into the global economy with the economic benefits thereof, 'there must be improvements in governance. Governments must be accountable and participatory; laws must be transparent; nonessential regulations eliminated; and the competence and impartiality of the legal system ensured.'[23] The question here is: to what extent should the IMF a non-state monetary institution dictate to sovereign states on their domestic governance structure as precondition for integration into the global political system? Are those requirements also applicable to industrialized states whose members control the decision-making rules of the IMF? Clearly, the African countries find themselves in the unpleasant position of owing private commercial institutions and other international organizations supported by the major powers in the international system and therefore, are susceptible to external impact from both states and non state actors. And, if any of them is unable to repay the loans without significant political and economic costs to the ruling coalition, the government's position of weakness offers international financial institutions a chance to link political reforms to economic ones without fully considering the logic of such linkage to the economic and political stability of the country, or even if the reforms can be implemented consistent with established criteria; it is the influence of power over weakness.

For example, the absence of resourceful indigenous elite in various African states makes the dishonesty of the external coalition and the extractive elites' failed policies possible. In the first instance, even though the external debts that continue to negatively impact infrastructural development, health, education and economic policies were incurred under the most spurious circumstances, neither the external coalition nor the ruling cabals could effectively trigger the odious debt principle or organize a debt-forgiveness strategy that translates into transformative change for the citizens. This is because the depth and magnitude of Africa's external debts[24] is such that some African governments, due to poor accounting practices, corruption and managerial problems, do not know the exact amounts of their external debts. Consequently, most of these governments simply resign public policies to the dictates of IMF-supervised reforms within the context of conditionalities that cut deep into social welfare policies such as health care and education that are taken for granted in industrialized countries. Clearly, the G-8 2005 meetings in Gleneagles, Scotland, came up with debt forgiveness promises, which remain only promises until actually fulfilled. What has not been addressed and indeed will not be substantively addressed by both the external coalitions and the extractive elites is the extent to which the governance institutions in most African states have decayed and cannot without radical reforms carry out its security and economic development functions. Thus, even if these debts are eventually forgiven, the expected impact will not be substantive or transformative on its impacts on the people as most of the affected states remain politically weak and incapable of establishing an efficient bureaucracy, merit-based civil service and effective protection for property rights and physical security of the citizens. Consequently, the promised debt forgiveness in Gleneagles will not be helpful because in the first place, most of the debts were not going to be paid back as most of the debtor states are economically not viable and, in the second place, most of the leaders remain self-interested rather than public servants committed to the economic, political and social well-being of their people.

Based on the UNDP Human Development Index, African states, especially south of the Sahara, are among the world's poorest states and significantly feature among the most heavily indebted poor countries. Empirically, since the imposition of SAP in 1980, external debt in Sub-Saharan African states has increased by nearly 400 per cent. Indeed, it is not just states in Africa that are burdened by the debt overhang. Generally, less developed states are paying more in debt servicing than they get in new credit. For example, between 1982 and 1990, the less developed states transferred a net $418 billion to the Northern industrialized countries in interest and debt repayments; and between 1987 and 1995 the IMF received $4 billion more in debt repayments from the most indebted and impoverished countries than it provided in new loans.[25] Specifically, African states now spend four times more on debt interest payments than on health care. For instance, by 1995, Uganda was spending $3 on healthcare for every $17 it paid in debt service most of which went to multilateral lending institutions. Similarly, between 1990 and 1993, the government of Zambia spent $37 million on primary school education but spent $1.3 billion on debt repayments. Repayments to the IMF alone were equivalent to ten times government spending on primary education.[26] Statistically, external debt per capita for Sub-Saharan Africa (SSA), excluding South Africa, is $365, while GNP per capita is just $308. Thus, on aggregate, external debt for SSA, excluding South

Africa was $203 billion in 1996, that is, 313% of the annual value of its exports; and with poor economic growth in the industrialized states, the situation is getting worse for African states, not better; and the promised debt forgiveness if reality, will be far from transforming the institutional decay into efficient and productive systems capable of resulting in economic and political development of the states without the commitment of strategic and visionary leadership.

Similarly, while SSA spends about 20 per cent of its annual export earnings on debt servicing, in 1996, it paid $2.5 billion more in debt servicing than it got in new long-term loans and credits. Thus, while the productive base is eroding as a result of decayed or decaying industrial outfits, problems with external reserve and consequently, plant closures, much of what is accrued leaks out to finance the standard of living of the already industrialized wealthy nations. Regrettably, Structural Adjustment loans that are supposed to enable governments to reform economic and governance institutions have mostly only enabled countries to continue to service external debts to western institutions and governments. However, as Soren Ambrose notes, structural adjustment programs 'have almost invariably caused increased poverty, unemployment, and environmental destruction and have usually led to an increase in the overall size of a country's multilateral debt,'[27] and of course, the opportunity cost forgone – educational, health and infrastructural developments – are mostly those that benefit ordinary people.

But, while the increase and therefore focus on debt servicing as a condition for further sourcing of external funding, loans and foreign aid directly impact the capacity of various African governments' ability to shape and implement public policies, it is fundamentally the absence of resourceful indigenous elites that the external effects on public policies are more pronounced. In other words, the domestic root of the debt overhang is a more important explanation of the persistent public policy problems in Africa than the fact of debt restructuring or trade barriers. Secondly, while the domestic factor offers a more plausible insight to persistent development problems in Africa and without concrete evidence of reform and, under the guise of restructuring, political and economic liberalization, the IMF continues to preside over the restructuring of existing debts that result in new borrowing by African states without verifiable and accountable policy reforms. The question is: which African state has truly met the conditions for reforms as initially laid out by the IMF? If none, why does the IMF continue to claim that African states are moving forward with reforms in governance and economic policies as evidenced by the continued restructuring of existing loans and access to new ones in Nigeria, Ghana, Kenya, Uganda and elsewhere? Rewarding African leaders on their political alliance to western interests rather than their domestic economic performance is profoundly dishonest and negatively impacts the well-being of African citizens.

The consequence of the foregoing has been an apathetic citizenry whose familiarity with marginalization, silencing and hopelessness amidst abject poverty have no regard for the state or its institutions and therefore negatively impact whatever intended policies the government may be willing to implement. Indeed, in various African states, especially in Nigeria, Angola, Uganda and Ghana, amongst others, citizens are often more apt to either steal or look the other way when someone else steals cables and/or steel structures scheduled for installing electricity or telephone lines because they see such items as belonging to 'the government.' The implication here is that the government and its draconian policies are enemies of the people.

Consequently, across the continent, especially in Sub-Saharan Africa, the lack of consistent and sustaining opportunities for informed and viable civic participation, irrespective of ongoing democratization processes, have left the masses feeling that the state and therefore formal authority is irrelevant to their lives. Hence, a culture of intolerance and general lawlessness permeates many urban areas, which have become even more pronounced in persistent but illiberal electoral politics. Thus, in many African states, the masses do not see themselves as part of the formal government and indeed are more likely to assume their primordial identities than state citizenship both for security and a source of national pride denied them by the absence of a national purpose guided by a vital indigenous elite. The problem here is that, such actions tend to translate into unwillingness on the part of these alienated citizens to pay taxes, consequently reducing the possibility of enhanced government revenues and therefore, the capacity to carry out such basic functions as making collective decisions in the interest of all.

Transcending External and Domestic Constraints to Transformative Policies

The challenge for decision makers in Africa is to structurally, institutionally and perceptually transform the state and government to become relevant and be seen as legitimate and relevant to the masses by making and implementing policies that have concrete and positive effects on ordinary citizens. Such a project is likely to result in a strategy for domestic revenue mobilization through acceptable taxation policies that the citizens will be willing to comply with because they could appreciate and relate to concrete and visible transformations in healthcare delivery, road construction and improvement in educational institutions and delivery of knowledge and information; issues most talked about and desired by the masses in Nigeria, Kenya, Togo, Rwanda, Sudan, Uganda, Ghana, South Africa and Tanzania, among other states. Indeed, as I traveled through South Africa, Nigeria, Ghana and Uganda, amongst other states between 2001 and 2002 and in 2004, I interviewed many ordinary Africans and was pleasantly surprised at their buoyant spirit and the clarity with which most formally educated, uneducated or poorly educated citizens like taxi drivers, market women, students, clerks and even the unemployed consistently argued that change in African states can only come about through a democratic system of governance that holds leaders accountable for their behavior. Many also advocated a stable political space where the citizens are free to pursue their individual and collective trades and interests without fear of state reprisals and/or criminal elements indiscriminately assaulting their lives. These goals will be realizable when: (a), the leaders invest in infrastructures that enable sustainable provision of electricity, healthcare delivery, education, road, communications and water supply; (b), develop the institutional structures that protect public and private property rights, which are essential for reforming existing corrupt practices that undermine the functioning of effective markets, human rights protection, and create external and domestic investor uncertainties; and (c), engage in policy frameworks that reform existing rent seeking practices that have continuously weakened and incapacitated various African states' ability to reverse the tendency for smuggling, engaging in black market transactions, evasion of taxation and a general attitude by public servants that perceive government service as opportunities for personal gains. All the above examples will increase the transaction costs of honest business activities in the region. As Brian Smith correctly notes, 'Absence of honest, impartial, efficient, and rule-bound bureaucracy enables corruption to flourish,' which politically, erodes the state's legitimacy and administratively, 'efficiency declines as officials respond to incentives to create scarcity, delay, and red tape, as scarce public resources are misallocated, as revenue is lost, and as public service morale is undermined by unequal access to one of the spoils of office.' Furthermore, Smith argues that economically, corruption inflates business costs, distorts demand for the allocation of resources and raises the cost of public provision when less efficient firms secure contracts with bribes; [and] socially, corruption strengthens inequality and has a disproportionate impact on the poor,'[28] which ultimately sustains the vicious cycle of instability and constant state repression. These unproductive strategies lead to poor policy choices implementation and therefore, poor development and program outcomes that perpetually undermine the spirit and humanity of every one, but especially of the marginalized and oppressed in many states.

In both advanced and less developed states, government policies are benefits to some and losses to others. But the process of choosing problems or issues that are deserving of decision makers' attention and how the leaders proceed with making those decisions will make a difference in terms of whether the policies are efficiently implemented to realize their intended goals. The strategy of selecting an issue or problem for the attention of policy makers reflects a process of political bargaining, compromise and consensus within a framework that *ab initio* accepts the existence of multiple issues, strategies, resources, interests and therefore alternative options as part of the decision-making process. In *Political Science in Theory and Practice*, Ruth Lane argues that the outcomes of issue-based battles are directly related to 'the power of strategically situated individuals to understand, confront, and change circumstances.'[29] The contextual framework could be an agenda setting arena where, for instance, an environmental non-governmental organization would like to see a tougher policy against pollution but is in conflict with companies opposed to such a policy. With expert knowledge on both sides, winning will reflect the difference between the resources available to each group. For most African states undergoing transitional processes from autocracy to electoral politics, the yearning of politically active individuals and civil society organizations remains the same – the need for an effective and efficient constitutional process that emerges from a national convention that helps resolve existing contentious issues amongst the nationalities strewn together by colonialism so that in a new dispensation, constitutional and democratic politics will truly guide public policies to progressively transform the lives of all citizens. Unfortunately, most of the instituted national conventions have produced no impacts on public policies. Indeed, in the case of Nigeria, the various reports out of the commissions are either 'missing' or the government simply refused to release the reports. For example, the report of the Oputa Panel that investigated the atrocities committed by successive governments against Nigerian citizens was locked in government secret vaults, until three years after its completion when the report mysteriously was released on the internet by a coalition of civil society organizations. Commissioning and releasing such a report as an instrument of public policy unarguably will put the country in question on a path of enthroning and sustaining constitutionally and institutionally/process-based rules of governance.

Analytically, the following diagram illustrates the directional outcome of such a constitutionally/democratically rule-based issue with contested benefits and whose resolutions are *ab initio* guided by ideas of indigenous elites and institutions based on transparency and accountability:

Rules Institutions		Rules maintained or changed
Individuals Resources	Politics	Individuals and Resources maintained or changed

Figure 15.1 Logic of Analysis of the Politics Model (adapted from Ruth Lane, 1997, p. 64)

Given existing rules and institutions, individual capacity to change them is largely dictated by the individual or group resources matched against those of the opposition in the context of politics.[30] As illustrated in Figure 15.1, the outcomes of such political processes proceed from maintained rules and institutions which support existing structures and people in power, or a changed rule and therefore, people, coalition or states also. In this sense, given the influence of resourceful indigenous elite committed to establishing a sustainable framework for public policies that not only preserve elite interests, but promote general welfare of the citizens, the institutional structures guided by such visionary leadership will hold everyone accountable based on the rules and consequently promote policies that invite the citizens to contribute their best toward building and strengthening their states. Ultimately, the outcome will reflect the knowledge the winners have of the rules, their resources and the weakness of the 'loyal' opposition in a given issue or policy; which in the end ensures that nation and state-building is only sustainable at the domestic level, guided by indigenous elites in coalition with the citizens.

The ruling elites in various African states have failed to understand the foregoing and/or install consequent ideas and policies. Thus African states remain unable to trust the institutions that they preside over; resulting in their preference for depositing their money in foreign bank accounts where property rights are respected and enforced and their inevitable penchant for seeking medical check-ups overseas rather than at 'home' where the medical facilities are either in decay or non-existent. Similarly, at the political institutional level, such leaders remain violators of their own rules as is demonstrated in their use of security forces to 'clear the road' before they can move from one part of the state to the other. These and other actions continue to weaken the states, its communities and their various constituents.

Thus, if resourceful indigenous elites were to emerge in various Sub-Saharan African states to establish: (a) sustainable frameworks for constitutional democratic political systems that respect and promote human rights, (b) excellence as the antidote to ignorance, discrimination, poverty and underdevelopment, and (c) promote citizenship as a rite of passage for all individuals within the frameworks of their laws, the likely consequence is a cathartic release of energy that will transform the psychological perspectives of the citizens toward the government and state and, without a doubt, progressive development and contributions by the citizens across the board. Implanting, disseminating and absorbing knowledge of the rules by which every citizen is expected to play the game of politics in such a new dispensation will unleash social interaction as a bargaining process such that public policy will *ipso facto* become a contest for creating and maintaining the rules and therefore, the values, norms and processes of maintaining and changing how society is structured and governed.[31]

In the same sense, both the indigenous elites and ordinary citizens accepting that 'the process of politics involves the pursuit of interdependent outcomes in the context of participants' beliefs about the importance and nature of just relationships, procedures, and outcomes,'[32] would have confidence that the laws and regulations are not only stable, predictable and enforceable, but will protect them and their property rights and therefore encourage ordinary citizens, the elites and foreign investors to commit their economic resources to developing the state. Thus, rather than the current system that alienates both civil servants and citizens, encouraging corrupt practices and unproductivity, such enabling framework will build and enhance the capacity of existing modern and traditional institutions to serve the citizens as individuals who have relevance both in their own perspectives and those of policy makers.

As individuals, policy makers tend to reflect the values of the community they represent while serving the preferred interests of a specific group. When public officials are not perceived as serving the interests of the majority, the maintenance of existing institutions within the enabling framework of a constitutional democratic system will change through the electoral process. Similarly, the resources different coalitions and participants are willing to invest in ensuring existing political rules and institutions or changing them becomes a function of how strongly the status quo is preferred or not. Ultimately then, the emergence of a resourceful indigenous elite that establishes a framework for 'changing the rules of politics changes the incentives for political actors; ... changing incentives leads to changes in political behavior; [and]... changing behavior changes political institutions and their significance'[33] in ways that will transform how social problems are dealt with and resolved within the framework of public policy in Africa. Inviting meritocracy and competence to the public policy process at the indigenous and governance levels and insisting on productive outcomes through a recognizable and accountable framework will enable African states to move closer to stability and a more solid base that will benefit all Africans.

Notes

[1] Yes, there have been many national conferences and/or truth finding and reconciliation commissions; but except for the cases of South Africa and Ghana, most of these post-cold war national commissions in (at least from the elites perspectives) Africa (e.g. Chad, Rwanda, Uganda, Zimbabwe, Benin and Nigeria) remain highly fraudulent in their intent, and therefore, their outcomes are irrelevant as public policy instruments.

[2] See Helen V. Milner, (1997), *Interests, Institutions, and Information: Domestic Politics and International Relations* Princeton University Press, New Jersey and Thomas Oatley, 2004, *International Political Economy: Interests and Institutions in the Global Economy* Pearson Longman, New York.

[3] Jeffrey E. Cohen, (2004), *Politics and Economic Policy in the United States* Second Edition Houghton Mifflin Company, New York , pp. 4–5.

[4] Clark C. Gibson, (1999), *Politicians and Poachers: The Political Economy of Wildlife Policy in Africa* Cambridge University Press, New York 1999, pp. 9–10.

[5] For example, many of the extractive elites in Africa could use the windows of opportunity following the end of the cold war as well as the ongoing war on terrorism with focus on other regions to convert themselves into indigenous elites by institutionalizing accountable, transparent and innovative institutions and governance structures that advance the collective well-being of their states and the citizens while preserving the elites' existing wealth – whether illegally acquired or not – for in the end, those with wealth are safer in Africa than in Europe and/or North America where government fiscal policies can reduce their value without warning. Also, the extractive elites could truly immortalize themselves by actually constructing private structures/institutions for public good, e.g. through schools, institutional and university endowments. These will ensure that the educational and other institutions are functional in producing competent leaders and entrepreneurs for a sustainable state. They can also construct effective private health facilities for public use in their local governments and/or truly engage in entrepreneurial activities that will create honest and value added employments across the continent rather than investing or merely leaving their money in foreign accounts that sustain the standard of living of those that do not need them.

[6] Thomas Oatley, *International Political Economy: Interests and Institutions in the Global Economy* p. 13.

[7] This section benefits from my earlier work on the role of ideas and theory in public policy in Africa. See Kelechi Kalu, (2004), *Agenda Setting and Public Policy in Africa*: Ashgate, Aldershot, U.K. and Burlington, VT, see especially chapter 1.

[8] For different definitions of public policy, see Thomas Dye, (1995), *Understanding Public Policy*, Eighth Edition Prentice Hall Publishers, New Jersey, pp. 3–4. Dye argues that definition of public policy in the tradition of David Eastern, Harold Lasswell and/ or Charles Jones all boil down to decision makers' authoritative allocation of values.

Therefore, there is no need for an elaborate definition of public policy beyond whatever governments choose to do or not do. My view of public policy is consistent with Dye's perspective, but goes further to specifically probe whether or not the decision makers understand the structure and relevance of ideas that inform their choice of decision in a given domestic reality. In this sense, ideas are not simply important but central to agenda setting in public policy.

[9]   Thomas Dye, *Understanding Public Policy* p. 15. Also, see Yehezkel Dror, (1989), *Public Policy Making Reexamined* Transaction Publishers, New Brunswick, pp. xii–xxii. Dror argues that public policy making is informed by the expert knowledge of decision makers, but is greatly improved on if grass-roots initiatives and localization are accommodated (p. xvii). In this sense, sources of ideas and the domestic realities where the policies are supposed to help enhance the lives of people become important, especially where transformative change is desired as is the case in Africa.

[10]   See Kelechi A. Kalu, 'The Global Political Economy and African States,' (Kieh and Agbese, (forthcoming), and, also see Mahmood Mamdani, (1995), 'The Politics of Democratic Reform in Contemporary Uganda', *East African Journal of Peace & Human Rights*, vol. 2:1, pp. 91–101.

[11]   Thomas Dye, *Understanding Public Policy*, p. 31.

[12]   Part of this section relies on my earlier work on economic development and foreign policy. For a useful characterization of how ideas and coalition politics impact advanced and less advanced states in foreign economic policies and the effect of domestic governance structures in this respect, see Kelechi A. Kalu, (2000), *Economic Development and Nigerian Foreign Policy* Lewiston, N.Y and Lampeter, U.K, pp. 144–153.

[13]   See Miles Kahler, (1993), 'Bargaining with the IMF: Two-Level Strategies and Developing Countries', in Peter B. Evans, Harold K. Jacobson and Robert D. Putnam (eds) *Double-Edged Diplomacy: International Bargaining and Domestic Politics*. University of California Press, Berkeley, pp. 363–394.

[14]   Ibid., p. 367.

[15]   Ibid., p. 368.

[16]   Robert Putnam, *Double-Edged Diplomacy: International Bargaining and Domestic Politic*, p. 433.

[17]   However, the existing position of weakness of African states is largely because of lack of vision and strategic thinking on the part of the extractive elites. For example, given the small size of most sub-Saharan African states, resourceful indigenous elites ought to think in terms of erasing the colonially-imposed state boundaries such that, the entire continent can be remapped into five super states – centered around West Africa, Central Africa, South Africa, East Africa and North Africa. This will have the immediate effect of wiping out the existing external debts because the imposed states would have atrophied and with it, the odious debts incurred for private rather than public purposes. There will also be an immediate enlargement of the economies and therefore market influence of the new states. For the logic behind this, see Kelechi A. Kalu, (2003), 'An Elusive Quest? Structural Analysis of Conflicts and Peace in Africa', in Ernest Uwazie (ed.) *Conflict Resolution and Peace Education in Africa*. Lexington Books, Lanham, Md, pp. 19–38; also Kelechi A. Kalu, (2003), 'Globalization and Democratization in Africa: Problems and Prospects', in John Mukum Mbaku and Julius Ihonvbere (eds.) *The Transition to Democratic Governance in Africa: The Continuing Struggle*. Praeger, Westport, Conn, pp. 57–79.

18   See Robert D. Putnam, Diplomacy and Domestic Politics: The Logic of Two-Level Games, in Peter Evans, et. al. *Double-Edged Diplomacy*.

19   See Stokely Carmichael and Charles V. Hamilton, (1967), *Black Power: The Politics of Liberation in America*. Random House, New York, p. 75. See also, Paula D. McClain and Joseph Stewart Jr. (1995), *'Can We All Get Along?': Racial and Ethnic Minorities in American Politics*. Westview Press and Harper Collins Publishers, Boulder and New York, p. 127.

20   Robert Putnam's 'Two-Level Games' metaphor is relevant for understanding the argument here. Both Sub-Saharan African states and the industrialized countries play at two tables – the national and the international tables. And, as previously argued, the industrialized democratic countries may seem weak at the domestic level due primarily to coalition politics or the leaderships' need for re-election, but remain strong at the international level in contrast to African states who are strong at the domestic level through their control of the instrument of force and weak externally because of their small size politically and economically and more importantly, their incompetence in using all their viable resources in negotiating with the advanced states and in advancing policies that progressively transform the lives of ordinary citizens.

21   See Putnam, Diplomacy and Domestic Politics: The Logic of Two-Level Games, p. 436.

22   Ibid.

23   See Washington Report on Africa, Vol. XIII, No. 13, (July 15, 1995), pp. 5–8. The address which Camdessus delivered at the Society for International Development in Washington on December 14, 1995, is a fleshed out position on what Africa needs to do to avoid further marginalization in the global community of the 21st century. See 'Africa: Adjustment Through Cross-Fertilization,' in *IMF Survey*, (January 8, 1996) pp. 21–24. Some of the suggestions by Camdessus such as the need for regional economic integration in Africa, social expenditure that encourage female education, improvement in public infrastructures and prevention of corruption reflect serious rhetoric that casts the IMF as encouraging 'adjustment with human face.' Indeed, the inherent fallacy of composition in the wave of regional economic blocs and its expectation to lead to sustainable development in Africa is based on a faulty logic derived from the neoclassical economic theory which states that free market will lead to economic growth which in turn will create winners and losers, and the winners will form a domestic coalition composed primarily of a middle class capable of defending their economic gains within a democratic system of government that will ensure further growth in the economy and increased defense of property rights.

24   For data on impact of debts, see '50 Years is Enough' <http://www.50years.org/factsheets/debt.html> The discussion in this section relies on the data from the foregoing source with cross references to UNDP Reports and World Development Reports for various years. While there are other indirect and direct ways such as low funding for general health and specifically, AIDS research that growth, poverty and environment (GPE) constrains African states' capacity for transformative change, this analysis focuses on the connection between GPE and external debt, escalation of conflicts in Africa through illegal and illicit mining and marketing of diamonds and other natural resources by multinational corporations, and institutional governance constraints by the IMF, the World Bank and the World Trade Organization (WTO).

25   Ibid.

26   Ibid. Consistent with General Eisenhower's observation about the impact of the Military Industrial Complex on U.S. social policies, the money that is spent on debt repayment is

Ethics, Law and Society: Volume II

essentially a theft from social policies that should be benefiting the general public, rather than the few who accumulated the debts or benefit from the interest payments.

27 See 'Soren Ambrose in Focus piece on Multilateral Debt'
     <http://lists.essential.org/stop-imf/msg00223.html>

28 Brian Smith, 2005, State-Building, in Peter Burnell & Vicky Randall (eds.) *Politics in the Developing World* Oxford University Press, New York, pp. 155–170.

29 Ruth Lane, (1997), *Political Science in Theory and Practice: The 'Politics' Model*. M. E. Sharpe, New York.

30 The same rules would be applicable in a context in which the international political institutions such as the United Nations, World Trade Organization, the IMF and the World Bank are democratized. But, given that member states of those institutions, especially the advanced industrialized states remain guided by ideas of power politics in their relationship with others, the capacity of African states to influence policy outcomes in the international system will be greatly enhanced to the extent that resourceful indigenous elites' decisions are based on ideas that use competent citizens' intellectual skills to make policies that lead to transformative change in the lives of ordinary citizens who in turn will become productive and revenue generating citizens to further enhance the credibility and therefore power of the various states.

31 Ruth Lane, *Political Science in Theory and Practice: The 'Politics' Model*. M. E. Sharpe, New York, p.10.

32 Alan C. Lamborn, (1997), 'Theory and the Politics in World Politic', *International Studies Quarterly* vol. 41, p. 190.

33 Cited in Ruth Lane, *Political Science in Theory and Practice: The 'Politics' Model* , p. 78.

Chapter 16

The Child and Family Policy Divide

Clem Henricson

Introduction

There is a difficult and unresolved tension within social policy and practice in responding to the needs of children on the one hand and parents on the other; it pervades family law, government planning structures for children and parents, and almost every service associated with family life – health, education, criminal justice, financial support, child protection. This is a tension that is imbued with a variety of ideological influences including conservatism, welfarism, social liberalism, religious perspectives and theories of children's and human rights. It is a tension that also heavily mirrors social relations, for example the growing emancipation of children, the democratisation of family relations and an evolving liberal attitude endorsing a search for fulfilment in adult relationships.

This study, by Clem Henricson[1] of the National Family and Parenting Institute and Andrew Bainham of the University of Cambridge legal faculty, examines the child and family policy divide. It considers the nature of the interests involved, its causes and consequences, and formulates possible resolutions to the policy, administrative and legal difficulties emerging in this area. It assesses the relationship between child and family policy, considering trends associated with the pivotal Children Act 1989 and its consequences in the context of recent thinking and developments. One of the most significant of these is the Human Rights Act 1998, and the incorporation of the European Convention on Human Rights into domestic legislation, which has major implications for family support and children's and adults' rights. Central and local government and other child welfare agencies now have to work in this new and not widely understood environment, ensuring that policies and individual actions by public authorities comply with its requirements. The study looks at the child and family policy divide in the context of this and other significant national and international developments, such as the draft European Union constitution and the United Nations Convention on the Rights of the Child.

There will always be occasions, for example in relation to child protection, when there is a potential conflict of interests between children and their parents and families, where separate policies and actions are needed. There will also be circumstances in which there is a unity of interests, for example in respect of financial support to families. The study seeks to identify those areas of public concern that require a separate approach to children, and those that are better met by a unified approach to children as members of their families. Inevitably values will have a significant part to play in determining recommendations of this nature. The standard by which judgements are made in this report is not one of endorsing the supremacy of a specific set of interests above others, nor a simple utilitarian one – the greatest happiness of the majority of family members, but rather one which has as its aim maximising the well-being of all. Within this context it is guided by the need to uphold children's rights and the human rights of all members of the family, to promote child welfare and child protection, and to accommodate separate and common interests in the family. It is intended to promote a balanced and complementary set of services across the child family policy divide.

Method

As a policy analysis exercise, intended to instigate debate on the relationship between children's and family policy, the study was conducted through a review of documents across family law, education, criminal justice, child protection and financial support. The review encompassed documentation relating to the past twenty years in order to enable a picture to emerge of the trends and issues linked to the Children Act 1989, and its consequences in the context of recent thinking and developments.

In terms of scope and structure, the report sets the historical and international scene. It then moves domestic policy centre stage probing exemplary issues on the government's agenda to illustrate different aspects of the child family policy divide, and the role played by international rights stipulations in the UK. There is an exploration of the government's social inclusion and antipoverty strategies across the lifecycle; the counterclaims of early preventative family support and child protection; and the status given to children's agency and the dynamic determining the relative influence on children's outcomes of the state, parents and children themselves. There is then a section on the structures of government that relate to child and family policy and the degree to which they underwrite a synchronised approach. The concluding chapter discusses the proposition of intergenerational equality of interests as a policy yardstick. It advocates transparency – a recognition of interdependence and the conflicts that arise. It proposes a clear governmental response to the issues, and moots a fuller endorsement of international rights perspectives to achieve this.

This paper focuses on two of the issues – poverty and the lifecycle, and education.

Poverty and the Lifecycle

Combating social inequality is a core governmental function undertaken for humanitarian reasons and to preserve the social fabric and cohesion of the state. In broaching the relationship between child and family policies, the question arises as to how these endeavours should spread across the population age span. Is there a common obligation to all age groups? Should investment be led by prevailing poverty levels, or vulnerability, or the potential for making a long term impact on individual lives and in reducing the inter-generational cycle of disadvantage – or a combination of these?

From a human rights perspective there are issues around whether the government should be focusing on child or all poverty. From a children's rights perspective, it has to be asked whether one can split addressing the poverty of the family from children's poverty; where does the differentiation lie, unless, of course, the child has left home and is de facto independent? And critically in the world of real politic, it has to be posited that child poverty may have become the acceptable face of redistribution and that this may be leading the government in its responses.

Reducing Child Poverty

The UK government has a broad agenda on social exclusion. Julian Le Grand et al.[2] has described the Labour government as having had a comprehensive 'war on poverty', albeit that it has not been marketed as such. A range of measures have been undertaken to counter poverty in childhood and old age and against individual and area social exclusion.

As part of European Union administrative integration, the UK government, together with other member states, has produced a National Action Plan on Social Inclusion, most recently for 2003–5, which has the broad sweep of social inclusion and exclusion issues within its purview. Targeted groups at significant risk of social exclusion include, as well as children, – large families, ethnic minorities, disabled and older people – and key risks: living in a jobless household; living with persistent low income; living in a deprived community; and intergenerational poverty. There is clear evidence that the government's action across this broad spectrum of interests and concerns is having an impact. For example, we have witnessed a reduction in elder poverty, with some 1.2 million having been raised above the poverty line between 1997 and 2003/4.[3] The government's projection of its antipoverty strategy is nevertheless dominated by child poverty reduction targets. It is child poverty that is the lead issue in ministerial statements on social exclusion. In terms of secured outcomes and achievements, too, there has been a radical reduction in child poverty, which suggests its core aim status in government thinking. The Institute of Fiscal Studies has shown that since 1999 support for families with children has grown by 52 per cent in real terms, and suggests that between 10 and 25 per cent of parents with children receive more government financial support than the estimated cost of their children.[4] Analysing the Family Resources Survey, Sutherland et al.[5] show that between 1996/7 and 2000/1 there was considerable poverty reduction in respect of children but less in relation to other groups. Countering this trend, there has been a considerable hike in pensioner income since 2001 with the introduction of the pension credit, but the thrust of government redistribution policies are still slanted towards addressing children's needs.

It might be said, however, that, despite these aspirations, the Government is promoting children's 'welfare' rather than 'rights' in its social exclusion strategies. Certainly, it makes scant reference to children's rights as a concept or to international frameworks such as the United Nations Convention on the Rights of the Child. There is no reference either in the anti-poverty strategies described in Every Child Matters, an absence sufficiently conspicuous to give rise to concerns being voiced by the House of Lords and House of Commons Joint Committee on Human Rights[6] (2003).

The Family or the Child?

While the reduction of child poverty is the government's principal social exclusion goal, in the event much of its activity entails support for the wider family in anticipation of enhanced child outcomes. Support for the child is channelled through the family. This is clearly the case with fiscal policy; tax credits and benefits are directed through parents. Even the 'baby bond', a capital asset entitlement for children at birth provided by the Child Trust Fund, is not accessible by young people until they are 18.

The Education Maintenance Allowance paid directly to disadvantaged young people to help them stay in education post 16 is an exception here, and there are, of course, supports in kind targeted directly at children that impact on poverty. Education and health are the obvious cases in point, and while these are long established services, the current government's investment in their enhancement is significant.

In balancing these two approaches to supporting children – reaching children directly or by family proxy, the government's response appears to have been largely pragmatic. While evidence has been cited that parents do pass the financial support they receive onto their children, there is perhaps insufficient discussion of children's agency or ways of improving the material benefits that actually reach children. There might, for example, be some benefit to be gained from considering a range of options for direct provision in schools that go beyond the offering of a piece of fruit for younger pupils and means tested school lunches of dubious nutritional value.

Public Debate and Differentiated Investment

The arguments supporting the government's prioritisation of child poverty are formidable. The UK had one of the highest rates in Europe when the Labour administration came to power.[7] It is also understandable that child poverty might be championed as the acceptable face of economic redistribution. In addition to these two factors, there may be an in principle argument to be made in favour of weighting social inclusion investment towards the age in life that is likely to derive the greatest long-term benefit from it, with 'benefit' defined here in terms of impact on lifetime and inter-generational poverty. With these inter-linked arguments, what is perhaps needed is in depth discussion of the background, principles, policies and associated rights relating to differentiated investment across age groups. This would provide the opportunity for the development of societal values that set childhood in the context of a lifetime's needs.

Rights and Education

The next example asks the question – how do we address the, sometimes, conflictual nature of children's and parents' interests? Their interests often overlap, of course, as with financial support. But there are occasions when they diverge, for example in relation to education.

> No person shall be denied the right to education. In the exercise of any functions which it assumes in relation to education and to teaching, the state shall respect the right of parents to ensure such education and teaching is in conformity with their own religious and philosophical convictions. (European Convention on Human Rights, Protocol 1, Article 2: Education)

This one stipulation in the ECHR encapsulates some of the predicaments in the tussle over parents' and the state's role in educating children. Education, laden as it is with values and torn obligations between the public and private face of bringing up children, is perhaps the sphere that illustrates most starkly the potential for child and parental interests to diverge. And it is where the state/child protective axis comes most demonstrably into play.

State or Parent

It is in education that the state takes over a significant parental function – that of inducting a child into the community, or at least a substantial part of that function. As Archard puts it:

> ... the state has a role as parens patriae to protect the interests of children and a further distinct interest in ensuring that any current generation of children become society's future functioning adults. The state must thus ensure that children are educated to a certain minimum extent so that they can act as citizens.[8]

Parents' Rights?

But parents also have a significant role, and not just a residuary one in guiding their children's upbringing. In Scotland it has been enshrined in legislation. The Children (Scotland) Act 1995 provides that parents have a responsibility and corresponding right:

- to safeguard and promote the child's health, development and welfare until the child reaches 16;
- to provide direction until the child reaches 16 and to provide guidance until the child reaches 18.

And they have from the European Convention on Human Rights, and arguably from commonsensical analysis, a role – even entitlement – to set norms of living and interaction that stretch from behaviour management to spirituality.

Those arguing the moral dimensions of the state's locus in children's education cite the importance of ensuring that its citizens can function as active participants in a democracy and are able to engage in the market of work, financial and social relations.[9,10] Beyond this, there are arguments that in a liberal society children are entitled to an 'open future', one where they are equipped to make choices across cultural, spiritual and economic spheres, and to be offered, so far as possible, equality of opportunity.[11,12]

Children's Interests

From the premise that the state has a legitimate aim to promote liberal democracy and the social welfare of its citizens, the questions to be asked are – what protection do children's interests require in terms of education? And – what are the circumstances in which parents' interests might diverge from that protective goal? Significant players here are – first parental negligence, or insufficient engagement to support the child in his/her education, and second counter conviction, for example a religious belief that a particular faith should be taught exclusively or a belief that moral guidance is being incorrectly or inadequately accommodated.

This and previous governments have long ago overruled the economic interests of the parent in taking a child out of school – at least pre 16. But in other areas there has been rather more ambivalence – religion for example. Arguably children should be equipped to have open futures – to be able to make choices, particularly in a country that has lurched from mono-cultural Christian traditions to multi culturalsim encompassing an array of religions and secular perspectives.

Though religious education has diversified there are concerns over a failure to teach critical appraisal – and increasing investment in religious schools is hardly conducive to children's open futures. The question has to be asked as to why we still pander to parents in allowing them to take children out of personal, social and health education?

The Child's Voice

Throughout the dynamic interplay in education between child welfare and parental engagement, one can detect a significant failure on the part of the government to accord sufficient space to children's views. The child's perspective is absent from school choice and receives scant recognition in school governance. It is parents and not children who determine participation in Religious Education and Personal, Social and Health Education.

This has been widely and adversely commented on by children's rights analysts in the field. Monk[13] writes of an 'almost total absence of legal recognition of children's rights in education..'; Freeman[14] notes their neglect in the education acts, many of which take cognisance of parents' agency and role in selecting and participating in the development of schools' policies. The main piece of legislation introduced by the New Labour administration underwriting education, the School Standards and Framework Act 1998, focused on standards and planning, and while, arguably, children were the beneficiaries of these, children's rights did not feature.

Conclusion: The Argument for a Rights Approach

Balance, credence to adults' as well as children's interests, recognition of children's need for support and protection, the legitimate claims of the wider community – have the tensions between these multiple claims been addressed by the government from a stance of considered balance and proportionality? The pattern that emerges from the examples discussed here, and more broadly in the full publication, can perhaps best be described as typified by pragmatism. It is a pattern that involves a juggling act from a beneficent perspective but without an established or transparent view of what the relationship between families, children's and community interests should be.

There have been some moves towards endorsing children's rights. There are increasing expectations that children's voices should be heard in governmental service decisions. A Children's Commissioner has been recruited for England, albeit belatedly, and the government has conceded to requests that the Commissioner should be under a duty to promote the requirements of the United Nations Convention on the Rights of the Child. However, the tardy, concessionary nature of the government's response denotes the hesitancy of its support for children's or indeed any rights. The government's commitment is more clearly aligned to children's welfare with itself, rather than externally driven rights obligations, in the determining role.

Nowhere is this more clearly demonstrated than in relation to education, where, despite the Government's much articulated and genuine commitment to enhancing education services, it has placed a restriction on the human right to education under the European Convention on Human Rights where pupils present behavioural problems. More broadly, the Government 's lobbying to remove the social rights dimension from the European Union draft constitution would have detracted from a range of rights affecting children including education.

Across the age divide, the evidence suggests that the Human Rights Act 1998 and the European Convention on Human Rights are not being taken into consideration in family and children's policy in as meaningful a way as they might be. They are not a significant point of reference in investment decisions and in the direction of policy promoting child protection and family support, in the involvement of parents in childcare and adoption proceedings, or in contact and residence decisions in cases of parental separation.

The laudable achievement of the government in reducing child poverty offers a further indication of a welfare rather than a rights directed political philosophy. A rights formulation would suggest anti-poverty programmes directed across the life cycle, albeit targeted at points of risk. It would suggest the establishment of a minimum income standard and clearly enunciated service entitlements. These have not been established.

The absence of a rights approach guiding the relationship between the interests of children and families is significantly in evidence around concessions to that ill defined attribution parental autonomy, which in some circumstances one sees perversely preserved at the expense of children's rights.

In education, for example, parental choice of school and religious education for their child has been questioned as undermining children's rights. Mitigating circumstances might be adduced in relation to the former in that choice of school is largely a process driven to try and enhance school effectiveness through competition. Religion, however, remains a significant and emotive point. There are question marks over the curtailment of children's agency through the continued endorsement of parents' power to direct their children's religious education. Overall in education the Government's role in the parent child state axis is to support children's individuation and opportunity for self determination and fulfilment. But the relationship is seriously undefined and needs principled clarification.

The problem with a welfare approach is that it is slippery. It enables particular preoccupations to dominate at a particular time, without checks against the rights of all interested parties. Without a rights framework following the model developed by the European Court under the European Convention on Human Rights, which operates a tight rope balance between the rights and interests of children and parents, the possibility of slipping excessively in either direction is always there.

Rights provide a framework and point of reference for handling interests. Interests sometimes elide, but also compete, and their reconciliation, or in some cases the championing of one side or the other, is the stuff of politics. Rights provide a pressure point and facility for reconciliation. They flush individual and collective entitlements out into the open. And they create expectations of a balance of interests that cannot disappear so readily as it might under a discretionary welfare model of government investment.

Turning to family policy, the UK has never had a family policy and the consequences are significant. The resulting void has been filled by a child policy where, whatever measures may be taken in support of families, they are only done in the context of a stated public policy aim of enhanced children's outcomes. Child policy cannot be equated with family policy because, by its limited, focused nature, it implies the eclipse of adults' rights, and many inter-related aspects of family life are not catered for, such as elder care and adult inter-dependency.

Quite properly there is a multiplicity of government policies. The advantage of adding yet one more – family policy – is that, while indeed it would overlap with other policies, it would provide a forum for recognising and reconciling interests that exist in close proximity and have the potential for friction. Children's rights and family support would fall within its broad remit. It would facilitate the development of complementary responses. With a primary function of balancing interests, such a policy would benefit in terms of direction and transparency from a set of principles to guide its decisions. A rights approach, implementing the provisions of the Human Rights Act and United Nations Convention on the Rights of the Child creatively and with conviction, would provide these.

References

[1]   Henricson, C. and Bainham, A. (2005), *The Child and Family Policy Divide: Tensions, convergence and rights*. Joseph Rowntree Foundation, York.

[2]   Le Grand, J., Burchardt,T., Hills, J., Namazie, C., Smithies, R., Stewart, K., Sutherland,H., Piachaud, D. and Vizard, P. (2005), *Policies, Concepts and Measurement.* <http//sticerd. lse.ac.uk/case/research/>

[3]   Sutherland, H., Sefton,T. and Piachaud, D. (2003), *Poverty in Britain: The Impact of Government Policy since 1997.* Joseph Rowntree Foundation, York.

[4]   Adam, S. and Brewer, M. (2004), *Supporting Families: The Financial Costs and Benefits of Children since 1975.* The Policy Press, Bristol, in association with the Joseph Rowntree Foundation.

[5]   Sutherland, H., Sefton,T. and Piachaud, D., *Poverty in Britain: The Impact of Government Policy since 1997.*

[6]   House of Lords and House of Commons Joint Committee on Human Rights 2003, *The Government's Response to the Committee's Tenth Report of Session 2003 on the UN Convention on the Rights of the Child.* HL paper 187; HC 1279. The Stationery Office, London.

[7]   Ruxton, S. and Bennett, F. (2002), 'Including Children? Developing a Coherent Approach to Child Poverty and Social Exclusion across Europe.' Euronet, Brussels.

[8]   Archard, W. (2003), *Child, Family and the State.* Ashgate, Aldershot.

[9]   Gutman, A. (1987), *Democratic Education.* Princeton University, Princeton, NJ.

[10] Rawls, J. (1993), *Political Liberalism.* Columbia University, New York.

[11] Coleman, J. (1998), 'Civic pedagogies and liberal democratic curricula', *Ethics*, vol. 108, pp. 746–61.

[12] de Wizje, S. (1999), 'Rawls and civic education', *Cogito*, vol. 13, pp. 87–93.

[13] Monk, D. (2002), 'Children's rights in education – making sense of contradictions', *Child and Family Law Quarterly*, vol. 14, pp, 45–56.

[14] Freeman, M. (1996), 'The Convention: An English perspective', in M. Freeman (ed.) *Children's Rights: A Comparative Perspective.* Dartmouth, Aldershot.

Chapter 17

Children and Family Breakdown

Gillian Douglas

Introduction

For over 50 years, it has been recognised that family breakdown constitutes one of the greatest risks to their emotional and psychological health and development that children may face during their childhood.[1] This paper considers how family law and policy have responded most recently to this risk in the light of evidence about children's own perspectives on the matter.

In the UK, it is estimated that over a quarter (28 per cent) of children will have experienced their parents' divorce before they reach the age of 16[2] and the Government has stated that 'some three million of the twelve million children in this country have experienced the separation of their parents'.[3] Over two-thirds of the nearly 150,000 children in England and Wales who experience parental divorce each year are aged 10 or under and almost a quarter are aged under 5.[4] There is also an unknown, but growing, number of children whose parents cohabit rather than marry and these may face an even higher risk – possibly as much as twice as high – that their parents will separate.[5]

This paper assumes that, from an ethical point of view, it is right that the state should seek to minimise the harmful effects of parental conflict and separation on these children. It argues, however, that current policy initiatives may be taking us in an unethical direction, away from a focus on the needs and interests of children themselves, towards a pre-occupation with adult concerns, be they a desire to assert parental rights, or a wish to control public expenditure on court processes.

Evidence of Risk of Harm

The starting point is briefly to review the evidence we have regarding the risk of harm that children may face when their parents' relationship breaks down. The data reported here derive primarily from the major review of research conducted by Jan Pryor and Brian Rodgers for the Joseph Rowntree Foundation at the end of the 1990s.[6] It should be borne in mind that their primary finding was that most children do not suffer *lasting* harm, so the detriments considered below are neither inevitable nor universal, but they *are* potentially significant enough to prompt some form of policy response.

What are the potential disadvantages experienced by children in separated families?

The immediate distress felt by children at the time of parental separation usually fades over time, and most settle into a pattern of normal development. However, generally, adverse outcomes are roughly twice as prevalent among children of divorced, as compared with children in intact families. Children whose parents separate do less well financially as adults, less well at school, have more health problems, are more likely to leave home and have sex, have a child or cohabit, at a younger age, and more likely to smoke, drink or use drugs. But it cannot be shown that parental separation is the underlying *cause* of these.

Separated families, especially headed by a lone mother (as 9 out of 10 are), tend to have lower incomes, poorer housing, greater financial difficulties than intact families. *The magnitude of socio-economic disadvantage far exceeds that for all other outcomes.* This suggests that tackling family poverty could be as (if not more) important and effective a means of diminishing the risk of lasting harm as anything else.[7] We might wish to ask whether, ethically and productively, we would receive a better return from focusing on child support (be it from the state or the absent parent) rather than on the kinds of measures considered in this paper.

It does not seem that the *absence* of a parent figure is the most influential feature of separation for children's development. Rather, it appears that it is family *conflict* before, during and after separation, which is stressful for children, who may respond by becoming anxious, aggressive or withdrawn.[8] Exposure to interparental conflict appears to help explain why some children can adjust 'normally' whilst others do not. Harold and Murch have reviewed the studies exploring the link between conflict and maladjustment, and have pinpointed the importance of factoring in the child's perspective in understanding how exposure to conflict between parents adversely affects children.[9]

What do we Learn from the Child's Perspective?

Research such as theirs suggests, then, that if we wish to find ways of identifying children at risk and responding to their needs, we need to focus more closely on the impact of parental behaviour on children, and on children's understandings of what is happening to and around them. Such an insight is timely because it chimes with the recent major shift in thinking and policy making which recognises the child as 'actor', 'agent' and 'rights bearer'. The best international manifestation of this development is to be found in the United Nations Convention on the Rights of the Child, which was opened for signature in 1989. Art 12 is perhaps the best known provision in the Convention and assures

> 'to the child who is capable of forming his or her own views, the right to express those views freely in all matters affecting the child, [such views] being given due weight in accordance with the child's age and maturity.'

It goes on to require states in particular to provide the child with

> 'the opportunity to be heard in any judicial and administrative proceedings affecting the child, either directly, or through a representative or an appropriate body, in a manner consistent with the procedural rules of national law.'

The creation of art 12 has coincided with a burst of research which has indeed finally paid attention to what children have to say about the matters affecting them, and this chapter draws particularly on a study conducted by the author and colleagues at Cardiff University, which examined the views of 104 children aged 8 to 15, whose parents had recently divorced.[10] The findings are very similar to those obtained in other studies of similar children.[11]

The experience of separation

Many of the children we spoke to told us that they were well aware that their parents' relationship was in difficulties well before they separated. Many had witnessed an increase in the intensity and frequency with which their parents argued. Even where parents had attempted to hide their arguments from their children, the children often reported having listened to their parents arguing while they were in another room or in bed trying to sleep.

We asked the children whether and how their parents had explained to them what was happening, when one of the parties separated. It is interesting to note that, in our sample, children and adults recalled this process differently.

Table 17.1   Parent and child reporting whether child told about separation

Child reporting whether parent(s) told child about separation (n = 103)	Parent reporting whether parent(s) told child about separation (n = 99)
Yes 73 (71%)	Yes 98 (99%)
No 30 (29%)	No 1 (1%)

Nearly one third (29 per cent) of the children indicated that they had not been told by either of their parents about the separation, although 71 per cent reported that they had been told (in the majority of cases, by their mother). In contrast, every parent (except one) for whom comparative data were available indicated that they had, either severally or jointly, explicitly told their children about the separation. It should also be noted that where each parent talked to their children separately, the children often received two radically different kinds of explanations of what had happened, which often added to their confusion.

Of 102 children answering the question, 57 per cent reported that no one had explained to them what the breakdown of their parents' marriage might mean for them in the immediate and longer term and almost two thirds (64 per cent) reported that they were not asked for their views, opinions, or feelings about what was happening. Over two thirds of children (67 per cent) indicated that they thought they should have been asked. For a significant proportion of children, then, little by way of explanation or preparation had *effectively* been undertaken by parents, as far as children themselves were concerned. As one 13-year-old girl commented:

> It was like, 'Oh well, it's not really your problem; you're just not going to be affected by it. You don't have to go through all the divorce things'. But, no one seemed to realise I was sort of THERE. They were all concerned with what they were doing.

Making arrangements

We also asked how far the children had been involved in the arrangements that were made for them by their parents. Most of the children valued their absent parent and wanted their relationship to continue. They also feared the loss of friends and possibly having to leave their school. In attempting to hold on to as much continuity in their lives as possible and to recover a sense of normality, children were also anxious about the possibility of further deterioration in their parents' relationship, the prospect of their parents' future happiness and their own financial and domestic circumstances.

Of 102 children responding, only 44 per cent reported that they were consulted over the question of residence. Just under half (48 per cent) reported that they were consulted over 'seeing contact' and a slightly lower proportion of children (42 per cent) reported that they were consulted over 'staying contact'.

A number of children, especially the younger ones, recalled feeling excluded from decision making. As another girl, aged 11, for example, told us:

> Mum just said that, 'We've decided for you to stay here the weekdays, so that we can get you off to school, 'cos your Dad will be working and you will go and see your Dad at the weekend'. I just had to go along with it really.

Many children, of course, were well aware of some of the practical constraints that operated around decisions concerning residence or contact and understood there was little or no choice in the matter.

Notwithstanding these examples, there was an unambiguous message from the children to whom we spoke that they would have liked to have more say in decisions that affected their future. Children who were asked their opinions usually appreciated having been given the chance to have their say.

It is important to note that it does not follow that children should take these decisions by themselves. Despite most children reporting the need to feel they had exercised some influence over arrangements, they usually accepted that the final decision was not theirs. More importantly, a number were keen to stress that they did not want to be left with what they perceived as the burden of taking the final decision. Particularly in relation to residence, several children described the difficulties they experienced when asked to decide who they wanted to live with. These children usually felt torn between wanting to have their say and not wanting to hurt their parents' feelings.

Q: Which was the hardest part?
A: When we had to say who we wanted to live with, that was the hardest part because at the time, I didn't want to hurt my Dad's feelings or my Mum's feelings. I never ended up saying who I wanted to live with 'cos I was so afraid I would hurt somebody's feelings.
13-year-old boy.

What is Wrong with the Current Legal Response?

In the wake of heavy criticism and a successful lobbying campaign by angry fathers, the way in which the courts handle parental disputes arising from separation and divorce has been the subject of a great deal of investigation and there has been a sequence of reports and reform proposals which have culminated in a bill currently before Parliament; practice and procedural reforms introduced within the court process; and some pilot schemes to test out some ideas, mainly American in origin, designed to reduce dispute and enhance parental cooperation. The criticisms of the present system concern both the substantive law, and whether it discriminates against men, and procedural problems.

As to the substantive law, fathers have complained of bias against them and stereotyping of parental roles with an assumption that women are better carers.[12] There is no convincing evidence to support this criticism. It is certainly true that one can find statements in case-law to this effect. For example, in *B v B (Custody of Children)*[13] where the unemployed father had been caring for the child, the first instance judge considered:

> It is, in my view, in this case, plainly wrong and silly if the father were to remain unemployed in order to look after one 4½-year-old boy. The father's primary role must be by his work to generate resources which provide for the support and maintenance of his child and himself, rather than remain at home performing what traditionally is regarded as the mother role, that being made possible by support of the tax-payer's money.

It is also true that the large majority of resident parents are in fact mothers. But the cases where one finds dicta of this sort date from the 1980s and the higher courts have affirmed on several occasions that there is no presumption in favour of mothers, apart from in the case of babies (clearly, an infant being breastfed falls into a different category from other children).[14] The more significant feature of the case-law is rather that the courts tend to uphold the 'status quo' – that if a child is satisfactorily placed, there needs to be a good reason to uproot him/her. Since it is still the case that mothers tend to assume a primary caring role for children, the likelihood is that more mothers start out, at separation, with the children in their care. If there is no reason to suppose that this arrangement is damaging the child, there is no reason to move him/her and hence the mother will retain residence. Carol Smart and her colleagues, in a detailed study of court applications and orders, found no evidence that mothers are significantly more likely to be successful than fathers when contesting residence. [15]

One could equally note the strong opinion frequently voiced by the courts as to the desirability of the child continuing to have a meaningful relationship with both parents, regardless of who is the primary carer. As Wall J put it in *Re P (Contact: Supervision)*[16] 'It is almost always in the interests of the child whose parents are separated that he or she should have contact with the parent with whom the child is not living.' Indeed, mothers have complained, perhaps not quite so vociferously, that this principle or presumption carries excessive weight and leads courts to downplay the presence of domestic violence and to override the court's consideration of whether contact can in fact be carried out with due regard to the safety of both mother and child.[17] But again, there is much greater judicial awareness of this issue than in the past, and it has been the subject of guidelines set out by the Court of Appeal[18] and of a detailed consideration by the Lord Chancellor's former Advisory Board for Family Law.[19]

The other criticisms are procedural. First, it is said that the courts act 'in secret'. The fact that the courts hear cases in private and there are heavy restrictions on what can be reported or published about their decisions has led to claims that they are unaccountable. But it is worth noting that the European Court of Human Rights has upheld the present system as preserving the interests of the child, and in any event, judgments are increasingly given in open court.[20]

Secondly, there are legitimate complaints regarding the cost, complexity and delay inherent in family proceedings. The first of these – the cost – is indeed likely to affect men more than women, because they are less likely to be entitled to legal aid. This has meant that there are significant numbers of men having to act as litigants in person[21] or running up large legal bills (and since costs are not generally awarded against the loser in children cases, they do not recover their expenditure even if they 'win').

Affecting both parents – and the child – are the delays and sheer complexity of the proceedings in difficult cases. In one notorious case, Munby J commented on the 'absolute futility' of proceedings, involving a father seeking contact with his daughter, now aged seven, which had entailed 43 hearings (not counting adjournments), before 16 different judges, with 950 pages of evidence, over a five- year period. At the final hearing, the father had abandoned his application in the face of the mother's refusal to comply with orders made and a wish not to damage the child any further. Clearly, from a psychological perspective, five years in the life of a seven-year old constitutes a wholly disproportionate length of time to be arguing about arrangements with consequent uncertainty and instability. The case also reflects very clearly the vicious circle that can develop when contact is not secured early on.[22]

It should not be thought that all divorcing or separating parents take court proceedings, however. We are in fact referring to a very small minority of families. Government statistical data suggest that there are between 150,000 and 200,000 relationship breakdowns involving children each year and that in 80 to 85 per cent of these, the parents manage to resolve contact arrangements independently or do not seek resolution at all. In around 5 per cent of cases they do so with the help of mediation and in the remaining cases, around 10 per cent, they turn to the courts for assistance. It is estimated that around 10 per cent of *these* (ie about 2000 cases) are the so-called intractable cases where resolution is unlikely to be reached without court intervention.[23]

Much of the difficulty in such 'intractable' cases stems from enforcement problems and the other major complaint of fathers has been the courts' inability, or unwillingness, to enforce their orders.[24] A failure to comply with an order is a contempt of court, but the only sanctions are currently a fine or imprisonment. If a mother, for example, will not comply with an order requiring her to let the child see the father, a court must think long and hard before deciding to commit her to prison – for what good would this do the child? In some cases, it may be possible to transfer residence to the father[25] but where this is not possible, the courts' options are limited. But it is again worth noting the other side of the coin in this regard. Court orders are *all* notoriously hard to enforce, as claimants who have made successful 'small claims' against sole traders or, more pertinently, mothers seeking maintenance via the Child Support Agency can testify.[26] Research has also found mothers complaining of fathers *failing* to maintain contact with their children with consequent disappointment and distrust on the part of their children.[27]

Reform Proposals

None of this is to suggest that there is no need for reform of the current system. The fact that it is so disliked and can create such trauma for those caught up in it means that one cannot be complacent even if the substance of complaints may not always be convincing. What, then, has it been proposed should be done to rectify the position? The suggested reforms concern amendments to the law, changes in practice, and concentration on certain services and provision of resources. They emanate from the government, which has published a green and white paper,[28] with a consequent bill currently before Parliament.[29] However, they build upon proposals put forward by the Lord Chancellor's former Advisory Board on Family Law and the House of Commons Select Committee on Constitutional Affairs.[30]

Changes to law

The Children and Adoption Bill proposes some legal changes intended to improve the effectiveness and enforceability of court orders, but it stops short of any substantive change to the bedrock of child law – the principle set out in s 1 of the Children Act 1989 that the welfare of the child is the court's paramount consideration. In particular, the government rejected the argument from fathers' groups that there should be a legal presumption in favour of 'equal time' and 'shared care' of children. Rightly, it is submitted, the government argued that such a presumption risks overturning the paramountcy principle and places an obstacle in the way of decision-making for the benefit of the individual child. Equally, they rejected a call from women's groups that, where domestic violence is alleged, there should be a presumption of no contact until the safety of contact can be clearly established. The government were right to oppose any diminution of the principle that every decision must focus on the particular child – even though it seems clear that, in practice, courts often apply a formulaic approach to eg frequency of contact.[31] We should be aiming at encouraging parents to focus on the interests of *their* children in particular, and not on generalised outcomes which may or may not 'work' for others.

Instead, the Bill attempts both to encourage parents to comply with contact orders through the provision of support and educative measures, and to make disobedience more subject to effective sanction. As to the first approach, the bill would enable a court to make an order for 'contact activity directions' where it is considering whether to make a contact order.[32] Under such an order, a court could direct a parent, at any stage in proceedings prior to a final order being made, to undertake activities such as attending parenting programmes, classes and counselling or guidance sessions, or information sessions about arrangements for contact or mediation. The court could require a CAFCASS[33] officer to monitor compliance with the directions or the contact order itself, and report to the court on its progress and on any failure to comply, for up to one year.[34]

Should these supportive measures fail, then the court would be able to make an 'enforcement order' which would impose an unpaid work requirement – community service – on the person in default. Alternatively, the court could require a person who has caused financial loss to the other party through breaching a contact order to pay compensation up to the amount of the loss. The aim is to cover the kind of situation where, for example, a parent has paid for a holiday for a child but the resident parent fails to deliver the child up, or the parent has travelled to visit the child and contact is then frustrated.

Rather more dramatic measures which had been mooted earlier, such as electronic tagging, have been dropped from the Bill no doubt in recognition of the possible conflict with the European Convention on Human Rights, as being a disproportionate response to the problem.

Changes in practice

Apart from the new legislation, the government proposals concerning practice are not so much radical changes, but more attempts to drive forward and consolidate a number of initiatives developed over several years in response to the perceived inadequacies of the court system. For example, it proposes an accreditation system for family lawyers, in an attempt, presumably, to ensure that the work is done (at least when publicly funded) by those who have 'signed up' to the ethic of conciliatory practice which has been promoted by bodies such as Resolution – the former Solicitors Family Law Association – for more than a decade.[35] Lawyers practising 'collaborative law', an American innovation under which the lawyers and their clients agree that they will not take court proceedings and in the event of failure to settle, the clients will have to instruct fresh lawyers, are to be encouraged through the introduction of a pilot scheme – yet increasing numbers of lawyers are already training in this technique and attempting to practise it. The use of solicitors as a gateway to a range of forms of advice and support is to be continued through the Legal Services Commission's 'FAInS' (Family advice and information service) initiative which began in 2003, and under which some solicitors are franchised to act as initial 'GPs' who then refer clients on to other specialists such as counselors, the Court of Appeal Mediation Scheme (CAMS) or mediation. Mediation itself, which has been available on an ad hoc basis for nearly 30 years, but which has proved to be stubbornly resisted by many couples whom it could potentially help reach agreements, is to be 'encouraged' but not made compulsory as is common in the USA, much to the disappointment of many fathers' groups. In-court conciliation, under which parties are diverted to attempted settlement discussions with the assistance of a district judge and CAFCASS officer, sometimes with the attendance of the children,[36] is to be made available nation-wide. Again, such schemes have existed since 1977 but have been dependent upon local initiative and enthusiasm in individual courts and even by individual judges.

A more intensive approach to support, the 'family resolutions pilot'[37] is currently being piloted in three courts in England and is to be carefully evaluated. Drawing upon a similar scheme in Florida, it operates in three stages. When an application for an order relating to children is filed in the court, the parents receive a letter from the judge advising them to take part (the scheme cannot be mandatory under existing law). Each parent is invited to a group meeting to watch a video in which young people relate their experiences (an interesting example of how research like that I described above concerning children's perpsectives has had an impact). The hope is that parents will then realise better what their children are going through and be able to look at their needs rather than their own. The parents then attend a workshop on managing family conflict with the session focused on 'learning skills for conflict management'. The couple then meet a CAFCASS officer to discuss parenting plans and try to agree on their own. If the plan is agreed, it is put to the court which can approve it and end the case.

The role of the CAFCASS officer in this process is intended to be more supportive and less investigatory than is commonly their function, and in this regard, the pilot scheme is a pre-cursor to a general shift in focus for CAFCASS workers. The government seeks to move them away from report-writing and advice for the court, where the implication is that the case will be litigated and decided by the judge, towards involvement in conciliation and social work support with a view to producing a settlement between the parties. Alongside this shift, comes a very necessary difference also in the the way the judge is to operate. Here, the judiciary's own efforts to 'manage' cases more pro-actively are harnessed to the task. The President of the Family Division accordingly issued guidance, at the same time as the White Paper was published, in the form of the 'Private Law Programme'[38] which emphasises the importance of judicial continuity (one has only to recall *Re D* above to recognise the value of this), a firm grip on the timetable and careful control over the use of experts, the gathering of evidence and the promotion within the court process itself of opportunities for mediation and settlement. This view of the 'managerial court' presents a very different model of the role and style of the family judge to that which might have presented itself thirty years ago. But it remains to be seen whether the new stereotype will be of the no-nonsense, avuncular judge who seeks to bring the parties to a compromise that they can live with, and who can relate easily to the family's problems, or of an impatient, distant bureaucrat whose sole aim is to avoid having to decide matters for himself and who is determined to 'bang the parties' heads together' (surely one of the most offensive sayings used in the family justice system) so as to save time and costs.

Provision of services and allocation of resources

Whilst the above measures are targeted at the problematic minority of cases where the parents take court proceedings, the government has recognised that all parents may need help and support to get through the breakdown process in a way that minimises the risk to their children. Once again, its proposals in this regard are not new but reiterate findings made in previous studies and approaches already endorsed. Davis and Murch[39] found in the 1980s that divorced couples felt themselves trapped on a 'conveyor belt' to the ending of the marriage and wished they had known more about the consequences of divorce when they had first sought legal help. The Family Law Act 1996[40] accordingly would have required anyone seeking a divorce to attend an information meeting. The pilot study[41] undertaken to test out models for the provision of such meetings endorsed the view that there is indeed a need for such information[42] and although the Act was not implemented, the government did issue a series of leaflets intended to provide summary information to parents and their children about relationship breakdown,[43] and it also promoted a parenting plan, drawn from the Australian model, to encourage parents to consider and agree on very detailed arrangements for post-separation parenting, down to issues such as who will feed the goldfish and wash the football kit. Such measures are to continue to be promoted to parents with further support to be given for websites and helplines, the targeting of legal family help (legal aid) and inclusion of issues relating to family breakdown in Personal and Social Education curricula for schools.

These are all useful measures, though it is unclear as yet how much resource will be devoted to their promotion nor how the government can ensure that they are accessed by all those who need them. But although some lip service is paid to the involvement of children in all this (for example, some of the leaflets are designed for children and the government is investigating how to involve them in mediation)[44] the bulk of attention is very much on the adults and how to respond to their concerns. There is nothing in any of these proposals which would place the child centre-stage in the legal or extra-legal processes being developed. Indeed, all the signs are that the one feature of the current system which *does* seek to do this – the appointment of a guardian *ad litem* and lawyer for the child so that he or she can be separately represented,[45] is likely to remain restricted to the most intractable and serious of the minority of cases which themselves cause the greatest difficulty to the legal system. There is, in fact, provision on the statute book already for greater use of such a person,[46] and new rules on when they should be appointed in parental disputes are intended to come into effect by the end of 2005. However, concern that any significant expansion of such representation would overburden the system, both in staff and financial resources, has led to an attempt to discourage[47] these appointments under the present rules and it seems unlikely that greater resources will be forthcoming to reverse this trend.

Conclusion

The concern of the government to reform the system is well-placed and arguably overdue. It is clear that the current set-up has lost the confidence of many litigants, both fathers and mothers, and those professionally involved – not least some of our most senior family judges – have themselves recognised the present failings. But the *political* debate has been hijacked so as to shift the focus of attention away from how we might better settle the arrangements for individual children, and has become damagingly gendered in its tone. There is a risk that all the research evidence, and all the information we now have at our disposal concerning how children themselves are affected by, and view, their parents' separation, may be sidestepped in favour of implementing politically appealing and headline-grabbing measures which appease parents (or some parents) but fail to get to the underlying needs of the children in whose name they are said to be made.

Perhaps we need to go back to art 12 of the UN Convention on the Rights of the Child. This needs to be read in a broader, more sophisticated way than as a simple injunction to 'hear' the child. Rather, what art 12 requires is that we provide *a voice for the child*, rather than to hear *the voice of the child*. On this basis, the age, capacity, maturity or intelligence of the child – factors which would otherwise determine the weight to be placed on the 'voice' of the child under art 12 – are insignificant. Instead, the child's interests should be fully explored and expressed from that child's standpoint, and not from that of the conflicted and partial adults.[48] Such an approach appears ethically sound in respecting children as persons, and in the wake of what we know of the effects of separation on children, to have the potential to benefit children. As one young person in our *Divorcing Children* study put it:

Q: Is there anything that could be done, that would help you? By other people? Or... ?
A: *Probably, if more people understood what it was like to go through divorce, and if they knew what it was like to, experience how bad it was.*
Q: What sort of people would need to know?
A: *Probably more children would need to know. More adults would have to understand children's feelings; others have to understand what children feel. Not what they feel, but what the children feel about it.*
Q: Do you think any adults do understand what children feel?

A: *Some of them do, but a lot think 'well, they have feelings, but they don't care that much about it, because they're only kids, they don't like care' – but a lot of children do.suffer from it and they just don't know what to do. They're like me! They don't know what to do.*

Notes

[1] As long ago as 1947, Denning J recommended (in the *Report of the Committee on Procedure in Matrimonial Causes* Cmd 7024) a procedure for ensuring that children's interests are properly taken into account in divorce proceedings, and what is now in place (in s 41 of the Matrimonial Causes Act 1973) stems from a proposal of the *Royal Commission on Marriage and Divorce* Cmd 9678 (1956) para 372. For a full discussion, see Douglas, G. et al, 'Safeguarding Children's Welfare in Non-Contentious Divorce: Towards a New Conception of the Legal Process?' (2000) MLR 177.

[2] Pryor, J and Rogers, B. (2001), *Children in Changing Families: Life After Parental Separation*, Blackwell Publishing, p 4.

[3] HM Government, *Parental Separation: Children's Needs and Parents' Responsibilities: Next Steps. Report of the Responses to Consultation and Agenda for Action*, Cm 6452 (January 2005) at p 1.

[4] Hunt, J. and Roberts, C. (2004), *Family Policy Briefing 3 'Child Contact with non resident parents'* University of Oxford Department of Social Policy and Social Work.

[5] Harold, G. and Murch, M. (2005), 'Inter-parental conflict and children's adaptation to separation and divorce: theory, research and implications for family law, practice and policy' CFLQ 185 at 187, citing Hetherington, E. M., Bridges, M., and Insabella, G. M. (1998), 'What matters? What does not? Five perspectives on the association between marital transitions and children's adjustment' *American Psychologist* vol. 53, no 2, 167 at 184.

[6] Pryor and Rodgers, *Children in Changing Families: Life After Parental Separation.*

[7] For a vigorous argument to this effect, see M Guggenheim, (2005), *What's Wrong with Children's Rights,* Harvard UP.

[8] Harold G. T., Pryor, J. and Reynolds, J. (2001), 'Not in front of the Children? How Conflict Between Parents Affects Children' *One Plus One – Marriage and Partnership Research*, 2001. Also Cummings, E. M. and Davies, P. T. (1994), *Children and Marital Conflict. The Impact of Family Dispute and Resolution,* Guildford Press, New York.

[9] Harold and Murch, 'Inter-parental conflict and children's adaptation to separation and divorce: theory, research and implications for family law, practice and policy' at 194 and 193.

[10] Butler, I. et al, (2003), *Divorcing Children* Jessica Kingsley Publishing.

[11] See especially Smart, C., Neale, B. and Wade, A. (2001), *The Changing Experience of Childhood: Families and Divorce* Polity Press. Judy Dunn and Kirby Deater-Deckard, (2001), 'Children's views of their changing families' Joseph Rowntree Foundation.

[12] See the discussion by C Smart et al, *Residence and Contact Disputes in Court* vol. 2 (Research Series 4/05) (DCA, 2005) at 29–31.

[13] [1985] FLR 166, CA.

[14] *Re W (A Minor)(Residence Order)* [1992] 2 FLR 332, CA – the baby was under four weeks old at the time of the case.

15 Smart, C. et al, *Residence and Contact Disputes in Court* vol. 1 (Research Series 6/03) (DCA, 2003) at 16.

16 [1996] 2 FLR 314 at 328.

17 See e.g. Smart, C. and Neale, B. (1997), 'Arguments against Virtue; Must Contact be Enforced?' *Fam Law* vol. 332.

18 *Re L (A Child)(Contact: Domestic Violence)* [2001] Fam 260.

19 Children Act Sub-Committee, *A Report to the Lord Chancellor on the Question of Parental Contact in Cases where there is Domestic Violence* (2000, Lord Chancellor's Department). The definition of 'harm' under the Children Act 1989 has also been amended to include 'impairment suffered from seeing or hearing the ill treatment of another': s 31(9).

20 *B and another v UK* [2001] 2 FLR 261, *Pelling v Bruce-Williams* [2004] EWCA Civ 845, [2004] Fam 155.

21 See Moorhead, R. and Sefton, M. (2005), *Litigants in Person: Unrepresented litigants in first instance proceedings* DCA Research Series 2/05 p 67.

22 See further Trinder, L. et al, (2002), *Making contact: How parents and children negotiate and experience contact after divorce* Joseph Rowntree Foundation.

23 DCA, DFES, DTI, *Children's needs, parents' responsibilities, Supporting evidence for consultation* paper (2004) Cm 6273 para 8.

24 See Smart et al, *Residence and Contact Disputes in Court* vol. 2, Chap 6. The European Court of Human Rights has held that the state has a positive (but not absolute) obligation to facilitate contact between parent and child or risk a breach of the right to respect for family life under art 8: *Zawadkaw v Poland* 23 June 2005, ECHR (unreported).

25 As was done in *V v V (Contact: Implacable Hostility)* [2004] EWHC1215 [2004] 2 FLR 851.

26 See HC Select Committee on Work and Pensions, *The Performance of the Child Support Agency* (2005, HC 44) para 104. The Agency, as at 31 March 2004, reported outstanding debt of £720.16 million and a further £947.7 million as 'probably uncollectable from previous years'.

27 See Smart et al, *Residence and Contact Disputes in Court* vol. 2, pp. 80–83, R Moorhead et al, *The Advice Needs of Lone Parents* p 25.

28 HM Government, *Parental Separation: Children's Needs and Parents' Responsibilities,* Cm 6273 (2004); HM Government, *Parental Separation: Children's Needs and Parents' Responsibilities: Next Steps. Report of the Responses to Consultation and Agenda for Action,* Cm 6452 (2005).

29 The Children (Contact) and Adoption Bill was published in draft on 2 February 2005 for pre-legislative scrutiny by an ad hoc joint committee of both Houses of Parliament. The scrutiny committee published its report on 12 April 2005, and *The Government Reply to the Report from the Joint Committee on the Draft Children (Contact) and Adoption Bill* (Cm 6583) was published on 8 June 2005. The current bill is the Children and Adoption Bill.

30 See Advisory Board on Family Law: Children Act Sub-Committee, *Making Contact Work* (2002, Lord Chancellor's Department); House of Commons Constitutional Affairs Committee, *Family Justice: The Operation of the Family Courts* HC 116 (2005).

31 See Smart et al op cit, *Residence and Contact Disputes in Court* vol. 2, p. 28 and see also the position in Australia, Smyth, B. et al, (2004), *Parent-child contact and post-separation parenting arrangements* Australian Institute of Family Studies.

32 Adding s 11A et seq to the Children Act 1989.

[33] CAFCASS is the Children and Family Courts Advisory and Support Service. CAFCASS officers are trained social workers whose major role in private law cases is currently to investigate cases and report to the court with recommendations on outcome: see CAFCASS, *Annual Report and Accounts 2004–2005* HC 109 (2005, TSO).

[34] The bill would also make family assistance orders (which may be made under s 16 of the Children Act) more flexible by extending their maximum duration to 12 months and require the officer implementing the order to give advice and assistance about improving and maintaining contact.

[35] This will tie in with proposed additional restrictions on the availability of legal aid: see Graham, L. (2005), 'Public Funding – the *New Focus* Reforms.' *Fam Law* 650.

[36] Children over the age of 9 are already required to attend similar sessions at the Principal Registry in London: see *Practice Direction (Child: Custody: Conciliation)* [2004] 2 All ER 463.

[37] See Maclean, M. (2004), 'The Family Resolutions Pilot Project' *Fam Law* 687.

[38] President of the Family Division, *The Private Law Programme: Guidance* (18 January 2005).

[39] Davis, G and Murch, M. *Grounds for Divorce.* 1988.

[40] Section 8.

[41] Walker, J. et al, *Information meetings and Associated Provisions within the Family Law Act 1996: Final Evaluation Report* (2001).

[42] But it also found that participants wanted individualis
ed advice, not just information, as did R. Moorhead et al *The Advice Needs of Lone Parents* (2003).

[43] These can be downloaded from <http://www.dca.gov.uk/family/divleaf.htm>.

[44] M. Murch et al, *Safeguarding Children's Welfare in Uncontentious Divorce* (LCD, 1999, Research Series 6/99) found that mediators were wary of 'direct' involvement of children in mediation, preferring parents to communicate the fruits of mediation to their children themselves.

[45] Which may be directed by the court under the Family Proceedings Rules 1991 r 9.5.

[46] S 122 of the Adoption and Children Act 2002 provides for the addition of private law cases to the definition of 'specified proceedings' under s 41 of the Children Act 1989 under which a guardian *ad litem* must be appointed.

[47] See Guidance from the President's Office, 'The Appointment of Guardians in Accordance with Rule 9.5 and the President's Practice Direction of 5 April 2004' 25 February 2005.

[48] And see Wall LJ in *Mabon v Mabon and others* [2005] EWCA Civ 634 at para 43: 'My difficulty … is that the judge seems to me, with all respect to him, to have perceived the case from the perspective of the adults'.

Chapter 18

The Impact of Discrimination on Children

Elspeth Webb

Introduction

The 20th Century saw the growth of a global commitment to the promotion of children's rights leading to the United Nations Convention on the Rights of the Child (UNCRC) in 1989, and the establishment of Children's Rights Commissioners in many countries. In the UK the UNCRC has been used to inform strategy in government, and seen local authorities, NHS Trusts, public health authorities, and schools making use of the convention to inform local policies and services. But, despite this, there is a growing gap between rhetoric and policy; indeed it could be argued that since 1991, the year the UK ratified the UNCRC, the situation vis-à-vis the rights of children has worsened. Table 18.1 lists Acts of Parliament and local by-laws in this period that have disadvantaged children, and reduced their rights and civil liberties.

Within Wales, the first part of the UK to appoint a Children's Rights Commissioner (CRC), and despite a very public commitment to children's rights, the policy choices made by the Welsh Assembly Government (WAG) still indicate that children's needs are not prioritised. Consider, for example, the state of Child and Adolescent Mental Health Services (CAMHS). Following recognition of the serious underfunding of CAMHS over many years in England there has been a massive investment into these services – £440m. This equates per capita to about £26m in Wales, whereas what has been spent, at the time of writing, is under £2m. Although the Welsh CRC has highlighted the parlous state of CAMHS in his last two reports, there remains a huge shortfall of investment in these services. At a time when WAG has announced its intention to spend £30m on free prescriptions for adults aged 18–65, it is timely to ask what are the mechanisms by which children's issues are lost in prioritization and allocation of health service spending in the face of obvious and demonstrated need.

Why are we witnessing this apparent paradox, i.e. that as politicians and journalists increasingly integrate 'children's rights speak' into their rhetoric, policy seems either blind or hostile to children and young people? There are parallels between the children's rights movement, and that for the civil rights of Black citizens that began in the USA in the 1950s. It has taken over 40 years to begin to understand the mechanisms by which lives are affected by racism, and the forms racism can

Table 18.1 Acts of Parliament and local by-laws affecting children

Act/by-law	Impact on children and young people
1994 Criminal Justice and Public Order Act	Incarceration for 12- to 14-year-olds Repeal of 1968 Caravan Sites Act: local authority duty to provide sites, with serious consequences for the health and welfare of traveller children
1996 Asylum and Immigration Act	Detention of children, denial of benefits, and poor service access for children of parents seeking asylum
1998 Crime and Disorder Act	Anti Social Behaviour Orders, curfews, truancy sweeps
2003 Anti-social Behaviour Act	Penalty notices for disorderly behaviour (16 –17 year-olds with provision for 10 year olds and over)
2003 Sexual Offences Act	Criminalises sexual behaviour in under 16 year olds
2004 Children Act	Law confirms the 'right' to hit for parents
2005 Bluewater ban on 'hoodies'	Stereotypes children; restricts choice of clothes and freedom of access

take. Even as late as 1995, unrecognised institutional racism in the UK police led to the inappropriate and ineffective investigation of the murder of a Black teenager, Stephen Lawrence. We have hardly begun to address the relationship between children's rights and discrimination against children. This paper will explore what forms this discrimination can take, the mechanisms via which it affects children, and the nature of the effects, using health and health care as the context. A conceptual framework is developed – see Figure 18.1. The definition of 'a child' is as in the UN Convention i.e. those aged less than 18 years old.

The nature of discrimination

Discrimination can be direct or indirect. Indirect discrimination is the inequitable treatment of one group disadvantaging another, as opposed to direct discrimination in which the focus of discriminatory attitudes, actions and policies is the group itself.

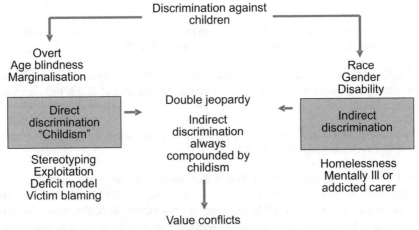

Figure 18.1 Conceptual framework for discrimination against children

Discrimination can act at the level of the individual, but can also be institutional. Institutional discrimination occurs when the structures or operating policies of organisations result in certain sections of the community being disadvantaged. This concept is most familiar as institutional racism[1], but can apply to any group disadvantaged by stigma and discrimination, including children.

Direct Discrimination

This can be manifest in the following ways:

Overt discrimination

In Britain the late 19th and early 20th centuries saw the beginnings of the exclusion of children from adult spaces, not for their safety or wellbeing but for the convenience of adults. This separateness of the child's world is now seen as a natural state of being. The resulting discrimination is so much a norm that it is both ubiquitous and unrecognised, with hotels in the UK routinely refusing access to children, and occasionally to dogs too. At the time of writing the Good Hotel Guide 'Editor's Choice'[2] includes the following text

> 'Restrictions No smoking: dining room, 1 lounge, some bedrooms. No children under 8. No dogs in house.'

Marginalisation

'Through their constructed otherness, children's status in British society is as non-persons relegated to a social, economic and political marginalisation'[3]

Marginalisation is when a group experiencing discrimination is not seen as part of the core business or service. In the context of health care it is not only a modern phenomenon:

' ...when sick children are admitted promiscuously with adults, the former never have so much attention paid them as the latter..'[4]

In 1994 the confidential local audits performed by the Audit Commission (S Farnsworth & B Fitzsimon, personal communication, 1994) and other research[5] revealed that the needs of children were not prioritised in health commissioning. Little has changed since.[6,7] When government first announced National Service Frameworks (NSF) for health, they did not include children. The children's NSF was agreed only after pressure was brought to bear on the government by NGOs, the media, and academics[8]; even so, unlike the disease centred NSFs which focus almost exclusively on adult services, the children's NSF is not accompanied by resources or investment.

Children are similarly under-represented in funding for research and development resulting in an inadequate evidence-base for much paediatric practice,[9,10] particularly evident in the development of new therapeutic drugs. Over two thirds (67 per cent) of 624 children admitted to wards in five European hospitals received drugs prescribed in an unlicensed or off label manner.[11] Although the problem is complicated by the ethical problems encountered around consent for child participation in trials,[12,13] it is largely profit driven. Drugs are not tested in children and thus not licensed for paediatric use. Even licensed drugs are prescribed off label 'resulting in children becoming therapeutic orphans sometimes with tragic consequences'.[13]

Age blindness

This is equivalent to colour blindness in racial parlance – treating everyone in the same manner, so ignoring or denying different needs. Such an approach can exclude children: for example, marina developments with inadequate barriers between toddlers and deep water.

Although huge strides have been made within the health sector to respond to the accommodation needs of children – providing facilities for play, and ensuring parents can accompany their children – there are still examples of poor practice, with shared waiting rooms in primary and secondary care in which carers have to spend considerable time with very young children in surroundings that are unsuitable and stressful.

The deficit model of childhood

Children are seen as immature, i.e. incapable or unfinished; simply on the road to adulthood rather than people in their own right. This is very evident in the field of participation of children's views, now almost an industry, with many departments of sociology studying the phenomenon, and no shortage of guidance: see references 14–18 for guidance within health services alone. [14,15,16,17,18] But again we find a gap between what is said and what is done: out of 509 trusts and health authorities in the UK just 27 consulted children on services for chronically ill or disabled children.[19] Only 11 of these went beyond consultation to meaningful participation in policy, with the other 16 cynically making use of children, somewhere between rungs 1 and 3 of Hart's Ladder.[20] At an individual level young people with serious illness have reported feeling marginalised in decision making.[21] Although there are problems in achieving full and meaningful participation, not least the competing rights of children and parents[21,22] children can be effective partners in the management of their own treatment[23] and there is plenty of convincing evidence from the Child-to-Child programme showing how children can contribute effectively to health alliances and transform their lives and health.[24]

Even older adolescents are denied the right to express their views in ways open to adults. At the start of the latest war in Iraq, many 6th form students aged 16–18 missed school to join anti-war marches; some of them were suspended or even excluded. A former Chief Inspector for Schools in England, when questioned on this on BBC radio, supported expulsion of these young people on the grounds that they were too young and too inexperienced to have a meaningful view on the war – this despite their being able to serve in the armed forces from the age of 16 years. Moffit[25] calls this 'a contemporary maturity gap' in which, in modern post-industrial societies, essentially mature individuals are infantilised by extended education and delayed work opportunities. For some young people this results in antisocial behaviours 'that are normative and adjustive'. This is an important issue. Around 25 per cent of British men under 25 will have accrued criminal records to accompany them through their adult life, of which over half will have been adolescent-onset delinquents.

Victim blaming

This term describes the phenomenon in which a vulnerable group is blamed when they experience disadvantage or harm.

Pedestrian injuries, a leading cause of childhood mortality, provide a good example. Children are blamed, with prevention strategies continuing to stress child behaviours, rather than addressing necessary and more effective changes in the structure of transport systems.

> The strength and pervasiveness of the ideology of victim blaming in child pedestrian injuries is explained by the special position that the road transport system holds in relation to dominant economic interests. Victim blaming ideology is a strategy that serves to maintain these interests at the expense and suffering of children.[26]

Another example is the 'Lolita' syndrome, in which children are blamed for their own sexual abuse. In 1993 a man found guilty of the rape of a girl, aged nine, was given two years' probation. The presiding judge said 'I have been provided with information which leads me to believe that she was not entirely an angel herself ...'.[27] Although Lord Taylor stated on appeal that this comment should not have been made, it is a view met elsewhere. On Alice Liddell, the girl with whom both John Ruskin and Lewis Carroll were infatuated, Prose writes 'what seems clear is that Alice was by no means a frail flower attracting these predatory bees; she pursued and actively encouraged their attentions'.[28]

Poverty provides the most pernicious example of victim blaming. During the 1980s much of the West moved towards more laissez-faire free market economies; some countries took steps to protect children from these developments whilst others did not.[29] The UK and the USA saw significant increases in the numbers of their child populations growing up in poverty, unlike many continental European countries[30] – see Table 18.2.

Table 18.2   Per cent of children living below national poverty lines[30]

Country	%	Country	%
Mexico	27.7	Austria	10.2
US	21.9	Germany	10.2
Italy	16.6	Netherlands	9.8
New Zealand	16.3	Luxembourg	9.1
Ireland	15.7	Hungary	8.8
Portugal	15.6	Belgium	7.7
UK	15.4	France	7.5
Canada	14.9	Czech Republic	6.8
Australia	14.7	Switzerland	6.8
Japan	14.3	Sweden	4.2
Spain	13.3	Norway	3.4
Poland	12.7	Finland	2.8
Greece	12.4	Denmark	2.4

Child poverty is thus a policy choice, despite the overwhelming body of evidence documenting the detrimental impact of poverty on the development and health of children.[31] For example, evidence shows clear links between life-course-persistent delinquency and abuse, poor parenting, relative poverty, and socially disorganised communities,[32,33] which ought to, but does not, inform both preventive and responsive strategies to this problem. Instead governments of all persuasions in the UK have tended to focus largely on a punitive approach. Other well documented consequences of relative poverty in rich countries include teenage pregnancy, drug and alcohol abuse, truancy, poor school performance and subsequent unemployment, for which these young people are also held responsible. We both condemn and blame children for these outcomes.

Stereotyping

Children can be viewed as poor witnesses, more likely to lie than adults. This has had serious consequences for vulnerable children in care, whose reporting of abuse was dismissed:

> the negative response (to complaints) … especially in relation to reports of physical abuse, justified the pervading cynicism of most residents in care about the likely outcome of any complaints that they might make.[34]

There is also a pervasive stereotype of distressed and disadvantaged children as inherently bad, a stereotype that has been both encouraged and exploited by politicians:

> During the election campaign I heard too often people talk about a loss of respect in the classroom, on the street corner, in the way our hard-working public servants are treated as they perform their tasks…People are rightly fed up with street corner and shopping centre thugs, yobbish behavior sometimes from children as young as 10 or 11 whose parents should be looking after them …, of the low-level graffiti, vandalism and disorder that is the work of a very small minority that makes the law-abiding majority afraid and angry. Tony Blair quoted in *The Times* newspaper, May 13th 2005.

The media is also guilty with significant consequences for policy – contrast its response to the murder of James Bulger to that of people killed by mentally ill adults, the most high profile of which was the stabbing of Jonathan Zeto by Christopher Clunis on a London tube station. James Bulger's death was just as much a health issue as was Jonathan Zeto's. But while the media argued that inadequate community mental health services, not Christopher Clunis, were responsible for Jonathan Zeto's death, it demonised James Bulger's killers, both of whom had experienced deprivation, neglect and abuse.[35] The link between James Bulger's death and a lack of child protection and child mental health services was not made, although professionals working in the area of child protection recognise that the interventions available for neglected and abused children, both in terms of post abuse work and in mental health promotion reached (and 15 years on still reach) only a fraction of those who could benefit.

Internalised discrimination

Discrimination can be internalised. A member of a group experiencing discrimination adopts and shares the views of a hostile society, thus seeing him/herself as inferior. A powerful example of internalised racism is provided by Mandela in his autobiography.[36] He describes an incident during a period of exile in which he panics on noticing that the pilot of the aeroplane in which he is travelling is black – even Mandela had internalised the view that a black person could not be capable of such a task.

Children also take on society's view of themselves – as someone adults can pass in a queue unchallenged, as people having nothing to say worth hearing, as lawful victims of physical assault.

Exploitation

As with any powerless group, children are vulnerable to exploitation by the powerful, i.e. adults. This may be private and secret, for example the sexual exploitation of children within families. It may be commercially driven, for example, child labour (including sexual exploitation), advertising aimed at, or using, children; or politically driven – in addition to the example given previously. Consider the exploitation of athletic prodigies in former Eastern Europe, given anabolic steroids in adolescence with serious consequences for their health.

Child labour is traditionally seen as a problem of low and middle income countries, but Field argues that we see emerging another equally exploitive form of labour – a tests and outcomes dominated education system, an 'insatiable schooling industry' of considerable economic value, and from which many people are making a great deal of money, with education as 'endless labour'.[37] Although Field is writing about Japan, her work has many resonances for children in the UK.

Indirect Discrimination

As children are dependent and powerless they are particularly vulnerable to indirect discrimination, in which their carers are disadvantaged as result of gender discrimination, racial discrimination, or the disadvantage many marginalised groups experience because they are poor, ill, disabled, or stigmatised for other reasons. Table 18.3 provides examples of how indirect discrimination affects children.

Children may of course experience, for example, racism and sexism directly – a possible explanation for the high exclusion rate of Afro-Caribbean boys in UK schools[38] and certainly the cause of the excess mortality of girls in India.[39] However, the focus of response strategies would still be to combat racism and gender discrimination, not childism per se

Multiple jeopardy

For children, indirect discrimination always compounds direct discrimination, with some children experiencing multiple jeopardy – see Figure 18.2.

For example, a child may be disabled, belong to an ethnic minority community, be living in poverty, and have a parent with mental health problems. Such a child will be victim to layers of discrimination, all of which will increase the risk of his or her rights being contravened. The effects of such multiple disadvantage may not be simply additive, but act in synergy to paralyse services and leave children in danger. There are many examples from the child protection arena in which layers of

Table 18.3   Indirect discrimination

Primary focus of discrimination	Mechanisms via which children are disadvantaged
Girls/women	Low pay; single mother households trapped in poverty Poor maternity provision: working mothers returning to work when babies are very young Reduced educational opportunities/expectations (in some communities)
Parents	No or little paternity leave[40] No parental leave for child illness (in the UK) Little acknowledgement of dual role of working parents in occupational law[41] Inadequate childcare services for young children Inadequate provision for prams in public transport – difficulty in accessing appointments
Black and ethnic minority communities	Increased risk of growing up in poverty[42] Increased risk of being in care (20% of looked-after population in England are non-white)[43] Poor access to health care[44] Inadequately protected from harm[45]
Asylum seekers	Poor health care In detention In poverty
Homeless families	Stigmatised; poor access to services; low uptake of surveillance and immunisation[46,47]
Disabled	Access difficulties; marginalised in policy
Mentally ill carers	Stigmatised; unsupported – children acting as carers[48]

complexity are associated with failures of the protection systems with devastating consequences for the children involved; for example child abuse complicated by:

- being in care[34]
- domestic violence[49]
- black or ethnic minority (BEM) status[50]
- BEM status and disability[46]
- BEM status and trafficking[51]

Figure 18.2 Multiple jeopardy

Value conflicts

This term describes when accepted values or moral belief are at odds with another set of values or beliefs both of which are valid within their own framework and context. In the field of child health there are four ways in which value conflicts may be manifest:

1. When for cultural, historical or religious reasons groups have widely differing moral frameworks and thus conflicting values. Examples include
    a. The conflict between parents who are Jehovah's Witnesses refusing to allow their child a blood transfusion, and the right of a child to appropriate treatment.
    b. Sex education in schools – the right of children to information may be in conflict with the withdrawal of children belonging to particular religious groups from the Sex and Relationships curriculum.
    c. Child abuse: A difficulty facing professionals in this area is the unresolved debate around whether child abuse is a relative or an absolute concept. Chand states: 'Overall cultural differences in the way families rear their children should be … respected, but where child abuse does occur it should be understood that this particular family has gone beyond what is acceptable not only in the British culture, but in their own.[52] But this relativistic approach, which leads directly to cultural deficit, is dangerous. It would mean that female genital mutilation (FGM) is not abuse since, in the context of the cultures in which it is traditional, it is perceived as a responsible act by parents ensuring their daughter a place in society, whereas it is recognised to be seriously harmful to children and outlawed by the UN Convention on the Rights of the Child.[53,54]

2. When, within a culture, accepted values in one area of activity are in contradiction to accepted values in another: For example:

a. Within the convention itself, the right to family life may be at odds with a child's right to protection from harm, and a child's right to freedom from exploitation may conflict with a child's right to work

b. At a macroeconomic level there is a tension between free market economics and the protection of children from poverty.[29]

3. When the needs or rights of one group are in conflict with those of another. For example:

a. Priority setting in health care in which resources are inadequate to meet the needs of the population. How does one balance the needs of disabled children for rehabilitation services against the needs of osteoarthritis sufferers for joint replacement surgery?

b. Where a parent's views on the medical care of a child may be in conflict with the views of the child, or perceived to be in conflict to a child's best interests, such as whether to continue or terminate a pregnancy in a 14-year-old girl, or when to terminate treatment in a dying or profoundly disabled child

c. Conflicts between the needs of different groups of children. For example, a child with severe learning difficulties and profoundly challenging behaviour has a right to family life and to educational inclusion. However, there are circumstances where this may be harmful to a sibling's health and welfare, or severely compromise the education of other children.

Value conflicts are often difficult to resolve, and may require the help of an independent advocate[55] or even of the courts. It is imperative in such situations to focus firmly on Article 3 of the UN Convention of the Rights of the Child – what is in the best interest of the child? Resolving conflicts of interest between groups of children is particularly challenging. Indeed the examples given here are not only unresolved, but unmentioned, unacknowledged and taboo. We need honest open debate.

Conclusions

Children's advocates need not only to identify when children are being disadvantaged but why and how they are disadvantaged. Without an understanding of how discrimination affects children it is not possible to identify the appropriate focus for action in any particular case. Is a particular child disadvantaged because she is a refugee, because she is disabled, or because children's services are marginalised and under-resourced? The conceptual framework developed here provides a tool to improve the recognition of discrimination against children, and help identify the precise mechanisms by which any child, or group of children, are disadvantaged.

Welfare systems for children must be able to recognise and respond effectively to complexity.

As a society we must become more informed and sophisticated both in recognising value conflicts, and in resolving them in ways that are child focussed and promote equity.

This paper is based on a presentation first given to the Annual Conference of the European Forum of Child Welfare, Limassol, May 2001.

Acknowledgements: to Caroline Willow, Children's Rights Alliance for England for Table 18.1 and for the quote cited in reference 35; to all the colleagues and masters students over the years who have contributed to my understanding and thinking in this area.

References

[1] Macpherson, W. (1999), *The Stephen Lawrence Inquiry* Volume 1, 46.25. <www.archive. official-documents.co.uk/document/cm42/4262/sli-46.htm> (accessed 27/03/03).

[2] <http://www.goodhotelguide.com/index.html> (accesssed October 2005).

[3] James A. 1993, *Childhood identities: self and social relationships in the experience of the child.* Edinburgh University Press, Edinburgh.

[4] Armstrong, G. *An account of the diseases most incident to children, from birth to the age of puberty, with a successful method of treating them.* 3rd edition, London: T Cadwell, 1783, *cited in* Dunn, P. M. 2002, George Armstrong MD (1719–1789) and his dispensary for the infant poor. *Arch Dis Child* vol. 87(3)**:** F228–31.

[5] Webb, E., Naish, J., MacFarlane, A. (1996), 'Planning and commissioning of health services for children and young people.' *Journal of Public Health Medicine* vol. 18(2), pp. 217–220.

[6] Viner, R.M., Keane, M. (1998), *Youth matters: evidence-based best practice for the care of young people in hospital.* Caring for Children in the Health Services, London.

[7] NCB 2000. *Improving children 's health. A survey of 1999–2000 health improvement programmes.* London: NSPCC, Children's Society, National Children's Bureau, 2000.

[8] Aynsley-Green, A., Barker, M., Burr, S., et al. (2000), 'Who is speaking for children and adolescents and for their health at the policy level?' *BMJ* vol. 321, pp. 229–32.

[9] Smyth, R.L. (2001), 'Research with children' *BMJ* vol. 322, 1377–78.

[10] AHCPR Policy on the Inclusion of Children in Health Services Research. *NIH Guide*, 1997; 26(15). Agency for Health Care Policy and Research. <http://www.ahcpr.gov/fund/ nih5997.htm> (accessed Feb 2003).

[11] Conroy, S., Choonara, I., Impicciatore, P., et al. (2000), 'Survey of unlicensed and off label drug use in paediatric wards in European countries' *BMJ* vol. 320, pp. 79–82.

[12] Stephenson, T. (2002), 'New medicines for children; who is protecting the rights of the child?' *Curr Paediatr* vol. 12, pp. 331–35.

[13] Sutcliffe, A. (2003), 'Testing new pharmaceutical products in children' *BMJ* vol. 326, pp. 64–5.

[14] BMA *Consents rights and choices in healthcare for children and young people* BMA 2000 London (ISBN 0 7279 1228 3).

[15] Brook, G. (1997), *Help me make choices too! Developing and using a framework to help children, with their families, to contribute to decisions about treatment.* Cascade; Issue 26. Action for Sick Children.

[16] Brook, G. (2000), 'Children's competence to consent; A framework for practice.' *Paediatric Nursing* vol. 12(5), pp. 31–5.

[17] DfES. *Core Principles for Involvement of Children and Young People* – Children and Young People's Unit, DFES 2001.

[18] NSPCC. *Two-Way Street Training Video and Handbook about Communicating with Disabled Children and Young People*. NSPCC. London 2001.

[19] Sloper, P., Lightfoot, J. (2003), 'Involving disabled and chronically ill children and young people in health service development.' *Child: Care, health and Development* vol. 29, pp. 15–20.

[20] Hart R. *Children's participation form tokenism to citizenship*. Florence 1992. UNICEF Innocenti Research Centre.

[21] Young, B., Dixon-Woods, M., Windridge, K.C., Heney, D. (2003), 'Managing communication with young people who have a potentially life threatening chronic illness: qualitative study of patients and parents' *BMJ*, vol. 326, pp. 305–10.

[22] Walker, N.E., Doyon, T. (2001), 'Fairness and reasonableness of the child's decision: a proposed standard for children's participation in medical decision making.' *Behav Sci Law* vol. 19(5–6), pp. 611–36.

[23] Emilio, J., Sanz, E.J. (200), 'Concordance and children's use of medicines.' *BMJ*, vol, 327, pp. 858–60.

[24] Pridmore, P., Stephens, D. (2000), *Children as Partners for Health: A Critical Review of the Child-to-Child Approach* Zed Books, London.

[25] Moffit, T.E., Caspi, A. (2001), 'Childhood predictors differentiate life-course persistent and adolescence-limited antisocial pathways among males and females.' *Development & Psychopathology* vol. 13(2), pp. 355–75.

[26] Roberts, I., Coggan, C. (1994), 'Blaming children for child pedestrian injuries' *Soc. Sci. Med.* Vol. 38(5), pp. 749–53.

[27] Attorney-General's Reference No. 13 of 1993 (Karl Justin Gambrill) (1994) 15: Cr. App. R. (S.) 292 CA (Crim Div).

[28] Prose, F. (2003), *The lives of the muses: nine women and the artists they inspired*. Aurum *cited in* Hughes, K. *Pas de deux*. Guardian Review 8/11/03. p. 15.

[29] Watt, G.C.M. (1998), 'Not only scientists, but also responsible citizens.' *J R Coll Phys Lond* vol. 32, pp. 460–65.

[30] UNICEF, 'Child Poverty in Rich Countries, 2005', *Innocenti Report Card* No.6. UNICEF Innocenti Research Centre, Florence. © The United Nations Children's Fund.

[31] Spencer, N. (2000), *Poverty and Child Health*. (2nd edition) Radford Medical Press, Oxford.

[32] Moffit, T.E., Harrington, H.L. (1994), 'Delinquency across development: The natural history of antisocial behaviour in the Dunedin multidisciplinary health and development study.' in W. Stanton and P. A. Silva (eds.) *The Dunedin study: from birth to adulthood*. Oxford University Press, Oxford.

[33] Farrington, D.P. (1995), 'The development of offending and anti-social behaviour from childhood: key findings from the Cambridge study in delinquent development.' *J Child Psychol Psychiatry* vol. 36, pp. 929–64.

[34] Waterhouse. *Lost in Care – Report of the Tribunal of Inquiry into the Abuse of Children in Care in the Former County Council Areas of Gwynedd and Clwyd since 1974*. Part VI: 29.30. London. The Stationery Office, 2000.
also at <http://www.doh.gov.uk/lostincare/20131.htm> (accessed 27/3/03).

[35] Morrison, B. (1998), *As if*. Granta. London.

[36] Mandela, N. (1995), *Long Walk to Freedom*. Abacus.

[37] Field, N. (2003), 'Education as endless labour' in H. Montgomery, R. Burr, M. Woodhead (eds.) *Changing childhoods: local and global*. Chapter 1, reading A; pp. 35–7. Open University/Wiley, Haddington, UK.

[38] ONS 2001 Permanent school exclusions by ethnic group: Social Focus in Brief: Ethnicity <http://www.statistics.gov.uk/STATBASE/ssdataset.asp?vlnk=6220&More=Y> (accessed 7/11/03).

[39] Khanna, R., Kumar, A., Vaghela, J.F., Sreenivas, V. and Puliyel, J.M. (2003), 'Commmmunity based retrospective study of sex in infant mortality in India.' *BMJ* vol. 327, pp. 126–30.

[40] MacDonald, R. (2003), 'Childcare for working parents' *(Website of the week). BMJ* vol. 326, p. 170.

[41] Leach, P. (1995), *Children First* Random House, London.

[42] Modood, T., Berthoud, R. (1997), *Ethnic Minorities in Britain: diversity and disadvantage*. Policy Studies Institute, London.

[43] DfES. Children looked after by Local Authorities Year Ending 31 March 2004 Volume 1: commentary and National Tables. HMSO 2005 also at <http://www.dfes.gov.uk/rsgateway/DB/VOL/v000569/vweb01-2005_1.pdf> (accessed Oct 2005).

[44] Webb, E. (2000), 'Health care for ethnic minorities.' *Current Pediatrics* vol. 10, pp. 184–90.

[45] Webb, E., Maddocks, A., Bongilli, J. (2002), 'Effectively protecting Black and minority ethnic children from harm: overcoming barriers to the child protection process.' *Child Abuse Review* vol. 11, pp. 394–410.

[46] Webb, E., Shankleman, J., Evans, M.R., Brooks, R. (2001), 'The health of children in refuges for women victims of domestic violence: Cross sectional descriptive survey' *BMJ* vol. 323, pp. 210–13.

[47] Tischler, V., Vostanis, P., Bellerby, T., Cumella, S. (2002), 'Evaluation of a mental health outreach service for homeless families' *Arch. Dis. Child* vol. 86, pp. 158–163.

[48] Wilson, J. (2000), *The Illustrated Mum*. Corgi, London.

[49] Owers, M., Brandon, M., and Black, J. (1999), *A Study of Part 8 Reviews Reports for the Welsh Office*. Centre for Research on the Child and Family, University of East Anglia, Norwich.

[50] Bridge Child Care Consultancy Services. (1991), *Sukina: An evaluation report of the circumstances leading to her death*. The Bridge, London.

[51] The Victoria Climbie Inquiry: report of an inquiry by Lord Laming London 2003: HMSO. Also at <http://www.victoria-climbie-inquiry.org.uk/finreport/finreport.htm> (accessed October 2005).

[52] Chand, A. (2000), 'The over-representation of Black children in the child protection system: possible causes, consequences and solutions.' *Child and Family Social Work* vol. 5, 67–77.

[53] Webb, E., Hartley, B. (1994), 'Female genital mutilation: a dilemma in child protection.' *Archives of Diseases in Childhood* vol. 70, pp. 441–4.

[54] Wynne, J. (1994), 'Female genital mutilation: a dilemma in child protection' (Commentary) *Archives of Diseases in Childhood* vol. 70, pp. 444–5.

[55] Webb, E. (2002), 'Health services: who are the best advocates for children?' *Archives of Disease in Childhood* vol. 87, pp. 175–77.

Chapter 19

Building Resilience:
Helping Vulnerable Children Cope

Tony Newman

On balance, data suggest that only about one third of any population of 'at-risk' children experiences a negative outcome … Two thirds appear to survive risk experiences without major developmental disruptions[1].

What is Resilience and Why is the Concept Important?

The concept of resilience is becoming more widely understood and increasingly comprises part of statutory guidance for child care professionals[2,3]. Unfortunately, while we now have a better understanding of the pathways that help build resilience through the lifecycle, we still lack a clear framework in which to develop effective strategies. We are programmed to notice abnormality before normality, deficits before assets and maladaptive before adaptive behaviour. Our tendency to focus on what is going wrong, rather than what is going right, leads inevitably to a pre-occupation with children who have problems, rather than children who have adapted successfully. A major lesson that we have learnt over the past half century is that child development is an interactive process, not a series of discrete stages in which children may become fixed, or to which they may regress. Early experiences do carry, in relation to later ones, more weight in determining developmental pathways, but only up to a point. A wealth of evidence from longitudinal studies indicates that while life chances are diminished by multiple adversities, children – and indeed adults – can recover if exposed to different circumstances, or are offered different options.[4] It has been observed for many years in the study of child development that adverse life events have contributed to psychiatric disorders in some children while others, faced with identical precipitating factors, have emerged unscathed.[5] The study of resilience exhorts us to explore ways in which we can learn from children who have the knack, as Robert Louis Stevenson remarked, 'of playing a poor hand well'.[6]

Resilience is a quality which, whether applied to materials, organisations, ideas or people, indicates a capacity to resist stress, cope with adverse conditions, and make the functional adaptations required when recovering from severe difficulties.[7] Three broad types of resilience tend to be described. The first type is represented by children who succeed, or do not succumb to adversities, in spite of their high risk status, for example low birth weight babies. The second type concerns children who exhibit maturity and coping strategies in situations of chronic stress, such as children of drug using or alcoholic parents. Thirdly, resilience may be exhibited by children who have suffered extreme trauma, for example through disasters, sudden loss of a close relative or abuse, and who have recovered and prospered. Resilience appears to be a dynamic rather than a fixed attribute, having the capacity to emerge in later life after earlier problematic periods.[8] Strategies which promote resilience reject a model preoccupied with pathology, damage, harm and the reinforcement of victimhood, and work towards a model based on strengths, challenges, adaptation and growth.[9]

There is a broad agreement as to the key features of resilience, which are summarised in Table 19.1.

Table 19.1　Key features of resilience

- Risk and resilience processes are cumulative – the presence of one increases the likelihood that more will emerge.
- If a chain of adversities can be broken, the majority of children can recover from even severe difficulties.
- Transition points in children's lives present both threats and opportunities.
- Managed exposure to risk is necessary if children are to learn coping mechanisms.
- Acute episodes of stress are – usually – less harmful to children than chronic difficulties.
- High self-esteem is important to the promotion of resilience, but it must be earned through the acquisition of socially valued competencies.
- The promotion of resilience involves trade-offs. The goal is effective adult adjustment not necessarily eliminating the legacy of all childhood trauma.

The Future is Unwritten

It is probable that a thing may happen contrary to probability.[10]

Despite our increased capacity to use large data sets to suggest correlations of varying strength between current adversities and future outcomes, our ability to predict individual destinations remains finite. Retrospective studies that attempt to make links between early events and later outcomes have proved less satisfactory than prospective studies, which have often failed to find the same strength of predictive association.[11,12] Data from the UK National Child Development Study (NCDS) indicate that half of all children who suffer from emotional and behavioural disorders at any time recover.[13] Even when confronted with 'the most severe stressors and the most glaring adversities', less than half of all children typically fail to pull through.[14] Put simply, if we had to rely on retrospective knowledge only, childhood would seem a more dangerous a place than it really is.

Processes which tend to promote resilience are usually described as being generated in the dimensions of the child, their family and the environment in which they live, as shown in Table 19.2.

The experience of stress in childhood may make individuals more resistant, or more vulnerable, to later psychosocial hazards.[15] Adversities that are accompanied by adaptation, mastery and the learning of new skills appear to equip children with an emotional disposition which renders them able to cope better with future problems. Early stress appears to programme responses at a hormonal level, with the nature of the response depending on whether or not the organism is capable of effective adaptation. Benefits have been reported by people who have experienced a

Table 19. 2   Processes associated with the promotion of resilience

The Child	The Family	The Environment
An easy temperament, active and good-natured	Warm, supportive parents	Supportive extended family
Female prior to, and male during adolescence	Good parent–child relationships	Successful school experiences
Age – younger or older depending on the adversity	Parental harmony	Valued social role such as a job, volunteering or helping neighbours
A higher IQ, or an aptitude for a particular skill	A valued social role in household, such as helping siblings or doing household chores	A close relationship with unrelated mentor
Good social skills with peers and adults	Where parental disharmony is present, a close relationship with either mother or father	Membership of religious or faith community
Personal awareness of strengths and limitations		Extra-curricular activities
Feelings of empathy for others		
Internal locus of control – a belief that one's efforts can make a difference		
A sense of humour		
Attractiveness to others		

wide range of adversities; their restorative strength appears to depend on the extent
to which the experience can be perceived as an opportunity for growth.[16] Where
stressors are excessive, or maternal attachment is damaged, the stress experience is
less likely to be followed by recovery, learning and growth. Where stressors are of a
manageable degree of intensity, caregivers are responsive and the child is comforted
or rewarded, the result is likely to be positive adaptation, as illustrated in Figure
19.1.

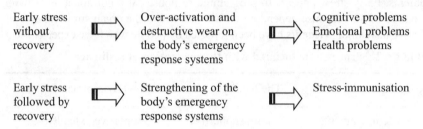

Figure 19.1   Risk and recovery pathways[17]

The Early Years

Protective processes have a greater impact on individuals and groups who are at
high risk; the well-attested effectiveness of early interventions makes the pre-school
years, especially the home–school transition, a prime site for resilience promoting
strategies,[18] as illustrated in Table 19.3.

Table 19.3   Processes promoting resilience in the early years

In the ante-natal period:
➔   Adequate maternal nutrition throughout pregnancy[19]
➔   Avoidance of maternal and passive smoking[20]
➔   Moderate maternal alcohol consumption[21]
➔   Maternal and child MMR vaccination[22]
➔   Social support to mothers from partners, family and external networks[23]
➔   Interventions to prevent domestic violence[24]
During infancy:
➔   Adequate parental income[25]
➔   Social support to moderate peri-natal stress[26]
➔   Breast feeding to three or preferably six months[27]
➔   Care from male partners[28]
During the pre-school period:
➔   Safe play areas and provision of learning materials[29]
➔   High quality pre-school day care[30]
➔   Links with other parents, the broader community and faith groups[31]
➔   Availability of alternative caregivers[32]

The Middle Years

School entry makes increasingly complex cognitive, emotional and inter-personal demands from children. For children facing multiple adversities, the best defence is a network of resilience promoting processes. Table 19.4 illustrates some effective strategies.

Table 19.4   Processes promoting resilience in the middle years

---

→   Services that are sufficiently flexible to accommodate a range of cultural and community specific behaviours[33]

→   Strategies that help children vulnerable to being 'left-out' develop social networks[34]

→   Creation and maintenance of home–school links for at-risk children and their families which can promote parental confidence and engagement[35]

→   The development of skills, opportunities for independence and mastery of tasks[36]

→   Structured routines, and a perception by the child that praise and sanctions are being administered fairly[37]

→   In abusive settings, the opportunity to maintain or develop attachments to the non-abusive parent, other family member or failing these, a reliable unrelated adult; maintenance of family routines and rituals[38]

→   In situations of marital discord, attachment to one parent, moderation of parental disharmony and opportunities to play a positive role in the family[39]

→   Help to resolve minor but chronic stressors as well as acute adversities[40]

→   Inclusive philosophies that promote positive motivational styles, problem-solving coping and discourage 'learned helplessness'[41]

Adolescence and Early Adulthood

Early adolescence is dominated by puberty, middle adolescence the growth of a distinct youth identity, late adolescence the transition to adulthood. These developmental phases involve biological, cognitive, social and personal identity transitions; these are shaped by earlier experiences and by discontinuities and unexpected turning points, as the individual matures and begins to make personal choices.[42] Table 19.5 shows a range of strategies, environments and social attitudes can help young people navigate successfully through this demanding chronological period.

Table 19.5   Processes promoting resilience in adolescence and early adulthood

→   Programmes that encourage emotional literacy[43]
→   Opportunities to develop valued skills through broad based curricula[44]
→   Programmes which encourage peer cooperation and collaboration[45]
→   Connections with cultural or faith communities[46]
→   Where parental separation occurs, opportunity to maintain familiar social rituals[47]
→   Support by fathers for both male and female children[48]
→   Emphasis in schools on educational achievements for vulnerable children[49]
→   Improve locus of control through valued household tasks or roles, part-time work outside the home, or volunteering[50]
→   Supportive social networks, prevention of social isolation, and registration with GP and dentist when living away from home for first time[51]
→   Opportunities to enter and be supported in the job market, and help to consider alternative options[52]
→   In early adulthood, opportunities to build supportive long-term relationships[53]

While we are only concerned with resilience promoting processes into early adulthood, it is important to note that positive transitions can take place at any time in the life cycle, should circumstances conspire to offer sufficient opportunities. Human agency is often a missing factor when life course trajectories are discussed in the academic literature. The longest ever follow-up study of young offenders, which reported on their circumstances some fifty years later, highlights the crucial role of structural turning points.[54] Drawing on the notion of 'side-bets',[55] small social investments of no particular magnitude individually, the study suggests that delinquent young – and not so young – men may choose different pathways because the accumulative importance of the 'side-bets' they have made is too great in total to contemplate losing. Men who 'made good' became embedded – often without deliberate choice – in structures, situations, and in relationships which offered nurturing and informal social control. The most powerful factor by far was the impact of marriage, or more precisely the moderating effects of a long-term commitment, both with respect to desistance from crime, but also in terms of emotional and physical health gains.

One Size Does Not Fit All

While active strategies to promote resilience have the support of a robust evidence base, it is crucial that we recognise the heterogeneity of children, problems and solutions. Emotional literacy may be a protective factor for people in many contexts;[56] for others, stoicism may also be associated with adaptive behaviour.[57] The intimate involvement of children and young people in decision making or their treatment plans may be a powerful resilience promoting process in some situations, in others, such involvement may have no bearing on the outcomes sought, or may be harmful.[58] We may even find some resilience promoting processes distasteful; for example, the stabilisation in male suicide rates from the early 1990s has been speculatively associated with the rise of 'lad' culture, and the accompanying opportunities for young males to strengthen their self-esteem.[59] Resilience may also be in the eye of the beholder; a withdrawn and passive young person may be seen as resilient by a youth justice worker and in need of treatment by a child psychiatrist.[60] Effective resilience promoting processes may sometimes be unpleasant for the participants, and utilise methods which may not have universal approval (for example, wilderness programmes for young offenders[61]). Maltreated children may develop strategies such as withdrawal and avoidance to minimise the impact of abuse, which may appear to indicate psychopathology, but may also constitute effective adaptation to unbearable circumstances.[62] More broadly, we may wish to cast a critical eye on what has been described as a 'corporate' approach to mental health promotion, where positive adjustment means producing, consuming, succeeding and avoiding risk-taking behaviours, and more radical or alternative lifestyle options are associated with deviance or psychopathology.[63] When considering programmes and interventions, we must be careful not simply to choose those that conform to our personal beliefs of what processes and outcomes are most desirable for children and young people. We need to take note of which processes – up-, middle- and down-stream – have the strongest evidence base, and what children and young people want for themselves. Consensual approaches are not always easy; for example, while school-based mental health support attracts strong support from professionals,[64] children themselves remain wary of on-site psychotherapy services.[65]

We have described the processes associated with the promotion of resilience in the dimensions of the child, their family and their community. Is there one domain that can be legitimately highlighted as an arena where the maximum leverage can be applied to the promotion of children's well-being? A recent authoritative review suggested that there is. While interventions that help build social capital, and which support the child directly are of great importance, the weight of evidence suggests that, overall, the most crucial arena is the parent–child relationship:

> For most children, parents represent not only the earliest but also the single most constant proximal socializing influences. Peer affiliations inevitably shift over time, as do teachers in schools and wider community influences. Thus, from the standpoint of promoting continuity of the protective factors that interventions bring into the lives of at-risk children, it is entirely logical to emphasize work with parents.[66]

Acuity v. Chronicity

Adults have often focused too much on acute, and too little on chronic stressors. In listing 'risk' factors that affect highly vulnerable children, it is easy to diminish the more common adversities that affect very large numbers of children. Most children may not be affected by the kinds of risks that make headlines in newspapers, but may be exposed to bullying, persistent parental conflict, or being 'left-out' in school. The latter, for example, is not just one of the main sources of unhappiness reported by children, especially in the middle years; it is also associated with damaged self-esteem and poorer educational outcomes.[67] In focusing on the most vulnerable groups, we need to keep in mind the impact on emotional well-being made by these less striking but no less distressing processes. Similarly, we need to recognise that while the prevalence of emotional and behavioural disorders is substantially greater in certain seriously disadvantaged social groups, the total burden of poor mental health for both children and adults lies predominantly *outside* these groups. Hence, targeted strategies, whatever their degree of effectiveness, can never hope to reach more than a small minority of children, presenting a compelling argument for a combination of focused and population level approaches.[68]

Conclusion

> What distinguishes the high-risk child from other children is not so much exposure to a special risk factor but rather a life history characterized by multiple familial disadvantages that span social and economic disadvantages; impaired parenting; a neglectful and abusive home environment; marital conflict; family instability; family violence; and high exposure to adverse family life events…[69]

Whether parents and politicians like it or not, many young people can – and will – smoke, drink, use illicit drugs, have sex, not get enough sleep or exercise, fail to eat their five portions of fruit and vegetables per day, visit dubious internet chat rooms yet still survive and grow into well-adjusted, emotionally healthy members of society. In many cases adolescence 'deviance' has to be lived with, not treated.[70] It is all too easy in a competitive welfare climate to put excessive emphasis on a particular risk factor without considering the unintended consequences of our actions, such as circumscribing children's lives and generating fear when we should be offering opportunities for growth and an optimistic vision of the future. We should at least take note of the increasing disquiet which has been expressed in a number of quarters at the alleged contemporary tendency to pathologize normative types of adversity. The boundaries between what is, and what is not, trauma, abuse and illness have, it is argued, become increasingly blurred.[71,72] It has been suggested that a culture of victimhood has developed which has promoted the construction of identities around the experience of stressful events.[73,74] These social pressures tend to inflate prevalence claims which may be supported uncritically by special interest groups. 'Abnormality' is defined statistically as being more than two standard deviations from the mean on a given measurement, which may be of height, weight, intelligence or psychological disposition. If we run enough tests of different kinds, we can label most of any population 'abnormal' on one measurement or another. A diagnostic label brings both potential harm and potential benefits. Benefits include the possibility of effective treatment, recognition and emotional support. On the other hand, a label may also bring stigma, social exclusion and the unnecessary medicalization of a social problem.[75]

In conclusion, we have suggested the dominant risk processes which jeopardise children's health and well-being are relationship associated; relationships with parents and carers, friends, and neighbourhoods. What young people worry about, as opposed to the risks they face, remains fairly constant; the three top ones are 'family', 'the way you look', 'friends' (for girls) and 'drugs' (for boys).[76] Supportive parenting (and supported parents), peers at school and at home that children look forward to, rather than fear meeting, and neighbourhoods that offer opportunities for challenge and learning, where children's movements are not unnecessarily restricted are the paramount factors affecting the well-being of the large majority of the UK's 12 million children. This is no reason to ignore the wider range of issues that affect children's well-being or the many specific issues that affect children in particular circumstances, but it is also necessary to focus our energies on what matters to children, as well as what works for them.

References

1   Kirby, L. and Fraser, M. (1998), 'Risk and resilience in childhood.' In M. Fraser (ed) *Risk and Resilience in Childhood: an ecological perspective*. Washington DC: NASW Press, p. 14.

2   Department of Health (2000), *Framework for the Assessment of Children in Need*. London: The Stationery Office.

3   Department for Education and Skills (2001), *Promoting children's mental health within early years and school settings*. Guidance. Department for Education and Skills, London.

4   Clarke, A. and Clarke A. (2003), *Human Resilience: a fifty year quest*. Jessica Kingsley, London.

5   Garmezy, N. and Rutter, M. (1983), *Stress, Coping and Development in Children*. McGraw-Hill, New York.

6   Katz, M. (1997*), On playing a poor hand well: insights from the lives of those who have overcome childhood risks and adversities*. Norton, London, p. xi.

7   Coutu, D.L. (2002), 'How resilience works.' *Harvard Business Review*. May, pp. 46–55.

8   Werner, E. and Smith, R. (1992), *Overcoming the Odds*. Cornell University Press, New York.

9   Greene, R.R. (ed.) (2002), *Resiliency: an integrated approach to practice, policy and research*. NASW Press, Washington DC.

10   From: Aristotle. *Poetics. XXVI* (trans. S.H. Butcher). Downloaded 25.09.05. <www.scholars.nus.edu.sg/resources/poetics/25.html.>

11   Murphy, L. and Moriarty, A. (1976), *Vulnerability, Coping and Growth: from infancy to adolescence*. Yale University Press, New Haven and London.

12   Hardt, J. and Rutter, M. (2004), 'Validity of adult retrospective reports of adverse childhood experiences: review of the evidence.' *Journal of Child Psychology and Psychiatry* vol. 45, 2, pp. 260–73.

[13] Buchanan, A. and Ten Brinke, J. (1998), *'Recovery' from Emotional and Behavioural Problems*. University of Oxford/NHS Executive Anglia and Oxford, Oxford.

[14] Rutter, M. (1985), 'Resilience in the face of adversity: protective factors and resistance to psychiatric disorders.' *British Journal of Psychiatry* vol. 147, pp. 589–611, p. 598.

[15] Rutter, M. (2002), 'Nature, nurture and development: From evangelism through science to policy and action.' *Child Development* vol. 73, pp.1–21.

[16] MacMillen, J.C. 1999, Better for it: how people benefit from adversity. *Social Work* vol. 44, 5, pp. 455–67.

[17] Adapted from: Bugental, D.B. (2003), *Thriving in the Face of Childhood Adversity*. Psychology Press, Hove, pp. 40 & 45.

[18] Reynolds, A.J. and Ou, S.R. (200), 'Promoting resilience through early childhood intervention.' in S.S. Luthar and L.B. Zelazo (eds.) *Vulnerability and Resilience: adaptation in the context of childhood adversities*. Cambridge University Press, Cambridge.

[19] Mathews, F., Yudkin, P. and Neil, A. (1999), 'Influence of maternal nutrition on outcome of pregnancy: prospective cohort study.' *British Medical Journal* vol. 319, pp. 339–43.

[20] Spencer, N. and Logan, S. (1998), 'Smoking, socio-economic status and child health outcomes: the ongoing controversy' in N. Spencer (ed.) *Progress in Community Health 2*, Churchill Livingstone, Edinburgh.

[21] Royal College of Physicians (1995), *Alcohol and the Young*. RCP, London.

[22] Hall, A. and Peckham, S. (1997), 'Infections in childhood and pregnancy as a cause of adult disease: methods and examples.' In M. Marmont and M. Wadsworth (eds.) Fetal and early childhood environment: long-term health implications. *British Medical Bulletin* vol. 53, 1, pp. 10–23.

[23] Stewart-Brown, S. (1998), 'Emotional wellbeing and its relationship to health.' *British Medical Journal* vol. 317, pp. 1608–9.

[24] British Medical Association (1998), *Domestic violence: a health care issue?* BMA, London.

[25] Benzeval, M., Judge, K.,Johnson, P. and Taylor, J. (1999), 'Relationships between health, income and poverty over time: an overview using BHPS and NCDS data.' in J. Bradshaw and R. Sainsbury (eds.) *Experiencing Poverty*, vol. 3. Ashgate, Aldershot.

[26] Olds, D.L. (1997), 'The prenatal/early infancy project: fifteen years later.' in G.W. Albee and T.P. Gullotta (eds.) *Primary Prevention Works*. Sage, London.

[27] Morrow-Tlucak, M., Haude, R. and Ernhart, C. (1988), 'Breast-feeding and cognitive development in the first two years of life.' *Social Science and Medicine* vol. 26, pp. 635–39.

[28] Cox, M., Owen, T., Henderson, V. and Margand, N. (1992), 'Prediction of infant-father and infant-mother interaction.' *Developmental Psychology* vol. 28, pp. 47483.

[29] Roberts, H., Smith, S. and Bryce, C. (1995), *Children at Risk? Safety as a social value*. Open University Press, Buckingham.

[30] Zoritch, B., Roberts, I. and Oakley A. (1998), 'The health and welfare effects of daycare: a systematic review of randomised controlled trials. *Social Science and Medicine* vol. 47, pp. 317–27.

[31] Runyan, D., Hunter, W., Socolar, R., Amaya-Jackson, L., English., D., Landsverk., J., Dubowitz, H., Browne, D., Bangdiwala, S. and Mathew, R. (1998), 'Children who prosper in unfavourable environments: the relationship to social capital.' *Paediatrics* vol.101, (1, Pt. 1), pp, 12–18.

32 O'Grady, D. and Metz, J. (1987), 'Resilience in children at high risk for psychological disorder.' *Journal of Paediatric Psychology* vol.12, 1, pp. 3–23.

33 Walker, S. (2002), 'Culturally competent protection of children's mental health.' *Child Abuse Review* vol. 11, pp. 380–93.

34 Asher, S.R., Parkhurst, J., Hymel, S. and Williams, G. (1990), 'Peer rejection and loneliness in childhood.' in S.R. Asher and J.D. Cole (eds.) *Peer Rejection in Childhood.* Cambridge University Press, New York.

35 Seal, H. (1997), *School Start Evaluation Report.* Wiltshire SSD, Trowbridge and Barnardo's.

36 Compas, B. (1987), 'Coping with stress during childhood and adolescence.' *Psychological Bulletin* vol.101, 3, pp. 393–403.

37 Webster-Stratton, C. (1993), *The Incredible Years.* Umbrella Press, Toronto.

38 Sagy, S. and Dotan, N. (2001), 'Coping resources of maltreated children in the family: a salutogenic approach.' *Child Abuse and Neglect* vol. 25, pp. 1463–80.

39 Hetherington, E.M. (2003), 'Social support and the adjustment of children in divorced and remarried families.' *Childhood* vol. 10, 2, pp. 217–36.

40 Smith, C. and Carlson, B.(1997), 'Stress, coping and resilience in children and youth.' *Social Service Review* vol. 71, 2, pp. 231–56.

41 Seligman, M. (1998), *Learned Optimism.* Pocket Books, New York.

42 McClure, M. (2000), 'Adolescence – the transition from childhood to adulthood.' in P. Reder, M. McClure and A. Jolley (eds.) *Family Matters: interfaces between child and adult mental health.* Routledge, London.

43 Steiner, C. (1997), *Achieving Emotional Literacy.* Bloomsbury, London.

44 Reynolds, D. (1997), *School effectiveness.* Highlight No. 157: National Children's Bureau/Barnardo's.

45 Brown, J., D'Emidio-Caston, M. and Benard, B. (2000), *Resilience Education.* Corwin Press/Sage, Thousand Oaks, CA.

46 Schapman, A.M. and Inderbitzen-Nolan, H.M. (2002), 'The role of religious behaviour in adolescent depressive and anxious symptomatology.' *Journal of Adolescence* vol. 25, pp. 631–43.

47 Hetherington, E.M. and Stanley-Hagan, M. (1999), 'The adjustment of children with divorced parents: a risk and resiliency perspective.' *Journal of Child Psychology and Psychiatry* vol. 40, 1, pp. 129–40.

48 Flouri, E. and Buchanan, A. (2003), 'The role of father involvement and mother involvement in adolescents' psychological well-being.' *British Journal of Social Work* vol. 33, pp. 399–406.

49 Jackson, S. and Martin, P. (1998), 'Surviving the care system: education and resilience.' *Journal of Adolescence* vol. 21, pp. 569–83.

50 Mortimer, J., Finch, M., Ryu, S., Shanahan, M. and Call, K. (1996), 'The effects of work intensity on adolescent mental health, achievement and behavioural adjustment: new evidence from a prospective study.' *Child Developmen.* Vol. 67, pp. 143–61.

51 Stein, M. (1997), 'What works in Leaving Care?' Barnardo's, Ilford.

52 Winfield, L. (2001), NCREL Monograph: Developing resilience in urban youth. Downloaded 25 March 2004. <www.ncrel.org/sdrs/areas/issues/educatrs/leadrshp/le0win.htm>

53 Kiecolt-Glaser, J.K. and Newton, T.L. (2001), 'Marriage and health: his and hers.' *Psychological Bulletin* vol. 127, pp. 472–503.

54 Laub, J.H. and Sampson, R.J. (2003), *Shared Beginnings, Divergent Lives: delinquent boys to age 70.* Harvard University Press, Cambridge, MA, p. 279.

55 Becker, H.S. (1960), 'Notes on the concept of commitment.' *American Journal of Sociology* vol. 66, pp. 32–40.

56 Goleman, D. (1996), *Emotional Intelligence.* Bloomsbury, London.

57 Moynihan, C., Bliss, J.M., Davidson, J., Burchell, L. and Horwich, A. (1998), 'Evaluation of adjuvant psychological therapy in patients with testicular cancer: randomised controlled trial.' *British Medical Journal* vol. 316, pp. 429–35.

58 Phipps, S. and Srivastava, D. (1997), 'Repressive adaption in children with cancer: it may be better not to know.' *Journal of Pediatrics* vol. 130, pp. 257–65.

59 West, P. and Sweeting, H. (200), 'Fifteen, female and stressed: changing patterns of psychological distress over time' *Journal of Child Psychology and Psychiatry* vol. 44, 3, pp. 399–411.

60 Rayner, M. and Montague, M. (2000), *Resilient children and young people: a discussion paper based on a review of the international research literature.* Policy and Practice Research Unit, Children's Welfare Association of Australia, Melbourne, Australia.

61 Wilson, S.J. and Lipsey, M.W. (1999), 'Wilderness challenge programmes for delinquent youth: a meta-analysis of outcome evaluations.' *Evaluation and Programme Planning* vol. 23, pp. 1–12 (available at: <www.vanderbilt.edu/CERM>).

62 Henry, D. (1999), 'Resilience in maltreated children: implications for special needs adoption.' *Child Welfare* LXXVIII, 5, pp. 519–40.

63 Weare, K. (2002), 'Work with young people is leading the way in the new paradigm for mental health.' *International Journal of Mental Health Promotion* vol. 4, 4, pp. 55–8.

64 Baruch, G. (2001), 'Mental health services in schools: the challenge of locating a psychotherapy service for troubled adolescent pupils in mainstream and special schools.' *Journal of Adolescence* vol. 24, pp. 549–70.

65 Roose, G.A. and John, A.M. (2003), 'A focus group investigation into young children's understanding of mental health and their views on appropriate services for their age group.' *Child: Care, Health and Development* vol. 29, 6, pp. 545–50.

66 Luthar, S.S. and Zelazo, L.B (2003), 'Research on resilience: an integrative review.' in S.S. Luthar and L.B. Zelazo (eds,) *Vulnerability and Resilience: adaptation in the context of childhood adversities.* Cambridge University Press, Cambridge, p. 533.

67 Arthur, L. (2004), 'Looking out for each other: children helping left-out children.' *Support for Learning* vol.19, 1, pp. 5–12.

68 Stewart-Brown, S. (1998), 'Public health implications of childhood behaviour problems and parenting programmes.' in A. Buchanan and B. Hudson (eds.) *Parenting, Schooling and Children's Behaviour* Ashgate, Aldershot.

69 Fergusson, D.M. and Horwood, L.J. (2003), 'Resilience to childhood adversity: results of a 21-year study.' in S.S. Luthar and L.B. Zelazo (eds.) *Vulnerability and Resilience: adaptation in the context of childhood adversities.* Cambridge University Press, Cambridge, p. 130.

70 Hurry, J., Aggleton, P. and Warwick, I. (2000), 'Introduction.' in P. Aggleton, J. Hurry and I. Warwick (eds.) *Young People and Mental Health.* John Wiley and Sons, Chichester.

71 Freeman-Longo, R.E. (1996), 'Feel good legislation: prevention or calamity.' *Child Abuse and Neglect* vol, 20, pp. 95–101.

72 Dineen, T. (2000), 'Manufacturing Victims: what the psychology industry is doing to people.' Constable, London.

73   Showalter, E. (1998), *Hystories: Hysterical Epidemics and Modern Culture*. Picador, London.

74   Furedi, F. (1998), 'Culture of Fear: risk-taking and the morality of low expectation.' Cassell, London.

75   Goodman, R. (1997), 'Child mental health: who is responsible?' *British Medical Journal* vol. 414, pp. 813–7.

76   Balding, J., Regis, D. and Wise, A. (1998), *No worries? Young people and mental health*. Schools Health Education Unit, Exeter.

PART III
BUSINESS AND
PROFESSIONAL ETHICS

Chapter 20

The International Financial War against Terrorism: Myths and Reality

Donato Masciandaro

The terrorism risk has heavily impacted the evolution of the international financial markets and their regulation. Right from 12 September 2001, a crucial query began to circulate with insistence within the world economy, and not just there: what will change for the banks and stock markets of the world after the apocalypse of New York?

Naturally, the initial summations dwelled on the painful observation of the costly tribute paid in human lives and on the unknowns linked to the possible crumbling of trust in the normal course of economic and financial activities.

Meanwhile, however, the world began immediately to question itself, with a longer perspective, on how this would affect a cornerstone of recent developments in the international financial markets: the 'neutrality' of the capital exchanged there.

There is no doubt, in fact, that the increasing fluidity of international financial interchange in recent decades has depended, all other things being equal, on the de facto 'neutrality' attributed to the capital handled in the markets, as far as its origin and final destination are concerned. Capital, in other words, has increasingly tended to have neither nationality, colour or odour: increasingly, it has been 'faceless' capital, moved exclusively by expectations of remuneration.

Nevertheless, in a context where the purpose of the war against terrorism had become a worldwide priority, assuming as an essential strategic objective the dismantling of the forms of financing to fundamentalist groups, it was inevitable that authorities and international public opinion would become extremely sensitive regarding the exact origin and destination of that capital.

The design of financial regulations, national and international, had to accommodate the need to develop policies to prevent and combat the phenomena of terrorism. The financial war on terrorism, which was born of the experience of the international war against drugs and organized crime in progress for at least the past two decades, was instituted on the basis of four fundamental assumptions.

The four postulates clearly emerge from an examination of the documents of the international organizations dedicated to the war on terrorism financing. In May 2002, for example, the OECD Council at Ministerial Level, affirmed that:

The scope for financial crime has widened with the expansion and increased integration of financial markets. Money laundering, terrorism financing and tax crime have to the changed in both nature and dimension. Today the potential for financial abuse can threaten the strategic, political and economic interest of sovereign states. Widespread financial abuse undermines the integrity of the international financial system and raises new challenges for policymakers, financial supervisors and enforcement agencies. In certain jurisdictions such abuse may go so far as to undermine the democratic basis of government itself.

And again:

Poorly regulated financial markets not only open up new opportunities for financial crimes but also threaten the stability of the international financial system. As new technologies reduce the importance of physical proximity to major on–shore financial centres, so a new generation of Offshore Financial Centres (OFCs) has emerged. Remote jurisdictions bereft of natural resources and too isolated to benefit significantly from the global economy have established OFCs characterised by strict bank secrecy, criminal penalties for disclosure of client information and a policy or practice of non–cooperation with regulatory, supervisory and law enforcement agencies of other countries. This new generation of OFCs has succeeded in attracting brass plate banks, anonymous financial companies and asset protection trusts.

Thus based on the analysis of the terrorism financing phenomenon, as summarized by us in the four postulates, that we will describe in the following pages, a global strategy to prevent and combat the phenomenon has been defined in the international forums, based on the identification of 'uncooperative' countries and territories and on the threat of sanctions against them unless they adopt credible policies to bolster their measures against the risks of facilitating the financing of terrorism and the laundering of criminal capital. The fulcrum of the financial war was represented by the policies of blacklisting instituted by various international organizations

Considerable work on the OFCs has been done by the Basle Committee, IOSCO, FATF, UN, OECD, and the G7 Finance Ministers. In 1999 the Financial Stability Forum established an ad hoc Working Group. The Group's Report was submitted on March 2000.

More importantly, in 1989 the G7 established the Financial Action Task Force (FATF). The FATF is an inter-governmental body whose purpose is to establish international standards, and develop and promote policies, both at national and international level, to combat money laundering and the financing of terrorism (FATF 2005). The FATF is currently comprised of 31 member jurisdictions and two regional organisations.

For the first time official 'blacklists' have been formulated including different countries all over the world. Looking at the action by FATF, this OECD-connected organization has now monitored up to 47 countries and listed 23 jurisdictions as Non-Cooperative Countries and Territories (NCCT). In October 2001, the FATF mandate was expanded to include policies to contrast terrorism finance. In June 2003 the FATF revised its Forty Recommendations for combating money laundering and terrorist financing, calling for special attention to business relationships and transactions with persons, including companies and financial institutions, from countries which do not apply the FATF Recommendations. During 2004–2005 the FATF has refined the Eight Special Recommendations on terrorism finance.[1]

The four postulates that represent the cornerstones of the international financial war against terrorism are the following.

First Postulate: Vulnerability to Terrorism Financing Risk – The world network that today represents the banking and financial industry, beyond the specific awareness of the majority of individual intermediaries and professionals who work in it, is the linchpin of the mechanisms that permit the financing of international terrorism.

The banking and financial industry is physiologically vulnerable to the risk of becoming an instrument at the service of terrorist and criminal organizations, because of the accentuated phenomenon of information asymmetries. The banking and financial industry produces and distributes fiduciary services through exchanges in which at least one of the two parties, if for none other than uncertainty surrounding future events, lacks a complete and symmetrical quantity of important information regarding that exchange.

In most instances money laundering is ultimately channelled through financial intermediaries that are unwittingly parties to the final objective of the chain of transactions.

Authorities seek to limit the possibility of these illegal transactions by setting 'due diligence' rules on banks, who ultimately act as agents for governments. The willingness of financial intermediaries to assume a monitoring role will depend on two types of cost: the costs relating to establish a monitoring system and the reputational costs associated with the lifting of bank secrecy.

There is information asymmetry between the regulator and the bank. The difficulty in monitoring the degree of effort spent by banks to report suspicious transactions is compounded by the lack of clearly identifiable indicators of laundering.

The design of effective regulation must therefore consider the role of incentives on behaviour. The intermediaries must find it optimal to perform their function of 'agent' effectively. Given the characteristics of intermediaries as complex organizations and their numerous relationships with various supervisory institutions, the system of rules must exert a positive impact on the resources deemed important by the intermediaries.

The widespread presence of information asymmetries thus makes that industry particularly well suited to the needs of those like terrorist organizations who need to conceal the destination, and often the origin, of certain financial flows, financial flows of a particularly significant amount.

Furthermore, the vulnerability of the banking and financial sector concerns not only, or not so much, the forms of overt and legal intermediation but also the lesser known informal financial network, developed in recent years due in part to the growth of world migration flows. In 2004–2005 the FATF monitored the evolution of money laundering and terrorist financing methods, highlighting the following financial topics: alternative remittance systems; money laundering and human trafficking and illegal immigration; money laundering vulnerabilities in the insurance sector; wire transfers and terrorist financing techniques.

Second Postulate: Equivalence between Terrorism Financing Risk and Criminal Capital Laundering Risk – The mechanisms that facilitate the financing of terrorism are the same that permit the laundering of illicit capital by transnational criminal organizations.

The second postulate seems less robust than the first. On the one hand, the laundering of capital (money laundering) is conceptually different from the financing of terrorism (money dirtying): in the first case, the objective is to transform financial flows of illegal origin into licit funds, while in the second case the purpose is to channel financial flows toward an illegal purpose, whether their origin was legal or not.

From another viewpoint, however, in both situations there is an interest in reducing the probability that the parties and organizations conducting criminal activity will be incriminated. In the case of money laundering, the desire is to reduce the probability that the financial flows originating from criminal activities might lead to the identification of the organizations that derive benefit from those activities. In the case of money dirtying, the intention is to decrease the probability that the identity and structures of the international terrorist associations will be discovered through tracking of the flows of financing.

And we must not forget that investigations have often determined that terrorist organizations finance themselves through the production and trafficking of illegal goods and services, such as drugs and arms, so money dirtying activity tends to overlap that of money laundering.

Thus the mechanisms and channels that permit the financing of terrorism do not perfectly coincide with those for the laundering of capital from organized crime but may overlap them and intermingle with them. On this respect, it is interest to note that in 2005 the FATF started to explore the symbiotic relationship among money laundering, terrorist financing and corruption.

Third Postulate: Offshore as a Catalyst of Terrorism Financing Risk – The mechanisms of financing terrorism and laundering criminal capital can function in a world financial network, because in that network there are 'weak' nodes or 'black holes' represented by offshore financial centres (OFCs).

The theme of the potential vulnerability of the world financial network due to the presence of OFCs was been explored with various methodological approaches.

Firstly, beginning with the financial aspects, we began by observing that the onshore countries, represented by the major industrialized countries, view as vulnerable those countries and territories whose regulations are relatively accommodating compared to their own, in the sense that greater risks exist that money-laundering or terrorism financing transactions can be concealed.

But why do the offshore financial centres possess these lax regulations? We answer the question by applying the latest instruments of economic, institutional and political analysis. The two key terms are a surplus of economic benefits that the OFCs receive by having lax regulations, which forcefully clashes with a deficit of political legitimacy in the directives of the onshore countries and international institutions, as perceived by the OFCs.

Thanks to an empirical analysis,[2] it was demonstrated that the OFCs display relatively uniform structural characteristics, economic and institutional: they are countries and territories of modest wealth, poor in natural resources, with a strong dependence on the income produced by their banking and financial services, devoid of particular problems associated with terrorism risk and organized crime risk. Therefore the laxity of their financial regulation ultimately becomes a case of free lunch for the OFCs: the anticipated benefits of laxity, in terms of increasing the value produced by the financial industry, are evident, while they do not perceive the anticipated costs, represented by greater risks of increasing terrorism and organized crime. Furthermore, the action suggested by the international organizations suffers from a marked lack of legitimacy, in the eyes of jurisdictions that express more or less accentuated and consolidated forms of national sovereignty.

Thus, more than the robustness of the third postulate, which is tautological per se – OFCs are those jurisdictions defined as such by the onshore countries – it is crucial that the analysis casts some light on the economic and political causes that may explain the birth and development – past, present and (alas!) future – of countries with relatively lax financial regulations.

Fourth Postulate: Equivalence of Offshore Centers as a Catalyst of Terrorism Financing Risk and Fiscal Damage Risk – The weak nodes in the network are particularly dangerous because they not only facilitate the financing of terrorism and the laundering of capital criminal but also facilitate unfair fiscal competition among sovereign nations.

The fourth postulate is false. The decision of a few countries and territories to institute highly advantageous taxation policies, in some cases highly aggressive, and the relative determinants do not coincide with those to adopt lax financial policies, although areas of overlapping and partial coincidence do exist. Using a graphic image, the set of fiscal OFCs does not coincide with the set of financial OFCs, although there is an area of intersection. Fiscal competition, if regulated by the principles of transparency and correctness, tends to be different from financial laxity.

On the theoretical level, while a relative consensus exists regarding the potential damage of financial laxity, the same cannot be said for fiscal competition. Various theories exist regarding the possible effects of tax competition. To attempt a summary, we might identify two opposing positions: on the one hand, the advocates of perfect fiscal competition, on the other, the supporters of total tax harmonization.

The supporters of perfect tax competition are those who feel that capital must be completely free to circle the globe, in search of the most advantageous tax regime. The possibility of capital to arbitrate freely among various national regulations becomes the key to an increasingly efficient allocation of resources. In other words, they are proposing the perfect demand of arbitrage: each citizen, in every nation of the world, must be free to choose the tax regime for his own capital. In parallel, each nation must have the possibility of providing a perfect supply of arbitrage, proposing its tax regime to capital throughout the world. The basic idea is that competition will punish the less efficient countries, characterized by harsher tax regimes, and thus reduce the risks of 'country failure', to the advantage of all.

The advocates of tax harmonization, on the other hand, stress that the individual and collective advantages of perfect competition can be exalted only by those who conceal the 'market failures' that characterize the real functioning of the markets, national and international. First, the presence of various forms of transaction costs and information asymmetries make the actual mobility of the individual production factors, and the capacity of choice of the various categories of citizens, highly heterogeneous and variable from country to country, so the demand for arbitrage, if satisfied, might in reality produce allocation inefficiencies and inequalities.

At the same time, the supply of arbitrage and competition among tax regimes must take into account that for each country, especially if it is characterized by a democratic regime, the design of public intervention, and therefore the relative fiscal burden, does not respond solely to the criterion of efficiency but must also consider other public priorities, which may be summarized as equity and sustainability.

Furthermore, the absolute neutrality of capital, in the sense that its origin and destination are irrelevant, can no longer be affirmed, especially since 11 September 2001, so the international objective of safeguarding integrity against the risks of capital contamination by terrorism and organized crime must be taken into account. This is another reason, therefore, for not allowing the debate on tax competition to coincide with that on the war on terrorism and organized crime.

Summing up, do the various analyses developed in these years suggest common guidelines for the design of international rules for the financial war on terrorism? The possible indications, useful on both the microeconomic and macroeconomic levels, revolve around four fundamental words: specificity, information, benefits and legitimacy.

Firstly, the phenomenon of terrorism financing has a specificity of its own, linked to the coexistence of three characteristics: firstly, the transnational, damaging and illegal nature of the destination of the financial flows. Fiscal arbitrage and money–laundering operations are also transnational phenomena. There is a widespread consensus on the damaging nature of financial flows produced by crime. The origin of those flows is illegal, while in fiscal arbitrage, which arises from forms of evasion, neither the origin nor the destination of the funds is illegal, just the decision not to contribute part of the funds to tax revenues. The specificity of financing terrorism must always be borne in mind, since the definition of policies for preventing and combating it, national and international, must not passively follow the schemes of action devised in the past for combating organized crime or tax evasion.

Secondly, it is evident that the more widespread information asymmetries to the detriment of various categories of authorities (sectoral, investigative, inquiring) are in the banking and financial industry, the more developed and effective the financing of international terrorism will be. A necessary, but not sufficient, condition for designing effective rules and enforcement at both the national international levels is the generation and collection of relevant information.

But the production and collection of relevant information – and this is the third point – can never reach satisfactory levels unless it places us in the perspective of providing proper incentives to the various players involved, starting with the individual intermediaries and operators, passing through the authorities and arriving at the countries, be they onshore or offshore. Combating the financing of terrorism must be beneficial at all the various levels that are potentially involved in a rather complex operation of terrorism financing.

The theme of benefits is thus strongly intertwined with that of information. There must be clear separation between the objective of information accessibility in the financial and economic system and the potential collaboration of financial intermediaries, and operators and companies in general, in the generation of useful information.

This difference is fundamental. The first objective is to enable authorities investigating a suspect to collect relevant financial information effectively: this means being able to access information with minimal time and cost, thanks to the availability of the information assets of intermediaries, companies and professionals ('passive collaboration').

A second, more ambitious objective is to activate inverse channels of information from economic agents to the authorities ('active collaboration'). In general, the action of active collaboration involves expected costs to economic agents – in terms of reputation, efficiency, reprisal – that are much higher than the expected benefits, and the path to follow is certainly not that of sanctions, including criminal sanctions, that seem perhaps unjust, undoubtedly ineffective. Rather, to increase the active collaboration from the economic agents involved, the path to take with decision is that of incentives and mutually agreed regulations, especially where sovereign offshore jurisdictions subject to blacklisting are concerned. On this point, the economic and institutional analyses developed in a recent volume[3] stimulate at least three considerations.

We have emphasized that countries deemed lax have some uniform structural elements in common, while there are significant differences between those countries and those judged accommodating on the fiscal level, hence three indications for designing international prevention and enforcement policies.

Firstly, the financial blacklist must be formulated and updated with particular care, so as to avoid errors in the formulation of relative incentives or sanctions. Secondly, the fact that a country simply brings its formal rules into compliance does not automatically mean that it is not a potentially lax country on the financial level, since the incentives to laxity in the war on terrorism may have deep-running structural, economic and institutional roots. In 2005 FATF removed three more countries (Cook Islands, Indonesia, Philippines) from the blacklist of NCCTs. The current NCCT list includes Myanmar, Nauru and Nigeria.

It has been argued that the overall result of the blacklisting mechanism is positive, since transparency regarding which countries do not comply has important effects in the financial markets, increasing the market pressures on the NCCT countries. But why is it, then, that in these years various jurisdictions, notwithstanding the blacklist threat, delay or fail to change their rules, confirming their non-cooperative attitude (*reluctant friend effect*)? Furthermore, it is true that most jurisdictions placed on the black list have enacted regulatory measures in an effort to be removed from it. But is regulatory reform sufficient to prove that a country has really changed its non-cooperative attitude (*false friend effect*)?

Thirdly, the international community must seek to act positively on these roots with specific country-by-country policies, precisely because the degree of laxity and its rationale may not be identical from case to case. It is not a case that in June 2003 the FAFT explicitly recognized that countries have diverse legal and financial systems and so all cannot take identical measures to achieve the common objective to combat money laundering and terrorist financing.

But, most importantly, the theme of financial regulations mutually agreeable to both the onshore and offshore countries leads us to the decisive question of the political legitimacy of the action by international institutions. The more each country and territory, active or passive party to the action under an international code of conduct for the war against the financing of terrorism, recognizes the political legitimacy of the international institutions guaranteeing that code, the more effective the code will be. The legitimacy problem is not restricted to the blacklisting phenomena; for example how can one clearly distinguish a political movement from the list of terrorist organizations that the United States and other industrial countries issue?

Economic benefit and political legitimacy are therefore the pillars on which to build rules for governing international capital flows that observe the cardinal principles for the proper functioning of a market economy: efficiency and integrity.

References

[1]   Financial Action Task Force, *Annual Report 2004–2005*, Paris, 2005.
[2]   Masciandaro D., *Global Financial Crime,* (ed.) Ashgate, Aldershot, 2004.
[3]   Ibid.

Chapter 21

Ethics and Advertising

Geoffrey Klempner

Introduction

Human beings are world creators. One of the worlds that human beings have created is the world of money, commodities, trade, exchange. To me, it's a world full of beauty and ugliness in equal proportions, messy, flashy, exotic, scary. No one who has made their home in this world would see this the way an outsider – and being a philosopher makes me by definition an outsider – can see this.

I regard the business arena – the world of buyers and sellers, bosses and workers, producers and consumers, the world of *money* – as nothing less than an ontological category, a way of Being. It is not accidental to who we are. It defines the way we relate to each other and to the world around us. But it is not the only way of Being. There are other ways, and the most fundamental of these is ethics.

Ethics, as understood here, is defined by the *I-thou* relationship:

> When I engage another person in moral dialogue, there are not two parallel processes of practical deliberation going on, his and mine, but only one. (Contrast this with the case of a 'dialogue' between politicians or traders, where each is privately deliberating how to gain the upper hand.) In opening myself up and addressing the other as a thou I am already committed to the practical consequences of agreement, of doing the action which, by the combined light of his valuational perspective and mine is seen as the thing to be done.[1]

As a professional metaphysician, I am fascinated by the idea that human beings can belong to more than one world, or move between worlds. Anthropologists who 'go native' in order to study their subjects more closely have an inkling of what I am talking about. We live in the marketplace and also outside it. We can play the various roles assigned to us in the game, or we can stand outside our economic personae and observe ourselves from an ethical point of view. The only difference between us and the anthropologist is that, most of the time, we don't realize that we are doing this.

In my recent article, 'The Business Arena',[2] I put forward three propositions, as a 'prolegomenon to a philosophy for business':

> Business and commerce take place in a frame, an arena defined by unwritten rules.

> Within the business arena, *normal* ethics is suspended.

The aim of a philosophy for business is to understand the rules that define the business arena, in other words, to grasp from an ethical perspective *how business is possible*.[3]

To claim that in the business world 'normal ethics is suspended' is not to deny the validity of rules of conduct, such as fairness and honesty. Without these universal rules, these values, the game could not be played. However, these obligations fall far short of the demands of ethics, as I have defined it here.

Advertising: For Good or Evil?

But how fair is the business game, really? On the face of it, producers and consumers have a very different view. The marketplace is not a level playing field, and the chief culprit is advertising.

Here are three charges levelled against advertisers:

They sell us dreams, entice us into confusing dreams with reality.

They pander to our desires for things that are bad for us.

They manipulate us into wanting things we don't really need.

All this can be summed up in the popular sentiment that advertisers cynically use a world of fantasy and illusion in an attempt to control us.

Most people who express this sentiment, however, would add that *the attempt doesn't succeed*. We see through the ruse. (Or, at least, it is always other people who seem to have the wool pulled over their eyes, never ourselves.) That is a claim to take with a big pinch of salt.

In recent times advertising has become increasingly regulated by codes of practice. These codes may be adequate to curb the worst excesses of advertising. It is much harder nowadays for advertisements to get away with telling outright lies. But they still fall far short of answering these three indictments.

That suggests the following question: suppose that you were an advertiser who wanted to be truly *ethical* and not just *legal*. What would you have to do? Let us look at each of the indictments in turn.

Selling Dreams

Let me start with a personal example. What initially attracted me to philosophy was the life of Socrates. In the same way that few, if any Christians could live the way Christ lived, so few if any philosophy students are capable of emulating the life of Socrates. I knew this. *I was sold the dream of philosophy.* And I am glad for that. I don't feel I was cheated. Plato, the greatest of all salesmen for philosophy, seduced me – along with countless thousands of students before and since – with his brilliant dialogues depicting the life of his mentor.

Gilbert Ryle in his book *Plato's Progress* (1966)[4] argues that the dialogues were performed live. You can see audiences of Plato's dialogue *Phaedo* sobbing, or swooning as Socrates calmly drinks the hemlock, with words of reassurance for his gathered friends, facing death with courage and dignity.

The dream is not extraneous to the product. It is part of the complete package. The treasure that is the collected works of Plato has added to the value of philosophy, not just through novel arguments or its addition to the storehouse of human knowledge but through the sheer seductive power of Plato's storytelling. Living and breathing the atmosphere of the dialogues we become more, we become better, we are enhanced.

But is that also true out there in the commercial marketplace, where humans barter their love of material goods, succumb to the dreams that advertisers sell? It is very tempting to say no. It is so easy to take the moralistic high ground. Yet, as I want to argue, that would be a serious error.

Anyone who is serious about deconstructing the dream world of advertising should start by considering the meaning of *fashion* and *style*, not as illusions that human beings fall helplessly victim to, but as part of the scaffolding of human culture. A world without fashion or style would be obnoxious, alien, brutal – in the true sense of being fit only for brutes.

Think of the clothes one wears as a kind of advertising. To say that the appearance that clothes create is a mere illusion is to class a well cut or well designed suit with cod pieces and false breasts.

A philosopher might object that my example of the 'dream of philosophy' is not fair. Philosophy is an ideal. Advertisers try to sell us material *things*. The two could not be more different. I totally disagree.

Philosophers, so quick to analyse, look at an object as a mere bearer of physical properties, or as a tool with a function, or, possibly, one of those rare objects that attains the status of a 'work of art', a bearer of sheer disinterested aesthetic value. None of these ways of analysing an object explain *why we love things*. All parents know how children lust for toys. We grow up. We put away childish things. We do not lose that lust, we merely look for different things to attach ourselves to, to project our emotions onto. This is normal, not pathological behaviour.

Object-love is one of the most profound facts about our *human* relation to the world. That is something Freud saw.

These are passing observations (as Wittgenstein would say) concerning the 'natural history of mankind'. It ought to be seen as surprising, worthy of note, in the same way as we ought to be surprised at the capacity of the human imagination to be captured by storytelling, by fiction. Maybe Martians are not so lucky. Pity them.

In the commercial world, there are plenty of examples of manufacturers who believe passionately in their product. Apple Macintosh is the best example I can think of. Macs are good, not only because they function well, but because they are beautiful, stylish, designed with loving attention to detail (most of the time, anyway – there have been occasional, humorous exceptions when in the face of competition cost-cutting was allowed to take precedence over quality).

I am happy to buy into a dream I can believe in. But not one that has been cynically created with the sole aim of making me spend my money.

So is this true? – 'As an advertiser, it's OK to sell a dream if you believe in it too.' When a consumer buys an Apple Mac, the value of the product is not just its beauty and functionality, but the love that has been lavished on it. The image that the advertisers have created is not only true, but also enhances the pleasure of using the product.

But we are on risky ground here. Consider the religious cults who send their followers on the streets seeking converts. They believe in the dream that they are selling too. Even if the dream selling is not done cynically, it all too easily becomes an attempt to brainwash, to control.

A campaign which Apple ran a couple of years ago featured 'real people' explaining why they switched to Macs and recounting the misery of badly designed, unreliable PCs. The campaign backfired because PC users found it offensive, while Mac users resented being patronised. They were rudely awakened from the dream.

Pandering

We tell a child, 'You'll feel sick if you eat that second chocolate bar.' Yet advertisers are only too willing to sell us as many chocolate bars as we can eat – or, whatever our particular vice may be.

In today's climate, as a would-be ethical advertiser, there is no way you could accept a cigarette advertising account. With the current problem of binge drinking in the UK amongst young people, one would have to be very careful in accepting a drinks account. I have yet to see a drinks advert whose message was, 'Enjoy our beer – but don't get drunk!'

Advertisements can set out with the laudable aim of educating people. 'Eat our cereal because it's low in fat and high in fibre'. This is good advice, offered, however, not in a spirit of social conscience but as part of the sales pitch. If consumers were less sensitive to such appeals to improve their health and life style, then advertisers would not waste time and money making them.

Ever-resourceful advertisers have even found ways to openly admit that their product is bad for you. A recent advert for meat pies portrays impressively overweight men – a construction worker, a welder, a tyre fitter, a fireman – as everyday 'heroes'. A potentially damaging admission is turned round into something positive with the clever use of humour. A *real man* likes his beer and pies.

This illustrates the important point that advertisements can be very *knowing* – showing an awareness of the ethical issues which marketing that particular product raises, while at the same time deftly deflecting criticism. We are not offended because we get the point, we smile at the irony – and we buy the product.

Manipulating

Suppose you are a deodorant manufacturer who has conceived the idea of an ethical advertising campaign. It goes without saying that the deodorant has got to work effectively, as claimed. It should not contain chemicals which are bad for your health (when the product is used according to instructions). This is more or less where we are now, in relation to current rules on advertising.

But what does it mean for a deodorant to be effective? On a hot day, you will be more confident in the company of other people, because they will not be able to detect your body odour. Critics of deodorant advertising have pointed out, however, that although it is true that the deodorant has the power to prevent odour, and this is a ground for extra confidence, the reason why it is a ground for confidence is at least partly due to a belief or attitude which has itself been inculcated by advertising.

'Body odour' (B.O.) is one of the classic phrases invented by advertisers, embodying the concept that any natural human smell is, or ought to be regarded as offensive. It is hard to question a belief when it has become part of language itself. If you have B.O. that is something bad, by definition. B.O. is unpleasant and offensive, because being offensive is part of its concept. But that begs the question whether all bodily odours are unpleasant, or only some.

So let us take our imaginary scenario from here:

> The ethical deodorant marketing team take the brave decision to question this assumption. The design and advertising of the product will be based around the idea that there are pleasant as well as unpleasant bodily odours. The chemists are asked to come up with a product which gets rid of the unpleasant odours while not masking the pleasant ones. After extensive research and testing, the product is launched.

The campaign is a great success. The concept captures the public imagination, better than anyone had dared hope.

However, a new trend emerges from the on-going market research. A significant proportion of the people questioned express a willingness to try a product which enhances their 'naturally pleasant' bodily smell. The chemists identify a complex blend of chemicals, some of which are capable of synthesis in a laboratory. The ethical marketing team now face a difficult dilemma.

How can it be wrong to market the chemically enhanced product, if this was what people want? The argument for not doing so is that it was the success of the first campaign that created the demand for an added 'natural bodily smell', where none had existed before. This is the very thing that the ethical advertising team had sought to avoid! Against competitors who show no such scruples, however, the ethical advertisers face a losing battle in the marketplace.

Conclusion

I raised the question whether it is possible to be an *ethical* advertiser – in the true sense of 'ethical', and not merely in the minimalist, legal sense of respecting the rules that govern play in the business arena, such as honesty and fairness.

I have argued that reflection on what ethics demands makes the hurdles impossibly high. The stark truth is that manufacturers and advertisers are as much controlled by the fickle consumer as in control. Rules can be set down concerning what is factually truthful, decent and fair. It is not the advertiser's job to make people better than they are, or want better things than they want. That is the work for politicians and preachers, or, possibly, philosophers.

A defence of advertising against unjustified demands is bound to be less spectacular than an attack. However, do not forget the point of all this. My aim is to defend ethics against pressures that would weaken or dilute its requirements in order to fit in with a so-called 'business ethic'. Ultimately, we are all members of the moral world, whatever games we choose to play, whatever other worlds we may inhabit. No one escapes ethics.

Notes

[1]   The Ethics of Dialogue. 1998, Wood Paths web site <http://klempner.freeshell.org/articles/dialogue.html>

[2]   Klempner, G. (2004), 'The Business Arena.' *Philosophy for Business* Issue 5 <http://www.isfp.co.uk/businesspathways/issue5.html>

[3]   Ibid.

[4]   Ryle, G. (1966), *Plato's Progress* Cambridge University Press, Cambridge.

Chapter 22

Self-Regulation and the Market for Legal Services

Richard Moorhead

Following an independent review,[1] the UK government has formulated plans to reform the regulation of the legal professions of England and Wales, which is likely to lead to a significant erosion of self-regulation and increased commercialisation of professional legal services.[2] Proposals to remove the handling of consumer complaints and impose an independent 'oversight' regulator to oversee the regulation of all legal service professions sit alongside proposals to permit outside ownership of law firms and the formation of multi-disciplinary practices. The complexities of the legal services market and the regulatory structure[3] give rise to a host of questions but there are three principal drivers of reform.

First is the increasingly vocal complaints of the competition authorities that the professions are a last bastion of anti-competitive practices. The Office of Fair Trading have issued a research report, a consultation and a response to consultation that make a consistent if somewhat simplistic competition case against the restrictive practices of barristers and solicitors.[4]

The second is the persistent failure of the solicitors' profession to regulate its own members with anything like the levels of competence which would ensure consumer confidence.

The third is the growing importance and complexity of external sources of regulation, and non-professional sources of legal regulation. A spaghetti junction of providers, systems of provision, and regulators has begun to sprawl across the policy makers' desk at the same time as the government has sought to stimulate market driven response to the general legal needs of the population.

Opening Up of Legal Service Markets: Competition and Quality – Quality and Professionalism/Voluntarism

The opening up of legal service markets to less restrained competition is an intriguing prospect and one on which there is a limited but growing amount of evidence. Lower costs and more innovative, responsive services is what we are led to expect by economic theory. To date the personal injury market is the main test-bed of this strain of policy making, though the opening up of the conveyancing market was an early predecessor that sought, with mixed success, to encourage competition. What lessons can we learn from the opening up of these two markets?

The briefest précis of the conveyancing reforms will suffice: solicitors firms, threatened with outside competition in the late 80s, cut their prices and began to compete with each other. Fixed price conveyancing was offered and the relaxation of the profession's advertising bans enabled consumers to shop around in a meaningful way on price (simply indicating hourly rates, the previous base of any competition, provided no means of ascertaining the actual price because consumers could not meaningfully predict how many hours a job would take and solicitors were reluctant to predict for fear of 'quoting' for a job). The substantial reduction in profits that would have been expected as a result of this price cutting was offset by the property market picking up with sufficient vigour to shield the profession from the worst effects of its reduced margins. Prices were set in a more fixed and transparent way but by reference to (rising) house prices. New entrants into the market, notably licensed conveyancers, were (and still are[5]) rather thin on the ground and have not challenged the dominant position of the solicitors' profession.

The main challenge to the profession's power has not come from alternative providers but from purchasers: financial institutions have for some time exerted a powerful influence as referrers of work, able to insist on reduced prices from shrinking panels of higher-volume producers often referred to as conveyancing 'factories' (with persistent allegations that volume and price is achieved at the expense of quality). In another vein, anecdotal evidence on the quality provided by high street conveyancers in more traditional-style firms suggests a rather depressing story of second class service for, in lawyers terms at least, fairly low levels of fees. The only comfort being that lawyers seem to offer a cheaper service and do a more professionally demanding, or at least slightly technical, job than estate agents.

The recent reforms of the personal injury market make the conveyancing reforms seem rather genteel. The (now) Department for Constitutional Affairs desired market solutions to access to justice problems. The Access to Justice Act 1999 effectively prevented legal aid from being granted to most personal injury cases and made the funding of personal injury work through 'no win, no fee' agreements much more attractive to claimants than they had hitherto been. The result was a shifting of the personal injury part of the legal aid sector into a peculiarly English brand of contingency fees, the Conditional Fee Agreement (CFA, no win no fee agreements). These agreements allow lawyers to be paid their normal fee plus a percentage uplift of that fee if they win a case. The uplift would normally be set based on an assessment of the risk that a case would be lost. The lawyers can thus use costs from successful cases to subsidise the cases that they lose.

If the litigant loses, the terms of the CFA ordinarily mean they did not have to pay their lawyer's costs. However, the principle that costs ordinarily follow the event, means that they are very likely to have to pay the costs of their opponent should they lose. This would be a major disincentive to taking cases and thus defeat the aim of encouraging people of modest means to take cases forward under CFAs which they could not otherwise afford. To meet this concern, insurance can be purchased to protect the litigant from the risk that they would have to pay the other side's costs.

The claimant solicitor lobby, for noble reasons, sought to ensure that (unlike the US system) the no win no fee agreement's success fee was not paid out of the claimant's damages (as they had been prior to the Access to Justice Act 1999), but could be recovered from unsuccessful defendants. Similarly, the insurance premiums could also be recovered. In a further innovation, the initial financing of the insurance premiums and certain upfront costs were met by financing arrangements ('magic bullets') which meant clients with a personal injury claim paid nothing at all. Claims handling companies, some not even employing CFAs, sought to roll these various fees up and claim them, along with advertising and other cost from unsuccessful defendants as part of the success fee plus premium payment payable alongside damages and ordinary costs.

There is an obvious lack of control over the setting of fee uplifts and insurance premium charges. Ordinary consumers have little or no incentive to control the level of these fees (even assuming they understand them) but insurers defending the claims brought by such claimants were incensed with what they saw as opportunistic behaviour on the part of claims companies and claimant solicitors. Satellite litigation ensued over the terms of such agreements and the costs that defendant insurers would have to pay out on the cases they lost to these claimants. The litigation threatened to paralyse the system leading to a series of 'big tent' meetings of insurers, lawyers, judges and policy makers and they have begun to thrash out solutions to some of the problems.[6] Meanwhile, two big players in the market imploded catastrophically and finance houses reportedly began to pull out of the magic bullet schemes. The fundamental problem was that a 'market' system had been created which was largely or apparently costless to the initial consumer, was mediated only by the commercial interests of the insurance companies.

This troubled history is enough to caution against an uncritical enthusiasm for markets in relation to professional services. Being credence goods, the marketing and purchase of goods is prone to information asymmetries and inefficiencies. One reading of the recent history of CFAs is an attempt by claims companies to exploit those problems for their own commercial gain. Solicitors too were demonstrably managing the system to their own advantage.[7] Insurers, through the use of satellite litigation about costs, also threatened huge cash flow problems on their opponents (claimant solicitors) as their taking of costs cases delayed payouts on thousands of claims.

Although it is only where clients' interests are aligned with insurers and solicitors that the system of CFAs promotes access to justice, it is important not to overstate the strength of this critique. For a substantial number of clients, particularly those with straight forward and cheap to run claims, the system works to provide them with cheap or costless access to legal services. It also only takes us so far in understanding the immediate concern of this paper. The events around the development of CFAs to self-regulation is the suggestion that economic pressures put professions under considerable strain (on occasion, it effectively prevents them acting in the public interest) but it also suggests a weakness in deregulation. The market response to information asymmetries appears, so far at least, to have been problematic.

There is further general evidence that economic pressures on legal service providers inhibit or reduce quality.[8] The quality of service received by clients under CFAs is a relatively neglected area[9] but anecdotal evidence refers to factory approaches to the 'farming' of claims, which are processed bureaucratically, without personal contact between lawyer and client. Substantial bodies of theory point to the risk of under settlement but actual evidence is more limited and mixed.[10] Claims handling companies have been criticised for their selling techniques. Their use of non-lawyers worries lawyers and hard-sell marketing techniques alienate some of the public. They have been criticised for rejecting claims when they ought not to (because cases are difficult to prove or expensive to run) and of encouraging unfounded claims which will succeed because of their nuisance value. In nuisance value cases, defendants pay unmeritous litigants to go away because the costs of a small settlement are lower than defending a case properly.

The complaint about lower levels of quality can be met in part by the argument that a market based system may deliver somewhat rougher justice but it opens up the system to a wider range of litigants than, say, the legal aid scheme did (being only available to the relatively poor). In other words: you get lots more slightly smaller bangs for your buck. Indeed, you get bangs without any (public spending) buck at all. Nevertheless it throws an important light on the need for regulation. Courts have confessed themselves somewhat inept at dealing with all the problems (see Lord Hoffman in Callery v Gray [2002] UKHL 28, for example) and the range of providers, lawyers and non-lawyers, and the rapidly developing commercial context underlines the need for wide-ranging but also adaptable regulation.

What is Wrong with Self-Regulation?

Many complaints are levelled at self-regulation. Professions, it is claimed with some credibility, set rules which they do not enforce or routinely ignore. Professional rules on conflicts of interest are routinely derogated from by City firms, through Chinese Walls and cones of silence, which suggest a very attenuated notion of traditional professional values.[11] The claim is that this is done because it is what the client wants, but there are suspicions that the commercial interests of large law firms are what is really at play. The Law Society's own management of Inadequate Professional Services is a case in point. The scheme was legislated by Parliament on the understanding that it was an informal system for resolving consumer allegations of negligence and other forms of poor service. Yet the Law Society's management of the scheme led to a system which routinely excluded complaints that smacked of negligence.[12] This was directly contrary to parliamentary intention and the basis on which the Law Society lobbied Parliament at the time. Both examples suggest rules and policies are finessed, or ignored, in favour of professional rather than public interests.

Secondly, professions routinely claim that self-regulation leads to higher levels of quality than can be gained from non-professional providers. This is a claim which has been shown to be false in a series of studies looking at how non (qualified) lawyers perform in doing work similar or identical to fully qualified lawyers.[13] The evidence suggests that it is specialism not professionalism that is a better guarantor of quality. The solicitors profession has recognised this through the promotion of specialist panels. This segmentation in itself indicates a wariness of the claim that a professional qualification is of itself a guarantee of quality; and it could be argued that it is the profession seeking to demarcate itself against other competitors.

Thirdly, it could be argued that self-regulation is in some ways sclerotic. The Law Society has moved tortuously slowly towards permitting referral fees for the introduction of business and also on the vexed question of Multi Disciplinary Partnerships. The issues here are not simple. Professional status is at stake, but there is genuine public interest concern too. Deregulating and permitting lawyers to have profit sharing arrangements with accountants, and the like may be a gateway to further Enron type scandals. The conflicts of interest already alleged where dominant purchasers of legal services use their muscle to reduce the number of firms who can provide their firms (finance houses and conveyancing; insurance companies providing legal expenses insurance cover; the Legal Services Commission and legal aid services; commercial muscle bypassing conflicts of interest regulations in commercial firms) may be magnified if such services are brought in house.

Fourthly, there has been a persistent and strong concern with the way that complaints handling has been dealt with by, in particular, the solicitors' profession. It is probably the highly visible and long running nature of this saga that is primarily responsible for the Clementi review.[14] Legal Service Ombudsmen have all raised the heat on the Law Society to improve but without notable success. The government too has been boxed in by the need to issue warnings and final warnings which, once breached, require action. Complaints handling has lacked resources, proper management, and independence.[15] Both professionals and complainants view the system as biased and inept.

Fifthly, professions are claimed to be better at promoting acceptance for reform amongst their members, being better placed socially to regulate actual behaviour through cultural pressure and persuasion. One such attempt to change the culture of the profession, was Rule 15. This Rule passed by the Law Society required firms to have their own complaints mechanisms and improve the information that they provide to clients on accepting instructions. The rule was either derided or misunderstood by a sizeable proportion of the profession.[16] Resistance took various forms including non-compliance and a grudging compliance, through prolix and incomprehensible client care letters being sent to clients which perverted the aims of clarity and good communication.

Is External Regulation Better?

If self-regulation is to be abandoned or watered down, one needs to consider the pros and cons of external regulation. The solicitors' profession is subject in various ways to external regulation. Courts, of course, exert some influence through various costs sanctions as well as other more social means of securing compliance with judicial ideas about case presentation and case management. Indeed, one of these thrusts of Lord Woolf's reforms of court procedure and pre-action behaviour was to encourage a less adversarial approach to litigation.[17] These changes have had some success[18] however, the fundamental point of the reforms: to reduce adversarialism and therefore make litigation cheaper and more accessible, was not met. Interestingly, the subsequent approach to this has been to adopt a partnership approach whereby lawyers, judges, policy makers and insurers come together to try and make a simpler, more workable and cheaper system. It is too early to tell whether such cooperative approaches have worked, but they suggest a resilience in the idea that trust and cooperation are essential to real regulatory reform.

There are other regulators. Indemnity insurers are, through the monitoring of claims histories and the demand for requirements such as risk management policies, able to affect the way that firms manage themselves but it is through the administration of legal aid that the Legal Services Commission has made the most concerted attempt to impose external regulation upon solicitor firms wishing to practice legal aid. An extensive system of quality assurance (the quality mark) require certain management procedures to be put in place as well as requiring that case work is supervised by someone with a degree of specialisation in types of cases being handled.[19] There is a growing body of evidence that the quality mark has improved the management of law firms[20] and some evidence that it has improved the quality of advice[21] but also that such systems do not remove a substantial minority of poor performers. Evidence suggested that upwards of one in five solicitor firms under the quality marks predecessor (LAFQAS) performed their work generally at levels below competence. Perhaps more worryingly still, about 30 per cent of cases handled by solicitors in a pilot (where the solicitors firms would be expected to be of higher quality) were of inadequate quality. Thus, external regulation may have achieved some improvements in quality but it has not led to a dramatic reduction in the amount of substandard work.

External regulation too has some side effects. It may be sub-optimal in imposing considerable transaction costs on suppliers. This is one drawback of the Legal Service Commission approach: where bureaucracy is amongst the reasons given for a recent exodus of firms from legal aid work.[22] Insurance led risk management policies have been interpreted by solicitors firms, as requiring them to turn away clients who they believe may be more prone to making claims against them. It is interesting to observe that, in spite of the received wisdom that complaints mechanisms are failing, solicitors fear the impact sufficiently for them to be on the lookout for clients who may be more likely to complain to ensure that they do not accept instructions from such people. Thus one of the hidden costs of regulation is the way that it impacts on access particularly for difficult or unusual clients.

There are other concerns about external regulation. The goals of organisations who conduct any form of external regulation need careful scrutiny. Insurers have purely commercial interests to protect. To them, risk aversion makes business sense but to the public interest where other values come into play this aversion may exclude sectors of the population or particular types of legal problem. Similarly, the Legal Service Commission's approach to quality is related to a need to match the level or quality to available resources. In one sense, this is inevitable and desirable: it must be the case that there is a sensible trade off between quality and cost. However, this trade off has been carefully managed and understood. There are issues of public governance and accountability to be considered: who decides how to strike the balance between quality and cost? And on what evidence? Similarly, the Commission's approach to quality has been shown to have significant impact on issues of access: raising quality may well diminish access independent of cost.[23]

There are other public policies reasons for wondering about the most appropriate home for regulation, more to do with protection of democratic principles, rather than instrumental concerns about the appropriate balance between quality, access and cost. Immigration tribunals issue 'certificates of concern' against practitioners they regard as behaving inappropriately. Highly respected immigration practitioners have indicated that they would regard such certificates of concern with ambivalence: both a badge of honour but also something likely to lead to problems with their funders. The implication of this is that they view 'quality concerns' as being used to stifle fearless, independent advocacy. Similarly, in relation to criminal work, the Home Office pushes an agenda centred around the control of crime and the need to process defendants quickly where as criminal practitioners are obliged to focus more on the needs of their clients and the protection of their legitimate rights. The setting of quality standards can critically affect how the balance between quality and efficiency is held.

Finally, it is interesting to note that several external regulators, the Legal Services Commission and the Office of the Immigration Services Commissioner in particular, have turned to peer reviewers as a way of measuring and regulating quality. In some ways this is a sharing of external and self-regulation. These approaches too involve an interesting melding of professional and institutional values. Some peer reviewers are concerned to ascertain whether or not solicitors have overcharged (e.g. in the context of cost compliance audits for the legal services commission) others are concerned to provide a more developmental role, and the legal services commission is developing peer reviewers as a final quality test to decide whether or not firms whose performances were worrying should or should not be able to remain within the legal aid scheme.[24]

Self-Regulation and Professionalism

In spite of the doubts about self-regulation, the notion of professionalism, the handmaiden of self-regulation, has powerful cultural appeal. Sociologists and ethicists, whilst sometime sceptical of its descriptive or normative force, do see professionalism as having an important aspirational potency.[25] It is very difficult to predict whether ending self-regulation would erode further ethical professionalism or whether such ethical professionalism stands independent of the mode of regulation. It is true that the solicitors' professional body the Law Society, does do certain amount of public interest work, lobbying in relation to law reform, for example and encouraging pro bono work. Whilst cynics might argue that this is a typical professional body seeking some kind of strategic advantage or reinforcing its high status image, it is difficult to be too censorious of activities which demand considerable energy and input from the volunteer lawyers that participate.

The Law Society has also sought somewhat modestly to change the culture of the legal profession by taking the lead in relation to client care. Research into the take up and application of Rule 15 discussed above painted a sorry picture of failure. This would seem to suggest that self-regulatory bodies are not successful at altering the culture of the profession certainly one as large and diverse as the solicitors' profession now is. However, we have no baseline against which to judge behaviour prior to the rule. It is possible that significant improvements were made but also that large levels of poor behaviour remain.

Let us assume for a moment that self-regulatory professions do successfully promote modest culture change and modest diversion of the profession away from self-interest and towards public interests. In the field of customer relations it has been pointed out that nevertheless the profession has not moved sufficiently to keep up with public expectations.[26] A social contract model of professionalism that sees the regulator as protecting the consumer from the information asymmetry caused by a professional, necessarily desires the pendulum to shift more towards what the consumer wants. As has been noted already, there are costs to the consumer in effecting that shift (the transaction costs of improved quality are inevitably passed onto consumers). A self-regulator is ill placed to persuade a sceptical public that their demands for quality risk prejudicing other interests such as the price they pay or the likelihood that a service will be available at all. If professional dominance of a market is based on trust,[27] and consumers are not satisfied that the trust is well bestowed, one basis of self-regulation falls away. Put this way, a persuasive case is made for some form of independent regulation. Independence necessarily means independence from professional self-interest but trust may also demand independence from governmental and commercial forces.

Some Concluding Thoughts: Is it Self-Regulation or Regulation we Should be Interested In?

Whilst much of the above analysis and debate focuses on the pros and cons of self-regulation, it is possible to see the debate in other terms. Any future regulator of the profession will need to think carefully about the techniques of regulation that it employs. The Legal Service Commission's success, albeit limited, may be due to the regulatory techniques it employed more than its independence from the profession. Equally, a new regulator (if there is to be one) has to perform a rather different task. A large part of its remit will be to satisfy disgruntled complainants, or to satisfy them as much as is reasonable, in the handling of their complaints.

The simple fact of independence may go some way to satisfy disgruntled complainants: one of their principal concerns is the inherent bias in having a system which has lawyers adjudicating on their own kind. Beyond that though, a need for regulators to respond rapidly and sympathetically to consumer complaints is obvious but it would also need to engage with lawyers and their values if it is to accurately adjudicate complaints. These complaints processes have typically been paper based affairs supplemented by telephone contact and telephone conciliation. Little focus has been placed on the nature of this process and their relationship to consumer satisfaction. Much more general work on the nature of fairness in the justice system has supported the importance of giving 'voice' to the lay participates in any law based process which they are subject to.[28] This may well suggest that a regulator should consider greater interaction with the complainants and consider, in particular, holding of hearings, virtual or telephone based perhaps, in appropriate cases. There are of course significant resource implications in so doing and considerable problems in holding hearings which involve a lay complainant and a professional respondent. Similarly the regulator will need to keep a healthy distance from legality and the courts. There is evidence that at least one ombudsman has had difficulty as a result of court intervening in the decision-making process.[29]

Furthermore, the complexities that arise in the fast moving legal services market, as illustrated by the conditional fee saga, suggest a need for a regulator who is powerful and adaptable and not constrained by professional interests. Some ombudsmen, although they avoid the nomenclature of a regulator, pride themselves on applying general principles without developing specific rules and thereby being highly adaptable to difficult and sensitive commercial and regulator problems.

The regulatory issues that this rather cursory discussion raises suggest that the problems of regulating professional service markets are not simply ones of independence, or self-regulation versus bureaucratic regulation. A number of values are at play: access, quality and cost are in tension and a regulator needs to balance the competition between these three values in a way that is optimal. Simply understanding what is optimal will be a tall order. The legal profession is adept at defeating regulatory strategies (this is after all what it is trained to do for its clients to a degree). Consumerist politics and the conspicuous failure of the solicitors' profession to respond competently to consumer needs challenge self-regulation but there is not an obvious model to put in its place.

Notes

1. Clementi, D. (2004), *Report of the Review of the Regulatory Framework for Legal Services in England and Wales*, Department for Constitutional Affairs, London.

2. Department of Constitutional Affairs, Norwich 2005, *The Future of Legal Services: Putting Consumers First*, Cm 6679, HMSO.

3. Baldwin Robert, Malleson Kate, Cave Martin, Spicer Sheila (2003), *Scoping Study for the Regulatory Review of Legal Services*, DCA, London.

4. See, in particular, OFT (2001) Competition in the Professions: A Report by the Director General of Fair Trading (OFT: London) at: <http://www.oft.gov.uk/nr/rdonlyres/e2v5ybukef4g57rpmlzhbvfp6gpdazsj4f5vpx53aconsxbdktvaq2733uwkwie3qtd74vd-sasfaqhptaviksuzizra/oft328.pdf>

5. There are about 850 licensed conveyancers and about 75,000 solicitors in provate practice (although only a proportion of those would do conveyancing work), See, DCA (2005) cited in note 2.

6. See the Civil Justice Council website for more details: <http://www.civiljusticecouncil.gov.uk/>

7. Yarrow, Stella and Abrams, Pamela (1999), *Nothing to Lose? Clients' experiences of using conditional fees?* Nuffield, London; Yarrow, Stella (2000), *Just Rewards? The outcome of conditional fee arrangements?* Nuffield, London.

8. Moorhead et al 2001, *Quality and Cost: Final Report on the Contracting of Civil, Non-Family Advice and Assistance Pilot*, Stationery Office, Norwich; Moorhead, R., Sherr, A and Paterson, A. (2003), 'Contesting Professionalism: Legal Aid and Non-lawyers in England and Wales', *Law & Society Review*, vol. 37, pp. 765–808.

9. Work on early conditional fee arrangements by Yarrow and Abrams being an honourable exception, see note 7 above.

10. See, Fenn, P., Gray, A. and Rickman N. (2002), *The impact of sources of finance on personal injury litigation: an empirical analysis*, LCD, London; Fenn, P, Gray, A., Rickman, N. and Carrier, H. (2002), *The impact of conditional fees on the selection, handling and outcomes of personal injury cases*, LCD, London.

11. See, Griffiths-Baker J. (2002), *Serving Two Masters: Conflicts of Interest in the Modern Law Firm*, Hart, Oxford Portland.

12. Moorhead, R., Sherr, A. and Rogers, S. (1998), *Compensation for Inadequate Professional Services, A Report to the Office for the Supervision of Solicitors*, IALS, London.

13. Contesting professionalism, cited in note 8; Genn, H. and Genn, Y. (1989), *The Effectiveness of Representation at Tribunals, Report to the Lord Chancellor*, (LCD); Kritzer, Herbert M. 1998, *Legal Advocacy*, The University of Michigan Press, Michigan.

14. There is one caveat to this claim. The Access to Justice Act 1999 introduced the power to appoint a Complaints Commissioner with power to set management targets and fine the Law Society. This power was invoked at the same time as the Clementi review was announced. A government concerned to give the Law Society one further chance could have invoked the power and seen what happened before appointing such a review.

15. See, Moorhead, R., Rogers, S. and Sherr, A. (2000), *Willing Blindness? OSS Complaints Handling Procedures*, Law Society, London.

16 Christensen, C., Day, S. and Worthington, J. (1999), 'Learned Profession? – the stuff of sherry talk': the response to Practice Rule 15? *International Journal of the Legal Profession*, vol 6, no. 1, pp. 27–69.

17 Woolf, the Rt. Hon. The Lord, (1996), *Access to Justice: Final Report to the Lord Chancellor on the Civil Justice System in England and Wales*, HMSO, July 1996.

18 Goriely, T., Moorhead, R. and Abrams, P. (2002), *More Civil Justice? The impact of the Woolf reforms on pre-action behaviour*, Law Society and Civil Justice Council, London.

19 The Specialist Quality Mark.

20 Bridges, L., Cape, E., Abubaker, A. and Bennett, C. (2000), *Quality in Criminal Defence Services: A report on the evaluation of the Legal Aid Board's pilot project on the contracting of criminal advice and assistance*, LSC, London: 2000; Sommerlad, H. (2002), 'Costs and Benefits of Quality Assurance Mechanisms in the Delivery of Public Funded Legal Services: Some Qualitative Views' (Paper to the LSRC International Conference, Oxford); National Association of Citizens Advice Bureau 2003, *Partnership Potential? Citizens Advice Bureau Views of the Community Legal Service*, NACAB, London.

21 Moorhead R. and Harding, R. (2004), *Quality and Access: Specialist and tolerance work under civil contracts*, The Stationery Office, Norwich.

22 Moorhead, R. (2004), 'Legal aid and the decline of private practice: blue murder or toxic job?' *International Journal of the Legal Profession*, vol. 11, 3, pp. 159.

23 Moorhead, cited in note 22 and Moorhead and Harding cited in note 21.

24 Seargeant, J. (2003), *Peer Review in Legal and Advice Services*, ASA, London.

25 See, for example, Abel, R. L. (1989), 'Taking Professionalism Seriously', *Ann Surv Am L*, vol. 41; Nicolson, D. and Webb, J. (2000), *Professional Legal Ethics – Critical Interrogations*, OUP, Oxford.

26 Legal Services Ombudsman (2002), *Reflecting Progress: Annual Report of the Legal Services Ombudsman 2000/2001*, LSO, Manchester.

27 Dingwall R. and Fenn, P. (1987), 'A Respectable Profession'? Sociological and Economic Perspectives on the Regulation of Professional Services. *International Journal of Law and Economics*, vol. 7, p. 51.

28 Tyler, Tom R. (1990), *Why people obey the law*, Yale University Press, New Haven and London.

Chapter 23

Corporate Responsibility for Children's Diets

Tom MacMillan, Elizabeth Dowler and David Archard

How to improve children's diets is one of the most pressing food policy questions of our times, in the United Kingdom and internationally.

Increases in diet-related disease are partly attributable to profound shifts in the ways children and families eat, which have occurred over the past two decades. More meals are consumed outside of the home and more food is purchased directly by children. Food products are also heavily promoted to children, targeting older children directly and tapping the 'pester power' of younger children.

Where children's diets were previously mediated by their families and by the state, children play an increasingly direct part in the food economy. They have become consumers of food, not only literally but also in a commercial sense. Children have a growing number of direct, market relationships with restaurants and food retailers.

The commercialisation of children's diets raises a serious problem. The capacity to regulate what children eat lies increasingly with the companies that make and sell food. Yet there are few ethical concepts and legal instruments to describe and to enforce the rights and responsibilities that come with this relationship between firms and children. As a society, we are poorly equipped to cope with children being consumers.

This paper asks how food companies might be held more responsible for their commercial relationships with children.

The Problem

The diets of children in the UK do not meet the nutritional standards recommended by government advisors (Parliamentary Office of Science and Technology (POST).[1] On average, British children are exceeding targets for saturated fat, processed sugars and salt, and they are not consuming the recommended quantities of fruits and vegetables.[2] Large minorities of children in the UK are deficient in vitamins A and D, and iron.

The incidence of diet-related ill health is increasing in children as in adults.[3] In 1996, 5 per cent of 6–15 year olds were obese, meaning that their large weight posed a serious threat to their health; by 2001, this figure had risen to 8.5 per cent. Obesity is also a risk factor for type 2, or so called 'adult onset', diabetes. In recent years, unprecedented cases of this condition have been found in obese children from ethnic groups without a recognised predisposition to the illness.

The human cost of overweight and other diet-related diseases is very great. A marginally obese young adult has twice the mortality risk of another whose weight is within the healthy range for their height.[4] In addition to the quantifiable health risks, children suffering from overweight are stigmatised, not only by other children but also by adults.[5]

The National Audit Office (NAO) estimates the public costs of obesity for adults and children in the UK to be at least £2.6 billion per year.[6] This includes the direct costs of treating dietary disease and the cost to the economy from lost working days. Rising levels of childhood obesity mean that these costs are likely to increase, because overweight adolescents have a 70 per cent chance of becoming overweight or obese adults.[7] The chair of the UK Food Standards Agency has described childhood obesity as 'a ticking timebomb'.[8]

Causes

It is clear both that children's diets are substandard and that diet-related ill health and obesity are on the increase. However, the link between the two is contentious. In particular, controversy surrounds the degree to which decreases in physical activity, as opposed to increases in the energy intake, are responsible for the rise in obesity.[9] Seemingly in favour of the view that 'sloth' and not 'gluttony' is responsible for this trend, is the annual National Food Survey of household consumption, which reports average diets to be improving on many counts.[10]

The answer, in practice, is that dietary changes *and* decreasing physical activity are doubtless both implicated in rising obesity rates. Indeed, the diet-or-exercise debate about the causes of obesity is something of a red herring. Irrespective of upward or downward trends, the fact remains that our diets, particularly those of our children, are sub standard. There are good health reasons for improving our diets and increasing our fitness whatever the link with obesity.

Nonetheless, the question of whether children's diets are bad but improving, or are actually deteriorating, is important in identifying the social causes of dietary ill health, and working out effective strategies for addressing them. And the indications are that, contrary to the impression given by the National Food Survey, the situation is actually getting worse. The recorded improvements in UK diet do not take full account of the growing proportion of food eaten outside the home. This is crucial, because food prepared at home is generally healthier, and lower in sugar and saturated fat, than food consumed elsewhere. Both the NAO and a United Nations expert consultation agree there is convincing evidence that the growing amounts of energy-dense and micronutrient-poor 'fast' foods, consumed outside the home, have contributed to rising obesity.[11,12]

The increase in fast-food consumption is just one aspect of a profound shift in the ways that children and families eat, which has occurred over the past two decades. Not only are more meals consumed outside the home, but more food is purchased directly by children, in and out of school, from vending machines and shops. Food products are also heavily promoted to children, targeting older children directly and tapping the 'pester power' of younger children.[13]

One can get a sense of this trend from changes in children's disposable income, consisting of pocket money, gifts and earnings. In 1982, the average annual income of UK 5–16 year olds was £91.[14] By 2001, their spending power had risen to £345, amounting to more than £3 billion nationwide.[15] According to the Wall's ice cream company, who conducted the survey, over half this money was spent on snacks and fizzy drinks! These figures do not even include some of the most significant food purchases that many older children make, which are for their meals at school.

The combined effect of such changes has been rapid social and economic upheaval in children's food habits. Where previously children's diets were mediated by their families and by the state, children now play an increasingly direct part in the food economy.[16] They have a growing number of market relationships with food manufacturers, restaurants and retailers, which take place in the home, in school and in the public places in between.

The commercialisation of children's diets raises a serious problem. The capacity to regulate what children eat is no longer confined as it once was, in large part, to the family and the state. It lies increasingly with the companies that make and sell food. Yet there is a near absence of ethical concepts and legal instruments to describe and to enforce the rights and responsibilities that come with this relationship between firms and children. As a society, we are poorly equipped to cope with children being consumers, particularly when it comes to their food.

The remainder of this paper briefly reviews some of the ethical issues raised by the commercialisation of children's diets. It identifies nine questions that warrant further work and discussion. As this is an early report of work in progress, we do attempt to answer those questions here.

Responsibilities

Defining children

A child has different capacities from those of a responsible adult, hence the special duties of adults towards them.[17,18] Yet children are different from adults, rather than just 'incomplete'. For instance, they are born with an innate preference for sweet tastes and they cannot fully sense aroma until the age of 4–5. This makes colour and texture prominent in food choice and marketing promotion.[19,20] Few under-7s can grasp the purpose of advertising.[21] What other social and biological factors differentiate children in dietary terms? How much do the responsibilities of adults to young consumers vary from child to child?

Parental duty and parental control

Public opinion that parents *ought to be* responsible for the diets of their children, in the sense of having a duty of care towards them, is commonly reported as the opinion that parents *are* responsible for children's diets, in the sense of controlling them as set out by Bristow.[22] Indeed, as parental control over children's diets has diminished, the ethical and legal language for describing the relationship of parents to children has shifted from that of parental rights over children to parental duties of care.[23,24] If parents discharge this duty by ensuring adequate home diets, can they also reasonably be held responsible for what their children eat outside the home? What are the responsibilities of food companies acting *in loco parentis*?

Collective accountability

Food industry groups reject the characterisation of energy-dense and micronutrient-poor foods as 'junk'.[25] They argue that there are no bad foods, only bad diets. This shifts responsibility off the manufacturer of a food, onto the people who regulate the different foods that children eat. But could food manufacturers be held collectively accountable for selling an unhealthy diet, via industry associations, broadcasters or 'gatekeepers' such as restaurants or supermarkets?

Justice

Consumer exploitation

Exploitation has been a core concern for research on the political economy production, but it remains marginal to the growing body of work on cultures of consumption. Thus, child labour in the food sector figures prominently in work on corporate responsibility, but there has been little research into whether companies exploit the vulnerabilities and special characteristics of children as consumers. What are the implications of Article 32 of the United Nations Convention on the Rights of the Child (UNCRC), which guards against 'economic exploitation'?[26] The UNCRC applies in the UK and to UK firms operating overseas.

Food poverty

There is a close link between dietary ill health and socio-economic status, including household income.[27] Food choice for lower income households is severely constrained by food availability and access.[28] Foodstuffs recommended for healthy eating often cost more than similar, unhealthy, equivalents.[29] Is it unjust or just unfortunate if the price premium for branded foods promoted to children exacerbates food poverty?

Best interests

The principle that, in action by any agency in respect of a child, the child's best interests shall be a primary consideration is a keystone of the UNCRC, the UK Children's Act, and child protection policy. There are acknowledged difficulties in interpreting this principle.[30] How might a best interests principle guide the regulation of food companies and the actions of parents in their provision of diets?

Autonomy

Food environments

Notions of individual choice and autonomy are prominent in discourses of body size. They underplay the social context of food retail and eating, as well as genetic factors, in overweight. Food advertising demonstrably affects what children eat.[31,32] Food promotion is an integral part of children's environments at home, at school and at most places in between. Research suggests that young children can self-regulate food intake when surrounded by nutritious foods, but overeat if surrounded by energy-dense snacks. How far do children inhabit an 'obesogenic' environment in which autonomous action amounts to self-harm?

Rights

Respecting the autonomy and rights of children does not mean satisfying their every whim.[33,34] Rather, 'it is something like the right to choose a life-plan and to control how it is implemented'.[35] Thus, parental and state regulation of the dietary 'choices' available to children can enhance the autonomy of children. Yet it is also crucial that children have a say in their diets and in food policies that affect them. Article 12 of the UNCRC states the rights of children to express views on matters that affect them, and that those views should be given due weight in accordance with age and maturity. What policies and actions would enhance children's dietary autonomy?

Stigma

Being overweight does not only compromise child welfare directly, through ill health, but also indirectly through stigmatisation. The stigma of being overweight is closely tied to the notion that it is a controllable condition.[36] (Schwarz and Puhl, 2003: 66). Even the adults from whom children seek help, such as parents, teachers and doctors, may believe that obesity or being overweight are due to lack of self-control and/or individualised psychological problems. Is there a gender dimension to stigma? How does this stigma relate to societal discourses of 'thin' body image and 'fat' eating?

Conclusion

We currently lack the means to hold food companies directly to account for their relationships with child consumers. As a result, the best efforts of regulators to do so seem tangential. Thus, attempts by the UK Food Standards Agency to control the promotion of foods to children have been condemned by the food industry for 'shooting the messenger' and failing to address the 'direct' causes of obesity. Meanwhile, campaign groups are concerned the measures proposed by the agency are too weak, because they are based on voluntary codes and industry goodwill.

There is an urgent need for robust means of ensuring that companies take responsibility in proportion to their control over children's diets. Specialists in food ethics, in family law and in corporate governance all have much to contribute to this project.

References

[1] Parliamentary Office of Science and Technology (POST) (2003), *Improving children's diet*. Parliamentary Office of Science and Technology, London, p. 19.

[2] Gregory, J. et al. (2000), 'National diet and nutrition survey: young people aged 4 to 18 years', Vol. 1. The Stationery Office, London.

[3] POST, *Improving children's diet*, p.24.

[4] Ibid., p. 27.

[5] Latner, J. D. and Stunkard, A. J. (2003), 'Getting worse: the stigmatization of obese children.' *Obesity Research*, vol. 11, pp. 452–6.

[6] National Audit Office (2001), *Tackling obesity in England*. The Stationery Office, London.

[7] POST, *Improving children's diet*, p.27.

[8] Revill, J. and Ahmed, K. (2003), 'The junk food time bomb that threatens a new generation.' *Observer*, November 9.

[9] Prentice, A. M. and Jebb, S. A. (1995), 'Obesity in Britain: gluttony or sloth.' *British Medical Journal*, vol. 311, pp. 437–9.

[10] POST, *Improving children's diet*, p. 21.

[11] Food and Agriculture Organisation & World Health Organisation (2002), *Joint FAO/WHO expert consultation: technical report series*, 916. WHO, Geneva.

[12] National Audit Office, *Tackling obesity in England*.

[13] Hastings, G. et al. (2003), *Review of research on the effects of food promotion to children*. Centre for Social Marketing, University of Strathclyde, Glasgow.

[14] Wall's (2000), *The authoritative survey on British children's pocket money*. Wall's, London.

[15] Unilever (2001), *Shifting fortunes for the nation's children*. Press release, October 5.

[16] Gustafsson, U. (2003), 'School meals policy: the problem with governing children.' in E. Dowler, and C. Jones Finer (eds.). *The welfare of food*. Blackwell Publishing, Oxford, pp. 685–97.

[17] Archard, D. (1993), *Children, rights and childhood*. Routledge, London.

18   Archard, D. & C. M. Macleod (2002), 'Introduction.' in *The moral and political status children*. D. Archard and C. M. Macleod (eds.), *The moral and political status children*. Oxford University Press, Oxford, pp. 1–15.

19   POST, *Improving children's diet*, p. 35.

20   Schwarz, M. B. and Puhl, R. (2003), 'Childhood obesity: a societal problem to solve.' *Obesity Reviews*, vol. 4, pp. 57–71.

21   POST, *Improving children's diet*, p.45–6.

22   Bristow, J. (2003), 'UK public: let parents decide what to feed their kids'. *Spiked*, November 11.

23   Blustein, J. (1982) *Parents and children: the ethics of the family*. Oxford University Press, Oxford.

24   Eekelaar, J. (1986), 'The eclipse of parental rights.' *Law Quarterly Review*, vol. 102, pp. 4–9.

25   Food and Drink Federation (2003). Promotion of food to children. *Press release*, November 9.

26   United Nations General Assembly (1989), 'Convention on the rights of the child.' *General Assembly Resolution 44/25.*

27   Dowler, E. A. (2001), 'Inequalities in diet and physical activity in Europe.' *Public Health Nutrition*, vol. 4, pp. 701–709.

28   Dowler, E. (2003), 'Food and poverty: insights from the UK.' in S. Maxwell, and R. Slater (eds.), Food Policy Old and New, special issue of *Development Policy Review*, vol. 21, pp. 5–6, 569–80.

29   POST, *Improving children's diet*.

30   Kopelman, L.M. (1997), 'The best-interests standard as threshold, ideal, and standard of reasonableness.' *Journal of Medicine and Philosophy*, vol. 22, pp. 271–89.

31   Food Standards Agency (2003), 'Outcome of academic seminar to review recent research on food promotion and children.' Food Standards Agency, London.

32   Hastings, G. et al. (2003), *Review of research on the effects of food promotion to children*. Centre for Social Marketing, University of Strathclyde, Glasgow.

33   Archard, D. (2003). *Children, family and the state*. Ashgate, Aldershot.

34   Brennan, S. & R. Noggle (1997), 'The moral status of children: children's rights, parents' rights and family justice.' *Social theory and practice*, vol. 23, pp. 1–26.

35   Ibid., p.16.

36   Schwarz, M. B. and Puhl, R. (2003), 'Childhood obesity: a societal problem to solve', p. 66.

Chapter 24

Do Toy Companies Really Care about Children? Evaluating the Ethics of the Toy Industry

Stephen P. Hogan

Abstract

Play is an essential ingredient of child development and traditional toys and games contribute considerably to encouraging healthy and safe play. The toy industry, like others targeting children directly, is under careful scrutiny to act responsibly in view of child vulnerability and attracts regular criticism about unsuitable products, promotional tactics, the encouraging of pestering, and its contribution to the peer pressure culture. But is this justified?

Based on qualitative interview data gained from senior managers in leading UK-based toy companies and focus groups of parents, this paper objectively examines the key ethical issues in the traditional toy industry, assesses the moral responsibilities of toy companies and influences on them to care about children, and examines the evidence and claims of the industry.

The findings highlight that care for children forms the core of many toy companies' values statements and there is evidence of caring in their attention to safety, product design and development, and to disadvantaged children. It is also evident, however, ,that in a challenging and competitive marketplace, companies are facing a difficult balancing act between doing 'what is right' and doing 'what works'. Despite the worthy practice in some areas, the pressure on profits is leading some toy companies to pursue questionable tactics.

Introduction

Play is an essential part of every child's upbringing and through play children learn amongst other things, 'sharing, receiving, giving and lending, anticipating, waiting and reciprocating, planning and organizing...'.[1] Although children's imagination can be fired by many commonly available objects such as sticks, blankets, and cardboard boxes in their play, children are often more inclined to play, and will play longer, when toys are available.[2] Furby[3] argues that within the contemporary matrix of consumerism, toys are a child's prototypical possessions – the first things that children learn to use, control, and derive pleasure from. Toys are important because they are, 'models of things that invoke in play the behaviours or skills required in later life'.[4]

There is some concern that today's children are at risk of 'play malnourishment'[5] as family lifestyles and structures change, leading to less parental involvement in child play, as sports played in schools decline, and as a general parental fear pervades society about letting young children engage in unsupervised play outside the home boundary. It could therefore be argued that the role of toys and toy companies in encouraging play has never been greater.

Toys are not just learning tools, but also provide enjoyment for children in a society that seems to give them less opportunity to play with others and more time to play on their own. Jean Jacques Rousseau is often credited with creating the modern notion of childhood and building on the ideas of John Locke and other 17th-century liberal thinkers. He described childhood as a brief period of sanctuary before we encounter the perils and hardships of adulthood. Abrams[6] argues that this sanctuary is seemingly becoming ever shorter as 'children silently and unobtrusively become the victims of capitalism, consumerism and the long-hours work culture'. Toys play an important part in making that sanctuary more pleasurable and toy companies have a responsibility to ensure that children do not become consumer victims through exploitation of their vulnerability and naivety.

This paper is based around the results of some recent qualitative research conducted amongst senior managers in twelve of the leading UK-based toy companies and four focus groups of parents with children under 10 years of age and examines the moral responsibilities of toy companies towards children as consumers, the ways in which the toy industry demonstrates care and concern about children, and considers the areas in which they could do more.

Ethical Issues in the Toy Industry

The traditional toy industry in the UK is valued at around £2.1 billion (at retail selling prices) making it one of the largest toy markets in the western world.[7] It comprises of all toys and games except consoles and electronic/computer games, which form a separate industry and are aimed at a generally older market. With around 82 per cent of all toys being purchased for children 10 years old and under, toy companies are highly dependent on making their marketing to them and their parents effective. The main categories of toys include action figures, arts and crafts, building sets, games/puzzles, infant and preschool toys learning and exploration, outdoor and sports toys, plush (soft) toys, and vehicles.

The toy industry in the UK has been growing steadily in value over the last five years but is facing a number of pressing challenges that threaten its longer-term potential. The toy market is highly competitive and price sensitive. The average selling price points have been falling in recent years which has forced most companies to look to cheaper labour economies for toy production, with China alone now manufacturing 80 per cent of all toys sold globally. Part of the price pressure comes from the retail market that is dominated by a handful of large powerful organisations. Argos, Woolworths and Toys'R'Us account for nearly half of all retail sales and wield considerable control and influence in the market. Toys are also predominantly 'fashion' items with short product life cycles of usually no more than a year. Companies therefore constantly need to invest in new product development and in creating new promotional campaigns. Finally, the consumer market itself is very challenging. The main toy recipients, children, can be fickle and difficult to predict, and research suggests that they are often now deserting traditional toys and games by the age of seven in favour of more sophisticated (adult) 'toys' such as mobile phones, televisions, computers and clothes.[8] The numbers of children are also declining with the UK population of under 12s set to fall by a further 5.4 per cent by the end of 2008.[9] A dilemma for the companies is the role played by parents and other adults in toy purchase decisions for children and whether to aim their promotional messages at children, in the hope of activating their negotiating and influencing skills, or at parents or other adults who ultimately endorse and fund most toy purchases.

In common with most industries targeting children, the toy industry is under careful scrutiny in many quarters and attracts some negative press and pressure group attention. This has highlighted a number of ethical issues.

The time and investment that most toys companies put in to the development of toys generally lead to few controversial products being launched in the market. Whilst there are some instances of distasteful products reaching the market (for example, a Barbie dressed in provocative lingerie) and occasionally a potentially dangerous toy slipping through the safety net (for example, the Yo-ball, banned in 2003), most concern seems to be around toys that lead to children's aggressive play (and a tenuous link to future anti-social behaviour), and the seemingly endless stream of character licensed toys and games linked to films, television programmes and books, most of which often offer only short-term play value.

Although the competitive market situation has contributed to lower prices (Crayola, for example, claim not to have had a price increase for seven years), pressure on profits has led at least one company to engage in price collusion. In 1993, Hasbro, the second largest toy manufacturer in the UK, was fined £4.95 million by the Office of Fair Trading (OFT) for fixing prices with some of its wholesalers, contrary to the Competition Act (2000). The company escaped a further fine when it cooperated with the OFT on a second charge of fixing toy prices with Argos and Littlewoods, who were subsequently fined £17.28 million and £5.37 million respectively.[10]

One of the more contentious ethical issues has been the promotion of toys and in particular the television advertising used by the larger companies to target children. With claims that British children are potentially exposed to as many as 20,000 advertisements per year, the highest level in Europe,[11] it is the volume of advertising rather than the content that mostly attracts the criticism. In recent years there has also be a swing away from traditional television and press advertising of toys as forms of promotion towards some arguably subtler and less regulated media such as children's websites for key brands and in-school marketing, where the distinction between providing educational value and the promotion of brand/sales message becomes more hazy.

The move to manufacture in the developing world has almost inevitably led to accusations of exploitation of toy workers,[12,13,14,15] although the British Toy and Hobby Association, whose members account for 95 per cent of market sales, has recently adopted the ICTI (International Congress of Toy Industries) charter, a global initiative designed to protect the rights, welfare and safety of those producing toys.[16] Environmentally, the widespread use of plastics and disposable batteries in toys has been criticised[17] and it is estimated that over 8.5 million working toys are thrown away each year in the UK, for which consumers must take a share of the blame. Such is the concern of the European Commission that it has included electronic toys in its Waste Electrical and Electronic Equipment Directive which will put the onus of toy recycling onto companies rather than consumers when it comes into force in 2006.[18] Most of the criticism aimed at toy companies, however, has centred on the morality of targeting young children, a segment made vulnerable by their immature shopping skills and cognitive abilities that limit their ability to make rational judgements about issues such as value or price, or fully understand marketing intent.[19] Television commercials aimed at young children (particularly preschoolers) have also been described as a clear case of coercion that cannot be condoned.[20] References to the vulnerability of children as consumers are common in the literature[21,22] with many arguing that they need to be treated as a special group in different ways to normal (adult) consumers[23,24] and that marketers have a special responsibility towards the vulnerable.[25,26] In considering what vulnerability means in a consumer context, Brenkert[27] distinguishes between being vulnerable (having the potential to be harmed in some way), being susceptible (easily influenced by someone or something), and being disadvantaged (impaired in transactions in the marketplace). Whilst there is little evidence to support that children come to much physical or psychological harm through playing with traditional toys and games, there is criticism that companies use children's susceptibility and limitations to support their own interests. Brenkert contends that any marketing campaigns that fail to ensure individuals are treated fairly are both unethical and unscrupulous.

Despite the often critical stance taken about targeting young children directly, there is some evidence of their increasing sophistication and abilities that the toy companies claim is often underestimated. Even before they can read, children as young as 2 or 3 years have been found to recognise familiar packaging and familiar characters in toys.[28,29] By 5 to 6 years, children begin to recall brand names[30] and almost all can distinguish commercials from programmes[31,32] although this does not necessarily translate into an understanding of the true difference between entertainment and selling intent.[33] An understanding of marketing intent usually emerges by the ages of 7 to 8 years[34,35] and from around 8 years of age, children can recognise the existence of bias and deception in advertising, no longer believing that commercials always tell the truth.[36,37] By this age, however, most children may well be moving away from traditional toys towards electronic games and other forms of entertainment,[38] and will still be vulnerable as consumers in other respects.[39]

It is therefore children under 7 years, in the prime of their toy playing lives, who may be most susceptible to commercial manipulation. Although toy companies argue that the promotions of toys for preschoolers are aimed predominantly at parents, any analysis of television commercials for toys placed around preschool programmes would identify many companies targeting messages at the preschool child. By targeting parents through their children, parents themselves seem to be being drawn into this vulnerability/susceptibility cycle as they strive to provide for their children's happiness and welfare, and to ensure their offspring are not disadvantaged in their peer groups. Changing societal trends and lifestyles (for example, homes with two working parents, high divorce rates of couples with children, and the growing numbers of single parent families) are also often resulting in less time for parent–child contact, creating feelings of guilt in parents which sometimes lead to an over-indulgence in acceding to child requests as some form of compensation.[40] All companies marketing to children are well aware of children's influencing and negotiating skills with parents and other family members (commonly termed 'pester power') and know that a toy request to a parent coming from the child is far more likely to result in a purchase than through any form of promotion they can aim at that parent.

The toy companies acknowledge that young children have limitations, but maintain that that they have rights as individuals. The United Nations' well-intentioned, but partly contentious, 'Convention on the Rights of the Child', ratified by the UK on 16 December 1991, gives children (anyone under 18 years of age):

- The right to say what they think about decisions other adults make that affect them, and to have their opinions heard (Article 12).
- The right to get, and to share information as long as it is not damaging to them or others (Article 13).
- The right to reliable information from the mass media (Article 17).
- The right to relax and play and join in a wide range of activities (Article 31).

(UNICEF UK Youth website, 2005)[41]

Such rights would appear to give commercial organisations at least some justification for both conducting research with young children (through listening to their views) and advertising products to them (through providing appropriate information via the mass media).

The toy companies do not deny that they take advantage of children's pestering skills but argue that such negotiation activities are a regular and natural occurrence in all family relationships and that, as parents always have the final say, it is they who should regulate children's demands. They also contend that children's requests are far more influenced by their peers than through any promotional activity that they can come up with, a view supported by Goldstein's research.[42]

Caring – Moral Responsibility or Astute Commercial Strategy?

It is only within the last two decades or so that many companies have finally woken up to the importance of 'relationship marketing', the nurturing of lasting relationships with their consumers.[43] Caring for the customer/consumer, as Liedtka[44] points out, has become 'the new corporate mantra... [because]... the new realities of the marketplace award competitive advantage to those whose customers feel cared for'. The toy market is no different in wanting to make its consumers feel secure about, and content with, their purchases but they face an additional challenge to many other consumer markets by having at least two sets of interests and care needs to address – children's, and those of parents and other adult toy purchasers. But what does 'care' really mean, how far should companies go in caring for their consumers, and do these relationship-building activities really amount to genuine care in a moral sense?

The word 'care' clearly has broad meaning and the care involved between a mother and child, often illustrated in the literature as 'care at its deepest level',[45,46] cannot easily be compared to the care involved between a commercial organisation and its consumers. However, because of the consumer limitations of children, toy companies do have a special responsibility to consider care not only from both the child's user perspective, but also from that of the parents as purchasers and guardians of the child's best interests. For a caring organisation, such responsibility would need to extend beyond mere compliance with the existing legislation, codes and rights designed to protect every normal consumer, but would require a corporate mentality and action programme that respects, considers and responds to children's unique needs.[47]

Noddings[48] (cited in Liedtka, 1996) makes an interesting distinction between caring *for* and caring *about,* suggesting that ethical caring only applies to those persons that we care *for.* She argues that people we care *about* represents only 'a verbal commitment to the possibility of care' but adds that we cannot care *for* those who are beyond our reach. This raises the question about how far most toy companies can care *for* (and therefore have an ethical responsibility towards) the young children who choose and use their products. With little direct contact with children who reside primarily in the home and school environments, does this make children beyond their reach? Marketing critics might argue that this is not the case, that television advertising is a proven way of reaching and influencing children in the home, and that schools are no longer the haven from commercial activity that they once were.

Building on Nodding's notion of caring, care is now considered as both a moral duty (caring *for*) and as a marketing/business strategy (caring *about*) in the context of the children's toy industry. Evaluative criteria have been selectively drawn from the ethical and marketing literature and matched against the claims and evidence of the toy companies (see Table 24.1).

Table 24.1 Notion of care in the context of the toy industry

CARING FOR	CARING ABOUT
Care as a Moral Duty	**Care as a Marketing Strategy**
Care for the disadvantaged/vulnerable	Relationship-building
Due care	Trust and loyalty
Product safety	Customer/consumer service
Treating people as ends, not just means to an end	Research, innovation and development
Protection of human rights	Product quality and safety
Self-care	Responsible promotion

Issues/Evidence

Company values

Investment in children's play

BTHA role/codes

Lion Mark scheme

ICTI code

Charitable deeds

Schools work

Educational products

Anti-social toys and games

Media Smart initiative

Care as a Marketing Strategy

In defining 'care' as a noun, Chambers dictionary uses terms such as 'attention and thoroughness, caution, gentleness, regard for safety, a responsibility, the activity of looking after someone or something' and as a verb, they define care as 'concerning oneself about someone or being interested in them'.[49] The toy companies would argue that they do very much care about children and can demonstrate meeting many of the above descriptors. They would also probably not deny that many of the caring things they do are done not just because they are the 'right' things to do, in a moral sense, but also because they make good business sense.

The toy industry, compared with many other child-focused industries, has a long history of relationship-building, with many parents (and even some grandparents) buying toys and games for their children (and grandchildren) that they played with in their childhood (for example, LEGO bricks, Barbie dolls, Hornby train sets, Scalextric, Monopoly, and Scrabble). The toy companies are conscious that if they act responsibly towards the current generation of parents and children, they can cement trust and loyalty for the future. As one manager point out the risks of being irresponsible are not worth it:

> We go over and above to make sure that our products are built, manufactured and marketed in the right way, because if we don't, we lose forty or fifty years of all the work we've built up in actually establishing these brands – they are our lifeblood! We don't do anything that would leave us open to suspicion, because it's not worth it… We don't do anything by the back door.

The toy companies argue that they serve a very important role in society by encouraging children to play and that care is shown through their extensive research, innovation and product development which utilise new technology, meet parents' wishes for more educational toys and lead to many new exciting ranges being introduced every year, to suit every budget. The companies interviewed also felt they acted responsibly by not offering replica guns or toys that would reflect 'real life' conflict or lead to aggressive play. Views ranged from those who would not even include cowboys with guns in their colouring books, to those who offered character models or figures with weaponry. These latter toys were rather bizarrely considered acceptable by the companies concerned because the characters were fictitious (rather than 'real life') and it was suggested that role-playing heroes is actually a healthy form of play.

Attention to quality and particularly safety were professed to be the companies' main concerns in producing toys and they pointed to the detailed toy safety legislation that exists and the fact that very few children in the UK are physically injured when playing with toys appropriately. Many of the companies highlighted their stringent quality assurance procedures that ensure products in the market are made to exacting standards, claiming that if there was ever a concern in the development process of a new toy, it would not be brought to the market, or that if there were the slightest concern about the safety of any product currently in the market, it would be recalled quickly, regardless of cost. Safety is also encouraged by the British Toy and Hobby Association (BTHA) who award a 'Lion Mark' to members whose products meet the most stringent European safety standards (BS EN 71). This mark can be displayed on packaging and in promotional literature.

The BTHA also play an important role in encouraging children's play and family play through an ongoing campaign. They work closely with playgroups' associations, toy lending libraries and others and produce consumer information literature on topics such as the value of play, understanding aggressive toys, toy safety, and toy advertising.

The companies provide service support. For parents and other adults, the larger companies have personal helplines for problems or queries. Some websites such as Leapfrog's carries advice to parents on how to maximise play benefits. For the children, a number of the leading brands have children's websites (for example, Barbie, Micropets, LEGO, and Crayola) to provide additional, safe and low cost entertainment. Others show caring in different ways. One company, for example, recognising the importance of a toy to a child, had created a repair facility that it termed the 'dolls' hospital'. If a doll needed repair, it was sent to the hospital and returned to the child with a note saying that, 'dolly has been very brave'. This was seen as important by the manager, recognising that the toy is not merely a child's doll, but also a friend.

Finally, the managers discussed the ways in which they claimed to promote products responsibly to children. They pointed to the many special provisions that children's toy advertisements must abide by, contained within the ITC's (Independent Television Commission) Code of Advertising Standards and Practices (1998, App. 1), which is designed to prevent unfair or misleading promotion. The low level of consumer complaints received by the ITC (now superseded by Ofcom) was forwarded as evidence of its effectiveness. Many also believed that their activities with schools combined well both educational and marketing purpose. One manager described a national schools' competition that her company had established that encouraged school children to design models using its construction toy kits and involved practising engineers going into the schools to judge the results. This, according to the manager, inspired children's learning in an important topic but one that otherwise might have been rather dull.

Critics might argue that many of these care claims have emanated not from the initiative of the toy companies or the industry body, but rather have been imposed on them by others (for example, national and regional government, consumers themselves, major retailers, the media, pressure groups, and so on). They might also question that if the quality and safety procedures are as effective as claimed, why there are still many product recalls from the market and how a potentially dangerous toy such as the Yo-ball, which had an elastic cord that could have become tangled around a child's neck, could have initially passed all the safety legislation and been introduced into the market?[50] And of course the trade body and all toy companies would promote more children's play. It is in their self-interest to do so!

Whilst the Lion Mark scheme is a positive attempt to encourage better toy safety, the consumer group research revealed that most consumers had seen the mark on packaging but had no idea of its meaning. Many of the parents interviewed objected to children's television advertising arguing that it would never be acceptable to them, whatever the regulations. A number would like to see a total ban on television advertising to children under 12 years, as in Sweden, or severer scheduling restrictions as in Greece for example, where toy advertisements cannot be broadcast on radio or television between 07.00 and 22.00h. The European Commission are also concerned at how many companies are using advertising to encourage pester power. The new 'Unfair Commercial Practices Directive', that comes into force in 2007, calls for stricter controls on advertisements aimed at children and bans any that include, 'a direct exhortation to buy or persuade their parents or other adults to buy advertised products for them'.[51] And finally, whilst there do appear to be clear benefits for all parties in appropriate joint company–school activities, such arrangements are often viewed as an uncomfortable mix. As one parent commented:

Marketing through schools surely cannot be right because your school should be somewhere where both parents and teachers trust the teachers to do the right thing. It would be seen as if the school is giving the nod of approval.

Care appears to be very much at the core of the companies' marketing agendas because the continuing support and custom of children and parents is their future. It is also in the interests of future generations of children and parents that toy companies make sufficient profit to survive independently and continue to provide the rich choice of products and value that they do today. The companies, whilst conscious of their wider stakeholder and societal responsibilities, are also clear on their priorities, as one director of a leading toy company admitted:

Delivering shareholder value is absolutely what we are about! Our number one priority, otherwise none of us would be here.

Care as a Moral Duty

In describing care as a practice, Tronto[52] emphasises its concern with thought as well as action. Before evaluating more of their activities, it is interesting to note the caring intentions contained within many of the leading companies' value statements.

LEGO's philosophy[53], for example, is that 'good play enriches the child's life – and its subsequent adulthood,' founded on the company values of creativity, imagination, learning, fun, and quality. In Binney and Smith's 'Vision and Culture',[54] they emphasize an obsession with consumer needs that requires employees, 'to constantly ask: What are the implications for the consumer?' For others, important values relate to children's development. Leapfrog[55] maintains that it is, 'passionately devoted to delighting and engaging big and little kids in a meaningful way that will inspire a lifelong love of learning'. Finally a number of companies refer to acting responsibly. Mattel's code of conduct[56] states that, 'as an organisation and individually, Mattel employees are responsible for acting with integrity, treating others with dignity and respect, being honest and fair in all transactions and constantly striving to do the right thing', while for LEGO, 'upholding the quality and ethical values and a consistency in all our actions that engender an ongoing feeling of trust', is important.

Whilst it has been suggested in the philosophical literature that individuals should act principally in their own self-interest[57] and businesses in their shareholders' main interest,[58] they also have a moral obligation to care about other key stakeholders such as employees, customers (intermediaries), consumers, and the wider community in which they operate.[59] Where consumers who are vulnerable in some way are treated as ends in themselves, this gives rise to a 'duty of care'.[60] The difficulty is assessing what constitutes an appropriate level of care for a commercial organisation. Soule[61] points out that possibilities range from non-interference to positive responsibility, bearing in mind the overarching imperative of looking after and not harming. The duty of protecting others' safety or *nonmaleficence* (not injuring – Ross[62]) would seem to be particularly important where children are concerned and companies should take all reasonable steps to ensure products are free from defects and are safe to use.[63]

Some of the toy managers described their work in the local community, particularly with local schools, while others spoke of their work with charities and the disadvantaged. Tomy, for example, works closely with the National Institute for the Blind in developing many of its toys, a particular cause encouraged by the Tomyama family. Other companies are involved in charity fundraising, such as the Early Learning Centre through its stores, and in cause–related marketing initiatives where there is a particular synergy. Vivid Imaginations, the largest British toy company, has raised £60,000 for the Royal Society for the Prevention of Cruelty to Animals through its 'Animal Hospital' range, and £30,000 for the 'Make A Wish Foundation' through its 'Care Bears' range, donating a portion of sales revenue.

At an industry level, the BTHA, is also working closely with preschool playgroup associations supplying toys, leaflets, and brochures on children's play, particularly in deprived areas of the UK, as well as special leaflets for handicapped, deaf, and blind children. The Association runs a 'Toy Trust' that annually collects charitable donations from member companies and raises funds through special events with proceeds donated to charitable organisations involved with disadvantaged children and their families. In 2004, the Trust raised over £152,000 for 90 different causes.

Interpreting Kant's views on duty, rights and responsibility[64] can lead to mixed messages about the appropriateness of targeting children. On the one hand, his second categorical imperative argues that people should be treated as ends in their own right and not as merely a means to an end. This would seem to indicate therefore that it is not appropriate for companies to target parental funds through their children. On the other hand, Kant, along with other libertarians, has also argued for ensuring the freedom and rights of every individual that might support the companies' policy of treating children as individuals with their own rights. So which view should have priority? As much of the basis for Kant's arguments rests on the notion of human beings' rational thought and action, therein perhaps lies the answer and one of the main limitations of young children. On this basis, companies would be wise to err on the side of caution.

One of the most widely discussed philosophical discourses about care is the Ethic of Care, emphasing the care-givers' responsibility to care for others. This theory is most closely associated with Gilligan's work on feminist morality[65] and a 'mothering' image of caring but perhaps has the potential for wider application in a business context. Liedtka,[66] in considering the Ethic of Care as appropriate for a caring organisation, argues that the aim of caring is the opposite to the stereotypical view of caring as fostering dependence. She believes that to care means to respect the other's autonomy and to work to enhance the cared-for's ability to make his or her own choices. The recognition of the importance of the need, for all human beings, to realise their capacities goes back to Aristotle. This view is significant in that it suggests that rather than bypassing children in their marketing because of their limitations, companies might play a proactive role, in conjunction with parents, in developing children's consumer socialization skills. The toy industry has recently become involved in the Media Smart media literacy campaign[67], an initiative that aims to educate children (aged 6–11 years), via schools and broadcast media in the home, to understand and interpret advertising so that they are able to make more informed consumer choices. Although this initiative also has an element of self-interest for the industries and companies involved, it does show some responsibility in trying to develop children into more knowledgeable consumers, an area currently missing from the National Curriculum.

A Caring Industry?

So do companies care in a moral sense or merely in a business/marketing strategy sense? Liedtka[68] is sceptical. For her, much current 'customer care' is impersonal, instrumental and object-focused. She questions whether companies really meet and address the care needs of their individual consumers or merely offer a set of pre-packaged solutions to problems in pursuit of the only end of significance to them – profit. And whilst many organisations excel at market transactions (producing standardised products efficiently and consistently, and marketing them aggressively), few she believes can really be described as 'caring organisations'. For her, a caring organisation needs an assembly of caring individuals whose efforts are supported through the organisation's goals, systems, strategies and values. A caring organisation would need to be focused entirely on individuals (not quality or profits), be undertaken as an end, not means to an end (such as profit), be essentially personal, and be growth enhancing for the cared for (moving them towards developing their capabilities).

It would not however be easy for toy companies to comply with all these conditions nor indeed for any consumer goods manufacturer. The need to generate profit for survival and the problem of having to demonstrate care at a distance through impersonal means of communication such as advertisements and websites may be difficult to overcome. Yet there are some worthy actions that toy companies take that appear to show care about and concern for their young consumers. There is a genuine passion for providing children with fun and enjoyment through playing with their toys and in many cases, the companies do play a valuable role in educating children through the development of important academic and social skills, as well as giving them guidance, confidence and encouragement, summed up by one manager:

> Play is a child's work at the end of the day and we are helping them to do things that will help develop their skills at lots of different levels.

There is also concern shown by the industry towards the disadvantaged children in society who do not receive piles of presents at Christmas and yet for whom play is just as important in their lives. The attention to care and to strong values amongst the sample companies can perhaps be part attributed to the influence of the founders and their descendants, many of whom are still involved in the businesses (for example, at companies such as LEGO, Tomy, BRIO, Vivid, and Flair). Others are perhaps influenced by the culture of their home countries. The Scandinavians have a history of protectionism for children, and in the United States, there appears to be a strong emphasis in many industries to post clear ethical statements and policies and to monitor and enforce them.

McNeal[69] has pointed out how difficult it is to market to children responsibly:

> Anyone can fool them, deceive them, cheat them. It takes a mighty good marketer to satisfy children's needs and wants and not do any of these things intentionally or unintentionally.

The toy industry however with its many long-established and highly regarded companies has in many ways an opportunity to become ethical innovators and set the lead for other child-focused industries to follow. Attention to safety, quality, play value, value for money and after-sales service as well as initiatives such as the Lion Mark scheme, the ICTI manufacturing code and involvement in Media Smart are all positive factors in this direction and have both moral and business worth.

Much remains to be done however if the toy industry as a whole is to be perceived as 'caring.' David Lipman the founder of JAKKS Pacific/Kidz Biz, a leading international toy company, recently declared that '...the public has a very bad perception of the toy industry and this needs to change'.[70] Many parents still view the industry sceptically not only because of its promotional activity targeting children, but also because of the unscrupulous activities of a few companies and managers, the general fears about the control of big corporations over everyday life and a growing cynicism about business practices.[71] It seems that because of time pressures and busy lifestyles, caring corporate practice needs to be better communicated to consumers, even if such care is pursued for philanthropic purposes. This might help breakdown what one parent described as the 'harsh and uncaring exterior' that she felt many toy companies have.

The general lack of profitability in the industry is a concern and should provide positive encouragement for the companies to care more in order to retain and win consumers' business. The reality though is that it may result in the opposite. Increased financial pressures are more likely to lead to shortcuts, more risks being taken and a greater chance of ethical abuses taking place. There is also likely to be more consolidation in the industry with fewer smaller toy companies and retailers and ultimately leading to less consumer choice. Already some of the larger companies are looking outside the industry for new opportunities and moving into other controversial markets (for example, links between Vivid Imaginations and McDonald's toys, Hasbro with Walkers crisps, and Lego with children's cereals).

The Legoland theme parks were also sold in July 2005 giving new parties access to the image of a leading and highly trusted toy brand.

Conclusion

There is always likely to be a body of opinion arguing that if commercial organisations really want to demonstrate care about young children, they must focus their marketing activities almost exclusively on parents and other adult toy buyers so that informed, rational toy purchase decisions can be made. But whether Swedish or Greek children have happier childhoods because of the restricted toy advertising or become more responsible consumers in later life remains unclear and any research may prove inconclusive as human ingenuity usually finds a way around regulation.

There is also an underlying assumption in this argument that parents would make better toy choices without the promotion-fuelled child influence. While parents might be able to discern information, value for money and marketing intent far more readily than their young offspring, many parents in the focus groups admitted to buying toys and games that they wanted (products remembered from childhood, products that they felt had an important education value, and products which they felt their children would like), without consulting their children, only to find that many were rarely, if ever, played with. Involving children in the marketing process, providing it is done responsibly and legally, that takes account of their limitations and fully involves parents or other guardians in the process at the same time, not only fulfils children's human rights but may also lead to better choices, better play value, and less environmental waste.

A caring children's industry needs caring parents to play their part, ideally with the support of the schools curriculum. Today's parents demand toys and games to support the development of their children's skills and knowledge to equip them for later life. Developing shopping/consumer skills at an early stage in life is another set of life-long learning skills and judging from the spiralling level of personal debt amongst adults in the UK, it is an area where more education at a younger age is urgently needed. Parents can also contribute to a more caring commercial environment if they are prepared to pay a fair price for their purchases. Developing better, safer products, improving communications, paying toy workers more and so on will normally incur greater expense for the companies. Whilst a growing number of consumers seem prepared to pay a premium for some products such as Fairtrade coffee or bananas, the evidence from the companies and parents suggests that consumers already consider toy prices to be high and expect them to fall rather than rise. As one senior manager commented:

> You cannot walk away from price-value. If you are not delivering price-value, sooner or later it will come back and bite you, however wonderful your brand is. If you are selling things to mums in Woolworths, the reality is that it's not a religious, sanctimonious purchase, it is a toy after all, and the majority of toys are rubbish anyway. How much room there is for a truly worthy toy in today's environment? – I don't know.

If the toy companies are not convinced that consumers really want more worthy products or are prepared to pay reasonably for them, this impasse may limit how much more care in the industry can grow. Throwing more money at companies is no guarantee that ethical standards will improve, but it may at least arrest the slide towards a selfish and uncaring society.

Notes

1   Kline, S.(1993), *Out of the Garden – Toys and Children's Culture in the Age of Television Marketing*. Verso, London.
2   Goldstein, J. (2004), *Making Time for Play 2*. Publication of the British Toy and Hobby Association, London.
3   Furby, L. (1980), 'The origins and early development of possessive behaviour', *Political Psychology*, vol. 2, pp. 3–42.
4   Kline, S., *Out of the Garden – Toys and Children's Culture in the Age of Television Marketing*, p. 15.
5   Cole, D. (2005), *The Concept of Play Malnourishment in the UK*. Report for the International Play Association.
6   Abrams, R. (2002), 'What is Childhood? – Part One', *The Daily Telegraph*, April 13, pp. 1–2.
7   BTHA Handbook 2004, British Toy and Hobby Association, London.
8   Key Note Limited (2004), *Market Report, Toys and Games*, 19th edn. April: London.
9   Ibid.
10 Rankine, K. (2004), 'Two toy retailers lose price fix appeal', *The Daily Telegraph*, December 15, p. 30.
11 Nielsen Media (2004), 'Junk food report', *Daily Mail*, May 1, p. 38.
12 National Labor Committee (2002), *Toys of Misery – A Report on the Toy Industry in China,* January 2002.
13 National Labor Committee (2002), *Toys of Misery – Made in China*, February 2002.
14 August, O. (2003), 'Step aside, Rudolph, Santa has gone east', *The Times*, December 19, p. 3.
15 Spencer, R. (2004), 'Unseasonal strife in Santa's little sweatshops', *The Daily Telegraph,* December, 22, p. 12.
16 BTHA Handbook 2004.
17 Ethical Consumer (2002), 'Toying with their Lives', October/November, pp. 10–15.
18 Wallop, H. (2005), 'Brussels lumps teddies with old fridges in waste ruling', *The Daily Telegraph*, January 29, p. 31.
19 Paine, L.S. (1996), 'Children as consumers: the ethics of children's television advertising'. in N.C. Smith and J. Quelch (eds.), *Ethics in Marketing*. Primis Custom Publishing (McGraw-Hill), New York, pp. 672–86.
20 De George, R.T. (1995), *Moral Issues in Business.* Macmillan, New York.
21 Mazis, M.B., Ringold, D.J., Perry, E.S. and Denman, D.W. (1992), 'Perceived age and attractiveness of models in cigarette advertisements', *Journal of Marketing,* vol. 56, (January), pp. 22–37.
22 Cohen, D. (1974), 'The concept of unfairness as it relates to advertising legislation', *Journal of Marketing,* vol. 38, pp. 8–13.

[23]   Brenkert, G.G. (1998), 'Marketing and the Vulnerable', in L.P. Hartman (ed.), *Perspectives in Business Ethics*, Int. edn. McGraw-Hill, London, pp. 515–26.

[24]   Smith, N.C. and Cooper-Martin, E. (1997), 'Ethics and target marketing: the role of product harm and consumer vulnerability', *Journal of Marketing*, vol. 61 (July), pp. 1–20.

[25]   Andreasen A.R. (1975), *The Disadvantaged Customer.* The Free Press, New York.

[26]   Goodin, R.E. 1985, *Protecting the Vulnerable* The University of Chicago Press, Chicago.

[27]   Brenkert, 'Marketing and the Vulnerable'.

[28]   Derscheid, L.E., Kwon, Y-H. and Fang, S-R. (1996), 'Preschoolers' socialization as consumers of clothing and recognition of symbolism', *Perceptual and Motor Skills*, vol. 82 (June), pp. 1171–81.

[29]   Haynes, J., Burls, D.C., Dukes, A. and Cloud, R. (1993), 'Consumer socialization of preschoolers and kindergartners as related to clothing consumption', *Psychology and Marketing*, vol. 10 (March/April), pp. 151–66.

[30]   Macklin, M.C. (1996), 'Preschoolers learning of brand names from visual cues', *Journal of Consumer Research*, vol. 23 (December), pp. 251–61.

[31]   Blosser, B.J. and Roberts, D.F. (1985), 'Age differences in children's perceptions of message intent: responses to TV news, commercials, educational spots, and public service announcements', *Communication Research*, October 12, pp. 455–84.

[32]   Stephens, N. and Strutts, M.A. (1982), 'Preschoolers' ability to distinguish between television programming and commercials', *Journal of Advertising*, vol. 11 (2), pp. 16–26.

[33]   Butter, E.J., Popovich, P.M., Stackhouse R.H. and Garner R.K. (1981). 'Discrimination of television programs and commercials by preschool children', *Journal of Advertising Research*, vol. 21 (April), pp. 53–6.

[34]   Blosser and Roberts, 'Age differences in children's perceptions of message intent: responses to TV news, commercials, educational spots, and public service announcements'.

[35]   Ward, S., Wackman, D.B. and Wartella, E. (1977). *How Children Learn to Buy.* Sage, Beverley Hills, CA.

[36]   Bever, T.G., Smith, M.L., Bengen, B, and Johnson, T.G. (1975). 'Young viewers' troubling responses to TV ads', *Harvard Business Review*, November-December, vol. 53, pp. 109–20.

[37]   Robertson, T.S. and Rossiter, J.R. (1974). 'Children and commercial persuasion: an attribution theory analysis', *Journal of Consumer Research*, vol. 1 (June), pp. 13–20.

[38]   Key Note Limited, Market Report, Toys and Games.

[39]   John, D.R. (1999). 'Consumer socialization: a retrospective look at twenty-five years of research', *Journal of Consumer Research*, vol. 26 (3), pp. 183–234.

[40]   Greenhalgh, T. (2002). 'Understanding family values', *Journal of Advertising and Marketing to Children*, vol. 4 (1), pp. 13–19.

[41]   UNICEF Youth Web Site. 'Summary of the UN Convention on the Rights of the Child'. < http://www.therightssite.org.uk/html/kyr.htm> (21.06.2005)

[42]   Goldstein, J. (1999). *Children and Advertising: The Research, Advertising and Marketing to Children.* Advertising Association, London.

[43]   Egan, J. (2001). *Relationship Marketing.* Pearson Education, Harlow.

[44]   Liedtka, J.M. (1996). 'Feminist morality and competitive reality: a role for an ethic of care?' *Business Ethics Quarterly*, vol.6 (2), pp. 179–200.

45 Held, V. (1983). 'The obligations of mothers and fathers'. In J. Trebilcot (ed.), *Mothering: Essays in Feminist Theory*. Rowman and Allanheld, Totowa, NJ.

46 Noddings, N. (1984). *Caring: A Feminine Approach to Ethics and Moral Education*. University of California Press, Berkley, CA.

47 Liedtka, 'Feminist morality and competitive reality: a role for an ethic of care?

48 Noddings, *Caring: A Feminine Approach to Ethics and Moral Education.*

49 Chambers Harrap (2005). *Chambers 21st Century Dictionary.*
    <http://www.xreferplus.com/entry.jsp?xrefid=11935576&secid=.-&hh=1> 22/08/2005.

50 Bird, S. (2003). 'Yo-ball toy banned for risk of strangling'. *The Times*, April 25, p. 9.

51 Browne, A. (2005). 'Ban on adverts that urge youngsters to pester their parents', *The Times*, February 25, p. 13.

52 Tronto, J. (1993). *Moral Boundaries: A Political Argument for an Ethic of Care*. Routledge, New York.

53 <www.lego.com/values>, (accessed 01/05/2004).

54 <www.binney-smith.com/page.cfm?id=20>, (accessed 14/05/2004).

55 <www.leapfrog.com/our_approach>, (accessed 14/05/2004).

56 <www.mattel.com/about_us/Corp_Governance/ethics.asp>, (accessed 14/05/2004).

57 Ross, W.D. (1938). *The Right and the Good.* Oxford: Clarendon Press.

58 Friedman, M. (1970). 'The social responsibility of business is to increase its profits', *New York Times Magazine*, Sept, p. 13.

59 Freeman, E.R. (1984). *Strategic Management: A Stakeholder Approach*. Pitman, Boston.

60 Crane, A. and Matten, D. (2004). *Business Ethics*. Oxford University Press, Oxford.

61 Soule, E. (1998). 'Trust and managerial responsibility', *Business Ethics Quarterly,* vol. 8 (2), pp. 249–72.

62 Ross, *The Right and the Good.*

63 Boatright, J.R. (2000). Ethics and the Conduct of Business, 3rd edn. Prentice Hall, Upper Saddle River, NJ.

64 Kant, I. (1785). *Grounding for the Metaphysics of Morals*. Reprinted in 1981. Hackett Publishing, Indianapolis.

65 Gilligan, C. (1982). *In a Different Voice: Psychological Theory and Women's Development,*. Harvard University Press, Cambridge, MA.

66 Liedtka, 'Feminist morality and competitive reality: a role for an ethic of care?

67 <http://www.mediasmart.org.uk/media_smart/index.html>

68 Liedtka, 'Feminist morality and competitive reality: a role for an ethic of care?

69 McNeal, J.U. (1992). *Kids as Customers* Lexington Books, New York.

70 *Toy News*, January 2003, p 55.

71 Varney, D. (2004). 'Loss of trust will hit firms where it hurts', *The Sunday Times*, March 14, p. 4.

PART IV
COMMENTARIES

Chapter 25

A Taste of the Orange Revolution: Ukraine and the Spirit of Constitutionalism

Jiri Priban

In November and December 2004, the Ukrainian 'Orange Revolution' was covering front pages of newspapers and media primetime all around the world. Was it a belated political change resembling the 1989 revolutions in the Soviet bloc countries, or a clash of geopolitical interests between the West and Putin's Russia echoing the Cold War logic?

The 'Orange Revolution', indeed, was strikingly similar to the East European events of 1989. Crowds were calling for the government's resignation. Activist groups – notably the youth movement Pora ('It's time') – demanded radical changes to the existing political regime and expressed their anger and complete distrust of the ruling élite which was massively corrupt and recruited from the old communist officials. Nevertheless, the corrupt regime was by no means totalitarian and resembled a lot more semi-authoritarian regimes typical of harassment of its critics and arbitrary use of power. Furthermore, the public protests were a response to the presidential elections which had been rigged by the state officials, yet monitored by international organisations and free in principle – something entirely unthinkable in the communist countries. Although the communist legacy heavily affected the independent state of Ukraine established after the split of the Soviet Union in 1991, one has to be careful comparing the political situation before and after the collapse of communism.

During the outgoing president Leonid Kuchma's ten-year rule, Ukraine was plagued by economic and political troubles and the allegations of politically motivated murders and illicit arms sales. Although Kuchma stabilised the ethnically and culturally divided state and eliminated the risk of a civil war between the Eastern industrial parts dominated by ethnic Russians (estimated 17 per cent of the total population) and the Western agricultural regions populated by ethnic Ukrainians during the 1990s, the legacy of his rule will be corruption, poverty, and political violence targeting the regime critics. One mark of this legacy is the disfigured face of the opposition's presidential candidate Victor Yushchenko who was poisoned by dioxin during the election campaign. Independent tests showed that the level of poison in the blood of Yushchenko was the second highest level ever recorded and he therefore had an extremely lucky escape from death in what was to be just a political battle.

Complaints that the West was meddling in Ukraine ignore that primary causes of the political crisis were internal and the public was responding to the unfair practices of the state officials. The confrontation between Russia and the West emerged only after international observers and the Organization for Security and Co-operation in Europe (OSCE), joined by the EU and the US officials, stated that the presidential election did not meet democratic standards. Despite president Putin's unprecedented support for the official candidate Victor Yanukovich and his two visits to Ukraine during the presidential campaign, Russia failed to achieve a strategic goal of keeping Ukraine within 'its sphere of influence' by supporting the old corrupt élite. The official Russian policy awkwardly supported the electoral fraud and, apart from Kuchma and his favourite Yanukovich, Vladimir Putin consequently became another loser in the whole affair.

The 'Orange Revolution' may hardly be perceived as an act of nihilistic destruction of the rule of law because it was triggered by a denial of one of the most fundamental constitutional rights – a right to free and fair vote. Protesters gathered outside the government's buildings because they demanded to reinstitute this right, yet completely distrusted the regime that was supposed to do it. It was therefore extremely important that leaders of the opposition followed a 'legalistic strategy' of going to the Rada, Ukraine's parliament, and then the Supreme Court to declare the presidential election void. No doubt the leaders learned an important lesson from the 1989 revolutions in Central and Eastern Europe which often used the strategy of 'revolution by a constitutional change'[1] and thus could win the public and international support and even avoid the biggest risk of the civil war and the split of Ukraine.

The rule of law and principle of legal and constitutional negotiations were absolutely central throughout the revolutionary process. Since the second round of the presidential election (on 21st November), Ukraine went through a series of parliamentary crisis sessions, the Supreme Court's ruling that the election was void (3rd December), and an agreement between Parliament and President Kuchma that was to bring political calm and constitutional change reducing the presidential powers and guaranteeing the fair presidential election scheduled for 26th December. Under the constitutional reforms approved by Parliament by an overwhelming vote of 402 to 21, the central electoral commission was reshuffled and the possibilities for falsification by voting from home and absentee ballots were substantially reduced. In return, the opposition agreed that the president would lose some of its powers, especially to appoint top executive posts except for the prime minister, defence and foreign ministers. The constitutional change means that the Ukrainian constitutional system of a presidential republic will be significantly transformed and adopt a number of features typical of parliamentarianism. Although responding to the pressure of the outgoing president Kuchma, the change may actually turn out to be beneficial for the Ukrainian constitutional system.

Necessary compromises in the constitutional reform should pacify the eastern parts of Ukraine supporting Victor Yanukovich and close ties with Moscow. At the same time, they should open access of the opposition to political power and initiate necessary reforms awaited by the public protesting against the existing regime and hoping to finally have democratic and accountable government. Whatever happens after the December election is fully in the hand of the Ukrainian people. The success of the opposition leader Victor Yuschenko in the repeated presidential election would be only a first, yet crucial step in eliminating the old political practices and making the political system publicly accountable and subject to the rule of law. Ukraine, the country of 48 million people, would certainly deserve it.

December 2004

Notes

[1] For instance, the rule of law and constitutional protection of legal certainty were highlighted as major principles of the regime change by the Hungarian Constitutional Court in the early 1990s. See especially its decision on retrospectivity of laws, No. 11/1992. (III.5.) AB of the Constitutional Court, *Magyar Közlöny,* no. 23 (1992): 935.

Chapter 26

Seroxat – The Power of the Pharmaceutical Industry. The Case for a Better Way to Research, License and Regulate Medicines

Sarah-Jane Richards

The old adage 'all publicity is good publicity' must surely be wearing thin for the pharmaceutical industry, especially for GlaxoSmithKline (GSK) which has been hit by a wave of adverse publicity and falling share prices following litigation in the USA over the safety of its anti-depressant, Paxil, which is known as Seroxat in the UK. However, it is not the prosecution of this company *per se* that has kept the firm in the public eye on both sides of the Atlantic, but allegations of a tardiness to act by health regulators. Both the Medicines and Healthcare products Regulatory Agency (MHRA) in the UK and the Food and Drug Administration (FDA) in the US have failed to take sufficient action on evidence that Seroxat, the most widely prescribed Selective Serotonin Reuptake Inhibitor (SSRI), can be addictive and cause suicide.

Parents of children that have attempted or succeeded in committing suicide have asked why their physicians were not warned of the risks associated with this drug. In seeking to answer this simple question, a picture has emerged of a flawed system of licensing and of reporting adverse drug reactions (ADR), a lack of independence of those responsible for drug regulation, and claims of fear by the government in challenging the marketing practices of the multi-nationals who threaten to move their empires overseas with commensurate loss of revenue and employment.

The serotonergic system has been associated with the brain's emotional centre since the 1980s, making serotonin an obvious target for investigation by the pharmaceutical industry in the quest for the next generation of anti-depressants. With both the tricyclic and benzodiazepine classes of anti-depressants issued with warnings of dependency properties and toxicity in overdose, general practitioners and psychiatrists were receptive to the new acclaimed, safer and non-addictive SSRIs. Of this new generation of drugs, Prozac developed by Eli Lilly & Co. rapidly became the market leader and maintained its dominant position throughout the 1990s. When the patent expired in 2001, Seroxat took its place as the market leader.

Conservative estimates derived from different sources of data suggest that four million people per year are prescribed Seroxat in the UK,[1] yet the evidence for efficacy (superiority over placebo) – the basis for any drug being licensed – has now been questioned, not just in the case of Seroxat but for other SSRIs too. Moreover, in June 2004 the New York State Attorney General, Eliot Spitzer sued GSK for concealing negative data regarding iatrogenic effects associated with discontinuance syndrome and suicide.

Seroxat was licensed in the UK on 11th December 1990 for the treatment of mild to moderate depression. By 1993, 78 Yellow Card notification reports of adverse withdrawal effects had been received by the Committee for the Safety of Medicines (CSM) and Medicines Control Agency (MCA).[2] This exceeded the total number of adverse reaction reports received for all of the benzodiazepines combined even though the SSRI's were represented as safer drugs. The CSM/MCA responded issuing a single paragraph statement in a newsletter to GPs reminding doctors of the need for gradual withdrawal. They failed to mention that often withdrawal symptoms were being mistaken for depression relapses, for which GPs were prescribing even higher doses of the drug.

On 9 January 1998, in the face of mounting adverse reports from users and GPs, Seroxat was re-licensed for a wider range of symptoms including depression accompanied with anxiety, obsessive compulsive disorder and panic disorder. Off label prescription included pre-menstrual tension and irritable bowel syndrome. This wider remit increased sales dramatically and for the first time people who had never been depressed or suicidal were being prescribed Seroxat. Unbeknown to them, they were exposed to the additional risk of dependency syndrome and a raised risk of suicide. No longer could depression, suicidal thoughts and acts suffered by these people be attributed to a relapse of their depressive illness.

By 2002, over 1000 Yellow Cards had been received by the CSM/MCA identifying adverse withdrawal effects.[3] At the same time, evidence of a discontinuance syndrome was being reported through case reports and published studies.[4,5,6,7] These events should have alerted the regulatory authority that there was a serious withdrawal problem with Seroxat. However, the CSM/MCA was quiescent and the Royal College of Psychiatrists reassured patients that there was no 'dependence' problem. Indeed, until mid-2003 the patient information leaflet continued to describe Seroxat as 'non-addictive' and failed to mention that patients could suffer suicidal ideation. Until 2002, GSK stated that 0.2 per cent of users suffered withdrawal difficulties. This increased to 0.7 per cent and then in 2003 they admitted 25 per cent suffered withdrawal problems.[8] However, this information was not positively communicated to GPs, who continued to reassure their patients that Seroxat was safe and non-addictive.

Several events occurred which played a key role in opening the door to Seroxat's adverse effects and which would eventually lead to a public enquiry. Firstly, the persistence by Director of Social Audit Ltd., Charles Medawar, in questioning the regulatory authorities' inaction over their failure to issue a medicines warning of suicide risk and addiction.[9] Secondly, members of the Seroxat User's Group wrote over 1000 letters to MPs and others in their bid to have an independent enquiry. No doubt this was not only influential in the MHRA's decision to undertake a review of

Seroxat but also in stimulating the investigative reporting of the BBC's Panorama team. As a result of such scrutiny, the public were able to observe for themselves how the medicines regulators interpreted and discharged their responsibilities and, with increased public awareness, the internet became the publishing focus of many personal accounts of addiction, dependency syndrome, suicidal thoughts and acts.

In October 2002, the BBC Panorama team revealed information that the adverse effects of suicidal thoughts and acts, and withdrawal problems vigorously denied by GSK had in fact been well known to its predecessors, Smith Kline Beecham, through their healthy control studies, prior to licensing.[10] Panorama revealed that Prof. David Healey, a psychiatrist and researcher at Bangor University, had for many years been concerned that the so called 'depressive relapses' experienced by Seroxat users were in fact withdrawal symptoms. On perusing the data comprising the Seroxat healthy control studies Healey discovered that these participants, who had never suffered from depression or suicidal thoughts or acts, started to experience suicidal thoughts on taking the drug, along with a cluster of distinctive withdrawal symptoms including the now well known symptom of 'electric zap' sensations in the brain.[11] Moreover, Prof. Healey reported his concern that results had not been published of a controlled experiment undertaken by GSK in which 85 per cent of healthy volunteers suffered adverse effects and one committed suicide. Prof. Healey claimed that GSK knew that approximately 1 in 60 adults on Seroxat made a suicide attempt while the figure for placebo was 1 in 550. It would therefore appear that GSK were aware of the risks Seroxat posed prior to their licence application. The question remains 'how could Seroxat have ever received the endorsement of the licensing authorities – the MCA (now MHRA) in the UK and the FDA'?

Licensing applications by pharmaceutical companies must be supported by the disclosure of all clinical trials conducted so that efficacy and adverse effects may be evaluated. The FDA has repeatedly denied receiving disclosure of the relevant control data. In the UK, the MHRA has declined to comment, stating that such disclosure is confidential. However, Richard Brooke, a lay member of the MHRA and chairman of MIND broke ranks with his colleagues in March 2004 and confirmed the suspicions of many – that the Committee for Safety of Medicines had been aware of trial data disclosed by SKB for more than 10 years about significant withdrawal effects if Seroxat was taken in doses exceeding 20mg yet in three successive reviews of the drug had failed to agree to taking any action.

Through the tenacity of a few concerned individuals, the case of Seroxat was eventually considered by the House of Commons' Select Committee on 14 October 2004.[12] Also during October 2004, evidence was presented to the Committee which challenged the independence of the regulatory authorities and told of too close a relationship between key members of the MHRA and GSK. For instance, the director of licensing at the MHRA was the worldwide safety director of GSK until 2001. For many years the Chairman of the MHRA was also sitting on Glaxo's scientific advisory committee. Although he did not vote, he took part in the Seroxat licensing discussions. It is alleged that other MHRA members have investments in GSK.

Charles Medawar and others claim that the practice of describing suicidal thoughts and acts in vague nomenclature is one method that has been used to disguise adverse effects. For example, 'suicide' repeatedly being described as 'emotional lability' in published reports, has been passed unchallenged by the MHRA. The Agency has not only failed to respond to the large number of ADR notifications received, but also not responded to the fact that Seroxat heads the World Health Organisation's league table of drugs from which it is difficult to withdraw.

On 23 February, 2004 Paul Flynn MP informed the House of Commons that, in correspondence received by him from GSK, the company had expressed the view that anti-depressants should be taken by half of the female population in the United Kingdom and a third of the male population; it wanted to see 25 million people taking anti-depressants.[13] This being the target, it is not surprising to hear that scientists employed in academic medical research are being sponsored by pharmaceutical companies, as indeed are some entire academic departments. Most scientists working in UK universities and medical schools are employed on short-term contracts and against this background of financial insecurity offers of funding by the pharmaceutical industry are gratefully received albeit at the risk of compromising scientific independence and integrity. There is even the suggestion that a significant proportion of the research literature on SSRI prescriptions to children may have been ghost written by the pharmaceutical company, with academics of standing agreeing to put their names to published reports.[14]

In 2003 the British Journal of Psychiatry published the proceedings of a debate entitled *Clinical trials of anti-depressant medications are producing meaningless results*. It reported the view that psychiatry is subservient to the drug industry and that clinical trials are valueless because of fundamental flaws in methodology and biased reporting. Moreover that 50 per cent of negative results are never published.[15] With the accusation that scientific data is being controlled by the pharmaceutical companies and that the MHRA comprises members who have financial investments in the industry, it appears that the public are not being protected against the profit-driven ambitions of 'big pharma' to achieve ever higher sales and to ignore legitimate concerns about safety and efficacy.

We need good medicines for many debilitating and disabling human conditions. However, the Seroxat story warns that there must be a better way of directing and regulating medicines, research and development. The primary focus must always be on the needs of patients for safe and effective drugs, which must never be sacrificed to the profit motives of the drug industry working hand in glove with government regulatory agencies equally concerned about reducing demands on the public purse.

November 2004

Notes

1   Paul Flynn in House of Commons transcripts of 23 February, 2004 (uncorrected transcripts).
2   Charles Medawar and Anita Hardon in '*Medicines out of control?*' published by Aksant, 2004.
3   Ibid.
4   Fava, G.A. and Grandi, S. (1995) *J Clin Psychopharmacol.* Oct. 15, (5), pp. 374–375.
5   Frost, L, Lal, S. et al. (1995) *Am J Psychiatry,* vol.152, (5), p. 810.
6   Rosenbaum, J.F., Fava, M., Hoog, S.L., et al. (1998) *Biological Psychiatry,* vol. 44, pp. 77–87.
7   Tobin v Smith Kline Beecham (2001) Wyoming, USA.
8   See Paul Flynn at note 1.
9   Charles Medawar and Anita Hardon in '*Medicines out of control?*'
10 BBC Panorama transcripts from website bbc.co.uk
11 David Healey Letter to Peter J. Pitts Associate Commissioner for External Relations, Food and Drug Administration *Re: Suicidal evidence not addressed by FDA*. Alliance for Human Research Protection: Feb 19, 2004.
12 House of Commons Health Committee – The Influence of the Pharmaceutical Industry, 14th October, 2004 (uncorrected transcripts).
13 See Paul Flynn at note 1.
14 Alliance for Human Research Protection – British Scientists Debate *Clinical trials of antidepressant medication are producing meaningless results*.
15 Thase, M.E. (1999) *J Clin Psychiatry* vol.60, Suppl 4, pp. 23–31; discussion 32.

Chapter 27

Doha Developments: The July Package and Agriculture

Julian Kinderlerer and Christian Lopez-Silva

The most difficult issue for negotiation in the last WTO Round, known as the Doha Development Agenda, has probably been agriculture. The programme of reform has been long, slow and complex. It started with the mandate provided by Article 20 of the Agriculture Agreement where countries agreed to take into account the experience in implementing the agreement and in particular, to look at 'non-trade concerns, special and differential treatment to developing country Members, and the objective to establish a fair and market-oriented agricultural trading system'. This was followed by the mandate of the Doha Declaration. Despite the Cancun Ministerial Conference in 2003, negotiations had stalled until a framework, known as the July Package, was agreed in Geneva on 31 July 2004.[1]

Last Round of Trade Negotiations: Doha Development Agenda

There are a number of negotiations taking place within the World Trade Organization (WTO), which is the international organisation dealing with the global rules of trade between countries. Most of the negotiations are now formally linked by the Doha Development Agenda which constitutes the latest WTO Round. This Agenda is meant particularly to take into account the needs of developing countries which constitute two thirds of the members of the WTO.

The Doha Development Agenda was launched in November 2001, at the fourth WTO Ministerial Conference[2] held in Qatar.[3] The Doha Declaration provides the mandate for negotiations on a range of subjects,[4] and other work including issues concerning the implementation of the present agreements.

Unsurprisingly, some subjects are more difficult to negotiate than others and therefore progress has not been even and not always even possible. Negotiations were stalled even after the 2003 Cancun Ministerial Conference which was considered a failure.

However, on 31 July 2004 member governments finally approved a package of framework and other agreements that were said to greatly enhance the chances of successfully completing the important Doha negotiations.

The previous deadline for concluding the talks (1 January 2005) was postponed to an as-yet unspecified date, at least until the sixth WTO Ministerial Conference to be held in Hong Kong in December 2005.

Undoubtedly the most remarkable progress during the negotiations was made on the difficult issue of agriculture,[5] which is highly sensitive for both developed and developing countries.

Agriculture Negotiations meet Doha

Up to 1995, General Agreement on Tariffs and Trade (GATT) rules were largely ineffective in disciplining key aspects of agricultural trade. Developing countries, in particular, have long insisted that direct and indirect subsidies for agricultural products were making it difficult for them to compete in world markets. The 1986–1994 Uruguay Round negotiations went a long way towards changing all that. The WTO Agriculture Agreement, together with individual countries' commitments to reduce export subsidies, domestic support and import duties on agricultural products were a first step towards reforming agricultural trade.

The reform strikes a balance between agricultural trade liberalisation and governments' desire to pursue legitimate agricultural policy goals, including non-trade concerns.

The Agriculture Agreement set up a framework of rules and started reductions in protection and trade-distorting support. But this was only the first phase of the reform. Article 20 of the Agriculture Agreement committed members to start negotiations on continuing the reform at the end of 1999 (or beginning of 2000). The 2001 Doha Ministerial Declaration set a new mandate by making the objectives more explicit and setting deadlines. Agriculture was made part of the single undertaking in which virtually all the linked negotiations were meant to end by 1 January 2005.

The declaration reconfirmed the long-term objective to establish a fair and market-oriented trading system through a programme of fundamental reform. The programme encompassed strengthened rules, and specific commitments on government support and protection for agriculture. The purpose was to correct and prevent restrictions and distortions in world agricultural markets.

Member governments commit themselves to comprehensive negotiations aimed at the so-called 'three pillars':

- market access: substantial reductions
- exports subsidies: reductions of, with a view to phasing out, all forms of these
- domestic support: substantial reductions for supports that distort trade[6]

The special and differential treatment for developing countries was made integral throughout the negotiations in order to enable developing countries to meet their needs, in particular, in food security and rural development. Note was also taken of the non-trade concerns (such as environmental protection, food security, rural development, etc) reflected in the negotiating proposals previously submitted during the negotiations

In March 2003, negotiators failed to meet a deadline for advancing technical proposals and ministers were not able to come to political agreements in September 2003 at the Cancun Ministerial Conference.

The July Package[7]

After protracted negotiations, the General Council of the WTO adopted a decision known as the July Package on 31 July 2004. The agreed package focuses on five areas of the Doha Declaration, namely, agriculture, non-agricultural market access (NAMA or industrial access market), development issues, trade facilitation and services.[8]

The framework for future agriculture negotiations, adopted as a separate Annex,[9] was widely seen as the main breakthrough.[10] The Group of Five Interested Parties (FIPs) that comprises the US, EU, Brazil, India and Australia, played a leading role and eventually agreed on a text that formed the basis for the final agreement. Members also agreed to make discussions on the sectoral initiative on cotton an integral part of the agriculture negotiations rather than treating the issue on a separate track.[11]

Annex A on agriculture simply lays down the basic pillars (market access, domestic support and export competition) and a framework for conducting future talks. Negotiations on modalities of substance, much of which has been left undetermined, will be a real challenge that Member States have yet to confront.

On Market Access, the language of the Decision reveals slightly more flexibility and stronger language in favour of developing countries when compared to earlier texts. The text retains the tiered formula which classifies tariffs into various bands for subsequent reduction from bound rates, the higher tariffs being cut more than lower ones. The actual modalities[12] remain subject to negotiation. The language only vaguely provides for 'substantial improvement in market access' for all products, mentioning that 'substantial overall tariff reductions will be achieved as a final result from negotiations'.[13] Although important compromises were achieved regarding sensitive products (more beneficial for developed countries) and special products (more beneficial for developing countries), much has yet to be determined.

The Doha Declaration called for 'substantial reductions in trade-distorting domestic support'. The Annex text accommodates both developed and developing country interests, particularly with regard to Blue Box[14] and the 'de-minimis' payments of the Amber Box,[15] major sticking points in the negotiations. The text includes concrete targets, at least for overall domestic support reduction and a cap for permitted Blue Box levels.[16] Language on Green Box (decoupled subsidies) remains largely unchanged from previous negotiations, only requiring a more transparent process for designating green box subsidies. Of particular interest is that national 'support for subsistence and resource-poor farmers' is recognised as being important.

The Doha Declaration called for 'reduction of, with a view to phasing out, all forms of export subsidies'. The Annex provides for significantly stronger language on Export Competition in favour of developing countries. In addition to providing for a 'credible end-date' (although yet to be agreed upon) for the elimination of export subsidies, it also includes within its ambit export credits and credit guarantees or insurance programmes.

In summary WTO Members have overcome the deadlock in agriculture negotiations – largely by putting off decisions but also by committing themselves to negotiations, which will impact on the whole WTO Round. This probably represents a major step forward. It is the fourth step of a long process, along a 'continuum' starting with the mandate, passing through the framework, to be continued by full modalities and hopefully ending with a final agreement.

September 2004

Notes

[1]   An excellent source of information and analysis on agriculture negotiations is offered by the International Centre for Trade and Sustainable Development at <http://www.ictsd.org/>

[2]   A Ministerial Conference is the organization's highest-level decision-making body according to the 1994 Marrakech Agreement establishing the WTO.

[3]   Since the creation of the WTO in 1994, there have been five Ministerial Conferences (Cancun 2003, Doha, 2001, Seattle, 1999, Geneva, 1998, Singapore, 1996), the next was due to be held in Hong Kong in 2005.

[4]   The 21 subjects listed in the Doha Declaration are: Implementation; agriculture; services; market access (non-agriculture); intellectual property; investment; competition; transparency in government procurement; trade facilitation; anti-dumping; subsidies; regional agreements; dispute settlement; environment; e-commerce; small economies; trade, debt and finance; trade and technology transfer; technical cooperation; least-developed countries; and special and differential treatment. Four of these subjects (i.e. investment, competition, transparency in government procurement and trade facilitation) are known as 'Singapore issues' and have a working group set up by the 1996 Singapore Ministerial Conference that has been studying them.

[5]   The negotiations in agriculture are difficult because of the wide range of views and interests among member governments. They aim to contribute to further liberalization of agricultural trade. This will benefit those countries which can compete on quality and price rather than on the size of their subsidies. That is particularly the case for many developing countries whose economies depend on an increasingly diverse range of primary and processed agricultural products, exported to an increasing variety of markets, including to other developing countries.

[6]   <http://www.wto.org/english/tratop_e/agric_e/negs_bkgrnd07_modalities_e.htm>

[7]   Available at <http://www.wto.org/english/tratop_e/dda_e/ddadraft_31jul04_e.pdf> on 24 August 2004

8 Regarding existing commitments in the rest of the Doha mandate, the agreement simply reaffirms continuing negotiations. However, regarding the Singapore issues, Members agreed to drop all but one issue (trade facilitation) from the Doha work programme, stressing that 'no work towards negotiations on any of these issues will take place within the WTO during the Doha Round'.

9 World Trade Organization WT/L/579 2 August 2004 (04-3297) Annex A: <http://www.wto.org/english/tratop_e/dda_e/ddadraft_31jul04_e.pdf>

10 Notwithstanding, Members also faced significant difficulties in finding compromises on industrial market access, cotton and development issues.

11 Following a deal struck between the US and four African countries (Benin, Burkina Faso, Chad and Mali) on July 29.

12 Which is the number of bands, threshold for defining bands and type of tariff reductions within each band.

13 Annex A paragraph 29.

14 In WTO terminology, subsidies in general are identified by 'boxes' which are given the colours of traffic lights: green (permitted), amber (to be reduced), red (forbidden). In agriculture, things are, as usual, more complicated. The Agriculture Agreement has no red box, although domestic support exceeding the reduction commitment levels in the amber box is prohibited; and there is a blue box for subsidies that are tied to programmes that limit production. There are also exemptions for developing countries (sometimes called an 'S&D box').

15 All domestic support measures considered to distort production and trade, except those in the blue and green boxes. These supports are subject to limits, the allowed 'de minimis' minimal supports. The reduction commitments are expressed in terms of a 'Total Aggregate Measurement of Support' (Total AMS) which includes all supports for specified products together with supports that are not for specific products, in one single figure.

16 In the first year of implementing the agreement, the text requires that Members reduce by 20 per cent their overall trade distorting support, which comprises the final bound total AMS (aggregate measure of support), plus the permitted de minimis levels, plus the permitted Blue Box levels. Such reduction is to be subject to a tiered formula that would cut subsidies 'progressively' with higher levels of trade-distorting domestic support making greater reductions. The Annex also provides for capping product specific AMS at average levels, based on a methodology to be agreed, in order to prevent circumvention of obligations through transfer of subsidies between different support categories.

Chapter 28

Lawyers and Ethicists Should be Careful When Talking About the Permissibility of Torture

Søren Holm

Harvard law professor Alan M. Dershowitz, a self-described pragmatist, said he believes the United States currently employs torture in some circumstances and will continue to do so. A public debate, he said, would ensure that top leaders, not servicemen and women, decide when it is appropriate. 'If someone asked me to draft the statute, I would say, "Try buying them off, then use threats, then truth serum, and then if you came to a last recourse, nonlethal pain, a sterilized needle under the nail to produce excruciating pain," he said. 'You would need a judge signing off on that. By making it open, we wouldn't be able to hide behind the hypocrisy.' Dershowitz said the judge might refuse to sign the order, creating a check that does not now exist. Arthur Caplan, an ethicist at the University of Pennsylvania, and the Rev. John P. Langan, a Jesuit priest and philosopher at Georgetown University, both said they believe torture can be used in some circumstances. 'I can imagine a few situations at the extreme where you might resort to torture,' Caplan said. Langan said he began endorsing coercive techniques such as sleep deprivation and lengthy interrogations after the 1983 attack on U.S. Marines in Beirut, which killed 241 people.

The quote above occurred in an article in the *Washington Post* on 11 May 2004. In the current paper I want to consider the cogency of the ethical arguments for the permissibility of torture in extreme circumstances and in the second part the arguments aiming to show that although torture may be morally acceptable in principle in very limited circumstances, there are good reasons to believe that we will never in real life know that we are in such a circumstance.

This paper is a philosophical paper and will therefore not engage with the legal questions raised by advocating the use of torture when there are firm prohibitions against torture in many authoritative human rights documents.[1]

The Philosophical Justification of Torture

The main argument for the ethical permissibility of torture in certain circumstances is either the straightforward utilitarian argument that allowing torture will promote the good, for instance by saving many human lives, or a more deontological argument that by planning to commit certain acts the persons involved forfeit their rights not to be tortured. In addition one might adduce a pragmatic legal argument that if torture occurs anyway it is better that it is regulated (the argument used by Dershowitz above).

In the quote above the extreme circumstances are not specified, but what is often discussed in first year ethics classes are what we could call 'the Bruce Willis scenario'. In this scenario the clearly evil terrorist has hidden a bomb in a place where it will kill many people but he won't tell us where it is, or how we can disarm it. We are therefore unable to call in Bruce Willis to cut the red (or was it the blue?) wire and save the world, unless we torture the evil terrorist.

Are these arguments for the acceptability of torture in extreme circumstances valid?

Well, the utilitarian argument is clearly valid, but it is only sound (i.e. valid with true premises) if one accepts the whole underlying utilitarian theory, and it may furthermore show too much, since it is not intrinsically important whether, for instance, only the guilty are tortured.

The deontological argument is, under certain conditions, valid as well; although we need much more explication to know exactly which acts it is that leads to forfeiture of the right not to be tortured.

The pragmatic argument is clearly invalid. From the (supposed) fact that the United States currently commits murder, does for instance not follow that it would be better that this practice is regulated. It may for instance be the case that it should not be regulated, but stamped out.

Let us, for the sake of argument, accept that one or more of the arguments justifying torture in extreme circumstances go through. Does that show that any currently occurring instances of torture are justified, for instance torture of supposed Al Qaeda leaders?

Not necessarily, there are a number of further complications to consider.

Epistemic Complications

The first set of complications is epistemic. Apart from the pragmatic argument both the utilitarian and the deontological argument require certain pieces of knowledge to be in place for the justification of torture to be complete.

We essentially need to know that we have the right person, that he knows something and that that knowledge is important and will allow us to save lives.

This knowledge is essential for the deontological justification of torture, because if we don't have the right person, he or she will not have forfeited their right not to be tortured and we are committing a terrible wrong by torturing someone who has a right not to be tortured.

For the utilitarian justification this knowledge is also important, although it is not absolutely essential to get it right. The utilitarian might say that we have to go on probabilities, but this is exactly the weakness of the utilitarian theory which will let us torture ten innocents so that one guilty person will reveal his secrets.

But how likely are we to have this kind of knowledge about the knowledge of the people we want to torture? In most cases we will not have knowledge of this specificity, unless our suspect is of the bragging kind, and we are therefore likely to torture a large number of bad people who have no valuable knowledge at all, which on all accounts is a very bad thing to do.

Time and Guilt

These epistemic concerns are linked to two other concerns, the first concerned with the time aspects of torture and decisions to torture, and the second with whether we should only torture the guilty.

If the justification for torture is that we can prevent some really terrible event from happening, this will often mean that we have to get the information we think the person has very quickly, before the event happens. We therefore have to decide to torture very quickly as well, and this means that normal procedures for determining even presumptive criminal responsibility may have to be abandoned. We simply cannot wait for the legal machinery to work, or if we want legal permission to torture this will have to be through an extremely brief legal process, probably without proper representation of the person to be tortured and without appeal possibilities.

But here it is worth noting that if torture was a punishment it would be a severe punishment that could in most legal systems only be imposed after a lengthy and thorough legal process.

This brings us unto our next question, should we only torture the guilty? Most would initially say 'Yes', there is something exceedingly horrific in the idea of torturing the innocent. But it will sometimes be more efficient to torture the innocent – a terrorist may 'break' more quickly if we torture his child than if we torture him, and it will often (probably in the vast majority of cases) be the case that because of the time aspects we discussed above we will not know whether the person is guilty of any serious crime at the time we torture them. By accepting torture we therefore necessarily accept torturing the innocent. There is no way of ensuring that only the guilty get tortured, and even if we get legal permission as Dershowitz wants, we will still end up torturing the innocent in a not insubstantial number of cases.

One Man's Terrorist is Another Man's Freedom Fighter

The current media discussion focuses on whether there are circumstances in which it is acceptable to torture terrorists, but we have to realise that it is very difficult to constrain the justifications that are given to 'bona fide terrorists'.

First, it is clearly the case that one man's terrorist is another man's freedom fighter. There is, for instance, no doubt that the US and its allies are occupying forces in Iraq (at the time of writing before the establishment of a legitimate new government), and that Iraqis are not terrorists just because they resist the occupation by military means.

Second, utilitarian justifications are unconcerned with the status of the person being tortured and only concerned with the results of torturing, and can therefore just as well justify torturing soldiers in a regular army as torturing terrorists, and we can probably imagine many situations where it would be highly advantageous to torture a captured enemy general. This clearly involves certain risks, if you start torturing the soldiers of the other side the other side might retaliate, but those risks may be acceptable, for instance, if you are in a situation where you are clearly winning the war in question.

Third, justice based deontological accounts will only protect soldiers who participate in just wars and not soldiers who participate in unjust wars.

Slippery Slopes

There are also at least two possible slippery slopes that we might slide down if we legitimise torture.

The first is the slope towards de-humanisation of those who order and perform torture. No one can inflict severe harm on another person without being damaged psychologically him- or herself (I hope).

The second is the slope towards the extension of torture from the extreme cases to less extreme cases.

The Fallacy of 'Clinical Torture'

Finally, there is the fallacy of believing that torture can ever be as 'clinical' as Dershowitz describes it. Torture is a messy business and to be effective the person being tortured has to believe not only that his torturers will cause him pain, but that they are willing to do anything imaginable. The torturer has at least to intend the complete annihilation of the personality of the tortured.

When we think of 'legitimate, legal torture', a category Dershowitz clearly finds to be cogent, we need to think of the full implications.

We might for instance need to consider whether torture should be televised live, like court cases and some executions in the USA, or whether states who allowed torture under the Dershowitz proposals should also fund torture research, or give out medals to exceptionally skilled torturers.

Conclusion

I hope to have shown that although many ethical theories can justify torture in extreme circumstances, in reality very few, if any cases will fulfil the criteria in the philosopher's idealised examples.

Ethicists and lawyers should therefore be extremely wary of stating the 'in principle' justification of torture. They may want to say 'Torture can be justified in very extreme circumstances, but these never occur in real life', but if they say that, they can be almost certain that the first part of the sentence will be remembered and the second part forgotten.

July 2004

References

[1] The UN 'CONVENTION AGAINST TORTURE and Other Cruel, Inhuman or Degrading Treatment or Punishment' has the following wording in Articles 1 & 2

Article 1
  1. For the purposes of this Convention, torture means any act by which severe pain or suffering, whether physical or mental, is intentionally inflicted on a person for such purposes as obtaining from him or a third person information or a confession, punishing him for an act he or a third person has committed or is suspected of having committed, or intimidating or coercing him or a third person, or for any reason based on discrimination of any kind, when such pain or suffering is inflicted by or at the instigation of or with the consent or acquiescence of a public official or other person acting in an official capacity. It does not include pain or suffering arising only from, inherent in or incidental to lawful sanctions.
  2. This article is without prejudice to any international instrument or national legislation which does or may contain provisions of wider application.

Article 2
  1. Each State Party shall take effective legislative, administrative, judicial or other measures to prevent acts of torture in any territory under its jurisdiction.
  2. No exceptional circumstances whatsoever, whether a state of war or a threat or war, internal political instability or any other public emergency, may be invoked as a justification of torture.
  3. An order from a superior officer or a public authority may not be invoked as a justification of torture.

Chapter 29

You Pays Your Money and You Takes Your Choice?

Joy Wingfield

Advertising Over the Counter Medicines

Is it ethical to promote the sale of medicines? Conversely, is any attempt to limit promotion a restraint of trade? In April 2004, the Medicines and Healthcare products Regulatory Agency (MHRA – formerly MCA, Medicines Control Agency) issued a warning to manufacturers and retailers that they were unhappy about 'multibuy' offers on certain Over the Counter (OTC) medicines [1]. These are perhaps more familiar to most us as 'buy one get one free' and '3 for the price of 2' offers. Until the last few years we did not see such promotions applied to medicines; why not?

From the early 1930s, the professional body for pharmacists (now the Royal Pharmaceutical Society of Great Britain) has attempted to establish a collective ethic amongst pharmacists that medicines were not 'ordinary items of commerce'. Successive Codes of Ethics made this point repeatedly and required pharmacists to regard all medicines (OTC or on prescription) with special respect and not as merchandise to be 'piled high and sold cheap'. Reams of words were expended in trying to describe how to sell medicines 'professionally' and much angst was incurred as each subsequent Code sought to square the Victorian ideal of 'professionalism' with an ever more competitive business environment and rising consumerism.

The law initially helped to maintain this position. Before the Medicines Act 1968, most medicines were controlled as 'poisons' which accurately reflected their capacity to both kill or cure human disease and ailments. As the decades progressed, despite increasing potency of medicines, more and more have moved from prescription only, to sales from pharmacies only (Pharmacy medicines–P) to sale from any retail outlet (General Sale List–GSL). It is well known that the public generally regard all OTC medicines as 'safe' and make very little distinction between those they can buy in a newsagent and those that can only be sold from a registered pharmacy with the legally required presence of a pharmacist. The courts further reinforced the special nature of medicines in the 1960s by applying Resale Price Maintenance (RPM) to all OTC medicines (as well as books, certain foods and many more goods). This meant that consumers would pay the same price for their medicines no matter where they chose to buy them; there was no incentive to bulk buy or shop around.

Competition and Loss of Resale Price Maintenance

By the late 1990s, however, the UK had eagerly welcomed the push from Europe to sweep away restrictive practices, open up 'closed shops' (including professions) and stimulate competition. The concept of competition is now perceived as good in itself. Consumers are anticipated always to benefit from reduced prices no matter what effect that may have on marginal shops and suburban general stores or on the prices paid to primary producers. To be sure, RPM on medicines maintained a guaranteed return on investment for pharmacies, including for those located in supermarkets or edge of town complexes and for many this enabled the business to augment the NHS dispensing service which since 1948 has been remunerated on a volume based – more prescriptions, more money – basis.

So in a rather heroic battle,[2] pharmacy interests managed to resist the demise of RPM on medicines until 2001, when the last of the rulings of the Restrictive Practices Court was abandoned.[3] Since then (subject to minor legal restraints[4]), all retailers could employ the full panoply of marketing devices to assist consumers to buy more, buy cheaper. At this time too, the MCA (as it then was) responded to the continuing tragedy of suicide by overdose of paracetamol or aspirin (but not ibuprofen). Of these, the first is by far the most likely to be fatal with doses as few as 12 tablets causing irreparable liver damage and probable death. Aspirin poisoning can be serious but suicides discovered early enough usually recover after gastric lavage; suicide is virtually unknown with ibuprofen, it has very low toxicity. Regulations[5] were brought in to restrict the pack size of these three GSL OTC analgesics and thus, it was said, to reduce the stockholding of them in the domestic medicines cabinets of would-be suicides. Regular purchasers of larger and cheaper packs found their wishes thwarted in pharmacies although cannier buyers could put several small packs in to their trolleys from supermarket shelves and clear the checkout with no challenges. The 'playing field' was definitely uneven but, still, the pharmacists in their pharmacies stuck by and large to the strictures still in the Code of Ethics not to promote medicines.

A level Playing Field?

The Office of Fair Trading also turned its attention to the pharmacy Code of Ethics. Suffice to say that every semblance of Victorian reservations about not touting for business, not promoting one's own professional services and, most significantly, not competing for trade with non-pharmacies was summarily lost from the 2002 version of the Code. The Code now really has very little to say on this topic save 'promotions for pharmacy medicines (not General Sale List) which seek to persuade consumers to obtain medicines that are not wanted or quantities substantially in excess of those wanted are considered to be professionally unacceptable'. And if you are not in a profession?

Our society is ambivalent about the status of OTC medicines. You and I (who know what we are doing) should be able to buy what we want, whenever and wherever we choose; others need protection. We want retailers to treat us as autonomous individuals but also to recognise when we are not. We expect pharmacists (as do pharmacists themselves) to have a duty of care towards us but don't have the same expectation of the forecourt attendant or the checkout assistant. So the MHRA is now concerned about the unwanted face of competitive pressures. Then I suggest legislation will be needed for **all** retailers. Expecting pharmacy to behave as a profession but compete as a retailer will continue to generate ethical anxiety for individual practitioners and further confuse the public as to why such distinctions operate at all.

June 2004

References

[1] Medicines Act Information Letter (Mail) MHRA Number 142 <http://medicines.mhra.gov.uk/inforesources/publications/mail/mail142.pdf> (accessed 27/4/04).

[2] Joy Wingfield, 'Don't treat medicines like fruit and veg!' *Pharmaceutical Journal* 2001, 266, 621 <http://www.pharmj.com/Editorial/20010505/comment/spectrum.html> (accessed 10/5/04).

[3] Editorial: Resale Price Maintenance at an end. *Pharmaceutical Journal* 2001, 266, 666-667 <http://www.pharmj.com/Editorial/20010519/news/news.html#1> (accessed 27/4/04).

[4] The Medicines (Advertising and Monitoring of Advertising) Amendment Regulations 1999 SI Number 267 <http://www.legislation.hmso.gov.uk/si/si1999/19990267.htm> (accessed 27/4/04).

[5] The Medicines (Sale or Supply) (Miscellaneous Provisions) Amendment Regulations 1999 SI Number 644 <http://www.legislation.hmso.gov.uk/si/si1999/19990644.htm> (accessed 27/4/04).

Chapter 30

Life After Death: My life After a Heart and Lung Transplant

Nicola Langlands

I am a transplant recipient, who is only alive today because of the death of another human being. This presents an entirely different perspective on the acquisition of organs, yet the process is equally complex and continues to lack strategic planning.

Whatever the circumstances for the trading donor or the terminally ill recipient, the common denominator is desperation. We are a universal society whose standard of living is driven by what we can afford, and therefore if members of such a diverse society can improve their quality of life by trading, then it would seem reasonable to expect that to happen.

It could be argued that a country that has the scientific technology and can foresee a need for transplantation as part of a health care package, should have been considering procedures to ensure a provision of organs from its immediate community, thus reducing the opportunity for people in Third World communities to compromise their lives, and the future of their families.

I had my heart and lung transplant in 1989, and I waited for 2 years to either become a priority due to a critical health condition or get a suitable donor. I am not sure what the reason was in my case, but I was told that the match was good for me. It would seem from the length of my second life, this was a good choice.

I am not able to reflect back to when I had my transplant, but my parents tell me that it was an exciting time because transplant technology was developing at such a rate, and not only adults but also children were being given the chance of a new life. My parents were at the point of desperation, and were being inspired by the new technology and influenced by the specialists who promised access to a 'normal' life for us all.

I use the term 'new life' because it was never an improvement on the old one. I feel this must be taken into consideration when regarding moral or ethical issues concerning the entire transplant process. The most significant affect on my life has been the psychological repercussions of having another person's heart and lungs. None can measure the significance of the heart as a focal point for ones life and soul. It is a very part of ones being, and when a foreign organ suddenly replaces it, there are no guides or rules to help you re-map your spirit. The term 'lost soul' has applied to me for many years, and the rules governing disclosure to donors has merely hampered the process of my internal growth and understanding.

The Harefield Hospital, Middlesex, England was a hive of activity and research, and people were coming from all over the world to access the technology and facilities. It was at this time that there should have been discussions and policies implemented to ensure a legal and consistent acquisition of organs. The role of the Transplant Coordinator would not be compromised, and there would be equal opportunities from all centres to acquire the organs they need.

I had a transplant because of a congenital heart condition, and many of the children at the time had similar conditions or cystic fibrosis or were stricken from a virus that attacked the muscles surrounding the heart. It has to be said that many of the children that had congenital conditions would now be able to have their hearts repaired. Surgery and drugs have advanced to such a degree that the drastic decision for transplant surgery is not so necessary. This must have reduced the demand for organs in children, and I can only surmise that the current demand is due to a lack of personal health care on the part of many adult members of our fast living society. We have an immediate problem that needs to be resolved, but we also have a preventative problem that will take much longer to manage, as it will in part be dependent on access to a media focused educational programme.

Whilst I am aware that an increasing number of people are suffering with heart disease, I fail to understand why hospitals like the Harefield, which command such expertise, have to be identified for closure. The hammer has been hanging over the hospital for the last few years, and from a purely personal point of view I have found this difficult to accept. I have been seeing the same people for the last 14 years, and throughout the hospital there is a wealth of knowledge and expertise that provide a holistic approach to patient rehabilitation. The hospital is easily accessible for patients and their families. It is also in a semi-rural environment that supports a programme for returning to health. If there is a move to increasing the number of organs available for transplantation then surely some thought needs to be given to maintaining existing areas of excellence. Low morale and reduced provision could have a significant effect on levels of care, which ultimately would have an adverse effect on me.

To return to the concept of a 'new life' is important if consideration is going to be given to what transplantation inflicts on many of its recipients. Whilst always happy to celebrate success, health providers must not simply recognise the statistics whereby the patient returns home alive. It is the quality of that life which needs to be considered, and indeed the extent of a 'normal' existence.

When I made my regular visits to Harefield I could reflect on the many photos of different transplant patients, and the dates of their surgery. They were pasted on the walls of the Transplant Outpatients, and it was good to see some of them making their regular visit with me. We were all at different stages of rehabilitation, and I have to say that the trend was towards poor health as opposed to 'normal' existence. It became apparent that the photos were being taken down each time I made a visit, and when all the photos were removed I had to believe that it was not generally good for patient morale, or maybe there was just a decline in the number of transplants taking place. I think that both of these reasons were accurate, but I would not say that the decline in transplants was wholly due to a lack of donors. It was apparent to me that there were very significant difficulties with transplantation that could not be addressed in the current climate, and there was a definite need for further research.

I was 13 and the world was my oyster, or so I thought. There was little in the way of preparation for what was ahead, and I am sure that if my parents had known more, then they would have found the words to tell me. The effects of the drugs were overwhelming, and to this day I still suffer from excessive hair growth all over my body, and shaking hands that prevent me from writing legibly. Steroids give me a bloated look, and in terms of living in a young society where street credibility goes a long way to enabling you to make and sustain friendships, I was certainly being disadvantaged. I remember telling my parents that I was fed up with sympathetic admirers, and was desperate for some real friends who liked me for what I was. But what was I? There was little general knowledge about transplants, and as far as my local community were concerned I was cured. This was also apparent when I made visits to the local doctor or hospital, and although we were told at the time that it would not take long before all hospitals were familiar with the complex needs of a transplant recipient, it was not to be. The training for local providers has not been apparent, and due to the fact that a small percentage of the local community have transplants, it would seem obvious that it may not be a viable way to spend professional development money.

Now I am an adult with a daughter and all the responsibilities that go with raising a family and managing a home, I am aware that there are additional difficulties that also limit my access to a 'normal' existence. The phrase 'you can do what everybody else can do' certainly didn't apply to my state of health and physical abilities, and now I recognise that it also does not apply to my opportunities to access the benefits that all young people enjoy when planning their life and securing a home.

These are some of the benefits that I am denied:

- a mortgage
- a life policy
- a bank loan
- holiday insurance

I have to exist on my disability benefits, as I am unable to secure a permanent job. I am seen as a liability in the workplace, and yet I am not recognised as being significantly disabled by the benefits agency to claim the full disability allowance. I am between a rock and a hard place, and see no way of improving the quality of my life within a wider society.

My family are my reason for living and they are the foundation for my acceptance as a 'normal' person. Megan, my daughter has given me the opportunity to become involved with a number of families who all see me for what I am and are genuine friends.

The commitment from hospitals to saving lives needs to be measured with what they are saving them for, and the role that they need to play to ensure that the world understands and includes people with these very special conditions. This should be part of their duty of care. They are saving a life and a future existence, which needs to be rich and fulfilled with each passing day.

Yes we do need to do something to formalise and legalise the acquisition of organs, but we also need to look at the concept that simply repairing the vehicle only gives it access to make the journey. The quality of the journey is entirely dependent on experiences gained along the way.

May 2004

Chapter 31

The Human Rights Act: Is it Working?

Philip A.Thomas

Giving people legal rights is one thing: making those rights work effectively for the benefit of the individual, the community and society at large is a separate and bigger issue. For example, the constitution of the US guarantees equality before the law but it needed Martin Luther King and 'black action' to begin turning paper rights into social reality.

In the United Kingdom the Human Rights Act (HRA) came into force in October 2000. Jack Straw, then Home Secretary, stated: 'These are new rights for the millennium. The Act is a cornerstone of our work to modernise the constitution. It is one of the most important pieces of legislation the UK has seen. But it should not be seen as a field day for lawyers. It will instead, mark a major change in the creation of a culture of rights and responsibilities in our society.' Big words and strong sentiments but has this legislation impacted significantly on those communities and individuals that are in greatest need of support? The gap between rich and poor has grown under the Labour government. We have the most unequal distribution of income in the EU (Greece excepted) with more than one in five people living on less than 60 per cent of median earnings. Regional differences remain stark with Wales continuing to lag behind other parts of the UK.

The very term 'Human Rights' delivers a powerful and positive message. This is legislation aimed to protect citizens from the abuse of state power and sustain the basic features of a democratic society. Thus, it is not about controlling or regulating society. Instead, it seeks to protect the vulnerable and the aggrieved against the excesses and improprieties of public bodies and state action or possible inaction. Redressing this enormous imbalance of power between the individual and the state is not easy. Consequently, the HRA benefits from the involvement of professional facilitators: solicitors. These are the people who have keys to the gates that open up access to the law. Their knowledge, experience and technical know-how helps you and me to access justice effectively and seek appropriate remedies for wrongs suffered. Those who are socially excluded are particularly vulnerable and particularly needy of professional support.

We know that the HRA has and continues to be employed by the few specialist human rights barristers' chambers and London based pressure groups. Test cases are advanced and sometimes won in the High Court and the Court of Appeal. For example, under article 3, (prohibition of torture, inhuman or degrading treatment or punishment) local authorities have an obligation to protect abused children. Under article 8, (respect for family life, home and correspondence) Thames Water Ltd., was held to have breached its duty to prevent flooding of property caused by inadequate sewers. There have also been cases affecting housing and education. The range of common, everyday disputes between the individual and public authorities which might attract the use of the HRA is considerable yet remains widely unknown to the general public. The Law Society estimates there are over a million disputes at any one time which could be resolved through the legal process but remain unresolved and are a continuing burden to the affected individuals.

On the other hand, the rich and powerful also use the Act, for example, to protect their privacy. Michael Douglas and Catherine Zeta-Jones tried to protect the commercial value of their wedding by stopping *Hello!* magazine from using pictures of the ceremony. In Canada publishing companies were successful in arguing that a restriction on soft porn magazines was a breach of their right to free speech. Soldiers involved in the killing of 13 civil rights marchers in Derry in 1972 have used article 2 of the HRA (protection of life) to remain anonymous whilst giving evidence to the ongoing Saville Enquiry. Clearly, the legislation is a two-edged sword.

So, who in reality owns the HRA: is it the state and the rich, famous and powerful or can ownership be claimed by the dispossessed who seek fair treatment in an unfair society? What is unknown is how the HRA has impacted on those on the lower end of the social spectrum and how high street solicitors to whom these people might turn have taken to the legislation.

In 2003 the author undertook a research project in the Cynon Valley to establish the level of awareness and usage of the Human Rights Act amongst local solicitors. In essence, I sought to establish what use they were making of this innovative legislation and if not, then why not. Twenty-one solicitors were interviewed.

The Cynon Valley was selected because of the prevailing social and economic conditions. It forms part of Rhondda Cynon Taff (RCT), which houses 8 per cent of the Welsh population. What is known is this area ranks towards the bottom of various social indicators both within Wales and also within the UK as a whole. There are significant health issues, some of which are produced or exacerbated by inadequate housing. Long term unemployment and poor academic achievement is another local issue. Twenty-seven per cent of pupils in RCT are entitled to free primary schools meals, which is 8 per cent higher than the average in Wales. Such figures are indicative of low-income families. The Cynon valley houses a community in crisis. Jobs are scarce and low waged; the levels of educational attainment are poor; there is a major drugs abuse issue; the local authority struggles to meet its statutory obligations through shortage of funds. The valley abounds with problems, some of which might be resolved through law and specifically through the HRA.

There are around 3,000 solicitors practising in Wales. Wales accounts for 5.6 per cent of the joint population of England and Wales but has 3.3 per cent of solicitors in practice. In Wales there is approximately one solicitor per 1,000 people and in England it is almost half that figure. Welsh firms are smaller and less profitable but one important question is whether they are able to handle the HRA which is new, challenging and totally different in terms of its conception and usage?

Our survey results identified a group of solicitors anxious to help their clients in what are becoming ever more difficult operating circumstances. The 'fat cat' legal aid solicitors, as described by Tony Blair, are extinct in the Cynon Valley, assuming this breed ever existed in the community. The profession is made up of predominantly Welsh people with two thirds of them born in the valley. The same percentage studied law in Wales and three quarters of the solicitors trained and now practice in the same Cynon Valley firm. Thus, there is a strong sense of local commitment and knowledge amongst these practitioners but at the same time this tight legal community has very little experience of practice elsewhere. There are concerns that feelings of belonging are insufficient to maintain the current numbers of law firms. Indeed, one solicitor said: 'there are going to be fewer lawyers in the Cynon valley in ten years' time. It is not a place where people like to live. It is not a place where you can get wealthy. It is not a place where you will sit in smart offices.' Legal wages are relatively low and staff recruitment is difficult. The contracting numbers of solicitors will be accompanied by contracting services. This is especially the case as the Legal Services Commission, responsible for administering public monies for legal aid, is seen as officious, bureaucratic and parsimonious. In a word, the solicitors believe that the commission is 'strangling' free or low cost legal services to the community. In a low waged community, as is the Cynon valley, publicly funded civil and criminal legal services are central to the legal practices. One solicitor commented: 'We are seeing a shrinkage of legal aid franchises and the clients were probably better off a few years ago. They were pointed in the right direction more quickly and had a better choice of firm.'

Within this depressing context the HRA has had very little effect or take-up by the legal profession. 'Initially we thought it was going to have a big impact but I think we can honestly say that it hasn't had a huge impact at all really.' Why should this be the case where so many people might benefit from its usage? Solicitors admitted that they were not properly aware or trained in the value and use of the legislation. 'There is a very low awareness of the HRA and it is not a topic that rises to the fore when we are talking amongst colleagues.' Training is expensive and takes solicitors away from their desks. In a practice where financial margins are tight, solicitors will focus on doing what they have always done, what they know best and what has historically made money. Innovation, experiment, new services and test cases are chancy and possibly expensive activities. Teaching old dogs new tricks is difficult at the best of times and these are not good times for legal practitioners.

Concerns were also raised about the willingness of local magistrates to take on board HRA arguments under, for example, article 6 (fair hearing) though criminal practice solicitors declared that this was the most commonly used section of the legislation. 'The magistrates in my view don't like you raising it. The magistrate's court is not largely interested in much law: it is not much interested in legal argument either. It is far better founded to deal with factual issues. It's not a particularly appropriate court to try and deal with many legal arguments.' Thus, solicitors are cautious about introducing new HRA arguments in court.

Where does this evidence take us? Clearly, the legal profession requires further training of a practical nature to show solicitors the value and utility of the HRA. 'If we were frankly a little bit more imaginative and did a little bit more digging and even a bit more thinking, I'm sure the HRA could be applied to a lot more cases than we do at the moment.' But the HRA must be placed within the context of a changing and uncertain legal profession. Local solicitors are unsure of their professional futures as publicly funded legal services are dramatically reshaped. In addition, new legal providers, such as Tesco may enter the market and undercut traditional services such as conveyancing and wills. Small firms of solicitors are disappearing in the valley and also in the United Kingdom. The general practitioner is under threat and with it comes a reduction of traditional legal services to the local community. New challenges and opportunities emerge and within this context the Human Rights Act remains open for debate and employment. It is truly the most important legislation that has been developed to support and protect those in greatest need. The immediate task is to make it known and make it work.

April 2004

Chapter 32

Fair Trials, Ethics and Saddam Hussein's Trial

Jason D. Söderblom

Introduction

How Saddam Hussein's trial is conducted will largely determine whether world opinion views the verdict as legitimate and will influence how history judges the United States (US), United Kingdom (UK) and Australian involvement in Iraq. The trial will also influence Iraqi jurisprudence for generations; for a rule of law compliant trial in turn promotes rule of law. Whereas, a trial that is contrived so as to avoid implicating foreign companies, foreign individuals and foreign governments will mark a return to the type of corruption that prevents democratic ideals taking hold in societies like Iraq.

The endorsement of fair trials has long been recognised. The 1215 Magna Carta states 'To no one will we sell, to no one will we refuse or delay, right or justice'.[1] In 1916, US President Woodrow Wilson stated 'Justice has nothing to do with expediency'.[2] In 1974, in response to calls for a trial for former President Nixon, US President Gerald Ford stated:

> The facts, as I see them, are that a former President of the United States, instead of enjoying equal treatment with any other citizen accused of violating the law, would be cruelly and excessively penalized either in preserving the presumption of his innocence or in obtaining a speedy determination of his guilt in order to repay a legal debt to society.
>
> During this long period of delay and potential litigation, ugly passions would again be aroused. And our people would again be polarized in their opinions. And the credibility of our free institutions of government would again be challenged at home and abroad. In the end, the courts might well hold that Richard Nixon had been denied due process, and the *verdict of history* would even more be inconclusive with respect to those charges arising out of the period of his Presidency, of which I am presently aware.
>
> But it is not the ultimate fate of Richard Nixon that most concerns me, though surely it deeply troubles every decent and every compassionate person. *My concern is the immediate future of this great country*. (my emphasis).[3]

The concept of a 'fair trial' and the 'immediate future (of this great country)' as Ford put it, are not competing concepts in democracies or would-be democracies.

The US, the UK and Australia have all acknowledged the interrelationship between fair trials, the rule of law and democracies. When Ford decided not to pursue a trial of former President Nixon it was because Ford – himself a lawyer – believed that Nixon would not receive a fair trial and the best interests of the nation were better served by no trial.

This chapter will not argue that Saddam Hussein should not be tried in a court. Nor should Saddam Hussein be used as the poster-boy for promoting fair trials and due process. Rather, by accepting that the merits of fair trials serve not only the defendant, but also the promotion of rule of law and related concepts of democracy, I argue for Saddam to be tried in a better court model, a hybrid court is in the best immediate and long-term interests of Iraq.

The defendant – Saddam – has a right to a fair trial, international law is adamant about that. Especially so, as the Republic of Iraq ratified the International Covenant on Civil and Political Rights (ICCPR) in 1976 and successor governments remain bound by it.[4] Article 14 of the ICCPR provides that any person charged with a criminal offence is entitled to 'a fair and public hearing by a competent, independent and impartial tribunal established by law'.[5]

Furthermore, Iraqi Shi'ites and Sunnis, Kurds, Kuwaitis and Iranians all deserve an accurate historical account of Saddam Hussein's and Ba'athists' atrocities. If the US and other nations are implicated in Saddam's atrocities then we should not condone an unfair trial to avoid political embarrassment for them. Rather, first-world democracies should lead by example.

History of Saddam Hussein and Ba'ath Government Atrocities

Since Iraq became independent from British rule in 1932 it has experienced eleven coups, and numerous international armed conflicts.[6] Those regimes and the coups upon them were usually accompanied by horrid violence and waves of corruption. When a small group of Ba'athist military officers seized power in July 1968, they quickly became more repressive than their predecessors. For over 35 years, Saddam Hussein and his henchmen employed violence and corruption for their own selfish purposes. Some 300,000 Iraqis are unaccounted for and are suspected to be victims of Saddam's regime.[7] The invasion of Iraq led by the US has ended Saddam's rule but has created new challenges in Iraq.

Establishment of a Court to Prosecute Saddam Hussein

The Iraqi Special Tribunal (IST) was established on 10 December 2003. In order to evade the stigma of the IST, which was setup through the an order issued by the Coalition Provisional Authority (CPA), the Iraqi National Assembly revoked the 2003 IST Statute in August 2005 and established the Iraqi Higher Criminal Court (IHCC) in its place.[8]

Saddam was caught in a spider-hole in Tikrit, Iraq on 13 December 2003. On 30 June 2004, legal authority of Saddam was transferred to the Iraqi interim government. Saddam first appeared in the IHCC on 19 October 2005, he pleaded not guilty to charges relating to the massacre of over 140 mainly Shi'ites in Dujail in 1982. The trial was then adjourned till 28 November 2005.

This chapter examines the charges against Saddam and explains why IHCC trials will be less than respectable in at least four ways. (i.) Holding the trial of Saddam and others in Iraq is a serious security risk for the defendants' lawyers and is dangerous for the IHCC judges. Flexibility on the location of the court should have been built into the Statute. (ii.) The court's jurisdiction is too narrow to extract the truth about foreign involvement in Saddam's atrocities. That foreign involvement would likely implicate the US in Saddam's atrocities. (iii.) The impartiality of the judges can be doubted so the trial will be perceived as unfair. (iv.) Despite some claims to the contrary, the standard of proof in the IHCC does not meet international standards for a criminal trial's 'standard of proof'.

Charges Against Saddam Hussein

In July 2005, formal charges were laid against Saddam. Those charges relate to the massacre in Dujail. Furthermore, on 10 September 2005, the Kuwaiti Justice Minister – Ahmad Baqer – stated that Kuwait has prepared its own indictment against Saddam for crimes committed during the 1990-1991 Iraqi invasion of Kuwait.[9]

Similarly, on 18 October 2005 the Iranian Minister of Justice Jamal Karimirad announced that Iran had sent its own indictment against Saddam to the Iraqi government, alleging Saddam committed atrocities during the eight-year Iran–Iraq war. According to Karimirad, Iran's indictment includes charges of genocide, murder, crimes against humanity and violating Islamic and ethical principles.[10]

Location for the trial of Saddam Hussein

On the surface, it would be an emotionally satisfying method of proceeding to hold the trial of Saddam in Iraq. After all, the crimes took place in Iraq so why not hold the trial there? Saddam's victims do deserve to see justice done *and* have it seen to be done. But a purely domestic trial is not the best way to accomplish those twin goals, for the following reasons.

First and foremost, any court convened and backed by an occupying army will be seen as meting out victor's justice – an expression of power politics – not the rule of law.

Many in the Arab and Muslim worlds are already predisposed to view the IHCC as illegitimate precisely *because* the US backs it, no matter how many procedural safeguards are built into the process. The IHCC (or the IST as it was then called) was established under the direction of the Coalition Provisional Authority (CPA).

Coincidentally or not, the court's formation was announced by the Iraqi Governing Council a week before Saddam's capture.

To be fair, there are safeguards built into Article 19 of the IHCC statute. They include provisions that 'All persons shall be equal before the Court', that the 'accused is presumed innocent until proven guilty before the Court in accordance with this Statute'; 'every accused shall be entitled to a public hearing pursuant to the provisions of the statute'; and the right to call defence witnesses and to examine said witnesses and prosecution witnesses and to present evidence that enforces his defense pursuant to this Statute and Iraqi law'.

But these safeguards are inadequate to legitimise the court in the eyes of many. The former US Attorney-General Ramsey Clark who joined the team of Jordan-based lawyers defending Saddam Hussein has described the IHCC as 'a creation of the US military occupation'.[11]

The perception of victor's justice is further reinforced as the Bush administration has shown little interest in conducting fair trials in other contexts. For example, international humanitarian and human rights law (e.g., the UN Covenant on Civil and Political Rights (ICCPR) and the Third Geneva Convention dealing with Prisoners of War) are being manifestly breached by the US at Guantánamo Bay.

Second, Saddam's defence team has renewed its call for a change of venue for his trial, this time asking UN Secretary-General Kofi Annan to pressure the US and Iraqi governments to relocate the trial to The Hague, Holland. The defence team cited security concerns.[12]

Security issues are dire. Already, five tribunal employees have been killed, as well as defence lawyers Sa'adun al-Janabi and Adel Mohammed Abbas.[13] On 27 November 2005, eight individuals were arrested for planning the assassination of a judge on the IHCC.[14] The identities of the majority of judges and staff have been kept anonymous. As a civil court (not common law), such secrecy affects the IHCC's ability to conduct thorough investigations.

Jurisdiction of the IHCC

The narrow jurisdiction of the IHCC gives the impression of victor's justice. Most nations' criminal courts can prosecute all crimes committed in their territories, whatever the nationality of the perpetrator; indeed, that is one of the manifestations of sovereignty. The IHCC, however, can only prosecute *Iraqi* nationals and residents: (Article 1(2) of the IHCC). The IHCC's territorial jurisdiction has been manipulated to ensure that American citizens cannot be tried for aiding and abetting Saddam's atrocities.

The narrow jurisdiction undercuts the Bush administration's stated desire for a complete and uncensored record of Iraqi atrocities and Saddam Hussein's role in them. It will be seen as a way for Washington to avoid embarrassing questions about its ties to the former regime.

A 'fair trial' requires the telling of the *whole* story. Iraqi history deserves a complete record of events, the most accurate narrative. If that means giving Saddam a forum to publicly adduce evidence of his previous liaisons with US governments (particularly during the 1980s, when he began acquiring and using biological and chemical weapons with Washington's acquiescence if not aid), then so be it. Establishing good governance and an effective judiciary requires that Iraq start its post-Saddam era with a clean slate.

Impartiality of the court

Article 36 of the IHCC Statute makes any member of the Ba'ath Party ineligible to sit on the IHCC. To be sure, many of the Ba'athist judges should indeed be disqualified. Yet, membership of the Ba'ath Party was a prerequisite for admission to judicial training under Saddam and does not necessarily imply that the member was a supporter of the Ba'ath Party or the government of Hussein. A requisite improvement to IHCC professionalism is that Ba'ath members have an opportunity for inclusion in the IHCC. Then the eligibility of former Ba'ath Party members should be assessed on a case-by-case basis with regard to their past performance and seniority of membership in the Ba'ath Party.

Standard of proof

The IHCC Statute does not elaborate on the standard of proof in criminal trials. However, one translation of the Law on Criminal Proceedings (with Amendments), Number 23 of 1971, Decree Number 230, Paragraph 213(A) states:

> A court's verdict in a case is based on the extent to which it *is satisfied* by the evidence presented during any stage of the inquiry or the hearing. Evidence includes reports, witness statements, written records of an interrogation, other official discoveries, reports of experts and technicians and other legally established evidence.[15]

A vague standard of proof or one that has an obscure meaning is insufficient to assure a justice or have justice being seen to be done. A 'fair' conviction must be based on a reasoned judgment that demonstrates each of the elements of the crime to an acceptable international standard of 'beyond reasonable doubt' as in common law systems or the 'intime conviction' as in many civil law systems.[16] Whereas, the IHCC's 'satisfaction' standard lacks common and civil law tradition and acceptance.

The IHCC standards of criminal responsibility also make superiors responsible for the actions of subordinates: Article 15(4), and allow soldiers to be convicted for following orders: Article 15(5).

Prosecuting soldiers for following heinous orders is wise, international law since the Nuremberg trials have not allowed a defence of 'following orders', although it may mitigate a prison sentence.[17] To be sure, I remain an advocate of prosecuting those who commit atrocities whilst following orders. The problem for the IHCC and its US sponsors is their double standard. The US does not apply the same standards to their own military as shown by US attitudes to the International Criminal Court (ICC), so why impose it upon Iraqis?

Complying With a Meaningful International Standard

The IHCC does not meet Washington's stated objective of conducting a process that 'withstands international scrutiny' at least as presently constituted.

An alternative course would be to move the trials to an international forum, such as the International Criminal Court, as the UN Security Council has the authority to do. Involving the ICC would increase the perception that a fair trial will ensue and that tough questions will be asked of US and other foreign governments', corporations' and individual complicity in Saddam's atrocities.

I concede that the ICC would somewhat disenfranchise Iraqis. Kingsley Chiedu Moghalu – the former legal advisor to the International Criminal Tribunal for Rwanda (ICTR) – rejects an ICC trial option for Saddam for this reason.[18]

Furthermore, if the US did not veto such an initiative, the ICC only has jurisdiction over crimes committed after the court came into existence (1 July 2002). Thus, it could not try Saddam and other defendants for some of their most notorious allegations including the use of chemical weapons on Iraqi Kurds in 1988.

Others have considered an ad-hoc criminal tribunal like the International Criminal Tribunal for Yugoslavia (ICTY) and the International Criminal Tribunal for Rwanda (ICTR) which uses international judges and is located in countries other than the location of the atrocities. But the ICTY and the ICTR are notorious for being behemoths that are expensive, slow, inefficient and somewhat ineffective.[19] Nevertheless, it would be erroneous to confuse the ICTY and the ICTR with the so-called second-generation international criminal justice as is the – hybrid – Special Criminal Court for Sierra Leone (SCSL).[20]

The adoption of a hybrid court comprised of Iraqi judges and international judges such as that used in the SCSL (with both international and Sierra Leonean judges) offers the best outcome for both Iraqis and others interested in prosecuting Saddam. It can achieve a rule of law compliant trials and simultaneously rebuild the Iraqi justice system and promote rule of law. The issue of retrospectivity that prevents the ICC becoming a viable option can be overcome by a SCSL model, which was empowered with retroactivity. The issue of the location for the trial is flexible under the SCSL model. The SCSL was located in Sierra Leone but could be moved to another state if Sierra Leone destabilised.

Unfortunately, a full hybrid court model as employed in SCSL has not been adopted in Iraq. The IHCC Statute offers no flexibility for its location which is seated in Baghdad with no mechanism to relocate: Article 2. The 2003 Statute of the IHCC (then the IST) had a capacity to create a type of quasi-tribunal and allowed the Iraqi Governing Council to appoint both Iraqi and international judges to the Trial Chamber and the Appeals Chamber. The international judges would only have an advisory and observatory capacity to ensure 'general due process of law standards'.[21]

That initiative would be at the discretion of the Iraqi Governing Council and makes the IHCC a quasi-hybrid tribunal.

A quasi-hybrid court could strike a balance between reviving Iraq's judicial system and compliance with rule of law standards. On one hand, the quasi-hybrid court would serve a rehabilitative role of reviving the local Iraqi judicial system through involving Iraqi judges. On the other hand, the advice and monitoring by respected international judges provides the crucial perception and legitimising fabric of fairness and impartiality. A quasi-hybrid court would also convincingly acknowledge that not all of Saddam's victims were Iraqi.

The 2005 Statute limits the ability to deploy a quasi-hybrid court that was not so worded in the 2003 Statute. Article 4(3) of the 2005 version provides:

> the Council of Ministers *may*, if deemed necessary, upon the President of the Court's proposal, appoint non-Iraqi judges who have experience in conducting trials of crimes stipulated in this law, and who shall be persons of very high moral standard, uprightness and integrity to work in the Court *in the event that a State is one of the parties in a complaint*. Those judges are assigned with the help of the International Community and the United Nations. (my emphasis).

Nation states are already parties to the most serious allegations against Saddam, therefore international judges may be appointed but for Article 7(2) of the IHCC Statute which states that the role of non-Iraqi nationals s*hall be to provide assistance* with respect to international law and the experience of similar Courts (whether international or otherwise).

This non-judicial role for non-Iraqi nations is fatal to the idea of an Iraqi hybrid court.

Furthermore, in the 2003 Statute (the Iraqi Special Tribunal) it was 'compulsory' to appoint non-Iraqi nationals as advisors or observers to the Tribunal Investigative Judges.[22] Whereas, the use of the word 'may' in the 2005 Statute does not create an obligation, rather it gives a discretion to the IHCC President and the Council of Ministers to appoint non-Iraqis.

Conclusion

As Iraqis awaken from the nightmare that was Saddam Hussein, global leadership through the rule of law is more important now than ever before. To promote a contrived trial of Saddam and other Ba'ath Party members will set a dangerously low standard for future Iraqi governments. We must be wary of reinventing Iraqi cronyism. Democracy requires more.

The vision for a strong rule of law in Iraq is further motivated by a vacuum in US security policy. We have seen a procession of *counter-terrorism* strategies employed by the US and their coalition partners, however there is a noticeable absence of cohesive *anti-terrorism strategies* to mitigate the growth of terrorism. A core notion within anti-terrorism discourse is the need for uniform adherence to the rule of law and all that it entails.

Criticisms and concerned assessments of the IHCC are already flooding in from reputable sources. Leandro Despouy, the Special Rapporteur for the Commission on Human Rights on the independence of judges and lawyers, addressed human rights standards in a report to the United Nations General Assembly.[23] Despouy states:

> The Tribunal's (IHCC's) power to impose the death penalty demonstrates the extent to which it contravenes international human rights standards... Because it was established during an occupation and was financed primarily by the US, its legitimacy has been widely questioned, with the result that its credibility has been tarnished... The Special Rapporteur urges the Iraqi authorities to follow the example set by other countries with deficient judicial systems by asking the UN to set up an independent tribunal which complies with international human rights standards.[24]

Geoffrey Robertson QC, who has worked on the SCSL and has trained Iraqi judges, has stated:

> ... it may be necessary to rethink the kind of tribunal (Court) which tries Saddam Hussein. It may be necessary to bring in an international component. It may be necessary to have the trial held outside the country if security cannot be guaranteed. But it's got to be an open process. The judges have got to be known and visible and so it will require a great deal of courage if the trials are to be held in the moral wasteland, as I say, that Iraq is at present.[25]

David M. Crane, the Chief Prosecutor for the SCSL has called the IHCC's legitimacy 'tenuous at best' because it was 'set up outside international norms'.[26]

Before Saddam was captured, many legal scholars called for a hybrid tribunal. When a hybrid model was not adopted, a quasi-hybrid model was lobbied for. The 2003 Statute of the IHCC allowed a quasi-hybrid model by mandating that non-Iraqi nationals be appointed to advise and observe on the due process of law. To those wanting peace and democracy in Iraq, the discretion (as opposed to an obligation) of the Council of Ministers on the advice of the President of the Court to appoint non-Iraqi nationals is a cruel blow to Iraq's future. Now we must hope that the Council of Ministers and the IHCC President exercise their discretion and pursue a trial that has justice both done and seen to be done.

March 2004 (revised November 2005)

Bibliography

Alexandria Samuel, 'UN Expert Assails Iraq Tribunal, says US, UK Anti-Terror Laws Undermine Rights', *Jurist Legal & News Research*, (Monday, 10 October 2005).

Anthony Dworkin, 'International Law: Saddam Hussein on Trial', *Crimes of War Project: ElectronicIraq.net*, <http://electroniciraq.net/news/printer2183.shtml> (accessed 12 November 2005).

Antonio Cassese, *International Criminal Law*, New York, Oxford University Press, (2003).

BBC (World News), 'Eight Held Over Saddam Judge Plot', *BBC World News*, (Sunday, 27 November 2005).

BBC News (World Edition), 'US Rebel Joins Saddam Legal Team', *BBC News* (World Edition) (Wednesday, 29 December 2004) <http://news.bbc.co.uk/2/hi/middle_east/4132505.stm> (accessed 15 November 2005).

Becky Diamond, 'Two Lawyers Dead. Can Saddam Trial Take Place?', *NBC News*, (8 November 2005) <http://msnbc.msn.com/id/9968466/print/1/displaymode/1098/> (accessed 15/11/2005).

Beth K. Dougherty, 'Right-Sizing International Criminal Justice: The Hybrid Experiment at the Special Court for Sierra Leone', *International Affairs*, Vol. 80, Issue 2, (March 2004), pp.311-328.

Brandon Smith, 'Ex-Official Warns Proposed Charges Could Weaken Iraqi Tribunal', *Jurist Legal News & Research*, (Tuesday, 11 October 2005).

Brian Stewart, 'Skeletons in the Closet', *The Canadian Broadcasting Corporation* (CBC), (16 December 2003) <http://www.cbc.ca/news/background/iraq/skeletonscloset.html >, accessed 15 November 2005.

Danielle Pletka, 'Trying Saddam Hussein: International Law, NGOs, and the Death Penalty', *Transcripts: American Enterprise Institute for Public Policy Research*, <http://www.aei.org/include/event_print.asp?eventID=729>, (15 January 2004).

David Shucosky, 'Saddam Defense Team Asks UN to Press for Venue Change', *Jurist Legal News & Research,* (Friday, 28 October, 2005) <http://jurist.law.pitt.edu/paperchase/2005/10/saddam-defense-team-asks-un-to-press.php> (accessed 15 November 2005).

Douglass Cassel, 'Trying Saddam', *World View Commentary No. 183*, Broadcast on World View with Jerome McDonnell, WBEZ 91.5 FM Chicago Public Radio (17 December, 2003).

Greg Samson, 'Iran Sends Saddam Indictment on War Crime to Iraqi Government', *Jurist Legal News & Research* (Tuesday, 8 October 2005).

Geoffrey Robertson, 'US Needs to Rethink Hussein Trial: Robertson', *Global Policy Forum* – Transcript of Interview between Tony Jones and Geoffrey Robertson on Australian Broadcasting Corporation (ABC) television, (17 November 2004), <http://www.globalpolicy.org/intljustice/tribunals/iraq/2004/1117interview.htm> (accessed 15 November 2005).

Gerard Ford, 'President Ford's Pardon of Richard Nixon', *Watergate.Info*, <http://www.watergate.info/ford/pardon.shtml> (accessed 15 November 2005).

Henry Weinstein, 'Law Experts Divided Over Legitimacy of Tribunal; Some Cite U.S. Influence and the Lack of U.N. backing. Others believe Iraqis are Within Rights', *The Los Angeles Times*, (20 October 2005).

Human Rights First, 'The Trial of Saddam Hussein', *Human Rights First website*, <http://www.humanrightsfirst.org/international_justice/w_context/w_cont_16.htm> (accessed 20 October 2005).

Human Rights First, 'A Fair Trial for Saddam Hussein', *Human Rights First website*, [27]<http://www.humanrightsfirst.org/international_justice/w_context/w_cont_15.htm> (accessed 20 October 2005).

Human Rights Watch, 'Iraq: Saddam Trial under Scrutiny', *Human Rights Watch*, (13 November 2005) <http://hrw.org/english/docs/2005/10/19/iraq11888_txt.htm> (accessed 13 November 2005).

International Center for Transitional Justice, 'Briefing Paper: Creation and First Trials of the Supreme Iraqi Criminal Tribunal', *ICTJ Website*, New York, (October 2005).

Iraqi Higher Criminal Court 2005, Pursuant to the Provisions of Articles 30, 33 and 48 of the Law of the Administration for the State of Iraq for the Transitional Period, (2005).

James Hider, 'Lawyer in Saddam Trial Murdered 'to hinder fair hearing', *The Times*, (22 October 2005).

Jason D. Söderblom, 'Iraq's Deposed Need a Hybrid Tribunal', *Lawyers Weekly*, (January 2004), p.11.

Jason D. Söderblom, 'Saddam Hussein's Trial: Due Process or Victor's Justice?', *Foreign Service Journal*, (May 2004), pp.15-17.

Jeannie Shawl, Saddam Pleads Not Guilty to Murder, Torture Charges, *Jurist Legal News & Research*, (Wednesday, 19 October 2005).

Jessica Martin, 'Is the Saddam Hussein Trial one of the Most Important Court Cases of all Time? Not necessarily, says International Law Expert', *University News: Washington University in St. Louis*, <http://news-info.wustl.edu/news/page/normal/6015.html> (accessed 12 November 2005).

Kingsley Chiedu Moghalu, 'The Iraqis Should Try Saddam, Not an International Court', *New Perspectives Quarterly*, Vol. 21, Issue 2, (March 2004), pp.29-31.

Law on Criminal Proceedings with Amendments, Number 23 of 1971, Decree Number 230, <http://www.law.case.edu/saddamtrial/documents/Iraqi_Criminal_Procedure_Code.pdf >, accessed 25 November 2005.

Magna Carta, (1215), website prepared by Seth Seyfried, University of Utah, <http://www.fordham.edu/halsall/source/mcarta.html> (accessed 15 November 2005).

MidEastWeb, 'The Iraq Crisis – Timeline Chronology of Modern Iraqi History', <http://www.mideastweb.org/iraqtimeline.htm> (accessed 15 November 2005).

Noam Chomsky, 'What a Fair Trial for Saddam would Entail', *The Toronto Star*, (25 January 2004), <http://www.chomsky.info/articles/20040125.htm> (accessed 15 October 2005).

Office of the United Nations High Commissioner for Human Rights, *Status of Ratifications of the Principal International Human Rights Treaties*, (as of 09 June 2004), <http://www.unhchr.ch/pdf/report.pdf> (accessed 26 November 2005).

Omar Sinan, 'Saddam's Defense Team Threatens to Boycott', *Yahoo News*, (Wednesday, 9 November 2005).

Sara R. Parsowith, 'Kuwait Seeks Death Penalty for Saddam under Own Indictment', *Jurist Legal News & Research*, (Saturday, 10 September 2005).

United Nations Office for the Coordination of Humanitarian Affairs (OCHA), 'Iraq: Saddam Hussein Goes on Trial, But Some Still Support Him', *IRIN News*, (20 October 2005).

Woodrow Wilson, Quote made on 26 February, 1916. Quote extracted from 'Text of Chairman Hyde's Remarks to Judiciary Committee Organizational Meeting', *US House of Representatives Committee on the Judiciary*, (5 January 1995), <http://judiciary.house.gov/legacy/003.htm> (accessed 24 November 2005).

Notes

[1]   Magna Carta, Article 40, 1215.

[2]   President Woodrow Wilson, 26 February, 1916 – Quote extracted from Text of Chairman Hyde's Remarks to Judiciary Committee Organizational Meeting, U.S. House of Representatives Committee on the Judiciary, 5 January, 1995, <http://judiciary.house.gov/legacy/003.htm> (accessed 24 November 2005).

[3]   Gerard Ford, 'President Ford's Pardon of Richard Nixon', *Watergate.Info*, <http://www.watergate.info/ford/pardon.shtml> (accessed 15 November 2005).

[4]   Office of the United Nations High Commissioner for Human Rights, *Status of Ratifications of the Principal International Human Rights Treaties*, (as of 09 June 2004), <http://www.unhchr.ch/pdf/report.pdf> (accessed 26 November 2005).

[5]   International Covenant on Civil and Political Rights, Adopted and opened for signature, ratification and accession by General Assembly resolution 2200A (XXI) of 16 December 1966 entry into force 23 March 1976, in accordance with Article 49.

[6]   MidEastWeb, 'The Iraq Crisis – Timeline Chronology of Modern Iraqi History', *MidEastWeb*, <http://www.mideastweb.org/iraqtimeline.htm> (accessed 15 November 2005). Coups or attempted coups in 1936, 1938, 1940, 1941, 1958, 1959, 2x1963, 1968, 1979, 1996.

[7]   Brian Stewart, 'Skeletons in the Closet', *The Canadian Broadcasting Corporation* (CBC), 16 December 2003, <http://www.cbc.ca/news/background/iraq/skeletonscloset.html>, (accessed 15 November 2005).

[8]   Article 1 of the Iraqi Higher Criminal Court 2005.

[9]   Sara R. Parsowith, 'Kuwait Seeks Death Penalty for Saddam under Own Indictment', *Jurist Legal News & Research*, (Saturday, 10 September 2005).

[10] Greg Samson, 'Iran Sends Saddam Indictment on War Crime to Iraqi Government', *Jurist Legal News & Research*, (Tuesday, 8 October 2005).

[11] BBC News (World Edition), 'US Rebel Joins Saddam Legal Team', *BBC News* (World Edition), (Wednesday, 29 December 2004), <http://news.bbc.co.uk/2/hi/middle_east/4132505.stm> (accessed 15 November 2005).

[12] David Shucosky, 'Saddam Defense Team Asks UN to Press for Venue Change', *Jurist Legal News & Research*, <http://jurist.law.pitt.edu/paperchase/2005/10/saddam-defense-team-asks-un-to-press.php> (accessed 15 November 2005).

[13] Carlos Hamann, 'Second Saddam lawyer killed', *News.com.au*, <http://www.news.com.au/story/0,10117,17188656-23109,00.html> (accessed 15 November 2005).

[14] BBC (World News), 'Eight Held Over Saddam Judge Plot', *BBC World News*, (Sunday, 27 November 2005).

[15] Law On Criminal Proceedings with Amendments, Number 23 of 1971, Decree Number 230, <http://www.law.case.edu/saddamtrial/documents/Iraqi_Criminal_Procedure_Code.pdf > (accessed 25 November 2005).

[16] Antonio Cassese, *International Criminal Law*, Oxford University Press, New York, 2003, p. 427.

[17] Ibid., p.427.

[18] Kinglsey Chiedu Moghalu, 'The Iraqis Should Try Saddam, Not an International Court', *New Perspectives Quarterly*, (2004), pp. 29–31.

[19] Beth K. Dougherty, 'Right-Sizing International Criminal Justice: The Hybrid Experiment at the Special Court for Sierra Leone', *International Affairs*, vol. 80, issue 2, (March 2004), p. 312.

[20] Dougherty, p. 311.

[21] Article 6(B) – *The Statute of the Iraqi Special Tribunal (2003)*, <http://www.cpa-iraq.org/human_rights/Statute.htm> (accessed 28 November 2005).

[22] Article 7(N) and Article 6(B) – *The Statute of the Iraqi Special Tribunal (2003)*, <http://www.cpa-iraq.org/human_rights/Statute.htm> (accessed 28 November 2005).

[23] Alexandria Samuel, 'UN Expert Assails Iraq Tribunal, says US, UK Anti-Terror Laws Undermine Rights', *Jurist Legal & News Research*. (Monday 10 October 2005).

[24] Ibid.

[25] Geoffrey Robertson, 'US Needs to Rethink Hussein Trial: Robertson', *Global Policy Forum* – Transcript of Interview between Tony Jones and Geoffrey Robertson on Australian Broadcasting Association television, (17 November 2004), <http://www.globalpolicy.org/intljustice/tribunals/iraq/2004/1117interview.htm> (accessed 15 November 2005).

[26] Henry Weinstein, 'Law Experts Divided Over Legitimacy of Tribunal; some cite U.S. Influence and the Lack of U.N. backing. Others believe Iraqis are Within Rights', *The Los Angeles Times*, (20 October 2005).

Chapter 33

Expert Evidence on Trial

Cathy Cobley and Tom Sanders

The Provision of Expert Evidence to the Courts

In recent years there has been a general sense of dissatisfaction with the system for providing expert evidence to both civil and criminal courts in England and Wales. In 1996, following a review of the rules and procedures of the civil courts, the Woolf Report concluded that the cost of litigation was too high, experts had become partisan advocates in court cases and their evidence lacked objectivity.[1] (Woolf, 1996). It was recommended that 'neutral' experts and those who were new to providing expert evidence should be actively encouraged. Conversely, the appointment of 'well-seasoned' experts with a reputation for supporting a certain position should be discouraged. Although practical steps, such as the disclosure of experts' reports and the holding of pre-trial meetings of experts to agree areas of controversy, have been taken to address some of these issues, fundamental concerns about the provision of expert evidence remain and these concerns are particularly evident in cases of suspected child abuse, as recent events have so vividly highlighted.

Child Abuse and Expert Witnesses

Whilst the courts may require the assistance of expert witnesses on a wide range of topics which may arise in almost any kind of legal dispute, expert evidence frequently plays a central role in cases of child abuse. Significant evidential problems can arise during court proceedings in these cases and the evidence of medical experts can often be crucial in determining the outcome of a case. Yet conflict between these experts is not uncommon, particularly in cases of alleged physical abuse, where evidence of causality, harm and future risk is often uncertain and contested. For several years there has been a continuing debate amongst professionals about the extent to which instructing several medical witnesses leads to the duplication of expert opinion and/or conflicting evidence in court.[2,3] However, in 2003 several events resulted in the attention of both professionals and the public being sharply focused on the role of medical experts in cases of child abuse. These events, which were well documented in the media, included the acquittal of Trupti Patel and the successful appeals of Sally Clark and Angela Cannings, all of whom had been accused of murdering their babies. Following these events, the reputation of Sir Roy Meadows, a formerly eminent expert witness in the field of child abuse, now lies in tatters. Sir Roy, a paediatrician who achieved wide recognition in 1977 for his work on Munchausen's Syndrome by Proxy and who was knighted in 1998 for services to Child Health, was an expert witness for the prosecution at the trial of all three women. The evidence he gave, which included incorrect statistical evidence and reliance on what has been dubbed 'Meadows law' ('one cot death is tragedy, two is suspicious and three is murder, unless proven otherwise'), has been subject to severe criticism. In July 2005 he was found guilty of serious professional misconduct for giving misleading statistical evidence in the case of Sally Clark and was struck off the Medical Register by the General Medical Council.

The intense furore surrounding the work of Sir Roy looks set to continue. In giving judgment in the appeal of Angela Cannings, Judge LJ in the Court of Appeal ruled that in future no parent who had lost two or more babies should be prosecuted if the case relied solely on expert evidence that was disputed by other professionals who believed that the death could have been caused by natural, if unexplained, causes. Following the judgment, Lord Goldsmith, the Attorney General, announced a review of 258 convictions of parents over 10 years for infanticide, murder and manslaughter (*The Daily Telegraph*, 20 January 2004). This in turn prompted Harriet Harman, the solicitor general, to announce that the review would extent to the civil courts (*The Daily Telegraph*, 21 January 2004). Although there was initially intense speculation that 'hundreds' of convictions would be quashed and 'thousands' of children returned to their families, the Attorney General's Review found cause for concern in only 28 cases (House of Lords Hansard 21 December 2004 col 1658) and only 26 of the 28,867 cases reviewed by local authorities were found to have involved disagreement between expert witnesses (*The Independent*, 17 November 2004). However, although many may not yet realise it, the potential impact of these events extends well beyond the cases which are now subject to review. The current system of providing expert evidence to courts relies on there being a sufficient pool of professionals in a particular field who have the necessary expertise and who are willing to act as expert witnesses. Although this will not be a problem in some areas, the number of medical professionals who are suitably qualified and willing to act as expert witnesses in cases of child abuse appears to have been dwindling alarmingly in recent years. The problem has been growing quietly in the background, rather like a ticking time bomb, and recent events can only serve to exacerbate the problem and, in effect, shorten the fuse.

Why Act as an Expert Witness?

Traditionally there have been a number of reasons why medical professionals may be reluctant to put themselves forward as an expert witness. These include barriers of a professional, practical and personal nature. The primary requirement for an expert witness is that a professional is suitably qualified and has the relevant expertise. Whilst there may be no national shortage of, for example, pathologists, the acute shortage of *paediatric* pathologists is a cause for concern, and this lack of specific expertise can cause problems if a child has died as a result of suspected abuse. The same is true of other medical specialities, such as radiology. Even if a professional has the necessary expertise, he or she must still be willing to act as an expert witness, but may be discouraged by the commitment required. Practising clinicians usually have a busy schedule, but acting as an expert witness takes time, particularly if the expert is required to give evidence at a trial. Court listings can be changed at short notice – a frustrating problem for all involved but especially clinicians who may find it impossible to re-arrange clinics and surgeries. Yet perhaps the most significant barrier to acting as an expert witness is essentially a personal one. Most medical professionals have only a limited understanding of evidential requirements and procedures in court and training on these issues is limited. This has traditionally resulted in a general reluctance on the part of medical professionals to become involved in litigation, particularly when they know that their expertise may be questioned and their opinions challenged. Recent events and the experience of previously eminent child abuse experts can only exacerbate this problem, leading to a further reduction in the availability of expert witnesses in this area. Indeed, it may legitimately be asked, who in their right minds would put themselves forward to act as an expert witness in a case of child abuse in the current climate?

What Does the Future Hold?

It may be thought that the above paints an unnecessarily bleak picture of the future and that the comments made are unduly alarmist. Admittedly, empirical research on the role of medical experts in cases alleging physical child abuse is very limited. Most attention has been focused on expert opinion from psychologists and psychiatrists in care proceedings, and scant evidence exists on the role of other experts such as paediatricians, radiologists, neurologists and neurosurgeons.[4,5] (Brophy & Bates, 1999; Vetere & Stevenson, 2001). Therefore further research in this area is an important first step, not only to test the claim that a significant problem exists, but also, if necessary, to help clarify the underlying reasons and suggest appropriate responses. These may include practical measures, such as support for more comprehensive training schemes to educate the medical profession about the legal process and the role of expert witnesses. This would need to be accompanied by greater flexibility in the working arrangements of clinicians to allow them to incorporate their duties as an expert into their daily routine and financial incentives to ensure that those who are prepared to act as experts receive adequate compensation. Resources would, of course, need to be found for any such practical measures but perhaps the most daunting task will be to bring about a cultural change. In cases of child abuse expert opinions will in future be subject to the closest scrutiny, particularly if a conflicting opinion is put forward. Yet effective child protection relies on the willingness of professionals with the necessary experience and expertise to come forward and provide evidence to the courts and so every effort must be made to tackle the increasing reluctance on the part of the medical profession to engage in an adversarial legal system where professional credibility is likely to be challenged and reputations can be so easily destroyed.

February 2004

References

[1] Woolf, The Right Honourable the Lord (1996), *Access to Justice: Final Report.* London, TSO.

[2] Wall, N. (1997), *Issues Arising from Expert Evidence Given by Psychiatrists and Psychologists.* In: Rooted Sorrows: Family Law.

[3] Wynne, J. (1999), 'Doctors as expert witnesses'. *Archives of Disease in Childhood,* vol. 81, p. 192.

[4] Brophy, J. and Bates, P. (1999), *The Guardian ad Litem, complex Cases and the Use of Experts following the Children Act 1989.* Lord Chancellor's Department, London.

[5] Vetere, A. and Stevenson, J. (2001), *The Use of Expert Witnesses: Useful or Useless?* Paper presented to the President's Interdisciplinary Conference 28–30 September 2001.

Chapter 34

Bhopal: The Disaster Continues

Dr Peter Wells

The original Bhopal incident in December 1984 was, by any standards, an awful disaster for the community within which the Union Carbide factory was located. Even now, some twenty years later, the initial reaction is sheer anger at the loss of life and appalling injuries suffered by thousands upon thousands of innocent victims.

At the heart of the issue is the question of the purpose of corporations in society. The tradition from which Union Carbide arose is that of capitalist minimalism: the Stanford maxim of 'the purpose of business is business'. This is the Anglo-American business model that places shareholder sovereignty above all else. The rationality of profit maximization is apparently immune to dissent, and is so deeply ingrained in our collective psyche, that we are unable to question this logic. Yet it is equally valid to argue that business cannot relentlessly pursue profit at the expense of all other considerations, indeed it is irrational so to do. More fundamentally, business is a social institution and, if it fails to serve social needs then it loses legitimacy.

The tragedy of Bhopal is that of a society without the control mechanisms, without the social, political, legal, economic and cultural mechanisms to control the excesses of capitalist minimalism. In this way Bhopal has become emblematic, it encapsulates and magnifies so many issues that were not only relevant then, but sadly are equally or more relevant today. Bhopal resonates with our sense of all that can go wrong, and then with the utter failure of those who suffer to find adequate redress. In this respect the devastation loosed upon the people of Bhopal by the Union Carbide factory, while it itself a terrifying incident, should not simply be seen in isolation as the unique outcome from a specific set of circumstances. Just as the problems at Enron have forced US financial regulators and institutions to rethink their approach to corporate governance and accounting, or indeed just as the attack on the World Trade Center met with the all-out 'war on terror' and Homeland Security, it is vital that Bhopal be seen in its wider context. Bhopal is therefore symbolic of:

- the plundering of local communities and their resources by large multinational companies regardless of the cost to those communities;
- the duplicity of standards that apply in some places but not in others;
- the global fluidity of capital, compared with the huge barriers erected against the movement of people;
- the abject failure of local, city, regional and national governments in developing countries to take on powerful multinational companies;

- the low value of a human life in developing countries compared with developed countries;
- the unforgivable lethargy of the system of redress for the victims of corporate carnage;
- the lack of local accountability or control;
- the lack of local knowledge or understanding about technologies, chemicals, processes, and many aspects of manufacturing that results in communities ignorant of what actually goes on in the factories around which they live;
- the way in which the poor and powerless of any country are always the victims.

In other words, Bhopal is symbolic of a sort of cultural collision that provides the raw ingredients for similar human and ecosystem disasters around the world.

China has sought to manage this collision with a 'one country, two systems' approach that allows the parallel coexistence of the state controlled industries and the inward investments of Western capitalist enterprises: it remains to be seen whether such institutional schizophrenia is viable. The need for investment for many countries is undeniable, but so too is the need for these countries to be protected from the negative consequences of such investment. Bhopal crystalized these problems into one devastating night, and hence made them visible. In the contemporary era perhaps the negative impacts are more diffuse, spread over space and time and so we don't see them. This does not mean that disasters no longer happen.

We are all still in thrall to capital. Individuals and companies generate wealth out of the societies within which they are hosted, but can abstract that wealth for themselves. We have acquiesced to a world in which the movement of money acts as a form of trans-boundary pollutant, rending apart cultures in the search for ever greater financial returns. The model of business in mainland Europe, while not perfect, at least recognizes that there is a social contract between business and the communities within which it operates. Strangely, many of these seemingly all-powerful companies vilified by the anti-globalization protesters are themselves horribly weak and ephemeral…and it is this vulnerability that in part drives the globalization process.

It is of course true that the world has changed since 1984. People in developing countries are probably better informed for example, while CNN can bring live footage of an unfolding catastrophe to the homes of millions in North America and Europe. Yet Bhopal has to be more than a fascinating case study in the epidemiology of poisoning by gas clouds. If we are to give the victims of Bhopal true justice it lies not simply in retribution or even financial compensation – although that is a right and proper place to start. Justice lies in creating the international legal controls and systems that treat the companies that commit these acts with the same vigour and resolve that is currently reserved for the followers of Bin Laden.

It is hard not to draw comparisons with the more recent disaster of the World Trade Center in New York. Both incidents resulted in enormous human suffering, in both cases people grieved for loved ones, yearned for explanations, and wanted the guilty to be called to account. In the Bhopal case, the initial incident has been followed by years of confusion and chaos, with a long struggle for retribution and recompense for people who were in any case among the poorest in the world. In New York, the initial incident triggered the huge, and obscene, expenditures on the invasion of Iraq and the paranoia of the Homeland Security regime.

January 2005

Index